D0122253

THE AMERICAN
NEWSREEL
1911–1967

UNIVERSITY OF OKLAHOMA PRESS : NORMAN

THE AMERICAN
NEWSREEL
1911 - 1967

By RAYMOND FIELDING

By Raymond Fielding

The Technique of Special Effects Cinematography (New York, 1965)

A *Technological History of Motion Pictures and Television* (Berkeley, 1967)

The American Newsreel, 1911–1967 (Norman, 1972)

International Standard Book Number: 0–8061–1004–X

Library of Congress Catalog Card Number: 73–177334

Copyright 1972 by the University of Oklahoma Press, Publishing Division of the University. Composed and printed at Norman, Oklahoma, U.S.A., by the University of Oklahoma Press. First edition.

791.43
F459a

180652

To *my Mother*

Mills College Library
Withdrawn

MILLS COLLEGE
LIBRARY

Mills College Library
Withdrawn

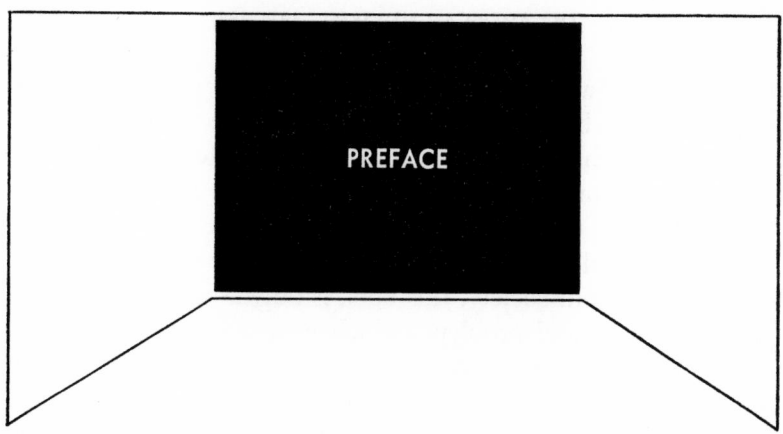

PREFACE

Most of the world's work gets done, I suppose, because human beings involve themselves professionally, legally, or psychologically in projects from which they cannot conveniently extricate themselves.

So it was with this history, which was started ten years ago as a concern of mine with the veracity of the motion picture newsreel. This concern, in time, became enlarged to embrace speculations about the newsreel's role in our society, its function in the motion picture industry, its survival for more than half a century, and its ultimate demise. What began as an affectionate glance at a disappearing institution evolved gradually into a critical indictment of a classic motion picture attraction which failed, in almost every way it could, to fulfill the promise which economic circumstances and an almost miraculous technology had provided for it. If the history which follows is noticeably hostile in its indictment, it is because I also loved the newsreel and, like many people, waited, with diminishing faith, for it to achieve some kind of maturity before it finally passed from theater screens in the late 1960's.

Any kind of motion picture attraction which survives for more than half a century obviously has some merit. If the statistics which I have gathered are even approximately correct, then somewhere around one-half billion feet of motion picture film were photographed by American newsreelers during that half century—

a good deal of which survives today in motion picture archives. Yet, despite its importance, what follows is the first history ever attempted of this historically important and tenacious motion picture attraction. And, like many other such histories, it will probably raise as many questions as it has answered.

For those readers who are concerned with the role of the information film in our society, this book is only a beginning, not an end. The issues and problems which were involved in the production of the newsreel are substantially those of the television news film. For that matter, many of the same people who made the newsreels are still peering through viewfinders, operating moviolas, and leaning over the editor's desk in today's television news operations. News is too important a matter to leave entirely to newsmen—at least in a free society. I hope that this book will encourage other critics and scholars to enlarge the investigation begun here.

The routes which I have traveled in this investigation have been devious but interesting. I have collected thousands of pieces of oftentimes conflicting information, viewed countless films, and interviewed many motion picture pioneers. It has all been enormously exciting for me, and I hope that my work in assigning historical form and meaning to this otherwise confusing series of events will intrigue the reader.

Extensive notes and citations have been provided which support the text throughout. They illustrate the varieties of evidence which I have accumulated and will help guide the scholarly reader through the labyrinth of my reasoning to the conclusions I have reached.

I am indebted to the many individuals who have assisted me along the way, all of whom, I trust, have been properly acknowledged at the appropriate places in the text and notes. In particular, I thank my good friend Richard MacCann, of the University of Iowa, who generously assisted in the editing of the manuscript and made useful suggestions for its improvement. I am also thankful to the following individuals and organizations who provided films, illustrations, and research materials: Edward Canstein, of Movietonews, Inc.; John Kuiper, of the Motion Picture Section of the Library of Congress; Bernard Karpel, of the Library of the Museum of Modern Art; George Pratt, of the George Eastman House Museum; Betty Franklin and Lillian Schwartz, of the Library of the Academy of Motion Picture Arts and Sciences; and the staff members of the Theater Collection of the New York Public Library; the Doheny Library of the University of Southern California; and the Theater Arts Library of the University of California, Los Angeles.

January 15, 1972   RAYMOND FIELDING

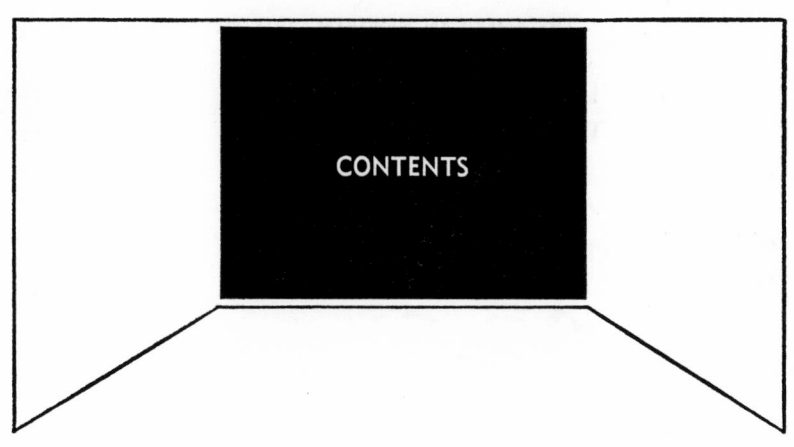

CONTENTS

ILLUSTRATIONS

THE AMERICAN
NEWSREEL
1911–1967

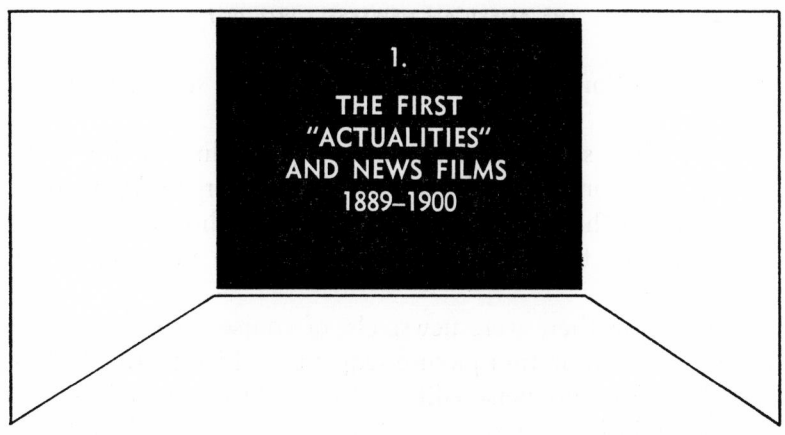

No scene, however animated and extensive, but will eventually be within reproductive power. Martial evolutions, naval exercises, processions and countless kindred exhibitions will be recorded for the leisurely gratification of those who are debarred from attendance, or who desire to recall them. . . . Not only our own resources but those of the entire world will be at our command. The advantages to students and historians will be immeasurable. Instead of dry and misleading accounts, tinged with the exaggerations of the chroniclers' mind, our archives will be enriched by the vitalized pictures of great national scenes, instinct with all the glowing personalities which characterized them.

W. K. L. Dickson, 1894[1]

The American newsreel, in case you have already forgotten, was a ten-minute potpourri of motion picture news footage, released twice a week to motion picture theaters throughout the country.

For more than half a century, from 1911 to 1967, it survived intact and unchanged, during which time it was as predictably a part of every theater's program as the Walt Disney cartoon and the Fitzpatrick travelogue.

As a form of journalism it provided predominantly photographic news coverage long before newspapers and magazines did, and from its loins sprang the vastly more sophisticated and thorough motion picture journalism which we see on television today.

It was often shallow, trivial, and even fraudulent. But sometimes it was wonderful—filled with vivid, unforgettable pictures and sounds of the people, events, wonders, and horrors which the free people of this century did their best to understand and confront.

Long before there were newsreels, of course, there were news films: individual motion picture sequences which pictured newsworthy events and personalities. News films were released as separate and isolated motion picture attractions, as frequently or infrequently as the cinematic availability of newsworthy events allowed. Unlike the newsreel, they had no fixed schedule of release and presented only a single topic.

And even before the news film, there were "actualities": short scenes of everyday people and events—unmanipulated activity of more or less general interest. It is with the humble actuality that one begins not only the history of the newsreel but also the history of all motion pictures.

When William Friese-Greene made his first motion pictures in 1889, he included scenes of London citizens in their best Sunday clothes, promenading through Hyde Park on their way to church. Fragments of the film still survive. It all looks very crude today, but it is remembered as one of the earliest actualities.

Six years later, in 1895, when the Lumière brothers gave the first public performance of their Cinématographe in Paris, it was composed of scenes of a similar nature, including "Lunch Hour at the Lumière Factory," "Arrival of a Train at the Station," "Rue de la République," "A Blacksmith," and "Bathing Beach." A year later, in 1896, Robert Paul's first program of projected films in London showed scenes such as "Shoeblack at Work in a London Street" and "A Rough Sea at Dover."

Unsophisticated audiences at first demanded little more of such films than the novelty of recognizable reproductions of familiar scenes, no matter how common and unspectacular. Newspaper

4

reviews of the period emphasized the novelty of the medium. The films were "so animated and real that one sat spell bound. The views were very clear and the action represented was so realistic that in several cases the audience could scarce restrain their wonder, and even startled surprise at the events which were flashed before their eyes."[2]

Such early actualities provided glimpses of contemporary life, brief in length and artless in their staging, structure, and composition. Soon theatrical artifice and manipulation, although of the crudest sort, were introduced, and simple stories of a fictional nature appeared. Theatrical film makers in particular are indebted to the prolific French film producer Georges Méliès, who from 1896 until well after 1910 produced ingenious story films which stimulated interest in the film as a dramatic art and provoked wide imitation by his competitors. Even Méliès, however, exploited the popularity of early actualities with his theatrical "re-creations" of major news events, including the assassination of President McKinley, the sinking of the *Maine*, the coronation of Edward VII, and the trial of Alfred Dreyfus. It was not until some years later that fictional dramatizations of any complexity began to challenge the appeal of the actualities.

In the United States the motion picture was not successfully projected onto a screen for commercial exhibition until 1896. Instead, it was viewed by individual patrons in peep-show instruments of varying design which first appeared around 1894, some based upon the original Kinetoscope of Edison, which employed positive motion picture film, others upon the Mutoscope patents, which utilized photographic cards. The effect in either case was to limit the presentation of motion pictures to individual viewing in side shows and amusement arcades.

On April 23, 1896, Thomas Armat, in association with Thomas Edison, presented what is considered to be the first successful motion picture show projected to a paying American audience, at Koster and Bial's Music Hall in New York City. Significantly,

Armat recalled several years later that the most popular film in the show was an actuality borrowed from Robert Paul, of England:

All the scenes shown, with one exception, were what might be called vaudeville turns, or stage subjects. A crowded audience applauded each of the scenes with great enthusiasm. The one exception to the stage scenes was an outdoor scene that Raff and Gammon had succeeded in getting from Robert Paul, who by that date was experimenting with motion pictures in England. This scene was of storm-tossed waves breaking over a pier on the beach at Dover, England—a scene that was totally unlike anything an audience had ever before seen in a theater. When it was thrown upon the screen the house went wild; there were calls from all over the house for "Edison," "Edison," "speech," "speech."[3]

The Armat showing was an immense success and helped establish the popularity of the projected film; still, many years were to pass before large numbers of permanent motion picture theaters began to appear, around 1905. Until that time the actualities or news films mentioned here were as frequently viewed by individuals in peep shows as by audiences in theaters.

Appraised by today's journalistic standards, the quality most lacking in these early actualities was newsworthiness, a shortcoming which producers sought to remedy once the novelty of the medium began to wane. Before long the newsworthiness of subject matter became a salable commodity; cameramen became as conscious of news values as newspaper reporters, and money was spent to secure exclusive coverage.[4] As early as 1894, Thomas Edison—who, with W. K. L. Dickson, is generally credited with the invention of the first practical motion picture camera in the late 1880's—invited to his New Jersey studio notable celebrities of the day to be immortalized on film by means of his crude Kinetograph. Sandow the Strong Man, Buffalo Bill, Annie Oakley, Bertholdi the Contortionist, dancer Ruth St. Denis, and other luminaries of the entertainment world were subsequently recorded by Edison's camera.[5]

If such early Edison films helped establish a market for scenes of newsworthy celebrities, other films, particularly from abroad, created a demand for motion picture coverage of famous events and worldwide scenic attractions.

Five months after patenting their Cinématographe in 1895 Lumière Brothers photographed what was apparently the first news film ever made in France—a record of the holiday excursion of the Congress of the National Union of French Photographic Societies. The film was made on June 10 and projected for the congress two days later.[6] Later in the same year the Lumière organization sent an employee named Francis Doublier and an assistant named Charles Moisson to Madrid to film a bullfight, and from there to Moscow for the May, 1896, coronation of Czar Nicholas II.[7] The conditions under which this very early news film was photographed are described by Doublier in a vivid account of the dangers which a news cameraman faced as early as 1896:

It was the custom that the Czar and Czarina go to a large field just outside of Moscow three days after their coronation to perform some sort of ritual, so I, wishing to film the incident, appeared at the field early on the day of the projected visit and set up my camera on some planks. I went down with the crowd to get some souvenirs made for the occasion—a goblet, and a scarf, with pictures of the Czar and Czarina on them—when a terrible panic was started. Out of a crowd of 20,000, some 6,000 [?] people were killed. I myself was trampled on and caught in the mob, but escaped without injury.[8]

During Doublier's stay in Russia he encountered one of the earliest known instances of news-film censorship:

. . . the police destroyed a film I had made of the Prince Napoleon, a member of the Russian royal family, because he had been photographed dancing with the lady of his affections, a professional dancer, and because no pictures of a member of the royal family could be shown on a screen without special permission from the authorities.[9]

Doublier was also one of the first motion picture cameramen to fake a news film—a practice which in time became as much the rule as the exception in the newsreel business:

The Dreyfus affair was still a source of great interest in those days, and out of it I worked up a little film-story which made me quite a bit of money. Piecing together a shot of some soldiers, one of a battleship, one of the Palais de Justice, and one of a tall gray-haired man, I called it "L'affaire Dreyfus." People actually believed that this was a filming of the famous case.[10]

About the same time, in 1896, the Lumière Brothers hired a second cameraman, Felix Mesguich, and sent him around the world to secure interesting footage.[11] Mesguich and Doublier became the industry's first roving motion picture correspondents. The many thousands of feet of film which they photographed in what were then exotic locales helped develop audiences' tastes for travel and scenic films.

In England the production of news films began as early as June 20, 1895, when British film pioneer Birt Acres photographed the official opening of the Kiel Canal by Kaiser Wilhelm II at Brunsbüttelkoog, as well as the Kaiser on parade shortly before the opening of the canal.[12] Assuming that the accounts of Acres' work on these occasions are accurate, his news films appear to be the first ever made of an event of international importance. A year later, on June 3, 1896, another British pioneer, Paul, in association with Acres, photographed the Derby at Epsom Downs (in the course of which Persimmon won the race for Edward, Prince of Wales, later Edward VII).[13] In a remarkable display of motion picture news-gathering initiative, the film was rushed through processing and screened at the Alhambra on the evening of the following day. Its success led to Paul's signing a four-year contract with the Alhambra to provide a regular fifteen-minute program of news films and comedies.[14]

Some writers have claimed that Paul's film of the Derby was the first news film ever photographed. It was, perhaps, the first to be photographed in England, but clearly it was preceded by Doublier's filming of the coronation of Czar Nicholas II in May, 1896, Acres' photography of the opening of the Kiel Canal in June, 1895, and Lumière's filming of the Congress of the National Union of French Photographic Societies, also in June, 1895.

From 1896 onward many European producers were active in the production of news-film items. Oskar Messter filmed news events for German audiences.[15] In France, Charles Pathé, of whom much was to be heard later in the newsreel business, released such newsworthy films as "The Czar's Arrival in Paris" and "March Past of the Light Cavalry," while another Frenchman, Léon Gaumont, photographed "Fourteenth of July Procession" and "Arrival of the President of the Republic at the Enclosure" in 1896.[16] In England, S. Mitchell photographed the Clyde Regatta and the King's Liverpool Regiment in 1898.[17] In the same year Cecil Hepworth photographed the Henley Regatta and its spectators, while Paul photographed the *Albion* launching disaster. Other exciting news films, photographed even earlier by unknown cameramen, still survive in the collection of the British Film Institute: 1896 scenes of the London Fire Brigade in action, the changing of the guard, and rush-hour traffic on London Bridge. Also of unknown origin are scenes of Queen Victoria's Diamond Jubilee in 1897, Gladstone's funeral in 1898, and other similarly notable events of the pre-1900 period.

The very early news films of the United States centered around prize fights. The prize fight was ideal subject matter for the early motion picture camera. It was popular with the male public and was not yet stained with scandal and criticism. Each fight was a complete drama in itself and was visually exciting. In addition, the entire action of the fight could be captured by one camera in a fixed position.

What appears to be the earliest of such news films was photographed in July, 1894, under the combined auspices of Thomas Edison, Gray and Otway Latham, Enoch Rector, and Samuel Tilden, Jr. The fighters were Michael Leonard and Jack Cushing,

9

the latter then contender for the lightweight title. The fight, although apparently a genuine match, was held expressly for the camera and enacted in natural daylight in Edison's "Black Maria" studio in West Orange, New Jersey. Leonard won the match.[18] Six rounds were photographed by means of a specially designed Edison Kinetograph that photographed up to 150 feet of film in one take.[19] The resulting picture, distributed by the newly founded Kinetoscope Exhibition Company and running about 1,000 feet in length, was shown at a New York Kinetoscope parlor in August by means of a set of six Kinetoscope peep-show machines—one round of the fight in each machine.[20]

It was a successful venture, and other prize-fight films soon followed. On September 7, 1894, the Kinetoscope Exhibition Company hired James Corbett, then heavyweight champion, to fight Peter Courtney, of Trenton, New Jersey. This time, however, Rector, production manager of the enterprise, is reported to have rigged the fight, timing it exactly to six one-minute rounds and prearranging for the favorite, Corbett, to knock out his opponent at the conclusion of the sixth round.[21] This early American news film appears to have the dubious distinction of being the first fake news film ever produced, preceding Doublier's "L'Affaire Dreyfus" by at least a year. The film was notable also for having involved the execution of an exclusive "star" performance contract—possibly the first one in the film industry—under the terms of which Corbett, the "victor," agreed to perform exclusively for the Latham-Rector group. He was reported to have been paid $4,750 for the two days' work involved in making the film. According to a contemporary newspaper account, the rounds lasted one and a half minutes each, and the rest period between rounds was two minutes, the length of time required to reload the camera.[22]

A year later, in May, 1895, the same organization presented a third fight film featuring "Young Griffo," and "Battling (Charles) Barnett." It was photographed by Otway Latham on the roof of Madison Square Garden, where bright sunlight was used to expose the relatively insensitive film.[23] The circumstances under which this attraction was presented to the public were far more important than the film itself. The Latham brothers, assisted by their father, Major Woodville Latham, and W. K. L. Dickson, had constructed a crude projector—first called the Pantoptikon, then later the Eidoloscope—with which they were able to project films onto a screen. The Griffo-Barnett fight was staged expressly for their first commercial screening, which took place on May 20, 1895, at 153 Broadway in New York City.[24] Although a projection process of grossly inferior design was employed, it can be argued—as some historians may wish to do[25]—that this was the first projected motion picture presented to a paying audience anywhere in the world, since it preceded the 1895 exhibitions of Lumière[26] and Armat[27] and the 1896 presentation of Paul.[28] If so, then the first commercial projected motion picture was a news film.

Still more fight films followed.* On March 17, 1897, Rector, formerly associated with the Latham brothers, photographed a genuine, newsworthy match between James Corbett and Bob Fitzsimmons at Carson City, Nevada. It was a bloody fight; in the fourteenth round Fitzsimmons downed Corbett with a blow to the stomach.[29] The match was photographed at ringside with three cameras, each of which—modified by Rector after the Edison design—was capable of fairly long takes. About eleven thousand feet of film were exposed, until that time probably the largest amount of film ever used to photograph a single attraction.[30] The film was presented to the public as a projected motion picture by Rector's Veriscope Company during the summer of 1897 and is reported to have made three-quarters of a million dollars for its owners.[31] It was followed almost immediately by a fraudulent and unauthorized re-creation of the same fight by film pioneer Sigmund Lubin, of Philadelphia, who employed two

---

* Apparently the first film shot by Herman Casler with the prototype Mutoscope camera in June, 1895, shows him sparring with his partner, Harry Marvin. The first Mutoscope film to attract any widespread attention from the press was of two professional boxers, "Professor" Al Leonard and his pupil, Bert Hosley, photographed on August 5, 1895, and reported by the press on August 10, 1895. See Gordon Hendricks, *Beginnings of the Biograph*, 15, 19, 21, and illustration 4.

freight handlers to impersonate the contenders.[32] The release of Rector's film was also followed by an early legislative attempt in Pennsylvania to ban prize-fight films. The attempt failed but portended the stringent regulation of prize-fight films which followed later. As Terry Ramsaye observed:

Until that picture appeared the social status of the screen had been uncertain. It now became definitely low-brow, an entertainment for the great unwashed commonality. This likewise made it a mark for uplifters, moralists, reformers and legislators in a degree which would never have obtained if the screen had by specialization reached higher social strata.[33]

Low-brow or not, despite a threat of state censorship and Lubin's imitation, the Veriscope film was eminently successful. It made a profit for its producers and stimulated further enthusiasm for the news-film medium. Suggested one editorial in a Brooklyn newspaper:

The man who could have predicted, at one time in our history, that an event of a prior month would be reproduced before the eyes of a multitude in pictures that moved like life, and that lightning would move them and light them, would have been avoided as a lunatic or hanged as a wizard.[34]

The success of Rector's film provoked similar fight-film ventures, the last major example of which—before 1900—was of the celebrated Jeffries-Sharkey fight of 1899. Before the filming of this event had been successfully completed, a number of leading film pioneers had been involved in the enterprise, some legally, some not. An illuminating and amusing insight into contemporary news-film ethics and the intrigues associated with this particular film has been provided in the memoirs of the late Albert E. Smith, one of the participant film makers. On his memoirs is based much of the following account.[35]

Until 1899, because of the relatively insensitive emulsions employed, motion pictures had to be made in bright sunlight. The early films of Edison had been photographed in his ingenious "Black Maria," a small studio with a roof which could be opened to admit sunlight. The whole studio was mounted on a turntable which could be rotated to move with the sun. Similarly, until 1899, prize-fight news films had to be photographed outdoors in bright sunlight to produce an image of satisfactory density.

In 1899, William Brady, a show-business entrepreneur, was manager of James J. Jeffries, contender for the heavyweight title. Brady had formerly managed Corbett, who had been defeated by Fitzsimmons in the fight photographed in 1896 by Rector's Veriscope Company. With Corbett's career ended, Brady turned to managing Jeffries. He arranged a match for him with Fitzsimmons, to take place at night at the Coney Island Athletic Club Arena. In the spring of 1899, shortly before the fight, Brady approached Albert E. Smith, one of the partners of the newly founded Vitagraph Company, and proposed that a news-film record be made of the fight. Despite the overwhelming problem of providing sufficient artificial light to film the event, Smith undertook to record the match for Brady. By the night of the event, June 2, 1899, Smith and his associate, J. Stuart Blackton, had arranged for one hundred arc lamps of special design, employing unusually large carbons, to be mounted around the ring. An auxiliary generator was employed in addition to the regular house current to provide the tremendous amount of electrical current required. Unfortunately, midway through the first round, the head of the generator blew off and the light level sank below that necessary to produce photographic images. The resulting films, which included Jeffries' eleventh-round knockout of Fitzsimmons, were ruined.[36]

Brady was enraged and blamed Smith for the generator failure. Appropriating the system of lighting as well as the lights themselves which the Vitagraph people had designed, Brady went to their competitor, Biograph, and arranged to have a match between Jeffries and contender Tom Sharkey photographed.* Shortly be-

* The Biograph cameraman of this event was "Billy" Bitzer, later to achieve fame as D. W. Griffith's cameraman.

fore the fight Smith and his associates, now shut out of the arena by Brady, were approached by James White, head of the motion picture department of the Edison Company. Without directly implicating Mr. Edison, White proposed that Smith, White, and other collaborators smuggle a camera into the arena and pirate scenes of the event. The Edison camera was far too large—the size of a small steamer trunk—to hide. The Vitagraph instrument, on the other hand, was reasonably small and portable. White, speaking for the Edison organization, promised to supply a cordon of Edison bodyguards to protect the group in the event of discovery and retaliation from the Biograph organization, which had already engaged a force of Pinkerton agents to safeguard the exclusiveness of their coverage. Fortunately for the conspirators, the legal status of the motion picture as a communications medium was not clearly defined at that time. Several years were to pass before a body of statute and precedent was established that effectively precluded piracy, copyright infringement, and violation of exclusive contractual agreements in the sports field.

The fight took place on the evening of November 3, 1899, again at the Coney Island Athletic Club. Shortly before fight time Smith and White were joined outside the arena by two enthusiastic assistants, an employee of Vitagraph named French and song writer Joe Howard ("I Wonder Who's Kissing Her Now"). Somehow, between the time the plans were made and the night of the event, the platoon of Edison bodyguards White had promised had failed to materialize. Nonetheless, the group decided to chance discovery and prepared to enter the building. It was decided that White, who was the largest of the group, would carry the camera strapped between his legs, hidden beneath his huge, flowing overcoat. The effect was predictably grotesque:

To allow leg movement the camera was turned length-wise. This caused a considerable bulge in the overcoat fore and aft, but there was nothing we could do about it. From a distance, White *looked like someone astride a small horse, or afflicted with an unseasonably severe case of elephantiasis.*[*][37]

Masked by the crush of spectators, the five men managed to enter the arena without detection and took their places in the ten-dollar-seat section, several rows up, overlooking the ring. This time over three hundred arc lamps had been mounted above the ring. The heat was so intense that the unfortunate fighters had to be shaded with umbrellas between rounds. "At one point the wiring became so hot that small chunks of ice were applied to the sizzling plug boxes and switches—sending a hot sprinkle down on the backs of the miserable warriors."[38]

Operating his partly hidden camera, Smith managed to film two rounds of the fight before the Biograph organization discovered his presence. Pinkerton agents tried to force their way to Smith but were driven back by the excited crowd intent upon the fight. Twenty-five rounds passed in what is remembered as an uncommonly bloody fight before Jeffries was declared the winner.

In the frenzied excitement which followed the fight, Smith, French, and Garrison escaped from the arena with their camera and film. White and Howard had long since deserted the group. Pursued from one part of town to another by promoter Brady, pugilist Jeffries, and a brace of Pinkerton agents, Smith finally made it safely back to the Vitagraph laboratory, where he developed the negative, left it upon racks to dry, and retired for a few hours' sleep. Awakened a while later by his partner, William Rock, Smith discovered that the negative had been stolen from the laboratory—not by Brady but by his own coconspirator, James White, of the Edison organization. Smith rushed across town to confront White in his office. In the midst of their argument Smith seized from White's desk a print of the film which the Edison group had already made and ran from the office, this time pursued by Edison employees, who failed to catch him. Recalling the turn

* Excerpts from Albert E. Smith, *Two Reels and a Crank,* which appear in Chapters 1–3, and are cited in the notes at the end of this book, are Copyright 1952 by Albert E. Smith, reprinted by permission of Doubleday and Company, Inc.

of events half a century later, Smith commented, "Despite my questionable position in the project, I always regarded White's seizure of the film as an unspeakable villainy."[39]

In the end, neither Brady (Biograph) nor the Edison organization profited much from their efforts. Brady delayed the commercial exhibition of the Edison film with a court injunction. However, Brady took so long releasing his own news film that public interest and response nearly disappeared.[40] Vitagraph, on the other hand, did nicely with its pirated version, which was booked by Riley and Woods, vaudeville producers, for forty weeks at two hundred dollars a week.[41] The only other film maker to profit from the event was Sigmund Lubin, who (as he had in the case of the Corbett-Fitzsimmons fight) released a fake re-creation of the fight, using impersonators for Jeffries and Sharkey.[42]

All three of the major film producers involved in the Jeffries-Sharkey fight of 1899—Edison, Biograph, and Vitagraph—were also engaged in more conventional news-film coverage, each in lively competition with the others.[43] Such evidence that survives—copyright records, newspaper accounts, reminiscences, and the like—indicate that Edison was far and away the most prolific producer of news films during the pre-1900 period. At first thought, this seems remarkable, considering the bulkiness of the first Edison cameras. Appraisal of the Edison output, however, reveals that its subject matter, almost without exception, lent itself to (1) thorough preproduction planning, (2) adequate time in advance of events for the mounting and preparation of the heavy camera, and (3) a static, never-changing camera position for the duration of the event. Such a camera was satisfactorily employed to photograph parades, posed "portraits" of celebrities, governmental ceremonies, embarkation and debarkation of troops by ship, and other similar scenes.*

* In time, cameras which the Edison organization used were reduced in size. According to Albert Smith, he tested Edison's "new light camera" while photographing the aftermath of the September, 1900, Galveston hurricane. Smith reported that this "light" camera of Edison's was still very much heavier than Vitagraph's machine.

One of the world's first news films was photographed by Louis Lumière in France on June 10, 1895. Actually a cross between the news film and an actuality, it recorded the not-too-newsworthy outing of members of the Congress of the National Union of French Photographic Societies at Neuville-Saint-Vaast. Two days later Lumière created quite a stir at a meeting of the congress, when he screened the footage for the members. (From the Museum of Modern Art, New York.)

From the beginning, sports events provided popular subject matter for the news film. This boxing match featured Billy Edwards, and was photographed by Thomas Edison in his "Black Maria" studio sometime before February 8, 1895. The film was viewed in peep shows. (From Eastman House Museum, Rochester, N.Y.)

The prize-fight match between Bob Fitzsimmons and Jim Corbett, held on March 17, 1897, at Carson City, Nevada. Corbett is on the mat at the left, and Fitzsimmons, the eventual winner, stands at the right. The fight was photographed by Enoch Rector with his Veriscope camera. Note the copyright notice painted on the edge of the ring. Such films as these played an important role in popularizing the early motion picture and in facilitating the technological sophistication of the medium. (From Eastman House Museum, Rochester, N.Y.)

The Prince's Derby at Epsom Downs, photographed on June 3, 1896, by the British film pioneer Robert Paul. The camera is located about 20 yards this side of the finish line. The horse at the left is Persimmon, who won the race for Edward, Prince of Wales (later Edward VII). In a display of motion picture news-gathering initiative remarkable for its day, the film was rushed through processing and screened at the Alhambra Theater in London on the evening of the following day. (From *Strand Magazine*, 1896.)

Some of the footage of the 1898 Spanish-American War was authentic; much of it was not. This photograph shows the pool, canvas backdrop, and miniature mountains and battleships which E. H. Amet constructed for his short re-creation of the sinking of Admiral Pascual Cervera's fleet in Santiago Bay, Cuba. (From *International Photographer*, 1933.)

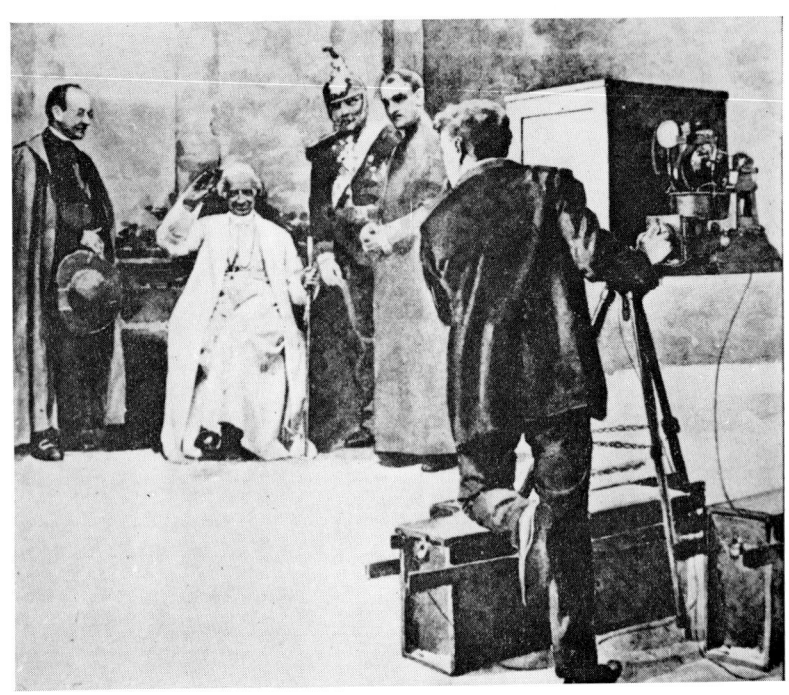

Despite their size and awkwardness Biograph cameras were carried all over the world as its operators searched for interesting subjects. Here a Biograph cameraman (probably W. K. L. Dickson) photographs Pope Leo XIII at the Vatican in 1898. (From Eastman House Museum, Rochester, N.Y.)

Facing page: The Boer War was one of the first military conflicts to be recorded on film. Following its outbreak in 1899, motion picture cameramen from many countries journeyed to South Africa to record it. Above: The cameraman is believed to be Joseph Rosenthal, of Charles Urban Trading Company of England. (From the author's collection.)

Below: The best coverage of the Boer War was photographed by W. K. L. Dickson for the British subsidiary of the American Mutoscope and Biograph Company. Here he is shown in the field in South Africa with the Biograph camera. With his horse-drawn cart and gigantic camera, Dickson became as much a fixture of the front-line areas as Mathew Brady had been on American Civil War battlegrounds forty years earlier. (From the author's collection.)

Above: The funeral of Queen Victoria in February,
1901, brought most of the crowned rulers of Europe
before news-film cameras. (From Museum of Modern
Art, New York.) Below: The coronation of Edward VII
of England in 1902 was faked by the French film pioneer
Georges Méliès for the Warwick Trading Company of
England. The elaborate reconstruction was intercut with
genuine footage of the exterior of Westminster Abbey
which had been shot during the ceremonies. According
to film historian Terry Ramsaye, the faked scene was
fatally flawed when the crown on "Edward's" head accidentally tilted, making him appear drunk. (From the
author's collection.)

Above: Catastrophes and disasters provided newsreel cameramen with their most exciting and popular subject matter. Few catastrophes were more spectacular than the San Francisco earthquake and fire of 1906, photographed by R. K. Bonine for a film released by the Edison Company. (From Museum of Modern Art, New York.) Below: San Francisco in ruins, also photographed by Bonine. This piece of footage is unquestionably genuine. (From Museum of Modern Art, New York.)

Some of the most spectacular footage of the San Francisco disaster was faked by film makers at the Biograph Company. They constructed a miniature set of the city, placed it in front of a backdrop, started the cameras running, and set fire to it. The film was immensely successful and was reported to have been convincing enough to fool contemporaries, including the mayor of San Francisco at the time of the fire. Here one of the technicians, F. A. Dobson, poses with the miniature for a production still. (From *International Photographer*, 1933.)

Among the more popular of the very early Edison films was a series of brief, exciting actualities of celebrated railway trains of the day, usually pictured dramatically rounding a curve or hurtling toward the audience at high speed. Included in the series were "The Black Diamond Express," "The Philadelphia Express," "The Chicago and Buffalo Express," "The Fast Mail, Northern Pacific R.R.," and "The Southern Pacific Overland Mail." The effect of such scenes upon unsophisticated audiences, at least in 1896–97, was said to have been spectacular.

In a not-too-thorough fashion Edison also covered the Alaska gold rush with scenes of the loading of miners' baggage, the sailing of the S.S. *Willamette* from the Klondike, a pack train in the Chilkoot Pass, and the washing of gold above Hunter, in the Klondike. Primitive sports coverage was provided, too, in Edison's films of the 1899 America's Cup yacht races, in which *Columbia* defeated *Shamrock I.*

The most interesting and enduring of the pre-1900 Edison films, however, were those photographed at the inauguration of President William McKinley in 1897. Although the camera rarely moved, the many subjects which passed before it were varied and historically significant. Among those pictured in the inaugural parade were retiring President Grover Cleveland, Governor Cook of Connecticut, the governor of Ohio, Buffalo Bill Cody, Vice-President-elect Garret A. Hobart, and, of course, President-elect McKinley. They were photographed being escorted by the Amoskeag veterans of New Hampshire, the Grant veterans, the Seventh and Seventy-first regiments of New York, the Sixth U.S. Cavalry, and marines from the cruiser *New York.* Following the parade, the first motion picture record of a presidential inauguration was made as McKinley took his oath of office. Solely on the evidence of the inaugural-parade films, however, we may say that Grover Cleveland was the first American president to be filmed by the motion picture camera while still in office. In all, at least four film producers of the day were said to have photographed the parade: Edison, Biograph, E. H. Amet, and Lumière.[44] The Edison coverage, as shown at the Central Church of Rochester, New York, was reported to have exhibited "several color effects" and was accompanied by the State Industrial Boys' Band.[45]

The second of the major film producers of this period, the American Mutoscope Company (later the American Mutoscope and Biograph Company, and still later the Biograph Company) became in time one of the most important of the early motion picture producers.* The Biograph Company utilized its own make of motor-driven camera, employing a film with an area eight times larger than that of Edison and an irregularly spaced system of perforations produced during photography which successfully defied Edison's patents. The Mutoscope negatives were printed on photographic cards and displayed in rapid succession in peep-show machines, examples of which still survive in some amusement arcades throughout the United States. Also, by September, 1896, positive motion picture prints were projected for audiences by the company with its own make of projector.[46]

Apparently the first news film by the Biograph Company was made on August 28, 1896. It showed Li Hung Chang, the Chinese diplomat, who had just returned to the United States after attending the coronation of Nicholas II in Russia.[47] About a month later, on September 18, Biograph's cameraman Billy Bitzer photographed an important news film which featured scenes of William McKinley before the 1896 election.[48] A column of the amusement page of the *New York Tribune*, allegedly written by a press agent for Hammerstein's Olympia Music Hall, where the film was screened, reviewed the film favorably:

Anybody who thinks that the enthusiasm of the modern music-hall audience is all for European singers of questionable propriety should have been at the Olympia Music Hall last night. The audience went fairly frantic over the pictures thrown on a screen. . . . The biggest part of the enthusiasm began when a view of a

---

* For the sake of convenience the firm will be referred to in this book as the Biograph Company.

McKinley and Hobart parade in Canton was shown. The cheering was incessant as long as the line was passing across the screen, and it grew much greater when the title of the next picture appeared: "Major McKinley at Home." Major McKinley was seen to come down the steps of his house with his secretary. The secretary handed him a paper which he opened and read. Then he took off his hat and advanced to meet a visiting delegation.[49]

Coincidentally, Abner McKinley, brother of the President, was said to be one of the major investors in the Biograph organization. It has been suggested that this business association led to the extensive coverage of the McKinley campaign, thereby imparting a distinctly Republican flavor to the early Biograph enterprise: "What with Abner McKinley's stock participation in the American Mutoscope and Biograph Company and its other "downtown" [Wall Street] affiliations . . . the Bryan cause [in the 1896 election] had not the remotest screen chance.[50]

Biograph photographed many other celebrities of the day, including William Jennings Bryan (long after the 1896 election), General Sir Herbert Kitchener, New York Police Chief Theodore Roosevelt, and Pope Leo XIII, the last filmed in the Vatican in 1898.[51] The Biograph Company also founded a British news-film branch with laboratories in Great Windmill Street in London. This subsidiary organization is said to have offered the first regular news coverage on film in England.[52]

Vitagraph, the third major company operating during this period, was also active before 1900, producing both genuine and fake news films under the direction of the company's founders, Albert E. Smith, J. Stuart Blackton, and William Rock.

During the years 1896 to 1900, Edison copyrighted more than 250 news-film titles and deposited them with the United States Copyright Office.[53] Inexplicably, neither Biograph nor Vitagraph appears to have copyrighted a single news film during the same period. Whether this omission should be taken as a reflection of their contempt for the primitive copyright protection which they frequently and successfully defied, a disregard for the value of their own product, or simply a lack of fear of infringement is not clear. It appears that a certain number of Biograph news films photographed before 1900 were not copyrighted till after the turn of the century. As for the uncopyrighted Vitagraph films, the Edison organization is known to have released several Vitagraph films and may have copyrighted them in the Edison name.

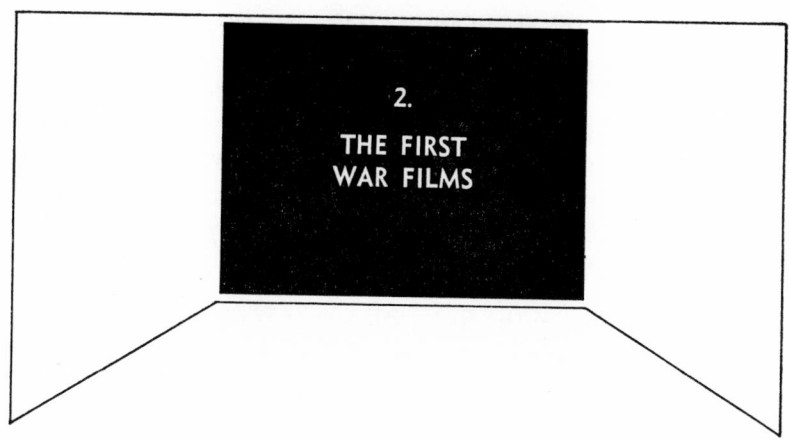

2.
THE FIRST WAR FILMS

In 1898 were produced the first news films of war—which is to say, the first filmed *records* of war rather than fictional dramatizations. In truth, in many of these early wartime films it is difficult to say where documentation leaves off and re-creation or outright fraud begins. Also, some question has arisen in the intervening years about the exact nature of the contributions made by various early motion picture correspondents. Some of these questions do not appear to be answerable at this late date.[1] This much seems certain—the Spanish-American War was the first war photographed by American motion picture producers, and a number of cameramen from several organizations covered it.

From the moment the American battleship *Maine* exploded in Havana Harbor on February 15, 1898, the war made good copy for both newspapers and film makers. As quickly as inflammatory, jingoistic editorials appeared on front pages, politically unequivocal film clips appeared on motion picture screens. One of the first and most successful of these was manufactured by Vitagraph on April 21, shortly after the declaration of war. Entitled "Tearing Down the Spanish Flag," this short, simple film showed a flagpole from which a Spanish flag was flying. The flag was abruptly torn down (by the hand of J. Stuart Blackton), and in its place an American flag was raised.[2] In the words of Albert E. Smith:

Projected on a thirty-foot screen, the effect on audiences was sensational and sent us searching for similar subjects. . . . The people were on fire and eager for every line of news. The New York Journal sold a million copies in a single day. The circulation of Pulitzer's New York World rose to five million a week. . . . With nationalistic feeling at fever pitch we set out to photograph what the people wanted to see.[3]

Edison was among the first with scenes from Colón, Cuba, of the funeral procession of victims of the *Maine* catastrophe,[4] as well as a scene of the half-submerged wreck of the ship.[5] Vitagraph finished the coverage with scenes of the burials at Arlington Cemetery. The Vitagraph footage ran for nearly three minutes:

We rented [the film] for a thousand dollars for two weeks to two promoters who were reopening a vacant opera house on Lexington Avenue, built before the present Metropolitan. For the first time, an orchestra accompanied a Vitagraph picture, making the most of the occasion with a soul-rending dirge. When it was over, the spectators filed wordlessly from the theater, faces grave, here and there eyes blinking furiously to press back the tears.[6]

Somewhat more exciting footage followed when Vitagraph and Edison filmed, at Hoboken, the departure of the Seventy-first National Guard Regiment for Tampa, the assembly point for the invasion of Cuba.[7] Vitagraph's film was processed within hours and was screened on the evening of the same day at Tony Pastor's Theater in New York:

That night at Pastor's the audience, enthralled with the idea of a war with Spain, saw their boys marching for the first time on any screen. They broke into a thunderous storm of shouting and foot stamping. Hats and coats filled the air. Never had Pastor's witnessed such a night![8]

Most of the competing film producers then in business—Edison, Biograph, and Vitagraph in particular—released films purporting to show activities of American troops in training, on their way to war, in the front lines in Cuba. Some of this footage was genuine; much of it was obviously faked. Insofar as copyright records are concerned, most of the titles belonged to Edison. Among those which appear to be genuine were films showing scenes of California volunteers embarking, Cuban refugees, the Tenth U.S. Infantry disembarking, United States troops landing at Baiquiri, an American wagon train en route in Cuba, American troops building roads near Santiago, transport ships at Tampa, and the embarkation of Teddy Roosevelt's Rough Riders for Santiago.[9]

The Edison news films which are classified as obvious fakes by historian Kemp Niver in his catalogue of pre-1912 copyright entries include the following films purportedly taken in Cuba and the Philippine Islands: the advance of Kansas Volunteers at Caloocan, the capture of trenches at Candaba, a Cuban ambush, an early-morning attack on an American position by Cubans, the retreat of Filipinos from trenches, the raising of the American flag over Morro Castle, a rout of Filipino soldiers, the shooting of captured insurgents, a skirmish of Rough Riders, United States infantry at El Caney, and United States troops and Red Cross staff in the trenches near Caloocan.[10]

Vitagraph, riding on a profit-making wave of war-film exploitation, followed Roosevelt to Cuba with its cameras and photographed scenes of the assault of the Rough Riders on San Juan Hill. In what was to become one of the first of many instances in which motion picture records contradicted written reports, Smith and Blackton's pictures of Roosevelt's attack showed not a theatrical sweep to the top but a slow, undramatic engagement extending over a long period of time. According to Smith:

The thin line of Rough Riders halted, fired, advanced slowly, more picking their way through the heavy thicket than charging. This was the assault. Nothing glamorous or hip-hip-hooray. . . .

It was not until Blackton and I returned to New York that we learned we had taken part in the celebrated "charge" up San

Juan Hill. Many historians have given it a Hollywood flavor, but there was vastly more bravery in the tortuous advance against this enemy who could see and not be seen.[11]

Seeking to improve upon the newsworthy but unspectacular nature of their authentic battle footage (released under the title "Fighting with Our Boys in Cuba"),[12] Smith and Blackton subsequently manufactured a fraudulent re-creation of the Battle of Santiago Bay in which Admiral Pascual Cervera y Topete's fleet was destroyed by American warships. Smith wrote:

At this time street vendors in New York were selling large sturdy photographs of ships of the American and Spanish fleets. We bought a set of each and we cut out the battleships. On a table, topside down, we placed one of Blackton's large canvas-covered frames and filled it with water an inch deep. In order to stand the cutouts of the ships in the water, we nailed them to lengths of wood about an inch square. In this way a little "shelf" was provided behind each ship, and on this shelf we placed pinches of gunpowder—three pinches for each ship—not too many, we felt, for a major sea engagement of this sort.

For a background, Blackton daubed a few white clouds on a blue-tinted cardboard. To each of the ships, now sitting placidly in our shallow "bay," we attached a fine thread to enable us to pull the ships past the camera at the proper moment and in the correct order.

We needed someone to blow smoke into the scene, but we couldn't go too far outside our circle if the secret was to be kept. Mrs. Blackton was called in and she volunteered, in this day of nonsmoking womanhood, to smoke a cigarette. A friendly office boy said he would try a cigar. This was fine, as we needed the volume.

A piece of cotton was dipped in alcohol and attached to a wire slender enough to escape the eye of the camera. Blackton, concealed behind the side of the table farthermost from the camera, touched off the mounds of gunpowder with his wire taper—and

*the battle was on. Mrs. Blackton, smoking and coughing, delivered
a fine haze. Jim had worked out a timing arrangement with her so
that she blew the smoke into the scene at approximately the
moment of explosion. . . .*

*The film and lenses of that day were imperfect enough to con-
ceal the crudities of our miniature, and as the picture ran only two
minutes there was not time for anyone to study it critically. . . .*

*Pastor's and both Proctor houses played to capacity audiences
for several weeks. Jim and I felt less and less remorse of conscience
when we saw how much excitement and enthusiasm were aroused
by* The Battle of Santiago Bay.[13]

Many years later "The Battle of Santiago Bay" was described
by Smith as Vitagraph's first "feature." It cost exactly $1.98 to
produce. In a speech before the members of the Academy of
Motion Picture Arts and Sciences, Smith recalled that "the press
was very good. The press said that the picture was even better than
the battle itself, so it must have been good."[14] Historian Arthur
Krows thought differently, however, after examining the film
many years later. His remarks provide an estimate of the gullibility
of early audiences:

*They tell stories today about contemporaneous audiences being
completely hoodwinked by this; but I do not believe that they
could have been—really. I saw the subject some years later, privately, as a curiosity. It was brazenly crude—even for then.*[15]

The war's conclusion did not escape Vitagraph's and Edison's
cameras. Late in September, 1899, the American cruiser *Olympia*
returned to New York Harbor, bearing Admiral George Dewey
fresh from victory over the Spanish fleet at Manila Bay. Smith and
Blackton stole aboard the cruiser and managed to photograph
Dewey walking near the stern of the ship.[16] Edison's cameramen
photographed the admiral visiting the State House in Boston,
leading a parade, and receiving welcoming committees in New
York and Washington. They also photographed New York City's

welcome to Admiral William T. Sampson's fleet following the Battle of Santiago Bay.[17]

Understandably, the Boer War (1899–1902) was more thoroughly covered by British cameramen than by Americans. The first footage sent back to England appears to have been taken by Edgar Hyman, who photographed the arrival of British troops at Cape Town.[18] He was followed shortly by John Bennett Stanford, Joe Rosenthal, Sydney Goldman, C. Rider Noble, and George Rogers, all of whom represented either the American-owned Warwick Trading Company or the Charles Urban Trading Company.[19] Additional scenes of troop movements in the British Isles and military activities far behind the lines in Africa were photographed by the British producers Cecil Hepworth and Robert Paul.[20]

By far the most intensive coverage of the war, however, was provided by W. K. L. Dickson, of former kinetoscope fame, who spent more than a year with the British forces as a motion picture correspondent for the British Mutoscope and Biograph Company, a subsidiary of the American firm. As mentioned earlier, Dickson, a British subject, had formerly been associated with Thomas Edison, with whom he invented the first practical motion picture camera in the late 1880's and early 1890's. In time Dickson left Edison and, after a brief association with the Latham brothers, went on to help found the American Mutoscope and Biograph Company. Early in Biograph's affairs he returned to England to work with the British subsidiary.

Almost immediately upon the outbreak of war Dickson left for Africa, sailing on October 14, 1899, aboard the *Dunottar Castle*. A fairly detailed description of his operating methods, problems, and successes survives in a series of dated dispatches which he sent back to England with his films.[21] Dickson's horse-drawn Cape cart, filled with photographic equipment, eating utensils, and sleeping gear, became as much a fixture of front-line areas as Mathew Brady's mobile darkroom had been on American Civil War battlegrounds forty years earlier.

The coverage Dickson secured for Biograph was surprisingly detailed and of good quality, considering the conditions under which he and his assistants, William Cox and Jonathan Seward, had to work. His coverage included trains of guns en route to Estacourt, armored trains with troops, remounted naval guns firing on the Boers, an ambulance corps, the Royal Fusiliers striking camp, various sorties, Boer prisoners, the Gordon Highlanders, the Battle of Ladysmith, and a number of so-called "living portraits" of military leaders, including Lord Roberts ("Bobs Bahadur") and Lord Baden-Powell. Dickson frequently accompanied the British artillery and on one or two occasions managed to photograph Boer soldiers as seen from the British lines. Most of the time, however, the awkwardness of his equipment—which had to be operated from his horse-drawn cart or a heavy tripod—precluded the intimate coverage which became common in later wars. Wrote Dickson on December 14, 1889:

We have made every effort to get a photograph of the Boer position, and the effect of the [cannon] shots, by means of the telephoto, but we were forced to give it up owing to the haze and indistinctness which made it impossible to focus properly. There are many other difficulties besides, all of which I hope to overcome in time.[22]

Many of Dickson's written dispatches described the unpleasant living and traveling conditions which he, like all other wartime cameramen who followed him, experienced when working near the front lines. He also described the manner in which permission was secured from military leaders to gain entry to front-line areas. Occasionally he was frustrated in these efforts. On December 7, 1899, he noted: "One military officer high in authority has done everything to block my path, and to prevent the world from seeing these views. I have yet to discover his motive."[23] Usually, however, he was able to secure passes and letters of introduction from such high officials as General Sir Redvers Buller and Cecil Rhodes.

In marked contrast to the manner in which the press was treated

35

MILLS COLLEGE
LIBRARY

in subsequent wars, Dickson enjoyed almost unimpeded access to high military officials, many of whom even confided secret plans for imminent military engagements so as to allow the film maker time to set up his equipment beforehand to cover the event. In one case a message from Colonel Kitchener was delayed en route for the convenience of the Biograph camera, "the operators kindly waiting until we got the machine in position before they sent the message."[24] Some of Dickson's own films for Biograph, which had been photographed earlier in Africa, were shipped to England, processed in London, and later shipped back and screened in Kimberley while Dickson was still engaged in wartime filming.

These early wartime news films were made in the best tradition of motion picture journalism. Like the troops whose activities he photographed, Dickson and his companions suffered risk of injury, disease, famine, and capture. Further, his safety as a noncombatant correspondent was by no means guaranteed if he was taken prisoner by the Boers.

During the same period at least two wholly American-owned firms, Edison and Vitagraph, also released footage of the British-Boer conflict. Most of the Edison footage seems to have been faked. However, Vitagraph sent one of its owners, Albert E. Smith, to Africa for a short period. There, sometimes in the company of Richard Harding Davis, he filmed not only the British troops but also the Boer forces.[25] The Vitagraph film was good enough to secure for the company an exhibition contract at Koster and Bial's Music Hall in New York City, a prize which Smith later stated was the only incentive for going to Africa in the first place.

3.
FAKING THE EARLY NEWS FILMS

Audiences of the late nineteenth century were apparently not too critical of what they saw, provided the picture moved. For every genuine news film photographed under difficult and sometimes dangerous conditions, an equal amount of energy was spent by the same producers to fake outstanding news events of the day. Generally, such fake news films fell into one of four categories:

1. Theatrically staged re-creations of famous events, based roughly upon the original but not intended or likely to fool audiences.

2. Realistically staged re-creations of famous events, based upon reliable information and duplicating insofar as possible the location, participants, and circumstances of the original. These films were generally designed to deceive audiences.

3. Rough re-creations of famous events, made without attempting to duplicate known particulars of the events. These films were also generally designed to deceive audiences.

4. Outright manufacture of unverifiable activities alleged to have been associated with famous events—always intended to deceive audiences.

All the clever re-creations produced by the French film maker Georges Méliès fell in the first of these categories. Among the many reconstructions produced by Méliès were the eruption of Mount Pelée, the assassination of President McKinley, the coronation of Edward VII, the Dreyfus trial, the sinking of the *Maine*, and the Greco-Turkish War.[1] These charming films, artificially staged and dramatically embroidered, were never meant to fool audiences. In those days the name Méliès was unequivocally linked with his slogan "Artificially Arranged Scenes."[2]

Sigmund Lubin's reproduction of the 1899 Jeffries-Sharkey fight provided an example of the second kind of fake news film.[3] Based upon newspaper accounts of the true event a fairly accurate reconstruction was prepared, using impersonators for the famous fighters. Lubin's efforts along these lines were not really frauds, since he released his films as "reproductions" rather than as records of the original events.

Both Doublier's "L'Affaire Dreyfus" and the Smith-Blackton reproduction of "The Battle of Santiago Bay" represented examples of the third kind of fake, roughly staged re-creations of famous events made without much attempt to duplicate any of the known particulars. Such fakes, certainly intended to fool audiences, were likely to do so only as long as pictorial coverage by competing newsmen was not available for comparison. With the passing of years, as competition increased and duplicate simultaneous coverage became common, this kind of fake, as well as the first two, practically disappeared.

The fourth kind of fake was the most common, the most difficult to detect, the most difficult to expose, and the most hardy—news-film footage of activities alleged to have been associated with famous events. The Corbett-Courtney fight of 1894 was undoubtedly the first fake film of any kind ever made. Not only was the fight expressly arranged for the news-film camera, but (as allegedly in the case of contemporary professional wrestling matches) the incidents of each round and the final outcome were prearranged. Another example of the manufactured news film was produced by Albert E. Smith while photographing the Boer War in Africa for Vitagraph. He wrote in his memoirs:

When I got back to the camp at Estacourt I sat down to figure out just what I had obtained with the camera and I saw that I had little of actual warfare, having been forced to remain at a distance beyond camera range. I asked a few of the British soldiers if they would put on Boer clothes and go through a few mock skirmishes, which they did. They fired a few volleys from behind boulders and went screaming past the camera in fine "forward charge" technique.[4]

Ironically, when Smith later photographed a really extraordinary event, the audience back in the United States did not believe him. The British employed huge railway freight engines, without tracks, to ferry loads across a river and to pull mired trucks and wagons out of the mud:

Huge railway freight engines steamed into sight! Enormous traction machines with the wide and high wheels and tremendous boiler. . . . That they were moving on land and taking part in a war in the very heart of Africa was almost unbelievable.

I photographed the snorting giants as they dragged huge loads across the ford and towed the mired wagons and guns out of the river. When the film was shown in New York, Vitagraph was accused of having faked the freight engine scenes. Our critics claimed it was not possible for engines to move without rails, much less on anything as rough as the African terrain at the Tugela.[5]

Apparently there was not a single major film producer in the period 1894 to 1900 that did not fake news films as a matter of common practice.* Sigmund Lubin practically specialized in

---

* Vitagraph continued to fake news films for many years. In 1911 the company produced a fraudulent war film which showed alleged atrocities committed by the Italians against the Turks. The fake was exposed, and the film caused such a commotion among Italian-American citizens, civic officials, and the motion picture trade press, that Vitagraph was obliged to remove the film from release and apologize to the Italian consul. One trade paper called the film "an abominable lie, and, as such, should be censored. . . . It was a disgrace to the Vitagraph Company, for the sake of pocketing a few dirty dollars, to bring out such a film, and, worse still, for the Patents Company to allow such a disgusting exhibition of disgraceful avariciousness to be released by the General Film Company." See *Moving Picture News*, December 16, 1911, p. 5, and December 23, 1911, p. 6.

fakes for a while, although he seems to have usually identified them as such in exhibition. Among his contributions to the art were reproductions of the following prize fights: Corbett and Jeffries (1899), Fitzsimmons and Jeffries (1899), Jeffries and Ruhlin (1899), Jeffries and Sharkey (1899), Kid McCoy and Maher (1899), Palmer and McGovern (1899), Corbett and Mc-Coy (1900), Fitzsimmons and Sharkey (1900), McGovern and Dixon (1900), Britt and Nelson (1905), Gans and Nelson (1906), Nelson and McGovern (1906), and Burns and Palmer (1908).[6]

One of the most ambitious frauds, already mentioned, was the Smith-Blackton re-creation of the Battle of Santiago Bay. Another film maker of the same period, Edwin H. Amet, was responsible for a second fake of this sensational event, in comparison with which—judging from the description of one who saw it—the Vitagraph version must have looked amateurish:

In miniature [Amet] . . . constructed the Bay of Santiago in a tub, with all the ships participating in the action, working them up with a great fineness of detail and equipping them with guns, all to fit exactly with the pictures and descriptions in the periodicals. The models were proportioned to the lens angle to create perspective with great accuracy. Electrically controlled devices supplied waves, and push buttons controlled the guns and ship movements.[7]

There is a legend—unverifiable, of course—which has survived in motion picture histories, that the Spanish government in Madrid purchased a print of Amet's film for its military archives, apparently convinced of its authenticity.[8]

The Edison organization was especially known for its many re-creations. Some of the ones done in miniature, such as the eruption of Mount Pelée and destruction of Saint-Pierre and the Bombardment of Taku Forts during the Boxer uprising in China, were easily identifiable as fakes because of their crudeness.[9] As for the company's coverage of the Boer War, one early biographer of Edison wrote in 1910:

. . . it is an open secret that for weeks during the Boer War regularly equipped British and Boer armies confronted each other on the peaceful hills of Orange, New Jersey, ready to enact before the camera the stirring events told by the cable from the heat of hostilities.[10]

Such Edison fakes, which fall into the fourth category above, were sometimes difficult to detect and expose, since neither recognizable locales nor identifiable individuals were pictured in them. In other cases, of course, the absurd histrionics of the actors and the impossible positioning of the camera in the very midst of hand-to-hand fighting revealed the fakes for what they were.

As for Biograph, the authenticity of Dickson's work in Africa has apparently never been questioned. Certain other Biograph news films are suspect, however. Of those few Biograph newsfilm titles copyrighted between 1900 and 1905, the following are certainly fraudulent: "Eruption of Mt. Vesuvius," "Battle of Mt. Ariat," "The Battle of the Yalu," "Reproduction, Nan Paterson's Trial," "Execution of a Spy," "An Execution by Hanging." A film called "Landing of U.S. Troops Near Santiago" is probably a fake.[11] The authenticity of Biograph's footage of the Spanish-American War in the Philippines was severely questioned by a contemporary critic in the May, 1900, issue of the *Rochester Democrat and Chronicle*:

[A view] . . . showing a trainload of British troops "en route" to join Buller at Frere Camp [during the Boer War] is apparently genuine. As much cannot be said for the alleged picture of American troops charging a force of rebels in the Philippines. If it is what it is represented to be, the camera must have been stationed just in front of the Tagalog position and in the direct line of fire, when the picture was taken. A Drill at Van Cortland Park would probably correctly describe it.[12]

Biograph was also known to have released an unusually detailed

41

fake of the San Francisco fire and earthquake, filmed in 1906 at the company's studios on East Fourteenth Street in New York under the direction of manager George E. Van Guysling.[13] A miniature of downtown San Francisco was built by Biograph employees Frank J. Marion, Joe Harrington, and F. A. Dobson. As the cameras turned, the miniature was destroyed by fire. A surviving still of Dobson at work on the miniature shows the great amount of detail which went into the construction.[14] According to Leslie Wood:

The buildings were made from cardboard boxes, and the yawning cavity which appeared to split the city in two was contrived from a base of modelling clay which was laid over already divided segments of cardboard which were pulled in opposite directions.[15]

Apparently the result, released to theaters shortly after the disaster, was convincing:

Eugene Schmitt, who was the mayor of San Francisco at the time of the fire, when he saw the picture, thought it authentic. And so did Senator James Phelan, the famous California U.S. Senator, who viewed the pictures at the Biograph Studios. Van Guysling offered the pictures for what they were worth; he neither claimed them to be authentic, nor did he claim otherwise. Prints from the picture sold to other movie makers with a profit to Biograph of about $35,000.[16]

Ironically but not untypically, an authentic motion picture record of the disaster which had been filmed by the early San Francisco film-exchange operator Harry Miles was said to have failed at the box office because it was released after the fake Biograph production.[17]

American film producers were not alone in faking news events—it was an international art. Britisher Robert Paul, for example, produced a series of *Reproductions of Incidents of the Boer War*, which were arranged under the supervision of an experienced military officer from the front and included such sequences as

"Bombardment of Mafeking" and "Nurses on the Battlefield."[18] The Sheffield Photo Company faked a scene from the Russo-Japanese War entitled "Attack on a Japanese Convoy." J. Williamson manufactured "Attack on a China Mission" in his own back yard and photographed other scenes from the Boer War and the Boxer Rebellion on a golf course.[19]

The British Gaumont Company also engaged in faking. One of the company's principals, Colonel A. C. Bromhead, in a lecture to the British Kinematographic Society in 1936, described Gaumont's faking of the "Signing of the Peace at Vereeniging in 1902":

Our little picture, which was ludicrously imaginative, showed actors posing as Lord Kitchener, Lord Milner, and the British staff with the Boer leaders—President Steyn, Smuts, Botha, de Wet, and others discussing dramatically and finally signing the Peace conditions. We included Lord Roberts and only found out afterwards that he had not been there.

Many other sensational staged topicals were made. The assassination of King Alexander and Queen Draga of Serbia, in 1903, was produced in a short, but meaty film....

Then there was a very effective film portraying the eruption of Mt. Pelée, and the destruction of St. Pierre, Martinique, in the year 1902.... Two or three did this—I think Pathé's was the best. It was an ingenious picture of models and firework display.[20]

The vividness and realism of the medium encouraged public confidence in its veracity. Time and time again the early critical literature stressed the accuracy and reliability of the motion picture as a documentary medium. As one 1911 writer put it: "Cinematography cannot be made to *lie*, it is a machine that merely records what is happening."[21] It took a number of years for this notion to die.

Fortunately for early producers, there were a number of factors working for the believability of fake news films.

First, the motion picture medium was so new that audiences

had little or no filmgoing experience to guide them in their appraisal of content.

Second, the quality of camera registration, optics, and film was so poor during the first ten years of the cinema that even the poorest re-creation could sometimes fool unsophisticated viewers. The best of the reproductions, "softened" as they were by the over-all technical imperfections of the medium, were good enough to fool experts.

Third, the length of such films, at least during the first few years, was so short—from a few seconds up to a minute—that only the sharpest-eyed patrons could detect errors.

Fourth, the lack of extensive pictorial coverage of newsworthy events, by both still and motion picture cameramen, rendered many early fakes relatively safe from immediate exposure. Without a variety of photographs or films for comparison purposes, audiences and critics had no way of knowing how the original event appeared.

Finally, some fakes were virtually impossible to detect and expose without evidence and testimony from the participants in the production. This was true of the fourth category of fake films, described earlier. In later years such "manufactured" news, in one form or another, probably provided more than 50 per cent of the scenes in an average newsreel. In this respect, of course, the problems of the news-film producer in satisfying his patrons seemed not much different from those of the newspaper editor. T. S. Matthews, former managing editor of *Time*, put the matter this way:

Most of the world's "news" is manufactured by the press itself: interviews with important men, reports on grave situations, press conferences, press investigations, political surveys, "informed speculation." ...

I remember once toting up the front-page news stories in a good provincial newspaper in America. Of the eleven stories on the page, seven had not happened at all. . . . If news is what happened yesterday, the newspapers print an awful lot of phony news.[22]

On the face of it, then, it seems possible to make a distinction between the "manufacture" of newsworthy events for legitimate news-gathering purposes and the outright fraudulent faking of news events which was such a familiar part of early motion picture production. Of peculiar interest was the candor and pride with which veteran news-film producers, both in recollection and in contemporaneous accounts, revealed the manner and frequency with which they fabricated the films. Such an apparent denial of traditional journalistic ethics suggests the likelihood that early motion picture news-film producers saw as their primary role and function not so much to provide accurate information for educational, political, or social action as to provide sensational visualizations of attention-compelling news events.

Be that as it may, the evidence of fraud in the early cinema seems abundant enough to justify unusual caution in appraising early news-film output. Early films have not always been evaluated by historians and documentarians with the care and suspicion that they deserve. For example, in 1926, Terry Ramsaye described what he considered the world's first genuine news-film scoop:

. . . a catastrophe was to bring a new flavor of verity into the pictures. On March 17, 1899, the Windsor Hotel in New York burned and forty-five persons lost their lives. Blackton and Smith covered the fire with their camera, getting short bits of film showing the burning ruins. Probably for the first time the motion picture camera pictured news in the process of happening.[23]

Unknown to Ramsaye, twenty-seven years earlier Smith had confided to the pages of his private journal:

March 30, 1899: Filmed miniature of Windsor Hotel fire with little rubber figures jumping out of windows of cardboard model. Ignited gunpowder for fire and smoke. Used toy squirt guns for streams of water. Film very successful among Vitagraph customers.[24]

4.

THE AMERICAN
SILENT NEWS FILMS

By the turn of the century the motion picture was a familiar but
not yet firmly established part of the American entertainment
scene. Used primarily at that time to augment stage and vaudeville shows, the motion picture was not to enjoy any kind of
permanence in America until the latter part of the first decade,
by which time many theaters had appeared which were devoted
exclusively to its presentation.

The introduction and early history of the motion picture news
film may be contrasted with that of other forms of pictorial
journalism, such as the illustrated newspaper and magazine. Although systems of photoengraving go back at least to 1839 with
the appearance of the first crude etched daguerreotype plates, the
art did not become sufficiently advanced to allow for photographic
illustrations in combination with type until the introduction of
the halftone (relief) engraving process later in the century.[1] The
first known halftone newspaper reproduction of a photograph
appeared in the *New York Daily Graphic* on March 4, 1880. It
showed a view of New York's Shantytown.[2] Other publications,
using the same process, cautiously followed with occasional photographic supplements.[3]

The advantages of halftone reproductions over artists' wood-
block renderings of photographs were not yet apparent, however,
and publishers were slow to exploit the innovation. Until the end

of the nineteenth century, although halftone engravings allowed for direct reproduction, photographs were used mostly as guides for newspaper artists in the preparation of woodcut or steel line-engraved illustrations.

This resistance to the obviously superior, faster, and cheaper photoengraving process is difficult to understand today. Newhall has written:

While Stephen Horgan was art editor of the New York Herald *in 1893, he suggested to its owner, James Gordon Bennett, that halftones could be printed in the paper. Bennett consulted his pressman who told him that the idea was impossible and preposterous. Horgan was fired.*[4]

It was not until January, 1904—by which time the commercial motion picture was already ten years old—that the *New York Daily Mirror*, "the first daily newspaper in the world to be illustrated exclusively with photographs," was introduced to the public.[5]

In view of the tardiness with which newspapers and magazines exploited the photographic medium, we can say that the motion picture news film—which appeared as early as 1895 and by the turn of the century was offering moderately effective coverage of newsworthy events—presented a form of pictorial journalism which was at least as advanced as the printed media. Indeed, the motion picture news film provided a predominantly photographic kind of news coverage long before most newspapers and magazines of the period began to do so.

But no matter how advanced, photojournalistically speaking, the turn-of-the-century news film may have been in comparison with contemporaneous newspapers and magazines, it was still a crudely fashioned medium of communication, and more than a decade was to pass before the introduction of the first American newsreel. Until that time the individual news films were frequent but unscheduled, highly topical in nature, local or regional in release, incomplete and unreliable in coverage, and necessarily geared to the unpredictable and fortuitous occurrence of news events.

But although the news events themselves were not predictable, the categories of subject matter into which they fell certainly were. It is significant that by the year 1900—less than four years after the commercial introduction of the projected motion picture and at least five years before the motion picture theater had become a permanent entertainment phenomenon—pioneer news-film producers had presented virtually every *type* of subject matter which was to characterize the newsreel for the next sixty years: catastrophe, international celebrities, pageantry and ceremony, sports, political and military events, technology, and spectacle and novelty. Henceforth newsreel content could nearly always be classified in these established categories.[6]

In the course of newsreel history, catastrophe, whether natural or man-made, has generally furnished the most colorful and dramatic subject matter. Newsreel producers understandably valued such subject matter highly and attempted to cover it regularly, often at great cost.

The first major catastrophe of the new century photographed by American film makers was the hurricane which on September 8, 1900, swept across business and residential areas of Galveston, taking five thousand lives and virtually destroying the city. In its wake a succession of giant tidal waves leveled what few buildings were left standing. As was so often the case in the history of the newsreel, coverage commenced shortly *after* the catastrophe. A 1901 Edison catalogue described the news-film operations:

At the first news of the disaster . . . we equipped a party of photographers, and sent them by special train to the scene of the ruins. Arriving at the scene of desolation shortly after the storm had swept over that city, our party succeeded at the risk of life and limb in taking about a thousand feet of moving pictures. In spite of the fact that Galveston was under martial law and that photog-

*raphers were shot down at sight by the excited police guards, a
very wide range of subjects have been secured.*[7]

According to Albert Smith, of Vitagraph, the footage was
photographed by him and released by the Edison Company.[8]
These scenes—prints of which have survived[9]—showed wreckage
along the Galveston waterfront, a panorama of the wrecked
orphans' home, rescue operations for the living, and search and
burial operations for the dead.

A year later, on September 6, 1901, another tragedy—this time
man-made—occurred during festive ceremonies at the Pan-American Exposition at Buffalo, New York. Both Edison and Vitagraph
were there on September 5 to film the scheduled events, which
included a review of troops and a speech by President McKinley at
the Temple of Music. Footage of that film still survives.[10] On the
following day, at a reception for the popular President, an
anarchist named Leon Czolgosz shot and fatally wounded Mc-
Kinley. Vitagraph's Albert Smith claimed that he was present at
the reception and photographed the assassination.[11] No such footage survives, however, nor have I been able to find a single reference—contemporary or later—to any exhibition of such film. I
suspect that this claim is an example of the "retroactive inventive-
ness" common among film pioneers in their later years.

Both Biograph and Edison filmed McKinley's funeral, concentrating on the presidential successor, Theodore Roosevelt, and the
burial at Westlawn Cemetery in Canton, Ohio. To conclude the
coverage, Edison filmed Auburn Prison at the moment of
Czolgosz' execution.

Among the many natural catastrophes of the first decade of the
twentieth century the San Francisco earthquake and fire of 1906
was undoubtedly the most dramatic. Although there was very little
coverage of the disaster at the time it occurred, a number of companies filmed the aftermath in the days that followed. The Edison
organization dispatched cameraman R. K. Bonine, who photographed what the Edison catalogue flamboyantly described as "a

series of pictures which have been universally admitted to be the finest on the market."[12] Vitagraph sent Albert Smith, whose footage was the first of a news-film nature that Vitagraph bothered to copyright.[13] As mentioned earlier, considerable fake footage of this event was produced by different individuals and organizations.

Other natural catastrophes of the period included the Italian earthquake of 1909, photographed by Vitagraph;[14] the eruption of Mount Pelée, faked by both Edison and Méliès; the Vesuvius eruption, filmed by Oscar Depue and faked by Biograph in 1906;[15] the Baltimore fire disaster of 1904;[16] and the Powers Film Studio fire of 1911 in New York City.[17] The Powers holocaust—a celluloid-film fire—was one of the first disasters of its kind to be photographed from beginning to end, in this case by the studio's cameraman, Al Leach. A description of the resulting film by the trade paper *Moving Picture World* suggests the manner in which sensation-seeking film exhibitors of the day perceived the appeal and contribution of the news film:

It is one of those pictures that will draw on its own merits and one that should be kept in a theater for more than one day, because those who see it are bound to return home and tell their relatives and friends what a wonderful fire picture they have seen. . . . Our advice to the exhibitor is to take it as quickly as he can get it, and keep it as long as he is allowed to, within the limits of reason. We have made some very strong statements on behalf of this film, but we do not think that they are strong enough. The Powers Fire picture is one that can be exhibited for years without losing its interest.[18]

During this period, when the novelty of film was sufficient in itself to persuade otherwise retiring notables to pose for the camera, a number of international celebrities appeared on motion picture screens. President Theodore Roosevelt is said to have been unusually cooperative with motion picture photographers, oftentimes pausing in the midst of official ceremonies to face the camera, bow, wave, gesture, grimace, and otherwise conform to the directions of newsreel men. He was photographed at both his inaugurations, at the White House, on a visit to Paris, with Admiral Perry, on his return to the United States from abroad, at a review of troops at the Charleston Exposition, at dedication ceremonies for the St. Louis Exposition, during a speech at a Fourth of July celebration, and on many other occasions.[19]

One of the most brazen hoaxes of the period involved the faking of Roosevelt's celebrated expedition to Africa in 1908. It was produced at the Chicago studios of Selig Polyscope at about the same time the former president was on safari. An illustrated article in *Collier's* magazine described production of the film but gave the impression that Roosevelt himself had participated in the reconstruction.[20] Historian Terry Ramsaye, drawing upon his personal acquaintance with Colonel William Selig, was able to prepare a somewhat more comprehensive description of the production details, which had included the hiring of a toothy impersonator of Roosevelt and the killing of an aged, peevish lion which had got out of hand on the set.[21] Colonel Selig carefully refrained from mentioning Roosevelt in the picture title or publicity. He simply waited until Roosevelt, on safari, really shot a lion and then released the film under the title "Hunting Big Game in Africa," to coincide with the newspaper headlines. Exclusive photographic rights to the genuine expedition had been assigned to the Smithsonian Institution, and it was said that Roosevelt was not amused by the fraudulent imitation—all the less so because of its considerable financial success.[22]

Roosevelt was still less pleased on another occasion when Vitagraph faked a film of the President's daughter, "Princess Alice." Roosevelt demanded that the prints be recalled from the theaters —which they were—and broke off the hitherto pleasant press relationship which the Vitagraph organization had enjoyed.[23]

Other celebrities of the period to whom footage was devoted included William Howard Taft—first as secretary of state and then as President, the Duke and Duchess of Cornwall on a visit to Canada, the Prince of Wales on a visit to Quebec, King Edward

PALACE THEATRE of VARIETIES

Manager   · · ·   **Mr. CHARLES MORTON.**

Assistant Manager and Treasurer   - - - -   **Mr. PHILIP YORKE.**

18/2/1901

Programme   H H H . H   **6d.**

1. OVERTURE ... ... "Oberon" ... ... *Weber.*	7.45
2. LA SERENADA TRIO.	7.50
3. GEORGE RIDGWELL. Baritone.	7.58
4. W. C. FIELDS. Juggler.	8.2
5. LEONIE ROY. Comedienne.	8.14
6. LITTLE GEORGE and his Canine Companion.	8.22
7. J. M. CAMPBELL. Mimic	8.34
8. "THE FOLLIES"	8.41

In a Selection from their "PEIRROT ENTERTAINMENT."
Messrs. H. G. Pélissier, N. A. Blumé and Lewis Sydney, Misses Evelyn Hughes, Doris Lind and Ivy Moore.

9. JOHN PEACHEY. Baritone.	8.58
10. HOWARD THURSTON. The King of Cards.	9.2
11. HENRI LEONI. Chanteur Français, will Sing:—	9.15

(*a*) "I Love you, Ma Cherie."   (*b*) "A Question of Age."
Written and Composed by Paul A. Rubens.   *Accompanied by* Herman Finck.

12. GOLEMAN'S CAT AND DOG SHOW.	9.27
13. Orchestral Intermezzo—	9.45

(*a*) "Pizzicato" ... ... *Delibes.*
(*b*) "Invitation à la Valse" ... ... *Weber.*

14. AQUAMARINOFF TROUPE of Russian Dancers and Singers.	9.57

| 15. | **THE MANHATTAN COMEDY FOUR.** | 10.12 |

16. **THE AMERICAN BIOGRAPH.** 10.24

Invented by **HERMAN CASLER**, of **New York.**

LIST OF LATEST PICTURES.

FUNERAL OF THE QUEEN:—
  The Cortege on its way from Osborne to Trinity Pier.
  Arrival of the Cortege at Trinity Pier.
  " Alberta" leaving Trinity Pier.
  The "Alberta" conveying the Royal Bier, and "Victoria and Albert," with Royal Mourners aboard, passing through line of Battleships.
  The Earl Marshal and Staff.
  Gun-carriage, Royal Mourners and closing Escort, Hyde Park.
  Blue Jackets drawing the Gun-carriage up to Windsor Castle.
  The Royal Procession on its way to open Parliament.
  The King and German Emperor passing through Hyde Park.

The German Emperor going to witness Launch of a Battleship. Kiel.
Scenes at Queen Wilhelmina's Coronation and Wedding.
Lord Roberts at his Headquarters receiving a Despatch from the Front.
Bloemfontein—
  Unfurling the Flag.
Naval Brigade Dragging 4·7 Guns into Ladysmith.
British Flag at Pretoria—Lord Roberts and Staff. A Courier arrives with Despatches from Heilbron.
Two of Britian's Heroes—Lord Roberts receiving Major-General Baden-Powell at Pretoria.
With the Flag to Pretoria—The Union Jack being hoisted at Pretoria on arrival of Lord Roberts, June 5th 1900.
Picturesque Panoramic Scenery in Canada.

The Music Composed by ALFRED PLUMPTON

| 17. | **THE THREE HAYDAS.** | 10.54 |

GOD SAVE THE KING.

MATINÉE Every **SATURDAY** at **2** o'clock. Full Evening Programme.

Children Half-price, Reserved Seats only.

Musical Director, Mr. **ALFRED PLUMPTON.**

The order and composition of this Programme may be varied as circumstances require.

DOORS OPEN 7.30. **COMMENCE 7.45.**

BOX OFFICE open from **11 to 5. TELEPHONE No. 1602** and **5050 GERRARD.**

The Pianofortes used at this Theatre are by Messrs. JOHN BRINSMEAD & SON,
The Mason & Hamlin Organ used at this Theatre is supplied by Messrs. METZLER & CO.
Floral Decorations by BAUMLER.

POPULAR PRICES.—PRIVATE BOXES from 1 to 2½ Guineas. FAUTEUILS (numbered and reserved) 7/6. ORCHESTRA STALLS (numbered and reserved), 5/-,
ROYAL CIRCLE Two First Rows (numbered and reserved) 5/-. ROYAL CIRCLE (unreserved), 3/-.
FIRST CIRCLE, 2/-. AMPHITHEATRE, 1/-.

The funeral of Queen Victoria was photographed by many pioneer film makers. The footage shot by the American Biograph Company and shown at the Palace Theatre in London on February 18, 1901, is described in this rare program. Also included were scenes of Queen Wilhelmina's coronation and of the Boer, the latter probably photographed by W. K. L. Dickson. The film presentation was accompanied by specially composed music. Note the rising young performer billed as No. 4 on the program.

VII with French President Émile Loubet on a visit to Paris, the Prussian Prince Henry with President Roosevelt on a visit to the United States, and Nicholas M. Butler at his installation as president of Columbia University.[24]

From the beginning the pomp and circumstance of state-sponsored pageantry and official ceremony, together with the appearance of international leaders and celebrities, provided ideal material for the newsreel camera. These pageants were good film subjects because of their color and interest and because of the relative ease and convenience with which the filming could be planned and executed. Notable events of this sort filmed during the first decade included the funeral of Queen Victoria in 1901,[25] the inauguration of President Taft in 1909,[26] the coronation of Edward VII in 1902 (also faked by Méliès),[27] the funeral of Edward VII in 1910,[28] the coronation of George V in 1911,[29] the funeral of Philadelphia Archbishop Ryan in 1911, and the Delhi Durbar ceremonies of 1911 (see below),[30] plus an almost unlimited variety of American parades—widely distributed in locale and generally insignificant, but celebrating a broad range of patriotic events sufficiently predictable, reliable, and colorful to ensure that they would remain favorite subjects for newsreel producers for decades to come.

The funeral of Edward VII, on May 20, 1910, was particularly well covered by both American and European news-film companies, including Pathé, Vitagraph, Hepworth, Warwick, Walturdaw, and Gaumont.[31] Pathé alone sent four cameramen to cover the event.[32] The funeral was rendered all the more newsworthy by the presence of many celebrities and members of royalty, including the widowed Queen Alexandra of England, King George V of England, Emperor William of Germany, King Haakon of Norway, King George of Greece, King Alfonso of Spain, King Ferdinand of Bulgaria, King Frederick of Denmark, and King Manuel of Portugal. Former President Theodore Roosevelt appeared as a special ambassador from the United States.[33] In Great Britain films of the funeral were released to local theaters within a few hours after the event. The American Biograph Company did its best to speed exhibition in the United States at a time when films had to be sent across the ocean by ship rather than by plane:

Within an hour after the Mauretania *docked on Friday morning a negative of the funeral of King Edward was delivered to the office of the Vitagraph Company by special messenger. An automobile was waiting to rush it to the factory and before midnight forty prints were on the trains speeding across the country. Five were exhibited in New York and Brooklyn theaters that same evening, viz., Gane's Theater, the Lincoln Square, Alhambra, Dewey and the Orpheum. We saw one of the prints just before going to press. It was clear in photography, the point of view excellent and the crowned heads of Europe and many notables were easily recognized. The 665 feet of film give an excellent idea of this event of worldwide interest and the Vitagraph Company deserve congratulations for the success of their enterprise.*[34]

Added an editorial in the *Moving Picture World*:

The exhibitor, then, . . . has an exceedingly fine opportunity for showing the public what an extraordinarily valuable agent the moving picture is for recording events of worldwide importance. . . . We cannot refrain from pointing out to the exhibitor that the exhibition of these films gives him an opportunity of further establishing his theater in the good opinion of the public. . . . Great funerals are, after all, not very common.[35]

Deadlines became increasingly stringent in the news-film business, and competitors spent almost as much money on processing and distribution facilities as on the original filming of news events. Kenneth Gordon wrote:

. . . many production records were broken, the laboratories working night and day. One of these speed records was made by Gaumont Graphic. They filmed the investiture of the Prince of Wales

at Caernarvon. On the pilot engine of the Royal Train were coupled a pair of large milk vans; these were turned into travelling dark rooms. The negative was developed, dried and rough cut, and a print was made on the way to London. As we sped along, every time we crossed any points, the developer, hypo and washing water would splash over and cover us. The developer was so low when we developed the print that it did not cover the frame, but the movement of the train saved the day, and the resulting film, nearly 1,000 feet in length, was shown the same night at the Electric Theatre, Marble Arch.[36]

Probably the most ambitious news-film coverage of this period was that arranged for the Delhi Durbar ceremonies in 1911, in which King George V was proclaimed emperor of India. Once again all major European film makers covered the event,[37] as well as the American Edison firm.[38] Newsreelman Kenneth Gordon wrote that coverage of this event was the first to be really well organized from start to finish: ". . . special stands were erected for the cameraman, who had to wear appropriate clothing—khaki when they were among the soldiers and top hats and frock coats when they moved in higher circles."[39] No expense was spared to secure interesting views, process the exposed film, and transport it back to European and American theaters:

Mobile laboratories were sent to India. A special kit was made in Paris, designed by M. Santau, chief of the Gaumont Laboratories. The developing frame was cut like a gramophone record in brass; the film stood up in the cuts, and a comb of brass was inserted in the top. Each frame took 200 feet of film, and fitted into a plated metal container which held the developer. The washing and fixing took place in bags of rubber waterproof cloth. The printing was by acetylene light which was more dependable than the local electric supply. About 200 prints were made before the negative was sent to London.[40]

By far the most interesting coverage, however, was the production of a three-hour color news film by the American-owned Charles Urban Trading Company,[41] using the Kinemacolor system, a complex process utilizing black-and-white film and rotating color filters before both camera and projector lenses. The film could be processed quickly and by the same method as that for black-and-white emulsions, and the quality of color was rather good.[42]

The resulting color newsreel, photographed by cameraman Joseph de Frenes,[43] was spectacularly successful and ran at many leading theaters throughout the world to capacity crowds. Green and Laurie reported: "In London the film was used to open its famed new showplace, the Crystal Palace. In New York it was presented at the Herald Square Theater with an orchestra, pipe organ and backstage choir."[44] Added Ramsaye:

In London Urban made elaborate and pretentious arrangements for the presentation of the Durbar picture. A vast stage set reproducing the Taj Mahal was built for the Scala theatre. Special musical scores were written for the pictures. The orchestra was augmented to forty-eight pieces."[45]

In attendance at the opening night in London were King George V, Queen Mary, Queen Alexandra, the Dowager Empress of Russia, and many other members of the nobility. The film also appeared at London's Alhambra Theater, where it was said to have run for over a year.[46] Kenneth Gordon, who photographed the ceremonies on black-and-white film for Gaumont Graphic, said later that "it was the colour version of this film, made by Charles Urban, that put newsreels [*sic*] in the big money class."[47] Ramsaye reported that within fifteen months after its release the film had grossed three-quarters of a million dollars.

From the beginning, major sports events were covered whenever possible because of their newsworthiness. After the newsreel was introduced in 1911 and it became necessary to manufacture news footage on schedule, sports events provided ideal subject matter, whether newsworthy or not. Highly visual and filled with action and movement, they were ideally suited to the motion picture medium. Occurring frequently and abundantly on national, regional, and local levels, they lent themselves to economical, preplanned, convenient filming. Competitive in nature and dramatic in staging, they offered maximum excitement and human interest to the average film patron while at the same time satisfying the needs of an immense established audience of sports fans throughout the country.

In later years sporting events were to provide the newsreel's largest single category of peacetime subject matter, by 1940 accounting for about 25 per cent of the total footage in newsreel releases.[48] During the prenewsreel period from 1900 to 1911, however, this subject was slow in appearing and establishing itself. One by one, different kinds of sporting events were filmed and presented to theater audiences.

The 1902 West Point–Annapolis football game, the 1903 Harvard-Pennsylvania game, and the 1903 Princeton-Yale game were photographed by Biograph.[49] The America's Cup races were filmed in 1901, 1902, and 1903 by Edison and Biograph, featuring the boats *Reliance, Shamrock III, Defender,* and *Columbia.*[50] In 1904, Edison photographed the intercollegiate championship track meet at Philadelphia and the intercollegiate regatta at Poughkeepsie, New York. In the same year Biograph filmed boat races on the Hudson River, a basketball game at Missouri Valley College, and auto races for the Vanderbilt Cup.[51] The World Championship Baseball Series was photographed by Essanay in 1908, 1909, and 1910.[52] By the time of the 1910 series, which featured the Philadelphia Athletics and the Chicago Cubs, preparations for both filming and exhibition were extensive. They were described in *Moving Picture World*:

> *Camera stands are being erected, while every facility for obtaining ideal views have been arranged. . . . Several camera men will be on the field in Philadelphia for the opening game and for the*

game the day following. Returning to Chicago, motion picture cameras of the Essanay Company will obtain the best plays of the final games. Announcement of the release date of the picture will be wired to all the licensed exchanges in ample time for the exhibitors to be informed. Special arrangements have been made at the Essanay factories to obtain prints of the films within the least time possible, probably within twenty-four hours after the terminating game.[53]

Whenever possible, news-film companies tried to include several different kinds of popular subject matter in one release. Essanay, for example, succeeded in combining both celebrity and sports appeal in 1909, when it released "Taft in Chicago and at the Ball Game." The film showed Taft "on his visit to Chicago . . . his welcome by 10,000 school children, his arrival at the National League Base Ball Park and . . . [his appearance] in the grandstand vigorously applauding and also on the diamond shaking hands with the players."[54]

Finally, the still popular but very controversial prize-fight film continued to appear on motion picture screens to the profit of film producers and the growing irritation of film critics, church groups, and legislators. Filmed events included scenes of Jeffries and Ruhlin in a sparring contest at San Francisco in 1901, Root and Gardner in 1903, Nelson and Britt at San Francisco in 1905, Gans and Nelson at Reno in 1906, O'Brien and Burns at Los Angeles late in 1906, Squires and Burns at Ocean View in 1907, and Jeffries and Johnson at Reno in 1910.[55] In addition were the many fake fight films manufactured by Sigmund Lubin.

The celebrated Jeffries-Johnson encounter of 1910, remembered by many sports fans as the "Fight of the Century," concluded in fifteen rounds with the defeat of the retired former champion, James Jeffries. It also reestablished the victor, Jack Johnson, as the first Negro heavyweight champion in the history of boxing.[56] The fight took place on July 4, 1910, at Reno, Nevada, and was photographed by the Vitagraph trio—Smith, Blackton, and Rock—for the General Film Company, which reportedly paid $150,000 for the exclusive rights.[57] The news film was a success and was said to have made a $300,000 profit.[58] However, it contributed greatly to the growing disrepute with which prize-fight films were regarded in many circles. Partly because of the racial issue, partly because of charges that Jeffries had been doped, and mostly because of an increasing distaste for fight films among civic and church groups, objections to exhibiting the film developed. Ramsaye wrote:

> Canon William Sheafe Chase of Brooklyn urged that Mayor Gaynor should take steps aimed at revoking licenses of theatres showing the pictures. . . . Theodore Roosevelt wrote a denunciation of the fight pictures for The Outlook, and announced he would advocate a law against fight films in every state where fights were forbidden.[59]

Finally, on July 31, 1912, Congress enacted the Sims Act,[60] which made interstate traffic in fight films illegal. Henceforth, until it was repealed in 1940, the Sims Act prohibited the transport of fight films which had been photographed in one state across its boundaries for exhibition in another state.

The prize-fight news film had long since served its purpose in the introduction, popularization, and technical sophistication of the motion picture medium. After the passage of the Sims Act it was absent from American motion picture screens for many years, although many ingenious attempts were made to circumvent the law. In 1916 entrepreneurs attempted to import pictures of the Willard-Johnson fight which had been photographed in Cuba. An optical printer of special design was mounted directly over the boundary separating Canada and the United States. The fight film was placed on the Canadian side, while fresh film was placed in the camera head of the printer on the American side. Only light rays crossed the border, and great care was taken to see that the original film at no time touched American soil. The event was

witnessed by officials, as the promoters intended. Federal indictment followed in what was intended as a test case. The jury subsequently disagreed, and on July 13, 1916, the case was dismissed.
However, the partners had apparently already fallen out over the
financial details of exhibition, and the film was never released to
American theaters. Subsequent fight-film promoters were not
always so fortunate, however. On March 30, 1925, a federal court
in New Jersey levied a fine of seven thousand dollars on promoters
Tex Rickard and Jap Muma and motion picture producer Fred
Quimby for a violation of the Sims Act.[61]

On the national political scene Biograph filmed the Democratic
National Committee at Esopus, New York, in 1904, while on the
international political and military scene Edison, Selig, and Biograph "covered" the Russo-Japanese War in 1904 with scenes of
the Battle of Chemulpo Bay (now Inchon), skirmishes between
Russian and Japanese advance guards, and the attack on Port
Arthur, all of which were "reproductions."[62] Both Edison and Biograph followed in 1905 with authentic footage of Admiral Richard
Mead and the peace envoys at the Russo-Japanese Peace Conference in Portsmouth, New Hampshire.[63]

The period from 1900 to 1911 was rich in technological innovation, and those inventions which lent themselves to photographic
visualization were frequently filmed by enterprising cameramen.
Such technological progress was honored by film makers in the
covering of the Pan-American Exposition of 1901 in Buffalo, the
Charleston Exposition of 1902, the Louisiana Purchase Exposition of 1904 in St. Louis, and the Jamestown Tercentenary Exposition of 1907, although far more film was spent on architectural
panoramas, military marches, and political speeches than on any
of the industrial, technological, and scientific displays these events
were meant to honor.[64]

Another subject of technological import was the opening of the
New York subway on October 27, 1904, photographed by the
Edison Company.[65] Scores of films were made showing trains,

boats, and automobiles, while the development of aviation was reflected in such films as those of Ludlow's aerodrome and aeroplane in 1905, and ballooning activities in 1902, 1903, and 1906.[66]

Scenes of spectacle and novelty augmented the coverage of genuinely newsworthy events and provided entertaining material for early news-film releases, just as they did for the newsreel after 1911. Such scenes were generally staged by the newsreel companies themselves or at least were subjected to extensive pre-production planning. Within this category fell four novelty items of the pre-1911 period, the first of which was filmed by Biograph in 1901.[67] Utilizing trick, "fast-action" cinematography, the film showed the dismantling and razing of the old Star Theater at the corner of Broadway and Thirteenth Street in New York City. By means of time-lapse photography, single-frame exposures of the wrecking operation were taken every four minutes, eight hours a day. When the final film was flashed upon motion picture screens, the dismantling of the building occurred spectacularly within the span of a few seconds. The effect was both startling and amusing.

Time-lapse cinematography was used for novelty's sake on other occasions. In 1902, Oscar Depue produced a sequence of such "crazy pictures," as they were called, while filming travelogues in Norway. He planted his camera on the bow of a steamer during a trip through the fjords from Vick to Ulrick, and by varying the speed of his camera to match the movement of the boat past the landscape produced a cinematic illusion of great speed over water. He repeated the stunt in 1907, when he took pictures of the entire 120-mile trip down the fjords. On the screen it lasted only three minutes.[68]

By way of sensation, Biograph released a film in 1905 entitled "The Hanging of Mary Rogers," which pictured the execution of a New England housewife convicted of drowning her husband. Biograph faked the footage with impersonators of Mrs. Rogers and the hangman and intercut it with genuine shots of the prison.[69] (Because of the possibility of a last-minute reprieve by

the governor of Vermont, Biograph wisely hedged its bet by producing, at the same time, a second version of the event in which
the prisoner's execution was commuted.) The film is noteworthy
not so much for its grisly subject matter as for the practice—perhaps used in film production for the first time—of producing
alternate endings beforehand. The practice survived in newsreel
production, particularly in political campaigns, to allow maximum
speed in releasing highly topical news.

There was at least one other item, produced by Edison in 1903,
which falls into this category. A paper print of it survives in the
collection of the Library of Congress. The film gives us an idea
of what film producers considered entertaining subject matter
around the turn of the century, and one cannot help wishing that
with the passing of time it might have disintegrated. It is titled,
simply, "Electrocuting an Elephant."[70]

5.

INTRODUCTION
OF THE
SILENT NEWSREEL

Question: Would it be a feasible scheme to endeavor to give *some of the news of the day in the form of motion pictures in the theaters? How long is the very shortest time in which a picture film can be prepared for exhibition after the view has been taken on the ground by the camera? Would the cost be prohibitive? Has it been done?*

Answer: It is quite possible to give each day a few items of the *news of a great city by means of moving pictures, and if regularly practiced and advertised it should be not only a feasible scheme but one promising profits.*

DAVID S. HULFISH, 1909[1]

Considering the important role which the news film played in the introduction of the motion picture and its undeniable popularity during the first few formative years, one is tempted to assume that this thread of popularity continued unbroken until the appearance of the newsreel in the second decade of the twentieth century. There is also some logic in assuming that, since the development of the news film culminated in the introduction of several news-reels between 1911 and 1918, a vigorous presold market for such an innovation must have existed. Neither assumption is correct, however.

Before 1900 the simple actualities and their news-film successors had been sufficiently novel to satisfy unsophisticated film patrons. Inevitably, however, the novelty of the medium disappeared. Motion picture audiences of the day became increasingly familiar with the "syntax" of film and were soon prepared for more complex cinematic innovations, whether along the stylized lines of Méliès' theatrical fantasies or the editorially revolutionary lines of Edwin S. Porter's naturalistic classic, *The Great Train Robbery*. With increasing success the style, form, and traditions of the theater were combined with the ultrarealistic rhetoric of film. In time, motion pictures replaced the legitimate stage as the major popular, national entertainment attraction—a replacement which was hastened and facilitated by the then current trend in the American theater toward realism of the Belasco brand.

The market for simple entertainment story films expanded with explosive force between 1905 and 1910. In 1905 the first nickelodeon was established by Davis and Harris in Pittsburgh. Within two years the theatrical trade paper *Variety* was able to report the operation of between four and five thousand such permanent theaters across the nation.[2] By 1908 there were eight to ten thousand theaters in the United States, and by 1914 their number was estimated at fourteen thousand.[3]

As the theatrical story film gained in popularity, however, the appeal of the news film declined proportionately. Evidence of this decline is provided by the copyright records of the period, which indicate a precipitous decline in news-film production toward the end of the first decade.* As Howard Lamarr Walls, former film archivist of the Library of Congress, has noted:

* No doubt other films were produced during this period which were not copyrighted. However, before the appearance of the first trade papers, around 1907–1908, there was no reliable record of film production other than the copyright records. Thus any theories about other, unknown productions of the period are speculative. Furthermore, the copyright entries, while undoubtedly incomplete, indicate clear trends in the kinds of films produced and the relative importance assigned to them by producers who took the trouble to copyright them.

The record pertaining to the newsreel type of film affords some surprise. The entries for these are rather profuse and important from 1896 to 1907, after which there are practically no entries during the period under consideration [1894–1912]. It is clear that by 1908 fictional entertainment had become an almost exclusive business with the industry.[4]

This greater emphasis on story-film production is demonstrated further by the proportion of articles and editorials devoted to different kinds of films in the trade magazine *Moving Picture World*, from its first issue in 1908 onward. Items devoted to the news film are conspicuous by their rarity in general and by their complete absence from many issues.

In view of the decline of the appeal of news films, it seems extraordinary that anyone ever bothered to introduce an American motion picture newsreel. Significantly, it was the American branch of a French organization—Pathé Frères—which finally did so.

During the first twenty years of motion picture history, the news film was far more extensively promoted in Europe than in the United States. The French firms were particularly active in presenting such materials in entertainment markets. They fairly well dominated the field through 1910 and remained influential until the outbreak of World War I, at which time entertainment-film production in France was severely curtailed.

It is interesting to speculate about the reasons for the comparatively greater popularity and exploitation of news films outside the United States during this early period. Two or three explanations suggest themselves. First, American film producers were inclined to favor theatrical fare over journalistic fare. In contrast to the French producers, the first American film makers tended to bring subjects to the studio rather than to take the camera to the subject, a practice which understandably favored theatrical manipulation rather than naturalistic documentation. Of course, the technological realities of the period favored such a practice. The early Edison and Biograph cameras were the size of steamer trunks and could not by any stretch of the imagination be considered portable. The French Lumière camera, on the other hand, was much smaller and was easily carried from location to location. During the first few years the French equipment lent itself to the convenient recording of newsworthy events in distant locations. The news-film content that resulted was as much the consequence of a technological imperative as of artistic inclination.

Second, by the turn of the century American taste in legitimate-stage entertainment had been conditioned by Belasco and his imitators, and theater audiences had come to expect and prefer ultrarealistic performances.[5] It was a taste which ultimately contributed to the decline of the American theater as popular entertainment, for, no matter how realistically a stage performance might be mounted, the motion picture could do the same thing far more convincingly, for much larger audiences, and at a far lower cost to the public. The American film succeeded in displacing the theater as a popular medium of naturalistic theatrical fare. At the same time, however, it inherited and exploited a theatrical tradition which was far more dynamic, economically speaking, than the photojournalistic tradition, which, as we have seen, did not develop fully until well after the turn of the century.

A third explanation for the tardy and indifferent exploitation of the news film in the United States lies in the geographical problems involved in getting timely news footage to local motion picture theaters at a speed competitive with the daily newspaper. As early as 1910 an editorial in the *Moving Picture World* described this problem:

The reason for the popularity of the topical picture in the British Isles . . . . [as well as, presumably, in France and in Germany] is simply this, that unlike the United States, it is not a country of magnificent distances. Practically the life of the nation, the ceremonial, official, sporting and public life is lived within a few hours of the capital, so that it is a comparatively simple matter for a film manufacturer to photograph an event of public importance in the day time, and have the pictures on the screen at the principal theaters in the evening. Thousands of miles in the United States separate the day's important happenings, so that it becomes largely an impossibility to photograph them, and show them on the screen the same night in the great centers of population.[6]

Whatever the reasons may have been, the newsreel was introduced in Europe far earlier than in the United States, and the French led in the field until the outbreak of World War I.

One of the oldest and most active of the French firms was Pathé Frères, whose founder, Charles Pathé, had begun his motion picture career as a salesman of cinematographic films in 1895. Out of his profits he purchased an early Lumière camera, with which he launched his career as a motion picture producer of both actuality and fictional film subjects, as well as a manufacturer of motion picture film and equipment.[7] His commercial rise was rapid. An article in *Image* states that "by 1907 Pathé Frères purchased and exposed about 30,000 meters of film daily; by 1909 about 70,000, by 1910 they built their own film manufacturing plant to accommodate their movie production."[8]

Pathé's film interests soon became global in scope. It was said that by as early as 1908 Pathé was selling twice as many films in the United States as all the American producing companies put together.[9] By the outbreak of World War I the company owned studios and manufacturing plants in several countries outside France, including the United States, and its films were exhibited throughout the world.

Toward the end of the first decade Pathé Frères undertook to introduce in Europe a regularly released reel of news-film subjects (that is, a "newsreel") under the Pathé trademark, the golden rooster. Available accounts of this venture are filled with contradictions; even those accounts which are nearly contemporaneous with the event differ widely in details. Such contradictions probably will not be resolved satisfactorily until an extensive study of the European newsreel is undertaken.

The idea for the newsreel is credited to Leon Franconi, Charles Pathé's American-based confidential interpreter. He is reputed to have had the inspiration while watching the inauguration of President William Howard Taft in a snowstorm in 1909.[10] Franconi urged his employer to introduce a weekly "magazine" of news events. Accordingly, in 1909 or 1910, Charles Pathé introduced a newsreel in Paris, entitled *The Pathé Journal*.[11] It first appeared in a theater owned by the Pathé Company, and located at 6 Boulevard Saint Denis in Paris. The theater was also called the Pathé Journal and was devoted exclusively to the presentation of newsreel material.[12] Léon Gaumont, another French film pioneer, soon followed Pathé's example and opened a similar newsreel theater called Société Éclair, a name which was later applied for a while to the widely distributed Gaumont newsreel itself.[13]

Around 1910, Pathé introduced his newsreel in England under the title *The Animated Gazette* or *The Pathé Gazette*.[14] A contemporary account refers to the attraction as a "daily service"—a term which was probably meant to indicate that the film was presented daily rather than prepared daily. The same account reveals that the London editor of the Pathé newsreel was a Mr. Steer and that it was exhibited throughout a circuit of English theaters to an audience estimated at over two million.[15] Other early British newsreels which followed included *Warwick Chronicle* (founded by Charles Urban), *Topical Budget*, *The Williamson News*, and the *Eclair Journal*.[16]

Historical accounts which have touched upon the introduction of the newsreel in America have been filled similarly with contradictions—all the more so since Pathé Frères *may* have released American issues of their European newsreels before introducing a distinctly American edition produced and edited in the United States. Some film histories, written many years after the event, confuse the French, British, and American editions of the Pathé newsreel and date the appearance of the American product as 1910. Even Leon Franconi, reminiscing years later, dated the appearance of the American edition as 1910.[17] However, this appears to be an error.

If there was a Pathé newsreel on the market in America in 1910, it was probably an imported release of the company's foreign newsreel edition, into which occasional shots of American events may have been cut. I suspect that much of the confusion in dating is the result of faulty recollections by Franconi late in his life. For example, in an October 29, 1939, interview in the *New York Times*, he stated that the American edition of the Pathé newsreel was released in the United States in 1910 and that it was followed almost simultaneously by the Vitagraph newsreel.[18] As we shall see later, Vitagraph's product did in fact follow Pathé's by only a few days' time, but in the late summer of 1911, not in 1910.

Indeed, there is considerable doubt in my mind whether the foreign edition of the Pathé newsreel was ever imported and released in the United States before the introduction of the American-produced edition in August, 1911. A page-by-page examination of all weekly issues of the *Moving Picture World* for the years 1910 and 1911 failed to produce a single reference to the release of any edition of the Pathé newsreel in the United States— foreign or domestic—before the introduction of the American-produced edition.

One argument for the possibility of an importation and release of the foreign edition of the Pathé newsreel before the introduction of the American-produced version is that some of the earliest issues of the American edition bore issue numbers well up in the thirties. For example, an issue of the American edition released on August 22, 1911—two weeks after the newsreel's introduction in the United States—is numbered 34.[19] A reel released in September, 1911, two issues later, is numbered 36.[20] Probably, however, the numbering refers to the incorporation of some footage in the American edition from issues 34 and 36 of the foreign editions. These numbers fail to prove that issues of the foreign editions were ever actually imported into the United States. Lacking any contemporary documentary evidence to the contrary, I have concluded that Pathé's foreign edition was never imported to the United States and shown here and that the very first newsreel seen by American audiences was Pathé's American-produced edition, which premiered in the United States on August 8, 1911.

To supply its regular American customers with theatrical story films, Pathé had established an American studio at Bound Brook, New Jersey, in April, 1910.[21] At that time Pathé was one of the organizations associated with the Motion Picture Patents Company, an American patents trust which sought to license and monopolize all motion picture production and exhibition in the United States through control of the camera patents of Thomas Edison or of those deriving from his patents. The distribution organization founded by the trust to serve its members was the General Film Company.[22]

In 1911, Pathé's American manager, Jacques A. Berst, proposed to the participating companies that

they should each furnish negative material for a news reel, these negatives to be printed, edited, titled and assembled at the Pathé offices in Jersey City, the finished product to be released through the General Film Company, and each manufacturer to be paid from the receipts according to the amount of negative received from him and incorporated into the weekly.[23]

Although the plan was favored by most of General Film's members, Vitagraph opposed it and so prevented its adoption. At the same time Vitagraph made plans to introduce its own newsreel series. Berst decided to undertake production independently of the General Film Company and ordered the immediate assembly and release of Pathé's first issue. In the July 29, 1911, issue of the *Moving Picture World* a full-page advertisement announced the forthcoming introduction of *Pathé's Weekly*—"A film issued every Tuesday, made up of short scenes of great international events of universal interest from all over the world. An illustrated

71

The first newsreel produced, assembled, and released in the United States was the French-owned *Pathé's Weekly*, the first issue of which was released on August 8, 1911. *Pathé's Weekly* not only was America's first newsreel but was, until the end of World War I, far and away its best. It survived for more than forty-five years. This announcement, the earliest known, appeared in the July 29, 1911, issue of *Moving Picture World*.

magazine on a film. The news of the world in pictures."²⁴ An
editorial in the same issue reported:

*Beginning on the first day of next month the moving picture
theaters of this country will go into active and, we believe, successful competition with the illustrated periodicals and magazines,
for they will be able to show the important news of the world not
in cold type or in still pictures but in actual moving reproduction.
The exhibitors will give their patrons no descriptions or photographs, but the things themselves, "just as they moved and had
their being." This novel idea, which will revolutionize pictorial
journalism the world over is called "The Weekly Journal," [sic] is
edited by the Pathé Frères, and will appear on the screens of the
moving picture houses every Tuesday.*²⁵

The first issue of Pathé's American-produced newsreel *Pathé's
Weekly* was enthusiastically reviewed by the *Moving Picture
World*:

*It would be difficult indeed to overestimate the importance of
this new feature in moving pictures, which will be sent out to
American exhibitors for the first time on August the 8th. The
confusion of tongues begun at the Tower of Babel bids fair to be
undone by this new institution. It will bring the continents and
nations together and work for a better understanding of one
people by another. To that extent it will do missionary work for
civilization of incalculable value.*

*The Pathé Journal [sic] makes its debut with a mixed program
of foreign and domestic events. The foreign events consist of
happenings in England, France, Russia and Germany. We see the
scenes and display of military splendor at the unveiling of the
monument to Queen Victoria in London; the presentation of the
colors to a regiment of French Zouaves at the Hôtel des Invalides,
in Paris; the visit of the German crown prince and his wife in St.
Petersburg; the highly interesting water jousts at Nizza, France,
and a big military review of the German troops at Potsdam. Of all*

73

the foreign features the last named is easily the most impressive. No amount of printed or spoken description could give us as clear and convincing picture of Germany in arms, as this film. For the first time we understand what is meant by the military prowess of Germany and the splendid physique and perfect drill and discipline of its soldiers.

Of American events, the most notable were the man-of-war, "North Dakota" lying at the dock in the Brooklyn Navy Yard, undergoing needed repairs; the annual horseshow at Long Branch and the Regatta at Saratoga Lake. All were fine and interesting, but the last named, showing as it does a great sporting event at the queen of American water resorts, was particularly attractive.

It is reasonable to expect that this unique feature, which in time will be developed to its fullest possible capacity, will prove of lasting value to the exhibitor. All preparations have been made by the Pathés to cover the entire country as thoroughly as the Associated Press covers it today. Who would not take part in the news of the world "just as it really happened" as part of the regular picture entertainment?[26]

Three or four issues later the Pathé newsreel was reported to have presented the following subject matter:

In No. 36, for example, [released early in September, 1911] the weekly continues its "royal progress" in its presentation of the "Crowned Heads" of Europe. A recent film presents Queen Wilhelmina of Holland as seen riding through the streets of Brussels while visiting in Belgium. The funeral of Queen Mary Pia, which took place in Rome recently, is very clearly portrayed. . . . From London comes the picture of Beaumont, "King of the Air," at the conclusion of his great all England flight. Vienna presents the most picturesque scenes in its "floral fete," which is very pretty. The whole world is represented in a picture of Jager-Schmidt boarding the "Olympic" in New York on the last stage of his "round the world in forty days" trip.

Another great voyage is shown by a picture of the 25-foot vessel

"Sea Bird" on its arrival in Rome, Italy, after crossing the Atlantic from America. Sydney, Australia sends a picture of the return of the Australian delegates from the coronation of King George V as they are given a rousing homecoming by their friends. From Turkey come pictures of the great fires which devastated a portion of the historic city of Constantinople. The fires in the famous forests of Fontainbleau, near Paris, are also shown.

America is represented by a series of views showing National Guard officers in camp at Fort Meyer, Virginia, a typical camping scene. The Aviation meet at Chicago presents some thrilling aeroplane ascents. Politics are not forgotten, as a picture of Congressman Rucker, of Missouri, brings to mind his near-fight in the House of Representatives in Washington a few weeks ago. Paris fashions for ladies are always an acceptable conclusion to Pathé's illustrated views.[27]

The number of prints of each issue during the first year reached ninety-five,[28] and they were released throughout the Keith-Albee and Orpheum circuits.[29] It was said that during the first year of its release *Pathés Weekly* contained an average of about 60 per cent American subject matter.[30] At first American coverage centered around events in New York, but gradually the company began reporting events in other parts of the country as the production staff was enlarged. In addition, *Pathe's Weekly* continued to draw upon the European coverage provided by its French and British offices. In the beginning Pathé released one issue a week, for which the publication deadline was 9:00 P.M. on Thursday evening.[31]

By this time the main Pathé studios were located at 1 Congress Street, Jersey City Heights, New Jersey, at the corner of Plank Road. The building was three stories high, and the news operation was located on the first floor, somewhat below street level. Pathé's processing laboratory was also located in the same building. At first, film was developed by rack and tank. Later, what was claimed to be this country's first machine developing equipment was installed in the building.[32]

The Pathé news camera was much lighter than the Pathé studio model, as was the tripod. The camera was about the same size as a Debrie camera, about six by eight by ten inches. The sides and back were of one piece, attached with a top hinge to the front section, three inches deep, which held all of the intermittent mechanism and the optical system. To open the camera, one swung the back section upward and over the front section, on its hinge, so that it rested on the front section, thereby exposing the magazines within—one on each side of the camera. The camera had a single, noninterchangeable 50mm $f/4.5$ lens. The camera was focused from the rear of the camera. The photographer viewed through a crude finder on the left side of the camera, in which a single-element meniscus lens produced a viewing image on a small piece of ground glass. Power was provided by a crank on the right-hand side of the camera. Pathé-brand film, both negative and positive, was used. The film was not too sensitive. Cameraman Arthur Miller recalled shooting ice-boat races on a bright, sunlit winter day with a camera aperture of $f/11$ at 16 frames per second.[33]

In those early days each newsreel cameraman developed his own new leads. Miller's territory covered Milwaukee, Chicago, Toledo, Cleveland, and Detroit. His particular enthusiasm was sporting events, at a time before exclusive coverage rights existed.

A cameraman's salary in 1912 was around thirty-five dollars a week, plus an expense account which could run as high as sixty-five dollars a week. For an unusually good job a cameraman might receive a twenty-five dollar bonus.[34]

On the average assignment a cameraman shot around two hundred feet. The important thing was to provide editorial continuity through selection of angles and coverage. Odd shots, no matter how pictorially interesting, were worthless. Properly edited, the footage was supposed to be capable of carrying itself after the explanatory titles had been presented.

The first supervising editor of *Pathé's Weekly* was H. C. Hoagland, who was also head of advertising and publicity for Pathé.

The first full-time cameraman engaged by Hoagland in 1911 was J. A. Dubray. By 1913 the staff of cameramen also included Victor Milner, Faxon Dean, Eddie Snyder, Berton Steene, Bill Harrison, and Ben Strutman, while the home-office staff, in addition to the managing editor, P. D. Hugon, included editors Emanuel ("Jack") Cohen and Al Richard.[35]

Within the first year the newsreel unit and its responsibilities had grown to such proportions that Franconi was appointed full-time supervising editor, replacing Hoagland.[36] Managing editors followed one another in rapid succession. In 1913, Franconi was apparently replaced by P. Allen Parsons,[37] who was succeeded in 1914 by William Helms, a New York newspaper man. Helms resigned in the same year, and Franconi again took charge. In 1915 he was given another assignment and was replaced by P. D. Hugon, the former editor of Pathés London *Gazette*. Hugon resigned the following year and was replaced by Eric Mayell, who was succeeded in 1916 by his assistant, Jack Cohen.[38] Cohen remained head of Pathé's newsreel for several years, during which time he introduced a number of innovations in the structure, coverage, production, and presentation of the American newsreel.

During the first years of its release the dependability and generally good coverage of *Pathé's Weekly* was further enhanced by the gradually improving quality of the photography. Within a year after its introduction, a contemporary reviewer could write:

It is a pleasure to note . . . the progressive value of the [Pathé] picture news. . . . It is also worthy of notice that the pictures themselves have greatly improved, better views and closer details together with much clearer pictures mark the advance of these most recent issues.[39]

In 1912, Pathé had eight full-time cameramen.[40] By 1914, so it was reported, Pathé was employing thirty-seven staff cameramen throughout the North American continent:

All told, the Pathé organization covering the world includes sixty different offices and studios in principal American and Euro-

pean cities. While each Pathé company is independent in a sense, they are all under the same general supervision and work in perfect harmony. . . . Not a week passes in which an aggregate of 15,000 feet of news film, sent from all over the world, is not received at the Jersey City plant.[41]

Pathé also occasionally provided footage released under the names of particular theaters in the New York area, including *Proctor's Daily News* and the *Strand Review*.[42]

The original American *Pathé's Weekly*, as the name indicated, was released once a week. By the end of the third year, however, a market existed for more frequent releases. Accordingly, on June 8, 1914, Pathé introduced a daily newsreel service to its customers. It was Pathé's plan to provide "each exhibitor who buys the service with the livest and snappiest news events of the world, in film lengths of approximately 200 feet, the minute prints of the events have been turned out of the Pathé factory in Jersey City—and at least once a day."[43]

An article in the *Moving Picture World* indicated that the daily news service was designed not merely to satisfy an apparent demand on the part of exhibitors but also to improve on the poor distribution service under which the newsreel had previously suffered. Pathé's relationship with the General Film Company was, by this time, no longer an amicable one. Pathé claimed that many exhibitors across the country were unable to obtain their newsreels from the distributor. In addition, by 1914 the General Film Company was also releasing, and tending to favor, a competing newsreel produced by the Hearst-Selig organization. By the time Pathé's daily news service was introduced, Pathé had already begun renting its product directly to exhibitors through its own exchanges.[44] The protection which the General Film Company had formerly enjoyed as agent of the Motion Picture Patents Company was gradually deteriorating. Independent film producers and exhibitors challenged the monopoly, prospered in their defiance, undertook expensive litigation against the monopoly, and provoked governmental antitrust actions which finally led to the dissolution of the Motion Picture Patents Company between 1915 and 1918.

Pathé's daily newsreel service was designed as a supplement to rather than a replacement for the weekly service and was intended for those exhibitors who were willing to pay additional rental fees for it. When the daily service was inaugurated, Pathé changed the title of the newsreel from *Pathé's Weekly* to *Pathé Daily News*. This rapid, daily distribution of prints was made possible by the use of "safety" motion picture film—a product of Pathé's manufacturing organization in France.[45] In contrast to the almost explosive nitrate film then commonly used for film prints, Pathé's safety stock was relatively nonflammable and could be sent through the mails for rapid delivery.[46] With the outbreak of World War I, however, the supply of safety film from France became at first uncertain and then practically unobtainable. Pathé ceased production of the daily service and returned to its regular weekly release under the revised title *Pathé News*.[47]

6.
PREWAR COMPETITION

Soon after *Pathé's Weekly* was introduced in the United States competing newsreels began appearing. The first of these—a monthly release—was produced by the Vitagraph organization and was entitled *The Vitagraph Monthly of Current Events*. The Vitagraph Company, as we have seen, had had a long history of news-film production in America, going back at least as far as 1898. Although its regularly scheduled newsreel did not appear until 1911, its previous news-film coverage had been frequent and thorough enough to merit occasional praise from film reviewers.

Vitagraph's persistence in producing news-film clips seems remarkable considering the exhibitors' general lack of interest in news films, the high cost of producing them, and the unrewarding financial returns. Indeed, there is a suggestion, provided in a contemporaneous editorial in the *Moving Picture World* that by 1909 Vitagraph's news-film coverage may have been conducted as a prestige item and carried as a loss by the company:

The Vitagraph Company are famed for their speedy handling of topical subjects. . . . It is an arduous and even risky task compared with the ease of the exhibitor who gathers in the dimes for exhibiting the film. . . . And if the Vitagraph or any other company confined their business to topical subjects they would soon go bankrupt, as the great expense attached, not to mention the con-

Less than two weeks after Pathé released the first issue of its newsreel, *The Vitagraph Monthly of Current Events* was introduced. It was a colorful but short-lived newsreel. This advertisement, the earliest known, appeared in the July 29, 1911, issue of *Moving Picture World*.

sumption of energy, is in inverse ratio to the amount of profit derived from the sale of film of this class.[1]

Vitagraph's plans to introduce a regularly scheduled newsreel were triggered by Pathé's proposal in 1911 to assemble and release a newsreel for the General Film Company, of which both Pathé and Vitagraph were members. Because of Vitagraph's opposition the original plan was abandoned, and Pathé set out to produce a newsreel on its own. So did Vitagraph, whose entry in the competition was first announced in an advertisement appearing in the July 29, 1911, issue of the *Moving Picture World*—the same issue in which Pathé announced its forthcoming *Weekly*.[2]

The first issue of *The Vitagraph Monthly of Current Events* was apparently released on August 18, 1911[3]—two weeks after that of Pathé. Vitagraph's notions of newsworthiness, as one might expect from its previous productions, ran along lines of strong action and sensational subject matter. The first issue featured "a head-on collision between two giant locomotives going 60 miles an hour. The iron steeds of the rail clash and tear into each other like two furious combatants. A sight that surpasses all imagination."[4] Added a reviewer in the *Moving Picture World*:

This thrilling scene, representative of such a death-dealing crash, with its destruction, smoke, steam, and attendant conditions seems especially peculiar from the fact that one can witness such a terrifying incident in perfect silence, the lack of noise never seemed so impressive as it does here. Whether such an event robbed of all its usually horrible and deathly results serves any scientific or other helpful purpose remains to be seen; it is, however, a novel picture.[5]

Vitagraph's Albert Smith later recalled:

The public greeted this edition of the Vitagraph newsreel with such enthusiasm that we immediately bought four old engines and rented an abandoned stretch of railroad track in New Jersey.

Our writers prepared several scenarios, building each plot around a train smashup as the big climax.[6]

Other Vitagraph action specials pictured a trip over Niagara Falls in a barrel by daredevil Bobby Leach and various sensational aeroplane feats by stunt flyer Frank Coffyn.[7] The Vitagraph newsreel was short-lived, however, and was merged with other newsreel interests (Hearst) within a year after its introduction.

In the wake of Pathé's success several modest newsreel enterprises were founded, all of which ultimately failed because of inadequate financing, poor quality, insufficient coverage, poor distribution, or lack of market. Regrettably, little accurate information survives with which the historian might document their short careers.

The *Gaumont Weekly*, a popular and successful international newsreel produced abroad, introduced an American version early in 1912 entitled *The Gaumont Animated Weekly*. At that time it was released by the Motion Picture Distributing and Sales Company. On July 24, 1912, within five months after its introduction, the American edition was discontinued.[8] (*Gaumont Weekly*, the international edition which was produced simultaneously in New York, London, and Paris, continued to be released in the United States until 1921, at which time it merged with *Kinograms*).

During the same period, 1912–13, *The Mutual Weekly* appeared, with Pell Mitchell as editor and Larry Darmour and Al Gold as cameramen. All three continued to play important roles in newsreel production long after the *Mutual* newsreel had disappeared.[9]

Another silent newsreel, *Kinograms*, survived somewhat longer. It was introduced shortly after the close of World War I by Charles Urban and George McLeod Baynes. The reel was originally distributed by the World Film Corporation, which from 1919 onward was owned by Lewis J. Selznick.[10] At one point it came under the control of Associated Screen News, a Canadian-controlled organization which during the early 1920's released a twice-weekly newsreel entitled *The Selznick News*.[11]

The Selznick News soon disappeared, but *Kinograms* hung on for a while. Beginning on January 30, 1921, the footage of the *Kinograms* and *Gaumont Weekly* newsreels were combined and released by Educational Film Exchanges, Inc., a firm which specialized in providing exhibitors with short subjects. The name *Kinograms* was retained for the newsreel, and the staff and operations of the concern were considerably expanded by Educational.[12] *Kinograms* provided lively competition for the next decade. So good was the newsreel that in 1919, New York's new Capitol Theater, then the world's largest motion picture theater, selected *Kinograms* as the exclusive news weekly with which to go into business.[13]

Some of the people associated with *Kinograms* over the years were managing editor Forrest Izard, assistant news manager H. E. Hancock, editor H. Butterfield, and cameramen George Doran, Fred Fordham, James Lyons, Frank Dalrymple, and Charles Sanwald.[14] After the industry's conversion to sound in the late 1920's, *Kinograms'* directors attempted to continue its release as a silent newsreel. The scheme was foredoomed to failure; *Kinograms'* studio closed its doors and went into receivership in 1931.[15]

The previously mentioned *Selznick News* was published by Lewis J. Selznick and was edited by E. V. Durling under the direction of Selznick's sons, Myron and David. The reel was first presented to the public on Easter Sunday, April 4, 1920. Among its innovations were newspaper-type headlines instead of conventional titles. It also claimed to be the only newsreel of the period which featured a woman's supplement.[16]

Examination of early trade papers and the memoirs and reminiscences of film pioneers reveals the names of still other newsreels which appeared briefly on motion picture screens and then disappeared for good. These included the *New York Weekly*, a local newsreel exhibited by Marcus Loew in New York City around 1914;[17] the *Celebrated Players Screen News*, released in

Chicago in 1921;[18] the *Item Animated Weekly*, produced by John W. Boyle in New Orleans in 1913;[19] *The Argus Weekly* ("The Argus Sees All"), produced in Hollywood in 1912 by Enrique Vallejo, Harry Revere, Dal Clawson, and Bert Longnecker;[20] and the *Golden Gate Weekly*, apparently released by Sol Lesser's Golden Gate Film Exchange in 1914.[21] Of interest, too, was an unsuccessful newsreel entitled *Newspictures*, introduced between 1915 and 1916 by Paramount.[22] It failed almost immediately, and it was many years before the company again ventured into the business with its more successful sound newsreel, introduced in 1927.

Because of their short lives, such productions as these failed to have much influence on the newsreel industry. During the same period, however, a far more tenacious competitor appeared which rivaled Pathé's leadership. This newcomer was certainly not the first American newsreel, but, as it happened, it was to become one of the most successful of them all. More important, it brought one of journalism's most celebrated names—that of William Randolph Hearst—into the motion picture industry as a newsreel producer.

As early as the autumn of 1911, Edgar B. Hatrick, head of photographic services of the Hearst organization, proposed that the company produce a newsreel in competition with the new Pathé and Vitagraph releases. At the time the proposal was not received with much enthusiasm. However, Hatrick's interest in the newsreel medium continued undiminished, and early in 1913 he produced for the Hearst organization a one-reel news film devoted to the inauguration of President Woodrow Wilson. The film was released in association with Harry Warner, later of Warner Brothers fame.[23]

During the same period Hatrick, representing the Hearst organization, began negotiations with the pioneer motion picture producer, Colonel William Selig, in an effort to merge the film-making and journalistic efforts of the two groups in the production of a motion picture newsreel. Colonel Selig had produced short news-film releases at least as early as 1903 and so was not unfamiliar with the problems of such production.[24] During the same period Selig maintained a close personal friendship with Moses Koenigsberg, then an executive on the Hearst *Chicago Evening American*.[25]

Finally, early in 1914, arrangements were concluded between the Selig Polyscope Company and the Hearst group for the mutual production of a motion picture newsreel to be called the *Hearst-Selig News Pictorial*. Ray Hall was appointed editor. The film was released twice weekly by the Selig Polyscope Company through the General Film Company in competition with *Pathé's Weekly*, which General also distributed. The first issue was apparently released on Saturday, February 28, 1914. An advertisement in the *Moving Picture World* during the following week was the earliest known announcement of the reel's debut:

Every week in the year, beginning February 28, 1914, the big events of the whole world will be caught in the happening by Selig moving picture cameras, operated by the trained news gatherers of Hearst's great International News Service which covers the entire globe, and these news pictures, throbbing with live news interest in every foot of film, will be released to you weekly.[26]

With the release of this series the Hearst organization began what was to become a long-term, if sometimes controversial, association with the newsreel business—an association which survived until the close of Hearst Metrotone operations in 1967. For some reason, however, the early alliance with Selig was short-lived and was concluded in December, 1915.

The following month Hearst entered into a new agreement with the Vitagraph Company whereby *The Vitagraph Monthly of Current Events* was discontinued and replaced with a new release entitled *The Hearst-Vitagraph Weekly News*, which was released semiweekly.[27] *The Hearst-Vitagraph Weekly News* foundered within a few months, however, and was abandoned. For a short

WHIZZ! BANG! SMASH!

Watch For Lucky Saturday, February 28th

Startling News Pictures of the World's Big Happenings Every Week

ON Saturday, February 28, the first big gun will be fired. On **Saturday, February 28**, you will see the first big result of Hearst's army of trained newspaper men working in conjunction with the famous **Selig Motion Picture Makers.** Every **week in the year,** beginning February 28, 1914, the big events of the whole world will be caught in the happening by **Selig** moving picture cameras, operated by the trained news gatherers of Hearst's great International News Service which covers the entire globe, and these news pictures, throbbing with live news interest in every foot of film, will be released to you weekly under the title of

 # HEARST - SELIG
NEWS PICTORIAL

This giant combination of the greatest newspaper organization in the world—in which are found world-famous correspondents and news gatherers who sense at a glance the vital, dramatic features in the thrilling events that happen every week—this giant combination of that globe-encircling newspaper organization with the **Selig Polyscope Company's** matchless facilities as producers, makes the HEARST - SELIG NEWS PICTORIAL the biggest event in the entire moving picture world to-day.

Get your orders in. Don't slip a cog on this. Don't be the **last** in your locality to exhibit a **real** news reel—BE THE FIRST TO SHOW THE HEARST - SELIG NEWS PICTORIAL.

MAKE YOUR BOOKINGS NOW!

SELIG POLYSCOPE COMPANY
CHICAGO

The Hearst organization entered the newsreel business early in 1914 with the introduction of the *Hearst-Selig News Pictorial.* For more than half a century Hearst's newsreel was released through or in association with several other companies, including Vitagraph, Pathé, Universal, and MGM. Hearst's name was dropped from the title around 1918. Note the use of the term "news reel" in this, the earliest known advertisement of the reel. (From the March 7, 1914, issue of *Moving Picture World.*)

period of time late in 1916 and early in 1917 the Hearst group apparently released its own films under the title *The International Weekly*.

On January 1, 1917, Hearst entered into another production-distribution alliance, this time with its rival, Pathé. Under the terms of a contract signed by E. A. McManus, of Hearst International, and J. A. Berst, of Pathé, all Hearst newsreels were released through Pathé's exchanges. The new product bore the name *Hearst-Pathé News* and was first released under that title on January 10, 1917.[28] The new association lasted for little more than a year, however, at the end of which both companies went their separate ways, each with its own newsreel release.

The Hearst name was also dropped from Hearst's own newsreel at this time, apparently because of the controversy over the publisher's alleged pro-German sentiments.[29] A new name, *The International Newsreel*, was given to the series. Hearst's use of the word "newsreel" in its release was probably the first occasion on which this term was used as part of a commercial trade name, although we do see it used as a descriptive term in a *Hearst-Selig News Pictorial* advertisement as early as March 7, 1914 (many years later the Hearst organization claimed to have used the term as part of its trademark as early as 1914).[30] Hearst continued to produce *The International Newsreel* for many years, releasing it during the 1920's through Universal Studios and, after the introduction of sound, through Metro-Goldwyn-Mayer Studios.

Following the split with Hearst in December, 1915, the Selig Polyscope Company continued producing newsreels under a different title. Colonel Selig joined with the *Chicago Tribune* early in 1916 in the release of a new series entitled the *Selig-Tribune*,[31] flamboyantly billed as "The World's Greatest News Film."[32] Herbert C. Hoagland left Pathé to become its general manager, and Lucien C. ("Jack") Wheeler, a former United States Secret Service agent, was appointed its first editor.[33] One of the innovations offered by this new Selig release was

This rare photograph shows Pancho Villa (far left) being photographed south of Chihuahua, Mexico, early in 1914, for Mutual Film's "exclusive coverage" of the Mexican revolution. The cameraman at the right is Charles Rosher, later a distinguished director of photography in Hollywood. (Courtesy of Lucille Kiester and the *PSA Journal*.)

No president was more photogenic than Theodore Roosevelt. He was often filmed during his administration and was said to be unusually cooperative with news-film photographers, often pausing in the midst of official ceremonies to face the camera, bow, wave, gesture, grimace, or otherwise follow the directions of the cameramen. Here he is photographed during a World War I rally. (From U.S. Signal Corps.)

President Woodrow Wilson, a much less photogenic and colorful man than some of his predecessors, photographed in his office during World War I. In those days of relatively insensitive film and primitive lighting equipment, it was a major achievement to photograph a president indoors. Wilson was probably the first president to be so filmed. (From U.S. Signal Corps.)

Owing to censorship and the reluctance of military officials to allow civilian cameramen near the front lines, most of the footage of World War I was shot by military cameramen (above and facing page), and much of what they photographed never reached theater screens. (From U.S. Signal Corps.)

Battle scenes of World War I (above and facing page). Newsreel coverage of the war was sketchy and inadequate by any standards, especially in comparison with the coverage of World War II and the television coverage of the Vietnam War with which later generations of viewers became familiar. (From U.S. Signal Corps.)

Much of the newsreel coverage of World War I was faked by film studios. The practice became so widespread and notorious that *Literary Digest* presented an exposé in its November 13, 1915, issue, describing the technical methods by which footage was manufactured. In the drawing above the magazine illustrated how powder-filled bladders were exploded underwater as costumed actors forded a stream.

Facing page: World War I scene from a sequence that definitely was not faked: the dramatic sinking of the Austrian battleship *St. Stephen* by Italian gunboats in the Adriatic on June 10, 1918. Seen in motion on the screen, the scene is startling. The ship is covered with hundreds of sailors scuttling across the upturned far side as the ship quickly overturns. (From Museum of Modern Art, New York.)

The last of the major silent newsreels was introduced in the fall of 1919 by Fox Studios. *Fox News* came on like thunder. It was the product of great energy, considerable imagination, and an initial investment of about five million dollars. In time it became the largest newsreel of them all and survived until 1963. (From *Exhibitors Herald*, July 15, 1922.)

Above: An unknown newsreel cameraman poses for a portrait in front of the automobile provided by his company. (From Fox Movietonews, Inc.) Below: Footage was transported from camera to laboratory by every known means of transportation—airplane, train, boat, automobile, and even dogsled. Some companies owned and operated their own aircraft. The cameraman in the shadow of the wing is Jack Painter. (From Fox Movietonews, Inc.)

Only those newsreels produced and distributed by the major studios survived. Along the way many small newsreel outfits appeared briefly and tried to compete. Here Bert Longnecker, at the wheel of the EMF, and Enrique Vallejo, at the camera, set out for a day's work on behalf of *The Argus Weekly*, a short-lived competitor founded in 1912 with the slogan "The Argus Sees All." (From *International Photographer*, 1938.)

Jack Painter, above, of Fox News, had a reputation as one of the most daring cameramen in the business. His camera is an unusual but popular invention of Carl E. Akeley, the taxidermist and explorer of Africa. In the trade it was affectionately known as the "pancake camera." (From Fox Movietonews, Inc.)

Facing page: Cameramen of the silent-film era *looked* like cameramen, with their knickerbockers, puttees, and turned-around caps. The cameraman at the right is C. J. Kaho, Fox photographer at Fort Worth, Texas. (From Fox Movietonews, Inc.)

Below: Roy Anderson, of *Fox News*, with his Debrie camera. (From Fox Movietonews, Inc.)

Excited by the romance and adventure of the calling, young men from all over the country were attracted to the newsreel business. This earnest young man was Kenneth Clyde Kilburn, *Fox News* staff cameraman from Eureka, California. (From Fox Movietonews, Inc.)

the flashing of a table of contents of the newsreel prior to showing the news pictures, in the form of a newspaper front page containing briefly written news stories, headlines and all, which are picturized a moment later. . . . Another innovation is the printing of these news briefs and picture titles in German and Italian, as well as English.[34]

The *Selig-Tribune* staff expanded rapidly. Within half a year after its appearance seventy-five film technicians were employed in its Chicago plant, and its cameramen were based in Chicago, New York, Washington, Los Angeles, San Francisco, Boston, El Paso, Portland, New Orleans, and Atlanta. An additional fifty cameramen, probably so-called stringers (free-lance workers), were reportedly located in London, Paris, Berlin, Petrograd, and other European cities. Despite its early promise and rapid expansion, however, the *Selig-Tribune* did not survive for long and was apparently no longer in business by 1917.

Other, better financed, more satisfactorily distributed newsreels appeared on the market and survived. In 1913, Universal Pictures introduced *The Universal Animated Weekly*, with Joseph T. Rucker, U. K. Whipple, and Frank Dart as its first cameramen[35] and Jack Cohn as editor (not to be confused with Emanuel "Jack" Cohen, the editor of Pathé). The reel was established as a weekly feature, and before very long enjoyed a reputation for dependable, thorough coverage.

Among the early scoops secured by the company was the filming in 1914 of the crew and officers aboard the British converted cruiser *Caronia*, which was secretly anchored off Sandy Hook, New York, during the early days of World War I, seeking to engage German ships leaving New York harbor.[36] Another exclusive Universal newsreel sequence, photographed in 1914 by J. M. Downie, pictured the siege of Antwerp.[37]

In an industry in which the mortality rate for newsreel companies was very high, the product released by Universal proved one of the most enduring of them all. After many changes in name, format, production (Hearst produced Universal's *International Newsreel* during the 1920's), and corporate ownership, Universal's newsreel was still appearing on neighborhood theater screens half a century later and did not finally close its doors until 1967, when it was America's oldest newsreel release.

The last of the major successful silent newsreels was introduced in the fall of 1919 by the Fox Studios. In time it became one of the most important of all and survived until 1963.

Fox News came on like thunder, the product of great energy, considerable imagination, and an initial investment estimated at five million dollars.[38] Among other things, it was apparently the first American newsreel to affiliate with a wire service—in this case, United Press. Under the terms of this association, UP gave its wire service exclusively to Fox. In addition, UP made available to Fox the assistance of its own reporters and photographers around the world.[39]

The Fox operation was divided into two sections: a feature department, headed by Ernest Howard Culbertson, and a news department, headed by Pell Mitchell (formerly in charge of the *Gaumont Weekly*). The first director of the operation was Herbert Ernest Hancock. The Pacific editor was Eugene Castle, of San Francisco, who many years later was to establish his own newsreel "magazine" for the home-movie market.[40] Originally the news department of Fox's operation worked out of offices at 3 West Sixty-first Street in New York City, and the feature operation was located at 130 West Forty-sixth Street. Later both moved to the new William Fox Building at Tenth Avenue and Fifty-fifth and Fifty-sixth Streets.

The first issue of *Fox News* was premiered on October 11, 1919.[41] New issues were thereafter released twice a week, on Wednesday and Saturday, to an audience estimated in 1919 at thirty million people.[42] Domestic rentals of the Fox product were supervised by Lewis S. Levin, while overseas sales were handled through Fox's foreign department.

Introduction of the Fox newsreel received an unprecedented

boost when a letter from President Wilson praising the introduction of the reel was made public.[43] How Fox Studios managed to secure this extraordinary commercial advantage is unknown. Ostensibly, Wilson's letter of commendation was unsolicited. In any event, as one of the trade papers, *Exhibitors Herald*, observed, "It is hardly to be expected that William Fox would allow a communication of this kind, coming from such a source, to remain hidden in the files of his office."[44] According to the same paper, this was the first time that a president of the United States had given personal attention and comment to a motion picture feature. Wilson's letter was soon followed by equally unprecedented commendations from five United States senators, two state governors, and the acting prime minister and the postmaster general of Canada.[45]

By October, 1919, Fox was reported to have overseas cameramen and representatives in Yokohama, Tokyo, Shanghai, Peking, Hong Kong, Canton, Manila, Honolulu, Wellington (New Zealand), Sydney, Melbourne, New Guinea, Borneo, Sumatra, Tibet, Russian Siberia, Irkutsk, Manchuria, Alaska, Stockholm, Dublin, Liverpool, London, Copenhagen, Le Havre, Paris, Bordeaux, Brussels, Lisbon, Madrid, and Rome.[46]

In 1922, Fox claimed to be served by 1,008 cameramen around the world—most of whom, of course, were stringers.[47] By that time the total amount of film pouring into its laboratories each week from around the world was estimated at sixty thousand feet.[48] The New York laboratory which Fox established on Fifty-fifth Street for its newsreel operation was considered one of the finest in the world. Separate toning and tinting departments were established there to provide color effects for selected news footage.[49]

Fox News was aggressive in securing exclusive footage of newsworthy events and rushing it to its theaters ahead of the competition. By its own report it presented seventeen uncontested scoops during the year 1921 alone. They included scenes of Mexican bandit Francisco Pancho Villa on his ranch; Germany's former crown prince in exile; interior shots from the United States dirigible *Roma*; the first "official" pictures of the Ku Klux Klan; aerial pictures of the Arkansas River flood at Pueblo, Colorado; the first airplane shots of the Grand Canyon; and scenes of the first flight from New York to Chicago. Extraordinary footage of Mount Vesuvius in eruption was also secured during this period by cameraman Russell Muth, who flew directly over the volcano and was nearly killed in the subsequent crash of his plane.[50] Less spectacular but substantively more important was a special feature released by Fox in 1922 in several installments on Japan's expansionist policies. Entitled *Face to Face with Japan*, the series attempted to answer the question, Does war threaten between United States and Japan?[51]

In the years that followed, the Fox newsreel consolidated and held its strong position in the field. Under the direction of Truman Talley and later under Edmund Reek it introduced the industry's first sound newsreel in 1929, following which it enlarged its staff, amplified its coverage, and pioneered new production techniques.

By 1918 four of the five major names in the history of the American newsreel had introduced their series: Pathé, Hearst, Universal, and Fox. The fifth, Paramount, was not to introduce a successful series until 1927.* From 1918 onward, although many other newsreel titles appeared briefly upon motion picture screens, the history of the American newsreel centered about the operations of these five major firms.

* In the late 1920's, MGM began releasing a newsreel under its own name. However, it was produced for the company by Hearst.

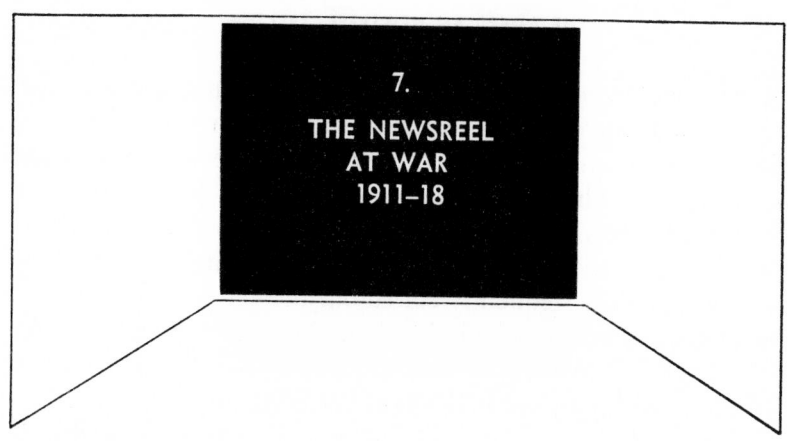

7.

THE NEWSREEL
AT WAR
1911–18

Of all the things which a newsreel editor hates, war is first. It is expensive, it is dangerous for the cameramen, and it seldom if ever produces pictures worth looking at.

THOMAS SUGRUE, 1937[1]

The history of combat newsreel cinematography by civilians is a chronicle of frustration.

I should remind the reader that we are looking at the fifty-year period of theater newsreel history which preceded the altogether remarkable war coverage we see on our television screens today. The quality and extent of today's coverage follows partly from the acceptance of television as a bona fide news medium by the communications industry, the journalistic corps, and the public. It also follows from recent technological breakthroughs in the miniaturization of camera and sound equipment and from the availability of communications satellites which allow daily transmission of news footage to the home front.

During the era of the theater newsreel military authorities generally discouraged coverage by other cameramen than their own. When they did permit civilians to photograph combat war scenes, they generally insisted on processing and examining the raw footage before it was released to producers and distributors (a practice still sometimes followed today). Censorship was rigorous, and shipment of the censored film to the newsreel com-

panies was slow and uncertain. Then, as now, much of the business of war and military endeavor was neither interesting nor
visual. Those scenes of actual combat which were of interest could
be secured on film only by daring cameramen who often took
greater risks than the combatants themselves to secure clear and
meaningful images. Finally, newsreel editors and local motion
picture exhibitors frequently edited out the very photographs for
which the cameraman had risked his life, for fear of shocking
audiences with violent or morbid scenes.

One of the few military conflicts before World War II which
received moderately good motion picture coverage was the Mexican revolution which followed the overthrow of dictator Porfirio
Díaz in 1911 by the constitutionalist Francisco Madero. The conflict continued undiminished for several years. Madero was over-
thrown in 1913 by Victoriano Huerta, who was in turn unseated
by Venustiano Carranza. Before this long-drawn-out conflict was
resolved, Carranza had been defied by his most important general, the colorful Pancho Villa. Villa made a raid on Columbus,
New Mexico, following which American troops were sent into
Mexican territory by President Wilson in a punitive expedition
against the general. Peace was finally restored in January, 1917,
with Carranza in power, but not without profound resentment in
many quarters over the American intervention.

Many features of the Mexican revolution seemed to lend themselves to motion picture coverage. The war ranged over a large
area, offering a variety of topographical features, while military
engagements frequently involved exciting cavalry charges, attacks
being made on horseback nearly as often as on foot. Further, many
of the leaders and participants were colorful, dramatic figures. All
the major American newsreel companies sent correspondents
south of the border, as did a number of smaller firms. Mathewson,
Wallace and Varges covered the war for Hearst,[2] Joe Rucker and
Sherman Martin represented Universal's *Animated Weekly*,[3] and
Fritz Wagner, Victor Milner, and a man named Steene photographed for Pathé.[4] However, because of the hostility of the mili-

tary authorities and the primitive conditions under which the cameramen lived and worked, it was not a particularly attractive newsreel assignment.

Pathé's Fritz Wagner was seized by rebel military leaders; his equipment, film, and money were appropriated, and he was thrown into jail. He escaped from prison on foot, starved for several days, and contracted severe dysentery from impure drinking water. He finally reached Mexico City, where he secured another camera and additional funds from the Pathé representative and again headed back to the battle area.

Wagner's relations with the Federalists were not much better. He reported:

I have seen four big battles. On each occasion I was threatened with arrest from the Federal general if I took any pictures. He also threatened on one occasion when he caught me turning the crank to smash the camera. He would have done so, too, but for the fact that the rebels came pretty close just then and he had to take it on the run to save his hide.[5]

Huerta himself edited out unfavorable scenes from Wagner's footage, all of which was required to be processed in Mexico.

Sherman Martin, cameraman for Universal's *Animated Weekly*, suffered similar unpleasantness. At Bermejillo he and other correspondents were continuously under fire for twelve days, during which time they lived on tortillas and rainwater. "Martin for five days was helpless from mountain fever, and once, for a thirty-hour stretch, war correspondents and photographers were without food or water."[6]

Much of the Mexican footage, photographed by such men as these, was genuine, acquired only through great personal discomfort and in the face of frequent and real danger. Other footage, however, was not. Surely the oddest feature of this revolution, at least from the photojournalistic point of view, was the manner in which Pancho Villa's army was covered from 1914 onward.

Villa's flamboyant military tactics and colorful personality were considered good copy by both newspaper publishers and newsreel producers. Augmenting Villa's adventurous leadership was his flair for self-aggrandizement and personal publicity. In the winter of 1913–14 he let it be known that the motion picture rights to "his" war were available to any American producer with enough showmanship to exploit the subject matter and the money to pay for exclusive coverage.

Harry Aitken, head of the Mutual Film Corporation ("Mutual Movies Make Time Fly"), entered into negotiations with Villa, and on January 3, 1914, a contract was signed in Juárez by Frank M. Thayer, representing Mutual, and Villa. The agreement called for a payment of twenty-five thousand dollars to the rebel leader at the time the contract was signed and a 50 per cent royalty on the earnings of the pictures.[7] In return Villa guaranteed not to "allow any other moving picture men except those of the company in which he is interested on the field during his battles."[8] Under the terms of this extraordinary agreement the Mexican general and one of America's largest film producers set out to produce artistically engineered combat scenes, employing a set of working rules which, so it was said, specified that, whenever possible, battles would be held during daylight hours and at such times as were convenient for the motion picture cameramen.[9] Charles Rosher, later a distinguished studio cameraman, and Carl Von Hoffman were two of the ten film technicians assigned by Mutual to photograph the war.[10] The cameras they operated were said by Aitken to have been specially designed for combat conditions.[11]

Throughout the campaign that followed, Villa fulfilled his part of the bargain. It was reported[12] that "Villa delayed his projected attack on the city of Ojinaga until the Mutual could bring up its photographic artillery. When the cameras had consolidated their position the offensive swept forward and Ojinaga fell to Villa and film."* It was rumored that prisoners of Villa were used as human

* It is interesting to compare this account with combat photographer Ted Genock's description of the attack and destruction of the Polish city of Gdynia by the Germans in 1939. The Germans delayed their attack long enough for their

targets in telephoto scenes showing the artillery scoring direct hits on enemy emplacements and, on the other hand, that many of the battles appearing on film were sham.[13] Whatever their authenticity, the films were enthusiastically received by audiences and profitably run by motion picture exhibitors.[14]

Editorial reaction in the press varied. The *New York Times* gravely observed:

> *No doubt the films thus secured would command the attention and the money of the multitudes, but even the most morbid seeker for horrors might be shocked if not by the sight of carnage, at least by the thought that it had been commercialized in this particularly cynical way.*[15]

On the other side of the Atlantic, British journalists took a less serious view. The *London Evening News* stated facetiously:

> *The introduction of the film on the battlefield can hardly fail in any case to have a remarkable effect upon the behavior of the troops. The soldiers will feel as individuals that the eyes of the world are upon them, and if a soldier feels tempted to run away the thought that he may be seen, bolting across the screen at home in the course of the next few days or weeks must surely exercise a great restraining effect. On the other hand, his heroic deeds will be done in the limelight and fully and permanently recorded.*[16]

Commented the *London Daily Citizen* in similar vein:

> *European governments, harrassed by their growing expenditures, could gain considerable revenue in a similar way. The right of filming the proceedings of the Hungarian Chamber should be worth a handsome figure; even the picture of the House of Commons on Budget night might save us the sugar tax, while a film of the Cabinet Council when the navy estimates were under discus-*

cameramen to move forward so as to be able to photograph backward, showing the German infantry and artillery in operation. See Ted Genock, "A Newsreel Man Shoots the War," *American Mercury*, August, 1942, p. 158.

Mutual Movies of the
Mexican War
Made by Exclusive Contract with
Gen. Villa
of the REBEL Army

FIRST reels just in—and being rushed to our branch offices.

These are the first moving pictures ever made at the front under special contract with the commanding general of the fighting forces.

Newspapers throughout the world are printing pages of matter about this war—and the amazing contract of the Mutual Film Corporation with Gen. Villa.

The public is clamoring for a sight of the pictures — which are far more exciting and sensational than any pictures of actual happenings that have ever been shown before.

Wire our nearest branch office for terms and reservations.

Heralds—and great one-sheet, three-sheet and six-sheet paper now ready.

MUTUAL FILM CORPORATION
Branches in
49 Cities   New York

A grimly humorous variation on war coverage was introduced in 1914, when Mutual Film Corporation bought the "rights" to the Mexican revolution. For $25,000 and a 50 per cent share of the earnings, General Pancho Villa guaranteed not to "allow any other moving picture men except those of the company in which he is interested on the field during his battles." The contract specified that, whenever possible, battles would be held during daylight hours and at times convenient for the motion picture cameramen. (From *Moving Picture World*, February 7, 1914.)

sion might pay half the cost of the navy without any secrets being betrayed.[17]

After the revolution ended, Villa remained a favorite subject for American cameramen, but he was rarely photographed because of his withdrawal from public life and his desire for privacy during retirement. There are amusing accounts, which do not seem worth recounting here, of the manner in which one American newsreel firm after another tried to secure photographs of the general at his ranch in central Mexico. Unsuccessful attempts were made by several different firms over a four-year period until cameraman C. J. Kaho, through subterfuge and at some personal risk, finally managed to photograph both the general and his estate.[18]

World War I was inadequately recorded from beginning to end by the civilian newsreel industry—not because of any lack of zeal but because of the many obstacles which were purposely created by military and civil authorities.

Long before the United States entered the conflict, cameramen found it almost impossible to gain access to front-line areas or even to film scenes of wartime preparation on the home front. In 1914 cameraman Rosher, at that time a British subject, stated:

It is impossible to get from England to the Continent with a motion picture camera. . . . Not only is it out of the question to get a motion picture camera out of England in the direction of any of the belligerent countries, but likewise it is not possible to get a motion picture camera into England and retain possession of it.[19]

Military authorities at the front forbade photographers to operate their cameras for fear of drawing small-arms and artillery fire. There are several accounts of newsreel cameramen, with their bulky, tripod-mounted cameras and long-focus lenses, being mistaken by the enemy for belligerents operating new and fearsome weapons.[20] At the same time government authorities in Britain,

France, and Germany restricted the filming and release of news-reels and other information for political reasons:

Though designed originally to keep information of military value from the enemy, this censorship also served to prevent the circulation of news, true or false, which might have an undesirable effect upon morale at home. Newspaper editors were given long lists of topics upon which they might print nothing; they were told the views they were to express on various other matters; and they were supplied with articles to print.[21]

During the early days of the war censorship was so stringent abroad that in Great Britain exhibitors were sometimes forbidden even to show films concerned with the European conflict. In their stead exhibitors ran old war dramas to help satisfy the public demand.[22] An article in the *Moving Picture World* indicated that much the same situation existed in the United States:

A series of old pictures showing the various armies of Europe in maneuvers have been taken from the shelves where they had been reposing in peace for many months or even years.

Old copies of Pathé's weekly and of other kinematographic news service bureaus have been ransacked and often duplicated just to offer the public something that might pass for war pictures. . . . In the big cities especially, where foreign-born inhabitants form a considerable part of the population, this demand for something that looks like war is undeniably great.[23]

Faking of World War I coverage was common. As early as September, 1914, John D. Tippett, London representative for the Universal Film Manufacturing Company, in a letter made public by the *Moving Picture World*, stated categorically that all war films being shown in theaters at the time were fakes:

Anything you see in America of any consequence is fake. I do not care what it is, if it is relative to the trouble now on the Continent. . . . Cameramen are absolutely forbidden to go anywhere near the points of interest. To get even small photographs is a most daring exploit. I understand some officers have given orders to kill every English correspondent, and many of them have made a practice of killing any person caught with a camera, irrespective of who he is. The story has never been told as to what happened during the last few weeks in Belgium, and men from America, and people from other neutral governments, have disappeared, and will never be heard of again.

One of my reasons for writing this letter was the reading of a trade paper advertisement. In my opinion the advertiser is very foolish to try to fool the American people in that manner with some old faked-up junk.[24]

The practice of faking newsreels, at least during the early months of the war, reached such proportions that in November, 1915, the *Literary Digest* published an illustrated description of the machinery and techniques employed in such war-film faking in England:

Agricultural laborers, farmers' sons, and village youths, drest in the uniforms of the British and German armies, are drilled in their new duties and initiated into the mysteries of disappearing bayonets, exploding fake shells, trench warfare, and make-believe "gassing." Stroll along a quiet, country footpath bordering some rolling grassland sloping to the sea and you may come upon a horde of yelling men whose spiked helmets and wicked-looking bayonets glint in the sunshine as they charge toward you. If you take cover nimbly and watch, you will see they are rushing a trench filled with khaki-clad British soldiers. You shudder involuntarily as you see those glinting bayonets sinking into human flesh three or four inches, but you find later that the points are protected with little felt buttons and that they are attached to the barrel end of the rifle by a spring that allows them to retract several inches upon striking a solid substance.

As the soldiers ford a stream in their mad charge, columns of water splash high into the air. . . . You wonder how it is that all

117

these country "supers" are not maimed or even killed until you find out that the water-columns are caused by electrically exploded bladders filled with gunpowder and hidden beneath the surface of the stream. As the charging "Germans" reach the opposite bank and make straight for the "British" machine guns, terrible explosions occur. They are the shells still "dropping" from the British artillery. The explosions are electrically controlled by a stage-director or producer, and are caused by burying small cans of gunpowder here and there under the ground to be rushed. At the proper moment the fake mines are exploded by throwing a switch or pressing a button, thus sending clods of earth, a cloud of smoke, and a dummy figure or two into the air. All the vivid effects of a big shell bursting on the ground are thus obtained. . . .*

So excellent are the pictures of modern "warfare" thus obtained by producers in rural Britain that the motion-picture theater patrons can not realize that motion picture men are not allowed near the firing-line in the theaters of war and that the restrictions imposed on the producers prevent them from obtaining the real thing in France.[25]

Genuine footage, although of rather poor quality and coverage, did appear from time to time. Two of the earliest American releases, already mentioned, showed the British cruiser *Caronia* lying off Sandy Hook, New York, in wait for German transport vessels, and the siege of Antwerp in 1914. Both of these early exclusives were photographed by cameramen for Universal's *Animated Weekly*.

At about the same time the American cameraman A. K. Dawson

---

* In another publication cameraman Cherry Kearton warned that, "if there are dense volumes of smoke and the soldiers fling their rifles up in the air, then die in a pose, such films are fakes. In warfare to-day smokeless powder is the only kind used, it being in universal demand because it does not give their position away to the enemy." See Kearton, quoted in Ernest A. Dench, "Methods by Which the European War Has Been Filmed," *Scientific American*, March 20, 1915, 277. A final, farcical note is added by historian Earl Theisen, who reported that night scenes of the battlefield were faked by intercutting negative rather than positive footage into the finished release prints. Earl Theisen, "Story of the Newsreel," *International Photographer*, September, 1933, p. 25.

In 1912, Universal's *Animated Weekly* was introduced. It soon became well established in the market, enjoying a reputation for dependable, thorough coverage. In an industry with a high mortality rate this newsreel proved one of the most enduring. After many changes in name, format, production, and ownership, it was still appearing on neighborhood theater screens more than half a century later. In 1967, when it finally ceased production, it was the oldest continuously released newsreel. (From *Moving Picture World*, January 10, 1914.)

secured permission from German authorities to photograph the German troops from behind their lines:

I had spent ten days . . . in traveling from the Carpathians to join the forces bombarding Przemysl. . . . My tent was finally pitched with the artillery. . . .

The range was about four miles so that our camp was continuously under fire. I was able to make moving pictures of the men bringing up the great siege guns, the work of setting them up, and the actual bombardment. . . . This lasted for days until the forts of Przemysl fell and we rushed forward to find that the great fortifications of steel and solid masonry had been turned upside down by the bombardment.[26]

The photographic quality of the World War I newsreels was generally poor, and the coverage was superficial. Occasionally, however—more by accident than by design—an unusually dramatic scene was captured. Collins reported one such sequence:

The camera was operated from behind the wall of a dismantled house which afforded partial protection for the operator. The film shows several men in a trench and firing steadily, when a stray bullet strikes one of them in the head. The soldier starts with the shock, and then slowly relaxing his hold on his rifle falls back and his eyes close. A companion several feet away crawls to him, administers first aid as best he can and then, taking him in his arms and boldly exposing himself to the enemy's fire, carries him away.[27]

Another newsreel sequence, photographed by subterfuge by a cameraman for the Eclectic Company (an American company owned by Pathé), showed the sacking and burning of Louvain. "Some of his pictures show the Belgian troops in their hastily made entrenchments. The retreat, the swarm of refugees and the start of the conflagration of the town are all shown."[28] Other films of war which managed to reach American theaters included scenes of fighting in the Aalst (Alost) and Antwerp areas, photographed by the Lubin Company,[29] and a magnificent sequence—unquestionably the most dramatic of the war—showing the sinking of the torpedoed Austrian cruiser *St. Stephen* in 1918.[30]

Specialized equipment and ingenious techniques were used to overcome the difficult conditions under which battleground cinematography was attempted. Understandably, long-focus lenses came in for a good deal of use. Such lenses allowed for the production of clear images of soldiers at a distance of up to six hundred yards. Among the technical innovations introduced during the war was the De Proszynski Aeroscope camera, which did not require the dangerous, time-consuming use of a bulky tripod.[31] This instrument, an invention of Kasimir de Proszynski, was the progenitor of all hand-held "self-powered" motion picture cameras. Until that time the average camera had been driven by a hand crank turned by the cameraman. In the Aeroscope the film was moved by a reservoir of compressed air. This charge of air was sufficient for the filming of several hundred feet of film. The reservoir was recharged by means of a foot pump, an operation which took about ten minutes. Although the camera weighed less than twenty pounds and was easily carried, it was large enough to hold four-hundred-foot magazines, enough film for seven minutes of continuous operation at the then-standard silent-film speed of 60 feet per minute.

An even more unusual feature of the camera was its stabilizing gyroscope, which automatically maintained horizontal stability. The camera was ideally suited for cramped usage on the battlefield, where it could be operated at eye level or held above the operator's head and safely projected upward out of the trenches.

The Aeroscope camera figured prominently in a macabre incident in the filming of the Battle of Verdun by the French cameraman J. A. Dupré. In the midst of the advance Dupré paused, apparently sat down upon the ground, rested the camera upon his knees, and started the mechanism going in order to film the battle before him. The camera had scarcely begun operating when Dupré was killed, either by a bullet or by shrapnel. The unharmed camera, automatically held level by its gyroscopic stabilizer, continued operating faithfully for several minutes, recording the battle long after the cameraman had died.[32]

Techniques used by wartime cameramen to secure important footage included climbing telephone poles and trees to obtain panoramic views of the action. In such manner a cameraman named Mason was able to secure what was described as an unusually good scene of the German army.[33] On another occasion a newsreelman named Bizeul hid himself in a second-story room of a restaurant in Ghent. He opened a window wide enough for the lens of his camera and from 3:00 to 4:15 P.M. secretly photographed German infantry as it passed through the street beneath him.[34]

Far more obnoxious to cameramen than battlefield dangers were the rarely evaded ministrations of the front-line censors, operating on behalf of the belligerents. Cameramen went to great lengths to try to smuggle footage out of Europe and back to American laboratories. Newsreelman Paul Rader made footage of an artillery battle between the French and the Germans and hid it in the cellar of a half-destroyed house. Several days later, after the battle lines had shifted elsewhere, he returned, picked up the film, and successfully smuggled it past military censors and back to his employer's laboratory.[35] Such a success was the exception rather than the rule, however, as bitter contemporary correspondence, trade-paper editorials, and correspondents' dispatches testify.

On April 6, 1917, the United States declared war on Germany and joined its allies as cobelligerent in the war. From that date onward American newsreel footage improved markedly under the administration of the United States Army Signal Corps. At the same time, coverage of the war by civilian cameramen diminished to the point of insignificance. The history of the combat-photography section of the Signal Corps, although inspiring and worth documentation, does not fall properly within the scope of this book, since it was only tangentially associated with the commercial newsreel industry. Nevertheless, because it sometimes furnished footage to civilian producers through governmental agencies, it seems worthwhile to review the relations of those agencies with newsreel companies.

On April 14, 1917, eight days after the United States declared war, President Wilson established the Committee on Public Information, charged with the responsibility of providing news, information, and indoctrination materials to the American civilian population. Because of the dynamic role which its chairman, George Creel, played in the conduct of the committee, it soon became known simply as the Creel Committee.

Dubbed "America's first propaganda ministry,"[36] the Creel Committee played a controversial role in bringing the story of the war, its aims, and its demands to citizens on the home front. The committee's *Official Bulletin*, filled with censored news dispatches and governmental pronouncements, was distributed to news services daily. Pamphlets, one of which had a total circulation of over six million copies,[37] were distributed. The National School Service was established to provide patriotic, "war-aim" information to schoolteachers on a periodic basis for retransmission to students.[38] A system of public-speaking engagements was established utilizing the Four-Minute Men, a nationally distributed group of volunteer speakers prepared to address large assemblies on government-selected topics in support of Red Cross, Liberty Loan, and Food Administration campaigns. The Four-Minute Men spoke for exactly that length of time at motion picture theaters across the country. "In exchange for an exclusive privilege of appearing on theater stages, the Four-Minute Men guaranteed the managers that they would get no other official demands for their facilities."[39]

Until the middle of 1918 war-film footage of an informational or historical nature was secured by the Signal Corps and turned over to the Red Cross, which released a few poorly made films. In March, 1918, the responsibility for utilizing Signal Corps footage was taken from the Red Cross and given to a new section of the Creel Committee, the Division of Pictures. The responsibilities of the new division included receiving, censoring, and editing combat motion picture footage from front-line areas and distributing it to newsreel producers. More than six hundred cameramen and technicians—all members of the armed forces—were engaged in securing combat photographs, both still and motion pictures, for release to theaters and press associations.[40] The task of utilizing photographic techniques for military reconnaissance, intelligence, and communication was handled independently by the Signal Corps.

Although war coverage by the militarily favored Signal Corps was certainly more extensive than that secured by civilian cameramen before America's entrance into the war, a rigorous censorship of raw footage by representatives of the Creel Committee prevented the release of much of the footage. One of the few groups privileged to view unedited footage was the Congress of the United States, for whose exclusive use two sets of projection facilities were built in Washington, one in a committee room in the House of Representatives, and the other in a room adjoining the Senate chambers.[41] For the average citizen, however, little material of real substance seems to have been released. Military setbacks were not shown, and politically favorable conclusions were not too subtly drawn from the available footage through editing and captioning.* The activities of the Committee on Public Information were never popular with the film industry or the working press. After the end of the war Creel came under harsh personal attack, which he sought to answer in his own history of the committee's work.[42]

In sum, despite the outstanding efforts of Signal Corps cameramen, a number of factors combined to render motion picture coverage of World War I thin and inadequate: the novelty of the motion picture as a journalistic medium and the failure of gov-

---

* For a study of the Creel Committee and its role as an information channel for the Wilson administration, see Elmer E. Cornwell, Jr., "Wilson, Creel, and the Presidency," Public Opinion Quarterly, Summer 1959, p. 189. Cornwell argues that "the activities of George Creel and his organization were a major factor underlying this growing tendency to see the Federal Government personified in Presidential terms."

ernment officials to accord cameramen the same privileges given newspapermen; the hesitancy of front-line military authorities to allow photography for fear of attracting enemy fire; the failure of the government to develop an efficient production and distribution system for war film; the almost complete lack of experience and tradition in combat photography; the exclusion of highly competitive civilian cameramen from front-line areas during most of the war; lack of equipment suited to battleground cinematography; and, most limiting of all, the presence of rigorous censorship by zealous representatives of the Creel Committee and the military services.

Fortunately for the American newsreel industry, World War I provided a training ground for professional film makers. Some of them remained with the newsreel business, while others went into Hollywood studios, where they achieved distinction as directors and cinematographers. Notable members of both groups include Joseph von Sternberg, Hal Mohr, Victor Fleming, Ernest Schoedsack, Farciot Edouart, Wesley Ruggles, Ira Morgan, Gus Peterson, Larry Darmout, Fred Archer, Faxon Dean, Harry Thorpe, Al Kaufman, George Hill, and Eddie Snyder.[43]

If civilian newsreel coverage of World War I was sketchy and inadequate, that of the Russian Revolution was practically nonexistent, owing to some extent to lack of interest in the Russian rebellion at a time when the major news headlines were being made in central Europe. The Bolshevik Revolution was simply overlooked in the worldwide chaos of the period. Even the Russians, during those first few violent weeks, failed to document their revolution on film. As the pioneer Russian film producer Alexander Khanzhonkov has written:

The February [1917] *Revolution was joyfully greeted by the film workers. Nevertheless, in the confusion everyone forgot to film anything on the first days. . . . Not until March 1st did the cinematographers collect their wits, and take their cameras out onto the streets.*[44]

Among the few American cameramen to bring back usable footage of the revolution were N. C. Travis and Donald Thompson. Travis was reported to have shot more than seventy-five thousand feet of film in eighteen days. In Petrograd he filmed the customs house under small-arms fire, as well as general mob violence and looting. In Minsk he toured the hospitals with his camera, and outside Minsk he filmed aerial engagements and trench warfare between Russians and German forces.[45] Thompson photographed scenes on the battleground and in Petrograd. He also secured footage of both Lenin and Trotsky.[46] Apart from such unusual scenes, however, American coverage of the Menshevik and Bolshevik uprisings was rare owing to journalistic problems intrinsic to the conduct of the revolution rather than to political censorship, which had not yet begun to function effectively. Within a few years, however, American newsreelmen would become unwelcome in many areas of the Soviet Union. Their photographic assignments would become occupationally hazardous, and their rare scoops newsreel classics.[47]

8.

THE POSTWAR
SILENT NEWSREEL

The already prosperous and influential American motion picture industry emerged from World War I stronger than ever. Almost overnight vigorous foreign competition—particularly from the French—had disappeared. During the war European film artists and technicians had been conscripted en masse into the armed forces, thus depriving the Continental studios of the talent and imagination which had helped establish their position in international film circles. Much of the energy of those technicians who remained had been directed into the production of government film projects. Hundreds of British and French theaters had been closed, destroying markets for films. Finally, the temporary closing of many film studios, including the Pathé and Gaumont facilities, had broken the back of the French film industry.

From the European film producer's point of view, any appraisal of postwar economic prospects was bound to be pessimistic. Wealthy American studios had begun to lure foreign artists to the New World; Continental audiences had dropped precipitously in number compared with those in the United States; European film makers had difficulty securing widespread release for their films in the United States; European studios and equipment were old and out-of-date; and new capital for speculative film investments was hard to come by.

More important in the long run was the artistic emergence and worldwide popularity of American films. Some French and British film makers ceased competition with the Americans altogether. In a move that had significance for the American newsreel industry, Charles Pathé set out upon a methodical and ultimately profitable dissolution of his entire film-production empire, selling off his studios, manufacturing plants, laboratories, equipment, and exhibition circuits scattered throughout the world.[1] Henceforth, although the Pathé name survived in American newsreel circles, it did so in association with American-owned interests. As French film historian Georges Sadoul observed, "The centre of world film-making deserted the banks of the Seine for the shores of the Pacific."[2]

The American newsreel industry set out upon a program of international coverage which within a short period of time had established its leadership in the international newsreel business. In one country after another American newsreel interests opened offices designed to provide a steady flow of newsworthy footage for American newsreel laboratories. In addition to increasing foreign coverage in the postwar period, newsreel producers undertook to reorganize their entire production system along journalistic lines to improve the quality of coverage, the efficiency of operation, and the speed with which footage was delivered to neighborhood theaters.

One of the individuals responsible for such reorganization was Jack Cohen, who after an apprenticeship with Eric Mayell had been appointed managing editor of *Pathé News* in 1916 at the age of twenty-two. In much the same fashion as a newspaper editor, Cohen "built" motion picture news stories, recognizing news values in events which were generally ignored, skillfully anticipating news breaks, and spending what were then considered lavish sums of money on a large international staff of cameramen to secure adequate coverage for quality editing. Often, when events lent themselves to preplanning, Cohen prepared elaborate scenarios before filming for the guidance of his cameramen and editors. Directives and travel orders poured out of his office daily as if from that of a commanding general, shuffling cameramen from country to country, alerting stringer photographers for impending news breaks, arranging for the collection and customs clearance of foreign footage, and marshaling in an ingenious and flexible manner all transportation media available for shipping negatives back to the American laboratories.

A contemporary account published in 1924 described the manner in which Cohen anticipated and arranged for the photography of the burning of Smyrna during the Greco-Turkish War:

> *One of his European staff, a Frenchman named Ercole, was at Vienna. Cohen cabled him to go at once to Constantinople. Ercole left the next day.*
>
> *. . . the Turks would not let him enter the city; so he got an airplane, flew over Smyrna, and made pictures from the air. Then, in spite of all obstacles, he managed to get aboard an Allied warship in the harbor, and with a long-distance lens made photographs of the terrible scenes on the water front.*
>
> *Meanwhile, Cohen cabled Ercole to rush his pictures to Paris. The latter, worn out by the experiences he had gone through, took his precious films by a special boat to the nearest European port, thence by airplane to Paris.*
>
> *There, the local staff worked . . . to get the films ready to be sent on the "Aquitania" to New York, but missed it by three hours. . . . They hired an airplane, chased out to sea, overtook the "Aquitania," and dropped the package of films on her deck. They had written on the package what was to be done with it.*
>
> *Then they cabled Cohen. And as the "Aquitania" neared New York another airplane went out to meet her, received the package of films, and delivered it to the laboratory. These pictures of the Smyrna tragedy were the first ones to arrive in this country.*[3]

Whenever possible, negatives were shipped air mail by special arrangement with the postal department whereby newsreel footage was given priority and special handling apart from other packages.[4] In many cases, however, the cameraman himself hand-carried valuable footage back to the laboratory, utilizing whatever transportation was available. Cohen described how exclusive footage of the Florida hurricane of the 1920's was brought to motion picture screens:

The Pathé News' cameraman was on the spot. Injured himself, as were thousands of others by falling walls, he nevertheless stuck to his camera and ground out . . . one of the most spectacular and marvelous pictures ever thrown on the screen, . . . walked miles with his film and then took an automobile to get to the nearest point from which a railway train could be boarded, out of the stricken area, and succeeded in getting to Jacksonville within twenty-four hours after the hurricane occurred.

At Jacksonville he was met by an airplane which had been engaged and transported to Atlanta, where a second airplane was being held in readiness to transport him to Charlotte. The cameraman had to be physically carried from one plane to another with his precious films in his hands and which he insisted on delivering personally to headquarters. The plane from Atlanta was forced down by a terrific rainstorm near Greenville, South Carolina, from where the cameraman then made a hurried trip by automobile to catch a fast train that took him to Washington. He was met there by another airplane which transported him to New York, thus bringing the first pictures of this terrible event to the screen within forty-eight hours.[5]

The speed with which such footage was rushed to theater screens was sometimes competitive with newspaper publication. Films of the inauguration of President Warren G. Harding were screened in New York theaters six hours after the President had taken the oath of office in Washington.[6] On another occasion, following the filming of the spectacular parade of the Twenty-seventh Division of the American Expeditionary Forces in New York, motion picture audiences watched newsreels of the first part of the procession while the parade was still in progress. Stuart Mackenzie described the mechanics of the operation:

Along the route of the parade, five or six expert camera men were covering it for the Pathé people. Each of them had an assistant with an automobile, in waiting. As fast as the pictures were taken they were rushed to the laboratory, developed, and screened. That is, they were shown on the screen in the projecting-room, so that the editor could see what they were, could have them cut if necessary, and could have the titles put on. That done, they were sent by messengers in motor cars to the theatres. The parade started at ten A.M. and at two P.M. the pictures were being shown in thirty New York theatres.[7]

The limits of rapid newsreel release were probably reached when Austrian Chancellor Johann Schober was photographed entering a European theater for a special motion picture screening. Hubl reported that Schober "was filmed as he entered the cinema and the print was shown on the screen at the end of the programme."[8] Compared with today's instant-replay techniques of television, such speed may not seem very startling, but to an audience of that time it was extraordinary.

Within a short period of time Cohen brought to Pathé's newsreel service a speed and efficiency of operation which became the envy of his competitors. The vigorous competition following World War I forced other newsreel companies to follow Pathé's example; they expanded their staffs, increased their budgets, and adopted high-speed production techniques.

By 1914 managers of the better theaters were taking great pains to present newsreels properly. A theater that took itself especially seriously subscribed to more than one newsreel, combined the best footage into one reel, and put its own name on it. Special scores were prepared for musical accompaniment. Volume 2 of the *Sam Fox Moving Picture Music Catalogue* of 1914 offered various original piano compositions intended as accompaniments for newsreels. The list of selections suggests some of the subjects which found their way onto motion picture screens in the newsreels of that day.

Part 1—European Army Maneuvers

131

Part 2—Funeral March
Part 3—Paris Fashions
Part 4—Aeroplane or Regatta Races
Part 5—Marathon, Horse or Automobile Races
Part 6—Exhibition (Flower, etc.)
Part 7—Explosion or Fire Scene

No one went to more trouble over accompaniments than S. L. Rothapfel, the "Roxy" of Broadway movie-palace fame:

For the Topical Special, or as it is best known, the "Weekly," we play absolutely according to the scenes used, the national airs of different countries and little bits of marches and waltzes that will fit the scene. Here, of course, we deviate from our regular adaptation and go back to playing the pictures.

We pay a good deal of attention to this portion of our program and I attribute the wonderful successes of our Topical Review to the musical accompaniment. Where organs are used the organ and orchestra work together in perfect harmony. The cues are given for the orchestra to give the score to the organ in which the organ, as a rule, plays the last four or five bars with the orchestra and slides into its own score without any noticeable break. The same thing occurs when the orchestra takes it away from the organ, thereby insuring absolute smoothness.[9]

A few years later, in January, 1918, Roxy anticipated the multi-image exhibition innovations of the 1960's and 1970's when he projected five newsreel films at once onto the screens of his recently opened Rivoli Theater in New York City. The series was entitled *The Rivoli Animated Pictorial*, and, according to a contemporary trade-paper review, it "called forth many exclamations of wonderment."[10]

By the mid-1920's the newsreel business had become a complicated but not necessarily profitable business.[11] It was estimated that between 85 and 90 per cent of the eighteen thousand theaters in the United States exhibited one of the six newsreels then available to a weekly audience numbering in excess of forty million people. For this service exhibitors paid as much as $100.00 or as little as $1.50 a week, depending entirely upon the type of run involved—that is, whether the two hundred prints made of each edition were sent directly to the theaters or were passed down from first-run to second-run theaters over a period of several days to two or three weeks.

The task of handling, processing, editing, and printing the flood of film which poured into the laboratories was a Herculean one. During an average week between thirty and thirty-five thousand feet of film found their way to each of the newsreel companies— as much as a quarter of a million feet a week for the entire industry. This bulk of film had to be edited into semiweekly editions by each company, each of which averaged between eight hundred and one thousand feet of finished, titled film with a running time of nine to eleven minutes. The two issues a week were called the "odd" and "even" issues, of which about five hundred prints were released throughout the country on Mondays and Thursdays.

The cost of newsreel production was a formidable one even for the largest studios, and the profit margin was slim or nonexistent. In 1925 the total production cost for the four newsreels in business averaged about $75,000 a week and the gross profit $115,000. By 1928, with six companies in the field and competition much stiffer, total production costs for all companies had risen to about $125,000 a week, while gross returns had shrunk to approximately $110,000. Much of the expenditure went into staff salaries. Each major organization maintained a permanent staff of about one hundred cameramen, internationally scattered, each of whom received $50 to $200 a week.

On the whole, according to veteran newsreel cameraman Sanford Greenwald, the newsreelman's lot was a pleasant one, particularly when compared with the hectic, hard-paced life which cameramen had to adjust to many years later, when they moved into TV news-film coverage:

In that era, a newsreel cameraman "led the life of Riley," he had a private office and a secretary in the film exchange of the company he was working for, entirely his own boss, his assignment editor was three thousand miles away in New York. . . . He had sole possession of a company car (a Chrysler New Yorker), gasoline, repairs and insurance all paid for by the company, and was allowed to put $10.00 a month for garage at home on his expense account, said account was unlimited. There were only five or six of these soft jobs in each large city, one from each of the five newsreel companies. When a cameraman was lucky enough to get one of these "positions" he couldn't be pried loose from it for at least twenty-five or thirty years, or was liquidated in a riot, an automobile or airplane crack-up, hit by a racing car, a parachute that forgot to open. The working conditions were better than perfect. . . . A good national or international story was scarce, and would happen only once or twice in two weeks, this made it possible for a man to call a friend at the A.P. or U.P. office in the morning to learn if anything was "cooking." If all was clear the guy could go fishing, play golf, or play at one of his hobbies, if he had one.

All this leads up to the fact that if you actually worked on a story a week the New York editors were happy, and very often it was two or three weeks in between working days, but the weekly pay checks came regularly from New York each week.[12]

Full-time employees were augmented by as many as 1,500 stringers, who would occasionally shoot footage on a free-lance basis, either on assignment or speculation. Apparently, in those early days before the introduction of sound, free-lance 35mm cameramen—both semiprofessional and amateur—provided a substantial amount of footage which found its way into newsreels. One company even published a handbook for free-lancers to guide them in their work, and occasional articles in early motion picture books and periodicals offered practical advice to amateurs on the photography and sale of newsreel footage.[13]

Occasionally the amateur's contribution was a major one; the only pictures taken of the spectacular collapse of the Tacoma Bridge during a severe storm were taken by a University of Washington physicist, F. B. Farquharson, who was present with his 16mm camera, studying structural stresses and strains at the moment of the collapse.[14] Before the introduction of sound, payment for such free-lance footage ranged from 50 cents to $2.00 a foot, averaging about $1.25. Unusually rare or newsworthy footage would bring as much as $100.00 a foot.

By 1922 the newsreel had achieved sufficient importance within the motion picture industry that *Exhibitors Herald* devoted a separate section of each issue to the current newsreel scene. In addition to reporting the state of the newsreel business and reviewing the contents of each major newsreel, the section also gave advice on promoting newsreels at the local level—tie-ins between local citizens and companies with different kinds of newsreels, advertising campaigns, newspaper publicity stunts, and so on.[15]

Professional personnel for the newsreel services were recruited, at least during the early silent period, mainly from the newsprint media—cameramen from the ranks of press photographers and editors from equivalent positions on newspapers.[16] As *Exhibitors Herald* described it: "The system in vogue is one not unlike the editorial rooms of a large daily publication. Here we have our managing editor, our news editor (city editor), our foreign editor, a copy desk and compositor, etc."[17]

The preponderance of journalistically trained and print-oriented personnel, together with the influence of the Hearst organization on the early news-film business, contributed in large measure to the distinctly newspaperlike structure and style of the American newsreel, with the fragmented succession of unrelated "stories," the titles composed in the manner of front-page headlines, and the practice of beginning each issue with the major news event of the day, followed by successively less important subject matter. After the introduction of sound in later years unionization of the newsreel industry and new management practices provided for the apprenticeship of motion picture rather than newspaper photographers, while editorships were assigned somewhat more frequently to experienced film makers than to newspaper veterans.

By that time, however, the style and format of the American newsreel had been irrevocably fixed along newspaper lines, a characteristic which should be considered less an intrinsic quality or necessity than the product of historical accident. The style and format of the American newsreel need not have been fashioned after that of the newspaper. The type of sound newsreel introduced by the Nazi government in the 1930's, for example, was considerably more dramatic and cinematic in style and structure, as was that also of the American quasi newsreel, *The March of Time*. For better or worse, the American newsreel took its structure, its style, its personnel, and many of its news-gathering techniques from the older newsprint media.

Despite such similarities, however, some distinct and significant differences in operation and purpose certainly existed. The news-gathering operations of the newsreel industry involved problems of transportation which the other press services did not face. The task of a newspaper reporter in acquiring information and transmitting it to his editor was much simpler than that of the motion picture cameraman, for, whereas the newspaper reporter trafficked in verbalized information about events, the newsreel cameraman set out to secure visualizations, of greater or lesser fidelity, of the same events.

The commodity handled by the reporter was an easily stored message which could be committed to memory or note pad until communication facilities were available to transmit it to the newspaper editor, in whose hands it was rapidly appraised, rewritten, and published for the reading public. In contrast, the news property handled by the cameraman was a perishable, physically bulky package of undeveloped film of a momentarily unknown value, which had to be laboriously and safely transported back to the laboratory for processing, viewing, appraisal, editing of a physical nature, printing, and distribution. Because of the nature of the medium, the newsreel cameraman's ability to bypass censors and overcome environmental obstacles was severely limited. The speed with which the film could be transported by rail or air could never compete with the speed of communication of written or oral messages by telegraph, telephone, or radio.

Apart from such operational differences, an equally important distinction should be made with respect to the purpose of the journalistic effort of the two media, at least as perceived by their practitioners. Whatever the average newspaper's limitations may have been, it was expected to offer a reasonably thorough coverage of all major daily news events at local, regional, national, and international levels. Its articles could run to any length, and could be subjected to indefinitely prolonged editorial elaboration and commentary. The newsreel, on the other hand, had a more or less fixed length, designed to fit conveniently into theater programs, and it was not expected to vary from that length. The most important news stories, if excessive in number and overlong, were abbreviated or omitted altogether to avoid running over the allotted time.

At the same time, a full measure of program footage was expected from week to week by exhibitors, whether or not the week's news warranted it, which meant that quasi-newsworthy footage had to be manufactured during journalistically lean periods. Although the practice of padding is common also to newspaper publication, its nature is far less readily apparent in print than on the motion picture screen. Lacking newsworthy information, the newspaper editor can provide a substantial amplification of yesterday's headlines. The production of such newspaper copy, intellectually derived and intangible in nature, is limited in quantity and quality only by the imagination of the editorial talent available. On the other hand, the newsreel editor, lacking physically tangible footage of newsworthy events, had to pad his ten-minute reel with either library footage, which was time-consuming to assemble and edit, or manufactured novelty sequences.

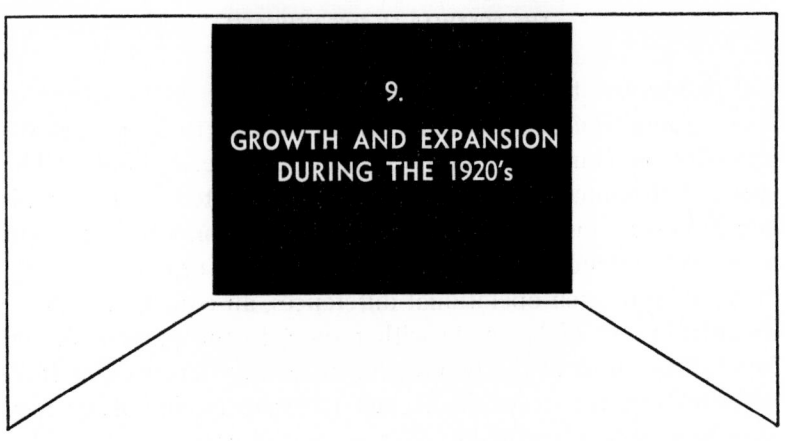

9.
GROWTH AND EXPANSION
DURING THE 1920's

In a competitive economy a news-gathering enterprise prospers in proportion to the energy and efficiency of its employees in securing exclusive news material, and in publishing what it gets in advance of its competitors. Perhaps the most notable characteristic of early newsreel production—and one which set the tone of the silent newsreel's style and appeal—was the intense competition among producers and cameramen to scoop their rivals. It was a characteristic which invites careful scrutiny, for it can be argued that the decay of competitive spirit in later years contributed substantially to the decline of the American motion picture newsreel. This competitive spirit, springing from motives of prestige or economic survival, can be traced to the very earliest days of news-film production and release. In fact, competition seems to have been particularly fierce even before the introduction of the American Pathé newsreel in 1911; in the early days each news-film release was unique and had an economic role to perform on the theater program.

We have already seen to what lengths such early film makers as Albert Smith were willing to go to secure newsworthy footage, as in the pirating of pictures of the 1899 Jeffries-Sharkey prize fight. Much early competition was a natural reaction to the common practice of buying exclusive newsreel rights to particular events. In some instances, as in Pancho Villa's sale of the photographic rights to his war, competition did not seem prudent. In other instances, when the consequences of detection seemed less severe, newsreel piracy was more the rule than the exception, and the acquisition by one company of "bought pictures" (exclusively purchased and assigned coverage rights to sports or news events) automatically provoked attempts at illegal coverage by the competition. Even before the newsreel was introduced, piracy of sporting events was so common that on one occasion race-track officials fired off smoke rockets at the start of the race to obscure the view of competing cameramen who were known to be operating in the area.[1]

Pathé was particularly belligerent in its assumption that exclusive reportorial rights to sports events could no more be properly sold to a newsreel company than they could be sold to a newspaper association. Accordingly, it set out to pirate every event that it could. On one occasion the Minerlava Company, a manufacturing concern, sponsored a beauty contest with eight contestants in Madison Square Garden. The newsreel rights were sold beforehand to one of Pathé's rivals. Pathé's cameraman Bob Donahue managed to bluff his way into the arena and onto the stage, where he photographed the entire event. Arrested by the police, he confounded the authorities with a legalistic maneuver and escaped with his footage of the event.

On most other occasions, however, bluff counted for little, and far more ambitious schemes were necessary to steal footage from the legitimate purchasers. Shortly after the American newsreel was introduced, one of the major film companies purchased exclusive rights to an important baseball game in New York City. A special police force was employed by the producer to detect and eject competing cameramen. Long before the game was underway, the guards had managed to uncover one rival photographer masquerading as a baseball rooter in the stands and operating a small, hand-held camera. The man was ejected from the ball park, but in the end one of his coconspirators got the pictures anyway by posing as a newspaper photographer and operating a rebuilt

Graflex camera in which a motion picture camera had been hidden.[2]

All the companies were engaged in piracy, of course. The organization which lost its exclusive coverage on the occasion described above later set up a camera on the roof of a building overlooking the Brooklyn ball park and began filming the game to which its former competitor had purchased motion picture rights. On this occasion the pirating concern was frustrated by the legitimate newsreelers, who set up mirrors on the field to reflect sunlight into the lenses of the rooftop cameras.[3] A similar attempt was made by newsreelers Ray Fernstrom and Joe Gibson to photograph the exclusively contracted 1929 World Series from a rooftop opposite Shibe Park in Philadelphia.[4] On still another occasion both Pathé and International Newsreel pirated a spectacular scene of an airplane taking off from the top of an office building—a stunt which had been set up at considerable expense by the producers of the Associated First National film "Stranger than Fiction."[5]

Motion picture producers were still forbidden under the provisions of the Sims Act from shipping prize-fight films across state lines. Nonetheless, preliminary events, including the introduction of the contestants, could be filmed and exhibited up to the moment the fight began. The Dempsey-Carpentier fight at Boyle's Thirty Acres in Jersey City in 1921 had attracted so much attention that even the preliminaries seemed newsworthy, and the rights were accordingly sold to a newsreel firm. The competition, led by Pathé's Jack Cohen, countered at once with plans to pirate scenes of the event. Unknown to the promoters, Cohen leased a rooftop opposite the open fight arena. He drained a large water tank at the edge of the roof and had a hole bored into it, through which he planned to have a cameraman secretly film the scenes below.

On the day of the event, however, some time before the preliminaries began, the promoters learned of the scheme and managed to buy the rights to the rooftop from the owner of the building. The police ejected Cohen and his associates from their vantage point minutes before the preliminaries began, whereupon the officials relaxed their vigil and made ready to take their own motion pictures of the event. Cohen, however, had had the foresight to station a second cameraman, Harfry Harde, on another floor of the building. In the confusion Harde was overlooked. Equipped with a seven-inch lens, he successfully filmed the entire contest, and immediately rushed the footage to the laboratory. According to Croy, "At half past eight it [footage of the preliminaries] was showing on Broadway. Other prints were put in an airplane and at twelve o'clock Sunday noon audiences in Chicago were seeing what the lens saw."[6]

This exciting but generally unprofitable conflict between bought-picture owners and pirates finally came to a head—and an end—in 1923 with the filming of the Zev-Papyrus horse race at Belmont Park.[7] Pathé, which usually played the role of pirate, offered fifty thousand dollars for the exclusive rights to the race. August Belmont, owner of the track, summoned Truman Talley, managing editor of Fox Newsreels, and invited him to bid against Pathé. Irritated by the discrimination against newsreelers as compared with members of the press, and foreseeing the financial ruin of the newsreel industry in a bought-pictures war, Talley refused and set to work, together with the Hearst Newsreel people, to end the practice once and for all.

More than forty Fox and Hearst cameramen were assigned to pirate the event. Several dozen very small, hand-held Sept cameras were purchased for the occasion and distributed to the cameramen, who were to infiltrate the track and mingle with the crowds. Long before the date of the race an old ice factory at the edge of the track was rented and outfitted with heavy cameras with telescopic lenses. Camouflaged platforms were built in the trees at the end of the track, and additional cameramen were stationed on them for a day or two before the race. Their meals were brought to them on a regular schedule. Two airplanes were leased and equipped with camera equipment for aerial coverage.

On the day of the race about two dozen Fox cameramen purchased tickets and entered the stands as paying customers, carrying the hand cameras under their coats. Eight more cameramen were smuggled onto the grounds in a horse trailer. As the race time neared, the cameramen in the icehouse, in the treetops, and in the stands readied their equipment. Finally, as a crowning touch, one of Fox's best cameramen managed to have himself sworn in as one of the deputy sheriffs assigned to guard the race track itself.

Pathé News, with a fifty-thousand-dollar investment at stake, had by no means been caught unaware and had planned appropriate countermeasures. At the moment the horses broke from the barrier and the race was on, more than one hundred smoke pots placed around the track were fired to obscure the competition's view. In addition, a Pathé plane laid a smoke screen over the entire track—which, as it happened, interfered as much with Pathé's photography as it did with Fox's and Hearst's. At the same time, large mirrors were brought into play by Pathé to reflect sunlight into the lenses of the Fox cameras operating from the icehouse and the treetops. A number of arrests were made of the masquerading cameramen in the stands, and their film was confiscated. In the end, however, Fox and Hearst got their film—five thousand feet of it—covering the entire race from beginning to end. The newsreels were successfully exhibited in the United States and abroad a full week before Pathé's legitimately secured pictures reached the screen.[8]

Talley's successful campaign virtually brought an end (until the advent of television) to the practice of purchasing or assigning exclusive newsreel rights to sports events in the United States, though abroad, particularly in Great Britain, the practice continued. In time the Davis Cup final was barred to all newsreelmen because of their refusal to pay what they considered exorbitant sums for the film rights.[9] The cost of such rights could vary from a few dollars for a second-rate tennis match to seventy-five hundred to ten thousand dollars for a major event.[10]

In 1935 competing newsreel firms had a real set-to during the filming of the Grand National Steeplechase at Aintree, England.

In earlier years Pathé News had bought the newsreel rights to this event, nonetheless having to put up with piracy by its competitors. In 1935, Pathé decided to try its own hand at poaching and declined to bid for the rights to the race. Exclusive rights were sold to Gaumont-British News and British Movietone (and through these two firms to the American newsreel companies Hearst Metrotone and Fox Movietone). This agreement left Pathé, Paramount, and Universal on the outside. Together they put up high towers on the outside course from which they could photograph the event with telephoto lenses.

When the British cameramen for Gaumont and British Movietone discovered the ruse, they rushed the towers and tried to shake off the cameramen. Police drove the attackers away, but one of them returned shortly thereafter and set off a still photographer's flashgun as the favorite horse in the race, Golden Miller, approached a small jump near the towers. The horse balked, threw its rider, and lost the race. A side effect was that British bookmakers saved about ten million dollars.

Though the incident was merely one more instance of rivalry between competing newsreel interests, as a consequence of the publicity British officials seriously considered abandoning the practice of granting exclusive rights.[11] Yet some years later much international ill will was generated against Great Britain when the government assigned to a British firm exclusive newsreel rights to the Olympic competitions.[12]

By the end of the 1920's sports promoters in both Great Britain and the United States had reached an agreement barring slow-motion cameras from sports events. On at least two occasions analysis of such footage revealed gross errors in the judgments of umpires and referees, resulting in complaints from sports enthusiasts and gamblers.[13]

Although the practice of buying exclusive rights was generally abandoned in the United States because of its cost and impracticality, other forms of newsreel competition continued during the period of the silent newsreel. In that intensely competitive era, zealous newsreel cameramen were not above sabotaging their fellow photographers to secure exclusive footage. Written accounts and testimony provide many examples of the rigorous and sometimes vicious competition that characterized the silent newsreel. Such competition was publicized by the newsreel companies as evidence of their zeal in securing newsworthy scoops for the public. It brought color and glamour to the business which was apparently enjoyed by the press, the public, and the newsreel cameramen themselves.

It was during the 1920's that the legend of the death-defying cameraman arose, fostered in large part by newspapers and periodicals. It was a legend with a great deal of truth in it, for, in fact, newsreelmen were an adventurous lot who regularly took extraordinary chances to secure exciting footage. Crippling accidents, maimings, imprisonments, and death were frequent in the business. That they were serious occupational hazards was evident in the unusually high insurance premiums which newsreel companies had to pay for their employees.*

The stereotype of the daring newsreeler is one which would probably have evolved whether or not the press had popularized it. The American newsreel devoted much of its program to the presentation of manifestly sensational pictures—footage which could only have been secured by daring photographers. Strikes, wartime battles, floods, hurricanes, explosions, recalcitrant celebrities, earthquakes, fires, and assassinations appeared on theater screens with impressive regularity.

At the same time, the newsreel organizations themselves did their best to publicize their cameramen's contributions. In 1922, Fox introduced a competition among its cameramen, the first

---

* Figures published in the late 1930's indicate that the premiums for cameramen on dangerous assignments ran about fifteen dollars a day and up to six thousand dollars a year for ten thousand dollars coverage. In addition, cameramen participated in group-insurance coverage, paid by their companies, in the amount of about four thousand dollars coverage for each cameraman. See Robert Desmond, "News About the Newsreel," *Christian Science Monitor Magazine*, September 28, 1938, 5; and Thomas Sugrue, "The Newsreels," *Scribner's Magazine*, April, 1937, p. 9.

144

prize of which was "a beautiful gold trophy of exclusive design and valued at $100 for the best THRILL pictures used by FOX NEWS."[14] The effect of this kind of promotion was to encourage dangerous but not necessarily newsworthy assignments, such as the filming of the building of the Golden Gate Bridge as seen from the support cables, or lions at the zoo as seen from within the cage—and then photographing the cameramen as they worked under such hazardous circumstances.

On one occasion Fox Newsreel editor Ray Hall even admitted to faking a newsreel sequence which showed a Fox cameraman photographing a rum-running operation off the coast of New England. In truth, admitted Hall, the cameraman was in no danger at all, since he had been welcomed along by the smugglers. However, he was photographed skulking about in such a manner as to suggest that the films had been secured at risk of life and limb. Ironically, when this footage was released in theaters, the unusually vehement public and official reaction led to a congressional appropriation of twelve million dollars to equip and strengthen the anti-smuggling arm of the United States Coast Guard.[15]

Within a few years after its introduction the American newsreel had become a hardy, if not particularly profitable, component of the exhibitor's program. Once it had been successfully introduced, however, the producers bore the responsibility of providing twice a week, week after week, ten minutes of exciting, newsworthy footage. It was a duty which was not easily discharged, for newsworthy footage was not always available. Before the introduction of the newsreel the news-film producer released his occasional specials only as news events occurred. After 1911, however, he had to provide footage on a regular basis, and if he could not secure enough genuine footage to fill the reel, then he had to manufacture it. The price which producers and audiences had to pay for permanent, regular newsreel release was a gradual erosion of authenticity and veracity in newsreel content.

Yet, despite the large amount of bogus footage of one sort or another presented by the newsreel in its silent years, its image as an inherently incorruptible medium persisted. There was—and still is—a peculiarly convincing illusion of reality in newsreel images. The testimony of our eyes seems so overwhelmingly irrefutable that only the strongest evidence to the contrary will convince us of cinematic fraud and deception.

The following quotations, selected from the popular press, trade papers, and critical literature of the silent film period, reveal an unmistakable assumption of trust in the veracity of the newsreel:

1900: *A written description is always the point of view of the correspondent. But the Biograph camera does not lie and we form our judgement of this and that as we watch the magic of the screen.*[16]

1911: *Cinematography cannot be made to lie, it is a machine that merely records what is happening.*[17]

1911: *The reporter with the pen will be superseded by the reporter with the camera. . . . The world will be treated to that rarest of rare things—a reporter who does not, in fact, who cannot lie. The events will come to us not as the policy of the paper would want to color them, but as they actually occurred.*[18]

1912: *The man with the camera holds an undisputed advantage over his* confrère *armed with notebook and pencil. He gives a truthful pictorial account of what takes place, not the garbled product of a vivid imagination.*[19]

1914: *The only real and incorruptible neutral in this war is not the type but the film. . . . It is utterly without bias and records and reports but does not color and distort.*[20]

1922: *Utter fidelity to life is the newspicture's distinctive attribute.*[21]

1926: *The newspapers may exaggerate on some news event that took place but the news reels present to us the happening in all its exactness.*[22]

1926: *The deadly accuracy and the vivid realism of the news film has brought it to the heights of purpose and utility which it now occupies. It has reeled its way into the confidence of millions of persons.*[23]

Further evidence of the trust which newspaper and periodical writers placed in the integrity of the silent newsreel is provided in the almost complete absence of critical attacks upon its over-all veracity. This was in sharp contrast to the flood of critical literature charging fraudulent manipulation of newsreel content which appeared in the 1930's, following the addition of sound to film. And yet, in fact, the average silent newsreel sequence was no more genuine than that of the sound newsreel.

If we are to gain some insight into the various sorts of manipulation practiced by silent-newsreel producers, we must first be aware of the different kinds of news events which demanded their attention. In 1926, Emanuel Cohen, editor of the Pathé newsreel, described what he considered the three basic kinds of news:

First, sudden news events like the Japanese earthquake, the Santa Barbara earthquake, or the Shenandoah disaster. These events happen suddenly out of a clear sky, you might say, and with no forewarning. . . .

Second, there is the field of impending events, which refers to those happenings which occur as a natural result of preceding events. A most notable example of this was the Smyrna fire, resulting from the war between the Turks and the Greeks in 1922. One could not foretell that the Smyrna fire would result, but by keeping close to the news scent of the situation it was apparent that some tragic occurrence was at least very likely, in one form or another. . . .

Third, we have the scheduled events. Events which are scheduled to take place on a certain day, such as the inauguration of a President, the World Series, or the Yale-Harvard game.[24]

To these three categories of basic newsreel subject matter Cohen could have added a fourth—that of "manufactured" news footage. Manufactured footage, at least during the silent-film period, appeared in four varieties. The first of these involved the staging or manipulation of components of an event at the time of their actual occurrence. For example, Lescarboura, in 1921, described the manner in which the inauguration of the airplane mail service between Belmont Park, New York, and Washington, D.C., might have been (and by implication was) covered by an experienced cameraman:

> The first thing a trained cameraman would do would be to secure a general view of the airplane used, including some action such as the mechanics walking about and inspecting the various parts. Next, he would ask the authorities to stage some suitable action, such as the handing of the mail bags to the aviator, and the aviator or his assistants placing them in the mail compartment. If no mail bags were yet on hand, dummy bags or anything resembling a mail bag would be used. Then he would secure some human interest snapshots, such as the aviator receiving a good luck horseshoe from some foreign aviation officer, the strapping of a map to the aviator's knee, or the wife of the aviator affectionately bidding him good-bye. Lastly, the cameraman would determine the probable direction of flight and place his camera so as to obtain a view of the airplane running along the ground and taking the air.[25]

What is described here might be considered the most "innocent" form of event manipulation, practiced not to deceive but to reveal the true nature of the subject matter through the acquisition and arrangement of meaningful pictorial story elements. Still, it represents a perspective once removed from the pictorial reality of the event as it happened or might have happened if the newsreel man had not been present. No matter how superficial such manipulation may be, the photographer has already left the imprint of his recording process upon the event itself. With the introduction of sound in later years, and as increasingly elaborate newsreel coverage evolved, events became more and more altered in their configuration by the inevitable presence of the cameraman. Finally, by the late 1930's and the early 1940's, many scheduled events, such as political appearances, conventions, and campaigns, were staged by their protagonists in such a manner as to conform to the requirements of newsreel coverage. An unusual and amusing variation on this sort of manipulation is said by Charles Reid to have occurred in England around 1915, on which occasion a newsreel cameraman set out to photograph a military and political celebrity, Colonel John E. B. Seely, during his participation in the dedication of a new hospital in London:

> Col. Seely was elected the honor of opening the new hospital, and was presented with a golden key with which to unlock the doors for the first time. After some preliminary ceremonies the time came to unlock the doors and the colonel inserted the key, only to find that it evidently did not fit, and he spent five minutes in a vain effort to unlock the new doors, during which time a motion picture photographer worked hard filming the colonel and his changing expressions of surprise, annoyance and wrath. At last he gave up the task and simply called for somebody to come and unlock the doors from the inside. The officials were very cross about the fiasco, and it was not until some time later that they learned that Col. Seely was adverse to having his picture taken, and the photographer being determined to secure a picture, he had plugged up the keyhole.[26]

A second form of manipulation involved the re-creation of a newsworthy event after the fact, using the same individuals that were originally involved. An early instance which created some controversy involved Louis de Rochemont, a young newsreel cameraman who was later to become famous as the founder and producer of *The March of Time.** In 1915 he covered the arrest of a German saboteur, Werner Horn, who was charged with demolishing a bridge at Vanceboro, Maine. De Rochemont and his competitors rushed to Portland, the scene of the arrest, only to

---

* De Rochemont began his career as a cameraman at the age of seventeen while still in high school.

discover that the actual incarceration had taken place earlier in the day. After his rivals had gone, however, De Rochemont persuaded the sheriff to re-enact the arrest. Both the officer and the saboteur obligingly performed for the camera, re-creating the scene. The footage was widely exhibited by both Mutual and Universal film companies.

Competing companies charged the young cameraman with fraud, but De Rochemont defended himself by claiming that the newsreel cameraman enjoyed the same privilege as the press reporter in re-creating the original event. It was De Rochemont's position then, as it was to remain later while he was producing *The March of Time*, that re-enactment was "frequently sharper and more detailed than the 'real' thing."[27] In time re-enactment became a fairly common practice in the newsreel business, providing attractively composed and rehearsed scenes which could be either presented by themselves or integrated with other genuine but inadequate coverage made at the time of the actual event.

A third form of content manipulation involved the manufacture of events for the newsreel camera—events which had no reality apart from the staging and which would never have otherwise occurred. Such footage was used with great frequency either to fill out the reel in lean weeks or to provide novelty and spectacle. In 1932 cameraman George Lancaster described how such an event was planned and filmed:

An active imagination is a handy asset for a newsreel cameraman when news is scarce. . . . Such attempts [at manufacturing news] usually involve stunts and require a lot of hard work in preparation.

Frequently it takes weeks to work up a gag. Of course first of all one must have a fixed idea in mind as to what would be a thriller or have screen value for entertainment. The next thing is to work it out on paper, contact the person or persons directly interested in the supplying of what one would need, which they usually do to the letter. It appeals to almost everyone to get into the movies.

One day while driving between Seattle and Portland on a weekly scouting trip to look around and get ideas I noticed two houses near the highway being wrecked by three men. I stopped and asked the owner if he was wrecking the houses. . . .

"It will take you months at the rate you are going. I can lay them flat in half a day if you want me to," I replied.

"Tickled to death to have you, but I can't afford to pay you."

"Okeh," I replied. "Pull the men off and I'll be back in a few days."

Following up my plan I got in touch with the commander of the tank division at Vancouver barracks. I told him about the houses and explained it would be swell practice for the men and tanks as well as give the War department a chance to see how the training is carried on.

The next day, as a result, the owner had his houses wrecked; the army got a good drilling; the public got an interesting news picture and a cameraman had hatched another idea.[28]

The last form of news footage manufacture involved the blatant faking of scenes of newsworthy events of celebrities, a practice which grew less and less frequent over the years. As the number of newsreel companies multiplied, it became more likely that any particular news event would probably be covered by two or more different organizations. For this reason the chances for successfully engineering a convincing fake which could compare favorably with footage of the original event grew correspondingly less likely. One kind of faking survived, however: the occasional impersonation of celebrities. Footage of internationally famous personalities was always widely sought and oftentimes presented problems in coverage. For example, cameramen who hoped to photograph the Prince of Wales soon learned that four formal "rules" or prohibitions governed such journalistic effort as far as the royal household was concerned:

(1) *His Royal Highness should not be photographed "close-up";*
(2) *His Royal Highness should not be photographed playing golf*

or indulging in other like informal sports; (3) His Royal Highness should not be photographed with ladies; and (4) His Royal Highness should not be photographed whenever he royally does not want to be.[29]

Cameramen sometimes yielded to their editor's demands for footage by staging impersonations. Tracy Mathewson, the official cameraman on the Prince of Wales's tour of Canada in 1920, described how he "covered" a royal fishing trip which he was not allowed to attend:

They refused to let me go along on a trout fishing trip into the mountains, because the Prince was resting and did not want to be bothered by cameramen. However, I did get a good shot of him as he started out. It occurred to me after he had gone that Doran, my assistant, was about the same build as His Royal Highness. We managed to scrape up an outing suit which looked like the one the Prince wore, dressed Doran up in it, and photographed him fishing up and down a stream with his back to the camera. No one who had not been there would have suspected it was not the Prince.[30]

In later years the practice of faking scenes of celebrities by employing impersonators was developed to a high degree of perfection by De Rochemont in *The March of Time*.

From 1925 to 1929 the era of the silent film drew to a rapid and unexpected close. In 1925 four major newsreel producers were in business. All of them released to a substantial number of theaters, and two of them were associated with major producing, distributing, and exhibiting organizations.

Fox Film Corporation, which had founded its newsreel service in 1918, continued to release its twice-weekly silent newsreel under the editorship of Truman Talley. The reel was filmed, edited, and released by the Fox Corporation.

Universal Studios also continued to release a newsreel series under its name throughout the 1920's, but under a production arrangement which differed from that of its founding. A few years after Universal had entered the field, its newsreel franchise was purchased—reputedly for one million dollars—by the Hearst *International Newsreel*, which contracted to produce, edit, and assemble three editions of the newsreel for Universal's customers. The three editions were entitled *Hearst News, Universal Screen Events,* and *Screen Telegram.*[31]

Pathé News, the oldest American newsreel, continued its release independent of the major feature film studios. In the main, it serviced the independent exchanges and theaters. In 1927, Emanuel Cohen resigned his position as editor of *Pathé News* and was succeeded by Ray L. Hall, originally a newspaperman who had at various times served as editor of the *Hearst Vitagraph Newsreel,* as one of the organizers of the *Hearst International Newsreel,* and as editor of *Kinograms.* Hall's assistant at this time was De Rochemont.[32]

Kinograms, founded shortly after World War I by George Baynes and edited by Terry Ramsaye, also survived throughout the last ten years of the silent film era, operated during this period by Educational Pictures, Inc., which specialized exclusively in short-subject distribution.[33] Through its thirty-six exchanges Educational Pictures distributed its *Kinograms* newsreel not only to independent theater chains but also to many theaters owned by those major studios which did not produce their own short subjects—notably Paramount and Metro-Goldwyn-Mayer.[34]

Toward the end of the 1920's, *Kinograms'* fortunes began to fluctuate wildly. The financial position of its parent firm had never been very sound, inasmuch as Educational Pictures did not own any theaters in which to exhibit its own product. In 1927, when Paramount and MGM finally began producing their own shorts and newsreels, *Kinograms* lost many of its exhibition accounts. With the introduction of sound—the success of which was not immediately apparent to many people—*Kinograms'* directors made an injudicious decision to continue with production of a silent newsreel. It was their plan to capture the "unwired" theater

Kinograms was the only American newsreel not associated with a major film company to survive for any length of time. Introduced shortly after the close of World War I, it provided lively competition during the next decade. When the film industry converted to sound in the late 1920's, *Kinograms* tried to continue as a silent release and then as a sound-on-disk, commercially sponsored newsreel. Both schemes were historically foredoomed to failure. In 1931, *Kinograms* ceased production. (From *Exhibitors Herald*.)

market when the other newsreel producers ceased silent production. Various peculiar and unwise financial and production innovations followed which, as will be seen in Chapter 10, led to a catastrophic loss for the parent company and the failure of the newsreel. Despite its erratic and eventually ruinous financial practices, however, *Kinograms* was a quality newsreel during the 1920's and newspaper critics who took the trouble to review the week's competition often rated it of superior quality.

Two more newsreels joined the competition in 1927 when Paramount (Paramount Famous Players–Lasky Corporation) and Metro-Goldwyn-Mayer introduced their respective series, a move designed in both cases to strengthen their financial positions as major producers capable of block booking complete theater programs.*

Pioneer newsreel editors Emanuel Cohen and Al Richard resigned from the staff of Pathé to head the new Paramount organization, taking many of Pathé's outstanding cameramen with them.[35] First presented to the public as a silent product, ("The Eyes of the World"), *Paramount News* acquired a voice shortly after the introduction of sound and became "The Eyes and Ears of the World."[36] Under Cohen's editorship Paramount quickly acquired a reputation for aggressive competition, worldwide coverage, photographic excellence, and frequent exclusive scoops of important news events. Such was the quality and extent of Paramount's coverage that five years after its introduction exclusive arrangements were concluded whereby the Associated Press secured many of its news pictures by making enlargements from Paramount's motion picture footage.[37] Even more important, Paramount was to build a reputation over the next few years for political fairness and reasonably mature commentary—characteristics which most critics were unwilling to assign to its competitors during the wrathful, polemically charged period of the 1930's.

---

* The MGM newsreel was a new name in the field. However, it was produced by the Hearst organization—one of the oldest newsreel producers in the business.

The effect of this new competition from Paramount and MGM was to reduce or eliminate profits for all the newsreel producers. In 1925, with four newsreels operating, the weekly net *profit* for all of the four was a meager forty thousand dollars. By 1928, with six companies in the field, the total net *loss* was estimated at fifteen thousand dollars a week.[38] It was at this point that Educational Pictures, the producer of *Kinograms* and the organization which felt the new competition most keenly, proposed to the other five newsreel companies that the group unite to form a newsreel combine or press association so as to lower costs and increase the efficiency of operations. The name of the proposed organization was to be Associated Newsreels, and it was rumored that Boston businessman Joseph P. Kennedy would head the merger. For reasons already mentioned, the Paramount and MGM newsreel companies rejected the proposal and elected to go their own highly competitive ways. Pathé, Fox, and Universal appeared moderately enthusiastic about Educational Pictures' plan. A complicated but equitable system of capitalization and financial support was finally worked out on paper. As economist Howard Lewis pointed out, the financial and operational advantages for the participants seemed attractive:

The president of Educational Pictures, Incorporated, who had originated this plan, believed that it would effect a marked reduction in the cost of newsreels in several ways. The number of camera men employed would be reduced greatly. Where formerly each company had assigned from 5 to 10 camera men to each important event, Associated Newsreels, Incorporated, would assign a force of 5 or 10 which would serve the needs of all 4 companies. It probably would be possible to cover the field more effectively with such a force. The expense of racing films to New York in an attempt to beat the other newsreel companies would be reduced, since only one airplane or other means of transportation would be used for the films of the 4 companies. It was believed that the total *cost to each company of producing a negative film laid down in New York would be reduced 50%. Estimating that each of the 4 companies which planned to form Associated Newsreels, Incorporated, had been spending about $10,000 per week for their negative films, one of the men who favored the plan pointed out that if each of the companies contributed $5,000 per week to the new company, the latter would have twice the amount spent by each of the companies in the past at half the cost to the separate companies.[39]*

It is interesting to speculate about what the long-range consequences of such a newsreel association might have been. Undoubtedly large savings in operating expenses would have been realized. On the face of it, too, the total amount of unduplicated footage of certain types of "scheduled" news events would probably have increased, allowing for smoother editing and more complete coverage. It seems just as likely, however, that such a move would have destroyed much of the spirit which newsreel cameramen and editors of the silent film period felt so necessary to ensure quality photographic coverage, the anticipation of news breaks, the securing of certain types of newsreel content, and the ingenuity and stubbornness necessary to follow through on difficult assignments. Lacking some sort of commercial incentive, the zest, zeal, nerve, and imagination which characterized the silent newsreel might have failed and decayed in the late 1920's, far earlier than it finally did, in the late 1930's and early 1940's. As is so often the case in show business, an increase in the efficiency of operations does not necessarily lead to an increase in the quality of the product.

Such speculations remain moot, however, for Associated Newsreels died a-borning. Any such scheme which did not provide for the participation of Paramount and MGM did not appear to be financially sound or commercially realistic. Furthermore, conflicting private interests appeared to be involved which, from the start, compromised the integrity of the proposal. As Howard Thompson Lewis concluded: "As in all cooperative enterprises, whole-hearted cooperation and loyalty were essential. No truly cooperative organization can succeed without them. It appears that they did not exist in the present instance."[40]

10.

INTRODUCTION
OF THE
SOUND NEWSREEL

Although the success of the sound film certainly surprised the entertainment world in the late 1920's, it would be an over-simplification to suggest that its technology burst unheralded upon an unsuspecting film industry. The sound film was as old as the silent film and in a sense even older. From its earliest laboratory origins, the motion picture had been conceived by Thomas Edison as an adjunct to his already successful phonograph. In October, 1888, Edison wrote: "I am experimenting upon an instrument which does for the eye what the phonograph does for the ear, which is the recording and reproduction of things in motion, and in such form as to be both cheap, practical and convenient."[1]

Following the invention and development by Edison and W. K. L. Dickson of the first practical motion picture camera (the Kinetograph), Edison manufactured and marketed a few Kineto-scopes which combined both picture and sound and were called Kinetophones. These were peep shows—the pictures could be viewed by only one person at a time. The sound was provided by a nonsynchronous phonograph recording and was heard by means of a stethoscopic-tube attachment which fitted the viewer's ears.[2]

During the years that followed, other inventors worked to per-fect a commercially practical sound-film system. Léon Gaumont, Georges Pomerede, E. H. Amet, William H. Bristol, Alexander Graham Bell, Sumner Tainter, Ernst Rühmer, Eugene Lauste,

J. T. Tykociner, Oskar Messter, and others contributed to the technology.[3] The two major problems were those of providing a positive, foolproof system of synchronizing picture and sound and amplification of the sound signal to allow for presentation of picture and sound to a fairly large audience. Over a period of years the amplification problem was solved, following Lee De Forest's invention of the Audion tube in 1906 and subsequent improvements in vacuum tubes and photo tubes. The synchronization problem was not so easily resolved, however, and at least two major systems were developed during the 1920's along entirely different lines. The first of these involved the mechanical gearing of a phonograph turntable to the camera's and the projector's intermittent movements. It was with such a system—known commercially as the Vitaphone—that *Don Juan* (premiered August 6, 1926) and *The Jazz Singer* (premiered October 6, 1927) were filmed and successfully exhibited by Warner Brothers, thus ushering in the sound-film era. Although this disk-recording system played a historically important role in the introduction of the new film form, it was wholly unsuited to commercial applications. The equipment involved was cumbersome in size, awkward in operation, and crude in engineering. The disks were fragile and had to be laboriously synchronized with each reel of film. Film prints which became torn or broken could no longer be easily repaired by splicing—an entirely new section of film had to be printed as a replacement to preserve synchronization with the phonograph disk. Most important, the disk-recording system did not allow for the intricate editing which had been developed to such a high art during the last few years of the silent film.

The other system, which was finally adopted throughout the world, provided for the printing of a sound track directly onto the same piece of film which carried the picture image. Although in its early years the sound quality was not equal to that of disk recording, it was commercially practical, it involved a minimum of equipment, it provided for absolute synchronism, and—following the subsequent sophistication of technique—it allowed for intricate and artistic editing of picture and sound. The sound-on-film system was pioneered by Lee De Forest between 1920 and 1924 under the trade name Phonofilm.[4] During the early 1920's, long before *The Jazz Singer* had made its spectacular debut, De Forest was screening sound films in a number of theaters using such a system. At that time producers were not interested in the process. As Kellogg states:

> *Perhaps the industry was prospering too well at the time, but judging from the initial coolness of film executives . . . it is easy to imagine that numerous imperfections which undoubtedly existed (as, for example, defective film-motion, limited frequency range, and loudspeakers that gave unnatural voices, and perhaps too, demonstration films that were uninteresting) contributed to loss of the impressiveness needed for doing business.[5]*

Beginning in 1922, Theodore Case and Earl Sponable collaborated—with Lee De Forest's aid—on a sound-on-film system of improved design. As early as July 25, 1924, Case produced an experimental sound-newsreel interview in which President Calvin Coolidge and Senator Robert F. La Follette appeared.[6]

After exhaustive testing Case's improved sound-on-film system was purchased by the Fox Film Corporation on July 23, 1926. The Fox-Case Corporation was founded to exploit the system commercially, and Courtland Smith was named president of the organization. The kind of motion picture attraction chosen by the new company to introduce its system was the sound newsreel. In 1926 the Fox Movietone Corporation was established, and on January 21, 1927—more than eight months before the release of *The Jazz Singer*—the first Movietone sound films were exhibited at the Sam Harris Theater in New York City.[7]

As was the case in the 1890's, the news film was about to play a role in the introduction of a major artistic and technological innovation. The first sound-on-film news film of any importance to be released commercially by Fox Movietone showed Charles Lindbergh's takeoff on May 20, 1927, at Roosevelt Field, Long Island, for his historic trans-Atlantic flight. It was part of an all-Movie-tone program premiered at the Sam Harris Theater on May 25, 1927, together with *Seventh Heaven*, a silent feature synchronized with music.[8]

As Frederic Lewis Allen's account of the Lindbergh feat suggests, a happier choice of subject matter could hardly have been made for the Movietone news film's debut:

> *Every record for mass excitement and mass enthusiasm in the age of ballyhoo was smashed during the next few weeks. Nothing seemed to matter, either to the newspaper[s] or to the people who read them, but Lindbergh and his story. On the day the flight was completed, the Washington* Star *sold 16,000 extra copies, the St. Louis* Post-Dispatch *40,000, the New York* Evening World *114,000. . . . He was greeted in Washington at a vast open-air gathering at which the President made . . . "the longest and most impressive address since his annual message to Congress."*[9]

The Lindbergh newsreel was an immense financial success. Although static in style, it offered satisfactory photography and good sound quality for the period. Even if it had not, it would probably have been a success anyway because of the sensational nature of the subject matter. The scene was photographed in a single, continuous pan shot at the moment of Lindbergh's take-off on a gray, overcast morning. The picture shows a group of by-standers milling around expectantly. A shout is heard, and the plane is seen, moving right to left, gathering speed to take off from the field.[10]

Subsequently the welcome-home ceremonies held for Lindbergh in Washington, D.C., were also photographed by Movietone's sound cameras on June 12, 1927.[11] Like the shots of the takeoff, the ceremonies were photographed with an immobile camera. The ceremonies lasted a full reel—approximately ten minutes.[12] The film shows Lindbergh, President Coolidge, and other officials on a reception stand in Washington. Coolidge delivers what is, for him, an unusually long speech of introduction.

Lindbergh then speaks very briefly. The film was arranged and executed without Lindbergh's prior consent. Later he was told by a friend that his appearance in a sound newsreel was not dignified and did not represent the appropriate way for an international hero to present himself to the public. Lindbergh rarely spoke again for the newsreel cameras.[13]

At no time during the speeches did the sound camera change angle, nor was the picture interrupted for cutaways or reaction shots; the motor was simply turned on, and the sound camera was allowed to run until the ceremonies ended.* The microphone even caught an official's order to the band to begin playing at the conclusion of Lindbergh's address. The scene was preceded by silent captions which elaborated upon the event. Apart from the voices of the participants and other natural sounds of the crowd, silence prevailed throughout both picture and captions—no music, no narration, no sound effects. Whatever it lacked in cinematic dynamics, however, it made up for with presence, immediacy, and an obviously unmanipulated reality. Permanently and movingly recorded were such details as Coolidge's old-fashioned elocutionary gestures and Lindbergh's intensely serious demeanor, halting manner, and occasional stumbling over words.

Fox's two Lindbergh films were really special news-film releases. It was apparently not until October 28, 1927, that the first all-sound reel of *Movietone News* was premiered at the Roxy Theater in New York City, containing the following subjects: (1) "Niagara Falls," (2) "Romance of the Iron Horse," (3) "Army-Yale Football Game at the Yale Bowl," and (4) "Rodeo in New York."[14] Six weeks later, on December 3, 1927, *Movietone News* was introduced by Fox as a regular feature to theaters throughout the country. The first issue contained three items: (1) The Vatican choir singing at the Tomb of the Unknown Soldier in Washington, D.C., (2) the dynamiting by engineers of the obsolete

---

* During the welcome-home ceremonies there are a couple of jump cuts which shorten the ceremony. Also, the camera cuts directly in, through a lens change, for a closer view, midway; however, the angle remains the same. The print upon which this analysis is based is the one in the collection of the Museum of Modern Art.

Conowingo Bridge in Maryland, and (3) the Army-Navy football game of 1927, which Army won, 14 to 9. The second regular issue of the Movietone newsreel, released December 10, 1927, also contained three sound-film subjects: (1) ground-breaking ceremonies for a new transept at the Cathedral of St. John the Divine in New York, featuring a brief address by Bishop William T. Manning, (2) a feature item about Miss Kathryn Sullivan, a San Francisco policewoman, and (3) the seizure and destruction of a cargo of rum by federal agents in Brooklyn, New York. The last sequence included a title which encouraged the audience to "Listen to it Gurgle."[15]

The newsreel of Lindbergh's Washington reception had been staged and produced for the Case-Fox Corporation by Jack Connolly, a former newspaper editor turned newsreelman. With Lindbergh and Coolidge captured on sound film, Connolly set out on an ambitious campaign to photograph other international celebrities for the Fox Movietone newsreel. Together with cameraman Ben Miggins and soundmen Harry Squires, D. F. Whiting, and Eddie Kaw, a good deal of sound equipment, and a newly constructed sound truck, he left for Europe, vowing to record the faces and voices of every important personality of the day. Within the next two years he very nearly succeeded.[16]

One of the first foreign political leaders to be photographed was Italian dictator Benito Mussolini, who, smartly outfitted in riding breeches, delivered a lively address in broken English to the "peep" of the United States (actually, the event was photographed on May 6, 1927, before the filming and exhibition of the two Lindbergh sequences).[17] Connolly personally coached Mussolini in his delivery, for the dictator did not understand English and had difficulty memorizing and pronouncing the words of his address. Finally Connolly wrote out the speech on a large card and, with the aid of American Ambassador Richard Washburn Child, held it just out of camera range where Mussolini could read from it. Everyone was pleased with the final recording—particularly Mussolini. "Your talking newsreel has tremendous political possibilities," he was reported to have said. "Let me speak through it in twenty cities in Italy once a week and I need no other power."[18]

A number of other major political figures and celebrities spoke for the Movietone newsreel. The first crowned monarch to appear was King Alfonso XIII of Spain, who delivered a brief extemporaneous speech in which he invited Americans to visit his country, "where there are no speed laws."[19] He was followed by King George V of England, the Prince of Wales, Marshal Ferdinand Foch of France, President Paul von Hindenburg of Germany, President Michael Hainisch of Austria, Prime Minister Raymond Poincaré of France, the Crown Prince of Sweden, David Lloyd George and Ramsay MacDonald of England, President William T. Cosgrave of Ireland, Queen Marie of Romania, King Victor Emmanuel of Italy, President Herbert Hoover, former President Coolidge, General John J. Pershing, Chief Justice William Howard Taft, former Governor Alfred E. Smith, Thomas A. Edison, and Sir Arthur Conan Doyle.[20]

One of the most amusing and unexpected remarks of the collection came from John D. Rockefeller, Sr., who was shown riding in his airplane, driving an automobile, and distributing new dimes to children. Just before the sequence concluded, Rockefeller unexpectedly turned to the camera and, in a memorable non sequitur, invoked God's blessing on Standard Oil.

Various stratagems were employed by Connolly to secure the cooperation of royal and political celebrities. King Gustav of Sweden, for example, felt it below his dignity to speak for the newsreels. Nonetheless, he gave permission for the cameramen to drive their truck to his tennis court and set up their equipment next to it. A complete sound sequence was then made of Gustav playing tennis, but he never spoke a word and he never looked at the camera; it was his wish to give the impression that the film had been made without his knowledge. On another occasion a hidden camera was used in defiance of official prohibition to film Crown Prince Humbert and Princess Marie José of Italy at ceremonies at the Tomb of the Unknown Soldier in Rome. Connolly camouflaged his truck and equipment some distance from the tomb and began photographing the ceremonies. Midway through the event he was discovered by the police, but just as they were about to arrest him an attempt was made on the life of Prince Humbert, and the authorities' attention was diverted from Connolly. Luckily, his camera and sound equipment had functioned throughout the excitement, and the entire assassination attempt was photographed, including the sound of the shot.

Probably the most popular interview film of all, however, was that of George Bernard Shaw, who was at first the most adamantly reluctant to appear for the Fox Movietone camera. One day in 1927 Shaw unexpectedly summoned Connolly and said that he would consent to speak, provided he was allowed to direct the production. Connolly agreed, and the result was one of the most charming newsreel appearances ever filmed. By Shaw's own "script" he was first discovered walking in his garden. As he approached the camera, lost in thought, he was suddenly "surprised" by the motion picture camera. Greeting the audience, he then began to ramble at some length on a variety of subjects. After assuring his audience that he was really a very harmless fellow, Shaw stated that he did not always have to appear so genial:

> Of course, I can put on the other thing. I—for instance [looking very stern]—now that is what I call my Mussolini stunt. . . . But now just watch; [changes expression] I can take it off. Now, Signor Mussolini cannot take it off. He is condemned, although he is a most amiable man . . . to go through life with that terrible and imposing expression which really does a great injustice to his kindly nature. But I—I can put it on and I can take it off and do all sorts of things.[21]

Despite the facetious nature of Shaw's words, they were widely reprinted and reviewed. Burns Mantle, of the New York Daily News, called it "the most impressive use to which the onsweeping movietone has so far been put . . . An hour's Shaw talk by movietone or even a half-hour's talk would provide a most stimulating adventure. Having seen the summer lightning of his smile, I want to hear him thunder."[22]

Unfortunately for Mantle and other perceptive viewers who had gained a brief but exciting glimpse of the sound newsreel's real potential, interviews of a longer and more substantial kind did not follow. Instead newsreel producers were satisfied to provide what was really only a continuation of the same sort of novelty celebrity footage that had filled the silent newsreels of previous years. At stake was a journalistic challenge and potential which was not to be met and exploited until the introduction of television.

Soon the style and structure of the sound newsreel began to change. In order to provide smooth transitions between sequences, editors added narration and music. Instead of presenting the raw, "single-system" recordings, technicians began mixing, or rerecording the original sound track with other tracks, to modulate the signal strength uniformly from shot to shot and to blend in other supplementary sound tracks in a smooth fashion. Also, whenever natural sounds were lacking in the original recording, editors added artificial or spuriously recorded sound effects from the rapidly growing newsreel sound library to add a bogus authenticity to the sequence. Sound engineer Warren McGrath described the complex technology that was involved in such an operation:

The newsreel synchronizer, or recording engineer, handles the final stage through which newsreel make-up proceeds. . . .

The editorial department furnishes the mixer with a "spot" sheet on which each scene of the newsreel subject is carefully listed in its proper sequence. . . .

Two music tracks are provided for most subjects. The tracks are prints of the same music negative but have "start" marks so placed that one is synchronized to start with the beginning of the picture and the other to finish with the end of the picture. The mixer must use a suitable spot during the recording to change over from the first music track to the second. This is usually done during sound effects, natural sound, or long periods of narration in order to mask the operation. . . .

*The newsreel sound crew consisting of two soundmen, a projec-
tionist, and the mixer, work as an efficient unit. . . .*

*Rehearsals completed, we are now ready for a take. A swift
resumé of the sound to be used on the subject might indicate that
two channels are required for music tracks, one for synchronized
sound effects, one for the continuous running loop machine, one
for the pick-up of field recorded sound from the picture film, and
a narration channel. Six channels which the mixer must manipu-
late in an average time of less than two minutes and with only
two hands. . . .*

*Although some lengthy subjects have taken as long as one hour
to score, the average time taken by the recording room, from the
start of rehearsals to the completed take, is less than 15 min.*[23]

The result of such technological manipulation was increased
smoothness of presentation and a more theatrical style. However,
every gain in smoothness appeared to be attended by a propor-
tionate decrease in authenticity, believability, immediacy, and
journalistic integrity. From 1932 on, the amount of original single-
system recording decreased markedly, to be replaced by studio-
recorded material. Increasingly, bogus sound effects were added to
scenes that had originally been photographed silent, and occasionally actual fraud and faking were employed in the manufacture
of otherwise significant sound-track content.

Because of the complexity of newsreel editing and processing,
every opportunity was taken to standardize studio procedures to
speed footage on its ways to neighborhood theaters. Engineer
J. A. Battle outlined the complete production process as it existed
in 1935:

*The cameraman reports the details of the story, including such
items as camera angles and the number of feet shot. This report is
attached to the film can and a duplicate is mailed at the same time.
From it the newsreel editors can have a suitable script prepared
for the commentator while the film is being developed. . . .*

Each story is assigned an identifying number when reviewed in

Telling evidence that the newsreel functioned principally as an offshoot of show business rather than journalism. No matter how grim or serious the news it recorded, there was always a pleasant zaniness to newsreel production. What could be more appropriate for the launching of Hearst Metrotone's new sound newsreel than a bevy of MGM chorus girls posing on one of its sound trucks? (From the British Film Institute.)

Some of the men and women who made *Pathé News* successful: editor Emanuel Cohen, head cameraman Albert Richard, cartoonist Bert Green, cutters Ethel Harrison and Nettie Menzel, and cameramen C. C. Pritchard and C. T. Chapman, all in Chicago; R. E. Donahue, K. W. Fasold, J. Bartone, and Henry de Siena, all in New York City; S. R. Pozio, in Paris; O. Aultman, in Texas; L. Wyand, in London; W. E. Hudson, in Seattle; J. P. Johnson, in Los Angeles; J. T. Baltzell, in Washington, D.C.; J. Coolidge, in Boston; L. C. Hutt, in San Francisco; G. Ercole, in the Far East; and H. D. Blauvelt, "on the road." (From *Exhibitors Herald*, November 13, 1920.)

PATHÉ'S WEEKLY

After World War I the major American newsreel firms reorganized their production systems, improving the speed, quality, and scope of operations. One of the individuals responsible for reorganization was Emanuel ("Jack") Cohen, who in 1916, at the age of twenty-two, was appointed managing editor of *Pathé News*. Within a short time Cohen had brought to Pathé's newsreel service an efficiency which was the envy of his competitors. Other newsreel companies soon followed his example, expanding their staffs, increasing their budgets, and adopting similar high-speed production techniques. (From the author's collection.)

The eyes of the world

COPYRIGHT MCMXXVII PARAMOUNT FAMOUS LASKY CORPORATION

EMANUEL COHEN
EDITOR

In 1927, just as sound was being introduced, Paramount entered the newsreel business with a product of its own, *Paramount News*. Pioneer newsreel editors Emanuel Cohen and A. J. Richard resigned from Pathé to head the new organization. First presented as a silent product ("The Eyes of the World"), the newsreel soon acquired a voice and became "The Eyes and Ears of the World." Paramount quickly acquired a reputation for aggressive competition, worldwide coverage, photographic excellence, and frequent scoops of important news events. Above: the familiar logo of *Paramount News*. Registered trademark of Paramount News. (From a front-page advertisement in *Moving Picture World*, April 2, 1927.)

The sophistication of newsreel cameras and recorders was a long, slow process, and truly portable equipment was not introduced until 16mm film became widely used in television news work. For more than two decades after the introduction of sound the average camera looked something like the one above: an N. C. Mitchell 35mm camera equipped for single-system sound, recorded directly on the film. The amplifier and recording unit shown were manufactured by the Art Reeves Company of Hollywood. (From the author's collection.)

The first sound-on-film recording equipment was heavy, bulky, and fragile. The tripod-mounted camera weighed as much as one hundred pounds, fully equipped, and the rack-mounted optical sound-recording equipment weighed as much as half a ton. Newsreel companies out-fitted trucks like this one to transport the camera, sound equipment, incandescent lights, and power generator or batteries. By contrast, today's high-quality hand-held camera-recorder ensembles weigh twenty to thirty pounds complete. (From the author's collection.)

Above: The first successful sound news film of consequence was filmed by Fox Movietone. It recorded the takeoff of Charles A. Lindbergh on his solo flight from Long Island to Paris on May 20, 1927. This very short scene was part of an all-Movietone program premiered at the Sam Harris Theater in New York on May 25, 1927. Although crude by present-day standards, it was an enormously exciting bit of sound-film reporting and thrilled audiences of the day. (From Fox Movietonews, Inc.)

Facing page: Fox Movietone also took sound cameras to the welcome-home ceremonies held for Lindbergh in Washington, D.C., on June 12, 1927 (above). Both President Calvin Coolidge (seated at Lindbergh's right) and Lindbergh (at the microphones) addressed the audience. At no point during this lengthy scene did the cameras cut to a different angle. Fox technicians simply turned on the camera and let it run until the end of the affair. It was static, but very intimate and exciting just the same. (From Fox Movietonews, Inc.)

Below: The title introducing *Kinograms'* silent coverage of Lindbergh's welcome-home celebration in New York. Note the newspaper-headline style of the title.

On October 9, 1934, King Alexander of Yugoslavia traveled by ship to Marseilles, France, to negotiate new political alliances. The French made his reception and motorcade the occasion for a gala celebration, and two Fox Movietone cameramen, the brothers Georges and Raymond Mejat, were dispatched with a new sound truck to cover the event.

Above: Before the motorcade begins, Alexander smiles and acknowledges the applause of the huge crowd greeting him.

Facing page: Suddenly, as the official limousine rolls along the crowded street, a Croatian terrorist jumps onto the running board and fires several shots at Alexander and his companion, French Prime Minister Jean Louis Barthou, mortally wounding them both. A moment later the assassin is cut down and stabbed to death by saber-wielding mounted military officers.

Below: King Alexander lies dying, surrounded by helpless officials. This footage is still the most spectacular of its kind ever photographed. The coverage was thorough and of excellent pictorial quality, and the sounds of the procession and attack were recorded throughout. (From Fox Movietonews, Inc.)

Newsreel cameramen lived colorful and sometimes dangerous lives. Crippling accidents, maimings, imprisonments, and death were common in the business, and newsreel companies did their best to publicize their cameramen's adventures. The effect of such promotion was to encourage hazardous but not necessarily newsworthy assignments, such as this coverage of skyscraper construction by a Pathé cameraman in the 1930's. (From British Film Institute.)

In the arsenal of equipment developed for newsreel work were extremely long-focus "Big Bertha" lenses, optically capable of bringing distant scenes to within a few feet of the camera. The lenses weighed almost as much as the cameras to which they were attached. Here a Pathé crew photographs a horse race in the 1930's. (From British Film Institute.)

For newsreel cameramen standard automobile sedans, such as this Ford V8, were often fitted with reinforced roofs and a suitable platform on which cameras and tripods could be mounted. This Fox cameraman is shooting a scene somewhere in England in the 1930's. (From British Film Institute.)

This $25,000 newsreel sound truck never made it back to headquarters. In 1934, Harry Tugander, of Paramount, took it to Salisbury, Maryland, to photograph attempts of a mob to lynch some prisoners being held by the police. In the rioting which followed, the mob attacked reporters and cameramen and pushed Tugander's truck and equipment into the Wicomico River. Paramount managed to cover the riots anyway, with additional equipment. (From *International Photographer*.)

On Memorial Day, 1937, several thousand CIO strikers held a demonstration march at the Republic Steel plant in South Chicago. They were met by 200 to 300 armed policemen. In the confusion someone fired a shot, and violence exploded. Ten people died from gunshot wounds, and many more were wounded. Paramount was the only newsreel firm to photograph the event. Seeking to avoid further involvement in an explosively controversial incident, Paramount decided to suppress the footage. The United States Senate Committee on Civil Liberties and its chairman, Robert M. La Follette, Jr., subpoenaed the footage, after which Paramount released the sequence in an issue of its newsreel. Chicago audiences never saw the footage, however; it was banned by police as "unfit for women and children to see." (Originally photographed by *Paramount News*. Published here by courtesy of Sherman Grinberg Film Libraries.)

If Theodore Roosevelt was the most photogenic president of the silent-newsreel era, Franklin Delano Roosevelt was certainly the most compelling presidential personality of the sound era. Through four terms of office his voice and face dominated the newsreel's political sequences, whether electioneering on the road or presenting one of his fireside chats. Above he is shown campaigning with Vice-President John Nance Garner. Below: the result. (From Fox Movietonews, Inc.)

the negative by the news editors. . . . About 20 per cent of the stories sent in are used for release. . . .

The selected stories are edited and cut, and a dupe negative and a lavender print are made. The dupe negative is made as a matter of precaution and, on occasion, is used to double the printing capacity to expedite the release.

The lavender "work" print is used for projection in scoring the comments, music, and sound effects if any are required. The commentator reads from a prepared script, and after a rehearsal or two the final sound negative is recorded. . . .

The preparation of the news begins one day prior to the release date, and an entire reel is ready to be printed within 18 or 20 hours. The news subjects are arranged in definite sequence prior to making the reel, and when the first half of the reel is scored, prints are run off. The second half follows as quickly as possible, so that the release print is generally made up of two sections spliced together. For checking, a rush print is made from the sound negative and lavender print. The combined print has a negative of the picture, but this is satisfactory for the purpose.[24]

The first two or three years of sound-newsreel release were financially successful. The Fox Movietone reel, for example, was released in four editions and did one hundred thousand dollars a week in business.[25] This financial success rapidly declined, however, as the novelty of the sound newsreel wore off and the sound screenplay feature gained popular favor. While the sound newsreel's profits dropped off, the cost of newsreel production rose precipitously because of the added expenses of sound recording. By 1939 average production costs for a typical newsreel release were estimated by Frederick Ullman, Jr., general manager of Pathé, to run as high as twenty to twenty-five thousand dollars a week.[26] Nonetheless, such was the initial popularity of the sound-film newsreel that, with one notable exception, by 1931 every major producer had converted to sound.[27] The exception was *Kinograms*, whose directors decided to pursue silent production on the assumption that the silent film would continue to prosper along with the sound film. George Baynes, president of the organization, stated in November, 1929, that "the success of a sound newsreel, to date, has depended on its novelty and its scope is so limited that it is impossible to show the public what they have for years been accustomed to in the news of the world on the screen."[28]

In 1927, Hearst's *International Newsreel*, which for several years had released its series through Universal, signed a new contract with Metro-Goldwyn-Mayer to produce another, entirely different silent newsreel for that company.[29] Two years later, in 1929, Hearst signed a new contract with MGM, under the terms of which Hearst produced two versions of its newsreel for MGM, the first a silent reel entitled *The MGM International Newsreel*, and a sound newsreel entitled *Hearst Metrotone News*. The first of these was introduced to the public on July 31, 1929, and the latter on September 28 of the same year.[30]

The new contract between Hearst and MGM left Universal without a newsreel. At that point *Kinograms'* producers contracted to produce silent-newsreel footage for Universal in addition to *Kinograms'* own independently distributed release.[31] At the same time Universal decided to hedge its bet by also introducing a sound newsreel of its own.

Kinograms' financial position gradually deteriorated. The number of motion picture houses which continued to run silent films diminished steadily, and *Kinograms'* bookings and receipts fell off. Finally, in 1931, Educational Pictures, Inc., the parent organization, restructured *Kinograms* as a sound-on-disk, commercially sponsored newsreel, thus anticipating commercial-television practice by a number of years.

Educational's plan was to release the new *Kinograms* advertising newsreel to motion picture theaters through the Allied State Exhibitors Exchange. Each issue would contain commercial advertisements for various manufacturers, including, so it was rumored, Camel cigarettes. Other sponsors that were mentioned included Listerine and Hygeinol Powders. The first issue of the new *Kinograms* was released to 2,980 theaters on August 28, 1931. The Warner-Brunswick disk-recording system was used, thus effecting a saving in royalties over the RCA Photophone (sound-on-film) system of one thousand dollars a week.[32] As far as is known, this was the only newsreel which was ever released with accompanying sound-on-disk.

The *Kinograms* advertising newsreel was a complete failure. The first few issues were given away to theater owners free of charge, the producer depending entirely upon advertising revenue to support the production. On November 17, 1931, Abram Myers, of Allied State Exhibitors, announced the failure of the newsreel after only nine issues. On December 15, 1931, a news bulletin announced that *Kinograms* was in the hands of the sheriff on attachments. Altogether, it had lost an estimated $110,000 for its backers.[33] According to Mr. Abrams, the project was abandoned

(a) because certain producers who had first brought advertising to the screen, abandoned the practice and made it unnecessary for the independent theater owners to engage in the practice as a measure of self-defense; and (b) because insufficient advertising of a kind which the leaders of Allied deemed appropriate for the screen was available to support the enterprise.[34]

A number of other, similarly ill-fated newsreels appeared and attempted to penetrate a market dominated by major studios. Sound or silent, national or regional—ultimately they all failed. These included *The Selznick News*,[35] *The [Henry] Ford Animated Weekly*,[36] *The American Newsreel* (which was edited and produced by Lowell Thomas),[37] *The Junior Newsreel* (for children),[38] *Eve's Film Pictorial* (for women),[39] *Iowa News Flashes*,[40] *The Chicago Daily News Newsreel*,[41] and the *All-American News*. The last of these was produced expressly for Negro audiences throughout the United States and featured news and feature material calculated to be of particular interest to black citizens.

Founded in November, 1942, the *All-American News* was

reaching an estimated audience of four million people by the end of its first year. In 1943, E. M. Glucksman, producer of the reel, stated that the series was run regularly in 365 of the nation's 451 Negro theaters. Quoting an Office of War Information survey, he estimated that "85 per cent of the negroes in five large cities get most of their news on negro affairs from . . . [this] newsreel."[42] Like the many other independent newsreel ventures which sought to break into the major-studio market, however, *All-American News* also finally went out of business.

Only one independent newsreel introduced in the 1930's survived. It was not, strictly speaking, a newsreel; it was not released to the theatrical market, and it did not compete with the five major reels. In June, 1937, Eugene Castle, a successful producer of industrial and advertising short subjects, introduced Castle Films' *News Parade* for the amateur, home-movie market.[43] It was estimated that at that time more than two million amateur American movie makers owned 8mm and 16mm projectors. Castle's *News Parade* featured genuine newsreel subjects from the major newsreel firms. The footage was reduced to 16mm and 8mm sizes for direct sale to amateurs. The first issue of *News Parade* featured the *Hindenburg* disaster; the second, the coronation of George VI; and the third, the life story of the Duke of Windsor. Castle Films prospered for many years in its production of newsreels and short subjects for the home-movie enthusiast. In the commercial theaters, however, only the five major newsreels managed to survive: *Fox Movietone News*, *Hearst Metrotone News* (later retitled *News of the Day*), *Paramount News* ("The Eyes and Ears of the World"), *Pathé News*, and *Universal News*.

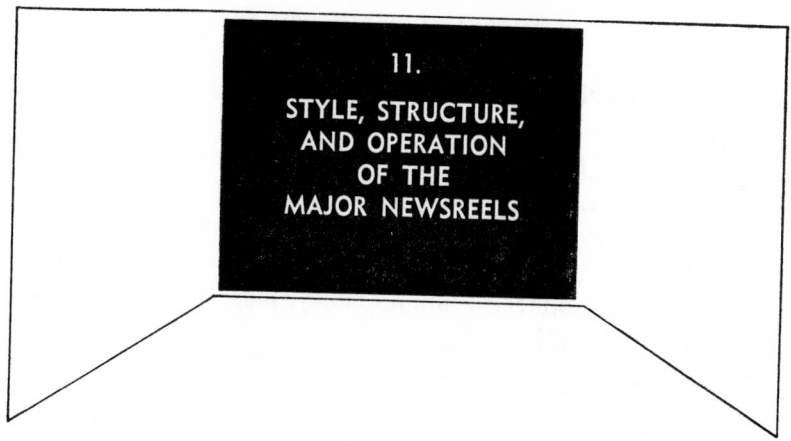

Within a few years after the introduction of sound each of the major newsreels had developed a fairly distinctive structure and style of presentation. From a vantage point of more than forty years it is not always possible to compare the operations, policies, and production practices of each of the firms, inasmuch as information bearing upon their work, although plentiful, does not always cover the same period of years. Also, the number of staff members, the administrative leadership, the "personalities" employed for narration, the content, the production techniques, the distribution and exhibition arrangements, the financial health or decay, and even the style and structure of each of the formats changed from year to year. However, the literature and testimony available from the 1930's suggest the following generalities.

Fox Movietone was the largest of the organizations, employing scores of cameramen and staffing the largest number of regional offices around the world.[1] Whereas the other companies depended to varying extents upon an exchange of footage with foreign newsreels to fill out their weekly releases, Fox Movietone was able to provide nearly all of its own material.

By 1935 the persons who supervised different territories of Fox's European coverage were Gerald Sanger, producer, and Sir Malcolm Campbell, editor, in Great Britain; Russell Muth in central Europe; Ettore Villani in southern Europe and the Near East;

Hans Pebal in other European countries; and Harry Lawrenson, foreign editor and make-up supervisor. All these employees operated under Ben Miggins, director of European operations. Bonney Powell was supervisor in the Far East. By 1937, Sir Gordon Craig had joined the overseas Fox team as British general manager. In the United States, Edmund Reek moved up to become general manager under producer Truman Talley. Jack Haney succeeded Reek as news editor, Harry Lawrenson continued as foreign editor, and Arthur de Titta joined the group as political editor.[2] By 1940 the company was reported to have cameramen in fifty-one countries and had nine producing centers in the important capitals of the world.[3]

Of all the American newsreel firms, Fox Movietone was best equipped for on-the-spot sound recording. In 1934 it was said that ninety-seven of the one hundred Movietone cameramen then on salary had complete sound equipment available to them, and they were expected to use it under all-but-impossible circumstances.[4] During the early years of sound, Movietone scored frequently with scoops and exclusive releases for which it always seemed to have money available. Back in the silent days, for example, Fox had spent more than twenty thousand dollars to get pictures of Roald Amundsen's polar flight back to American theaters ahead of the other competition. On other occasions Fox outbid its competitors and purchased film from amateurs. When the H.M.S. *Vestris* sank off the coast of Virginia in 1928, an amateur movie maker photographed the catastrophe with his 16mm camera. Managing editor Truman Talley sent an agent to the rescue ship in a power launch, equipped for negotiations with a checkbook and pen. By the time Fox's rivals met the amateur at New York's quarantine dock, the footage had already been sold. Fox's laboratory technicians subsequently enlarged it for theatrical release.[5]

When war between Ethiopia and Italy threatened in late 1935, editor Laurence Stallings personally headed a "Fox Expedition" to Ethiopia to cover what one of the trade papers described as "what promises to be a first class war." Two of Fox's top cameramen, Len Hammon and Al Waldron, joined Stallings, together with a brand-new specially outfitted sound recording truck. Other newsreel companies soon followed with their own carefully planned expeditions. In the contemporary descriptions of their news-gathering exploits, one feels an almost festive air as they set off to cover their first "real war" since 1918.[6]

The Fox reel featured a rigidly compartmentalized series of news categories, each of which had its own title and its own narrator. Lowell Thomas served as chief commentator for many years, while Lew Lehr narrated the novelty material, Louise Vance described the women's fashion footage, and Ed Thorgersen described the sports footage. All the narrators were identified and credited in the reel. This compartmentalization of content was first introduced in 1934, and some of the departments were supervised consistently by the same director or editor.[7] Vyvyan Donner, for example, staged the Movietone women's fashion sequences for many years.[8]

The structure of the other four reels was far less rigidly cast than that of Movietone, the make-up of their issues depending more upon the newsworthiness of the week's footage than upon the filling of predetermined categories.

Pathé News, edited by Courtland Smith (formerly head of Fox Movietone), provided for a weekly "Sports Department" in its release, experience having shown that there was always an abundance of such footage to fill out the reel week after week. Otherwise, the choice of content was contingent only upon its availability and newsworthiness. Beginning in 1935, radio announcer Harry Von Zell performed regularly as the "Voice of Pathé News." Teddy Bergman, a radio dialect comedian, announced the humorous and novelty material, and racing authority Clem McCarthy narrated the sports events.[9] During the 1930's, Pathé emphasized domestic news and frequently built short feature sequences around national issues. But during the early 1940's it relied heavily upon World War II military footage, almost to the exclusion of domestic footage.[10] Pathé benefited from the experience gained over its unusually long history, as well as from long-standing agreements with its own foreign subsidiaries and other overseas concerns by which they exchanged footage. During this period Pathé tried to tie up exclusive newsreel rights whenever possible. Although this practice gradually faded in importance, it was sometimes successfully employed. Shortly after the birth of the Dionne quintuplets in May, 1934, Pathé paid a handsome sum for the exclusive rights to take motion pictures of them. For several years Pathé cameraman Roy Tash was the official cameraman for the quints, and it was a long time before competing photographers were able to get close to them.[11] Shortly after the Sims Act prohibiting interstate transport of prize-fight pictures was rescinded in 1940,[12] Pathé was the first to tie up fight rights. One of the first of the fights, photographed for Pathé (RKO-Pathé) by Irving Browning, was the Lou Jenkins-Henry Armstrong world welterweight championship fight at the Polo Grounds in New York City.[13] Pathé had also secured its share of scoops, including cameraman Will E. Hudson's coverage of the Wilkins Arctic Expedition in 1927.[14]

During the silent period Pathé, like Universal and *Kinograms*, had serviced the independent-theater market. Its distribution system was described by Lewis:

Pathé pictures were sold in groups of varying numbers, depending upon the requirements of the exhibitors and the sales ability of the salesmen. The company endeavored, by all fair and reasonable inducements, to persuade exhibitors to contract for the entire number in the group. While the company never refused to sell an exhibitor less than an entire group of films, it did not permit an exhibitor to make his choice of one or more of the pictures offered in a group at a group average price. In the case of Pathé News, 104 issues, divided into 2 series, comprised the output for a year.

Of the 15,000 or so theaters considered as potential accounts, satisfactory distribution commonly constituted from 6,000 to 8,000 contracts on an individual picture.[15]

In 1931 the Pathé organization and RKO Pictures were merged into one organization by financier Joseph P. Kennedy.[16] The merger provided RKO with a newsreel with which to fill out its program in competition with the other major studios. The association lasted until August, 1947, at which time Pathé left RKO and began releasing through Warner Brothers.[17]

In 1937 the Pathé organization experienced a change in management when the president, Courtland Smith, and the general manager, Jack S. Connolly, resigned, together with a large number of their editorial and camera staff members. Leadership of the organization passed into the hands of the new president, Ned E. Depinet, and vice-president, Frederick Ullman.[18]

Hearst's *News of the Day* (originally *The Hearst Metrotone News*), edited by Mike Clofine, also pursued an antidepartmentalization policy with respect to its structure and style. Material was selected and arranged solely upon the basis of its availability and newsworthiness. Hearst used only one narrator for its reel. Until 1936 this role was played by Edwin C. Hill.[19] He was replaced by Jean Paul King of NBC when the Hearst series changed its name to *News of the Day.*[20]

As mentioned earlier, for several years before the coming of sound, Hearst's newsreel had been released through Universal. Beginning in 1927 it was released by Metro-Goldwyn-Mayer.[21] For a few years following the introduction of sound, Hearst was associated with both Fox and MGM at the same time. The Case-Fox Corporation controlled the sound patents which Hearst needed, and so an involved contractual arrangement was concluded (which lasted from 1929 to 1934) whereby *The Hearst Metrotone News* was released through MGM. Meanwhile, Hearst was also associated with *Fox Movietone News.*[22] Under this arrangement the Fox-Hearst Corporation was formed, and Hearst purchased an interest in Fox Movietone Corporation.[23] After October 2, 1934, the Hearst newsreel operated its own production facilities and was released solely through MGM.[24]

Hearst also collaborated briefly with Fox in 1929 in the production of a wide-screen newsreel entitled *Grandeur*, which in its content and style anticipated the semidocumentary presentation *Cinerama*. The premiere of the attraction was described in a news item:

New Yorkers who attended the first showing of Fox Grandeur Pictures, featuring double-width film, with the images projected on a screen as wide as the stage, must have realized that, nipping the heels of the talkie movement, another revolution is on the way.

They saw and heard the rushing waters of Niagara Falls, not in short, unrevealing glimpses, but in broad, natural perspective, as if they stood on the spot. A honeymoon, someone said, for a dollar. Instead of the unsatisfactory knot-hole view of a baseball game and tennis match, they watched the entire diamond and court and plainly saw the players' faces and movements. Had they been able simultaneously to see the same scenes on an ordinary screen, they would have realized that the new idea is nearly as superior to the old as the first movie was to a penny-arcade peep-show. . . .

What effect the invention will have on photoplay making remains to be seen. Its effect on news reels, however, is immediately apparent. It makes them decidedly better.[25]

Whereas most newsreels placed the decision-making responsibility in one man's hands, the production policy at Paramount News sought to prevent the superimposition of any one editor's personality upon the week's material. Instead, a board of three editors jointly determined daily editorial policy. During the 1930's these men were A. J. Richard, the general manager (formerly of Pathé); William P. Montague, the assignment editor; and William Park, the make-up editor. Various narrators spoke for the Paramount sound track, none of whom was identified to the public.[26] Paramount, with "The Eyes and Ears of the World," aggressively entered the sound-film competition of the 1930's, at first under the leadership of Emanuel Cohen. During the 1930's, Paramount scooped the competition with some regularity. As Earl Theisen noted admiringly:

Paramount News swept the world like a storm. The Paramount men trekked the outlands and reported, besides news, those things not generally known, those quaint habits of other peoples, bringing to the screen a liberal education in ethnology and geography.[27]

Paramount secured exclusive rights and coverage of Admiral Richard E. Byrd's 1929 expedition to the South Pole. Most resulting footage was later released by the parent studio as a special feature entitled *With Byrd at the South Pole*. The cameramen, Willard van der Meer and Joe Rucker, subsequently won the Academy Award for their photography.[28] In the middle 1930's the company prepared carefully for its coverage of the imminent European hostilities.[29] Paramount claimed to have enjoyed an exclusive arrangement whereby footage was secured from the Soviet government.[30] Paramount also scooped the competition with the first German war films, which it had secured directly from the German Ministry of Propaganda.[31] In all respects Paramount News was a formidable competitor.

Universal, a late-comer in the sound-on-film competition, managed to establish its own series successfully despite the strong competition which it faced and the peculiar production problems under which it operated. During the silent period Universal's newsreel had been produced by Hearst. For the first years of sound its silent reel (which was released to unwired theaters) was produced by *Kinograms* after the Hearst staff departed to join MGM. Universal then set up its own sound newsreel staff, headed by Charles Ford (later by Samuel Jacobsen). Within a few years, it had captured a substantial number of accounts in the independent market.

In contrast to the other major newsreels, which were well financed, Universal ran a thrifty, low-budget operation. Lacking the worldwide coverage of Fox, the exclusive tie ups of Pathé, the globe-trotting, costly zeal of Paramount, and the sound equipment and budgets of its competitors, Universal's editors decided to forgo actual sound recording and substitute studio-produced

sound effects, music, and narration. Announcer Graham Mc-
Namee was hired to narrate the reel.[32] Within the trade, because
of its penny-pinching operations, Universal's reel became known
as "The Five-Cent Weekly." As late as 1937 the company had
only four synchronized-sound outfits at its disposal for on-the-spot
coverage. Nonetheless, what Universal lacked in facilities and
budget it made up for with imagination, and the quality of its release was generally good. As it happened, Universal's decision to
keep on-the-spot recording to a minimum, although journalistically regrettable, was an economically wise one, for with rising
costs and the decline of the sound newsreel's novelty, all the newsreel companies eventually reduced the amount of first-hand sound
recording to a minimum and relied largely upon studio-produced
sound tracks.

Universal also secured occasional scoops, including spectacular
coverage of the arrival of the German dirigible *Bremen,* which was
photographed by Ray Fernstrom in 1928. The *Bremen* newsreel
coverage was noted for unusually rough and vindictive competition, including fist fights and attempted "sabotage" of cameramen. The footage which resulted was considered so important at
the time that a rival news organization was said to have offered
Fernstrom twenty-five thousand dollars for an interview.[33] Universal also scooped the competition with unusually fine coverage
of the Chinese-Japanese conflict during the 1930's, much of which
was photographed by Norman Alley and George Krainukov (who
later changed his name to Crane).[34]

During its history the Universal newsreel organization was
litigant in two important legal cases, each of which set precedents
supporting the freedom of the newsreel as a communications
medium. The first of the cases occurred in 1917, when Grace
Humiston, an attorney in a famous murder case, sued for invasion
of privacy, despite the fact that she had posed for the camera.
Following prolonged litigation, the appellate division of the
Supreme Court of New York ruled in favor of Universal, declaring
the newsreel's right to photograph people in the news.[35]

Several years later, in 1935, Mrs. Doris Preisler and her husband sued Universal Pictures Corporation and the Los Angeles Pantages Theater, asking $4,150,000 damages for mental shock leading to the loss of a prospective child, allegedly caused by the viewing of newsreel scenes of the corpse of gangster "Baby Face" Nelson. However, Los Angeles Judge Joseph Sprouls directed a verdict in favor of the newsreel company and the theater, pointing out that the audience had ample warning of the newsreel's contents through poster and newspaper advertisements.[36]

During the early 1930's some of the American firms introduced foreign editions of their sound newsreels, each recorded in the appropriate language and containing specially photographed and edited materials for the country in which it was to be shown. Fox Movietone, the oldest and most firmly established of the producers of sound newsreels, pioneered in the penetration of the foreign market. In England, the first *British Movietone* issue appeared on June 9, 1929, and was the first sound newsreel of any kind to be presented in that country. Denwar Sharar wrote:

This premier edition consisted of two items: the Derby, and the Trooping of the Colour. It created a great sensation, which was quickly followed in the second issue, when Mr. Ramsay Mac-Donald personally introduced his new Labour Cabinet to the camera and the microphone.[37]

For another *British Movietone* issue—the coronation of King George VI—nearly twenty-four hundred prints were made, of which five hundred were in color, to be exhibited in forty-one countries and in nineteen different languages. Over one hundred million people saw it.[38] Shortly after these first, special issues were released, Harry Lawrenson, Fox's foreign editor, set up permanent foreign headquarters in London, Paris, Sydney, Brussels, Rome, Prague, and Tokyo to produce original material, combine it with duplicate negatives of the week's footage from other production centers, record an appropriate narration, and release the finished newsreels to the different countries under such exotic titles as

Actualités Parlantes, Actualités Movietone, Fox Tonnende Wochenschau, and *Foxuv Zukoyv Tydenk.* The commentary was always in the language of the country of exhibition, except in the case of China, where, according to Davidson,

> there are so many local dialects that Lawrenson finally threw up his hands and sent a regular English-commentary reel. The ingenious Chinese have solved this problem by placing an interpreter in a chair alongside the screen in each movie theater. As the American commentator speaks, the Chinese interpreter out-shouts him in the dialect of the community.[39]

By 1946 the *Fox International Movietone Newsreel* was regularly exhibited in forty-seven foreign countries and in more than a dozen languages. At that time its worldwide audience was estimated at a staggering two hundred million a week.[40]

Paramount also had a widespread foreign audience in thirty different countries, including (before World War II) China, Japan, Germany, Russia, and even the South Sea Islands.

The financial arrangements under which foreign release was secured were usually complicated, oftentimes involving the founding of corporations which were jointly owned by American and foreign business interests. As the British Arts Enquiry report observed late in 1947: "Balance sheets of the newsreel companies are the private concern of their parent companies and no separate disclosures of newsreel budgets are made. It is therefore difficult to assess their financial position."[41]

In Great Britain, for example, the following financial alliances were known to exist in the mid-1940's:

British Movietone News—Twentieth-Century Fox (American)
British Paramount News—Paramount Pictures, Inc. (American)
Pathé News—Associated British and Warner Brothers (British-American)
Universal News—Produced by British Pictorial Productions, Ltd. (British) and rented through General Film Distributors, which also handles *Gaumont-British News.*[42]

An elaborate description of these relationships appeared following an inquiry into nontheatrical film production in 1947 on
behalf of the British Arts Enquiry and sponsored by the Darting-
ton Hall Trustees:

> *Financial inter-relation between these companies is known to
> exist. Gaumont-British and Twentieth Century Fox are related
> through the Metropolitan and Bradford Trust, which gives* Movie-
> tone *an entry into some of the Gaumont-British cinemas. The late
> Mr. Maxwell, who owned Pathé, also had shares in Gaumont. It is
> believed that Mr. Rank, who owns* Gaumont-British *and* Uni-
> versal News, *also has indirect interests in* Movietone *and* Pathé.
> Paramount *appears to remain completely the property of the
> American Paramount Pictures and to work in conjunction with
> Olympic Kinematographic Laboratories, an American-owned
> group.*
>
> *The affiliations with feature film companies assure monopoly
> distribution for the newsreels in the parent company's circuit, with
> the exception of* British Paramount News. *Paramount has only
> very few cinemas in Britain and its newsreel sustains itself largely
> through exhibition in a number of the independent cinemas
> which constitute approximately 75 per cent. of the 4,500 cinemas
> in the country.*[43]

Many American and foreign newsreel firms operated under
reciprocity agreements whereby they bought, sold, and exchanged
duplicate negatives of each other's weekly footage.[44] Both American and foreign firms suffered under mutually restrictive tariff
arrangements of a severe and discriminatory nature which contrasted sharply with the absence of such restrictions upon the importation of written or printed news. Both the American and the
foreign firms tried over a period of years to have newsreel footage
admitted by international customs officials as "educational material," but generally without success.

In 1937 the Fédération Internationale de la Presse Cinématographique and the Union Internationale de la Presse Filmée, with

the endorsement of the Motion Picture Association of America, petitioned the League of Nations for reduction or abolition of such restrictions. In his address to the delegates of the league, H. Piron, of Belgium, presented customs statistics in support of the petition:

Information obtained by us . . . indicates that charges for the importation of exposed films are: Francs 5 and 25 per meter on positive and negative film, respectively, in France; 5 and 3.5d per foot, in ordinary and in preferential tariff, respectively, the latter not applicable to the newsreels, in England; 2,000 R.M. per 100 kilos in Germany; 20 gold crowns (Austrian) per 100 kilos, in Austria; 20,000 slotys per 100 kilos, in Poland; 34 and 52 centimes per meter on undeveloped and on positive film, respectively, in Belgium; and 2 drachmas (in coin) per kilo in addition to a 75 per cent import tax, in Greece. The charges are somewhat complicated in the Netherlands but can be estimated in a general way as being in excess of one quarter of total value.[45]

Piron concluded: "These several instances demonstrate clearly . . . the heavy burden carried by the motion picture newsreels, whose box office value is measured in terms of only one or two weeks."[46] Apparently little or no tax relief followed this petition. On the contrary, as political tensions mounted during the 1930's, restrictions grew more stringent.

It was during this period that the first of the major American newsreel theaters were opened. Such was the initial financial success of the first sound newsreels and the enthusiasm generated by their release that on November 2, 1929, Fox opened the 544-seat Embassy Theater at Broadway and Forty-sixth Street in New York City and devoted it exclusively to newsreels.[47]

The idea of a newsreel theater was not new of course. The early Pathé news films were presented in just such a theater in Paris before 1910. Even earlier, in May, 1906, a news-film theater called the Daily Bioscope is said to have opened in London, next to Bishopgate Fire Station.[48] In the years that followed, many such theaters were established both in major cities and in small towns and were patronized by a large number of faithful, enthusiastic viewers.[49] By 1940, London alone was reported to have more newsreel theaters in operation than there were in all of the United States.[50]

In New York, Fox's Embassy Theater was originally intended to popularize the company's new sound newsreel and thereby overcome exhibitors' resistance to the five-hundred-dollars-a-reel charge Fox assessed for its product. W. French Githens, the local news editor of *Movietone News*, and Courtland Smith, the general manager, arranged a promotion scheme whereby thousands of people were mailed cards with quarters attached. The cards invited the addressees to attend the new theater during the opening week at Fox's expense. Thousands did attend, and the trade-paper advertisements that followed read: "The Embassy Newsreel grossed more than $11,000 in a 550-seat [sic] house showing only *Fox Movietone News*."[51]

Movietone ran the Embassy until December, 1933, when it was closed because of poor business. Githens (who had since become managing editor of *Pathé News*) and his partner, Carter Wood, Jr., organized Newsreel Theaters, Inc., on their own and reopened the Embassy as a newsreel house in 1934. From that time on, the theater ran the products of all the major newsreel companies and operated successfully for many years thereafter.[52] According to Githens, "We soon discovered that in Franklin Delano Roosevelt we had the greatest single attraction. Announcement of his fireside chats, which were always filmed, brought hundreds of patrons to the theater. Anti-New Dealers came to hiss. The vigorous years of the New Deal under FDR and the rise of Mussolini, Hitler, Stalin, and Chiang Kai-shek aroused great interest in newsreels. Each had his adherents in the city, who flocked to the Embassy Theater when their favorite was on the screen."[53]

In March, 1931, another newsreel theater, the Trans-Lux, also opened in New York City, managed by two former staff members of Fox Movietone, Courtland Smith (formerly managing editor of

Fox and then of Pathé) and Jack Connolly (who had arranged for most of Fox's successful early interview sound newsreels).[54] Many technical innovations were introduced at the Trans-Lux to lower exhibition costs. Their theaters were installed in ordinary rented store space, each containing about 160 seats. Rear projection was employed, patrons were admitted through a turnstile triggered by the ticket seller (thus eliminating the ticket taker), and house lights were left on at a subdued level to dispense with the need for ushers. Prices were kept low (about twenty-five cents), each complete show ran about forty-five minutes, and performances were continuous, thus serving both the inveterate newsreel enthusiast and the occasional downtown shopper.

The number of newsreel theaters in the United States was never to equal those in operation abroad. Nevertheless, several other houses opened during the 1930's in New York City, Newark, Boston, Philadelphia, and other cities on the East Coast. Both the Trans-Lux and the Embassy organizations established small chains of newsreel theaters.[55] A third major newsreel theater-competitor appeared in 1939, when a group of New York businessmen headed by Alfred A. Burger and Herbert L. Sheftel founded the Telenews Theater in San Francisco. It opened its doors on September 1, 1939, which was about as propitious a date for founding a newsreel theater as could have been chosen. Telenews' first program featured the German invasion of Poland.[56]

During the next two decades, Telenews opened a chain of thirteen similar theaters across the country and also set up its own newsreel-production organization to furnish footage to its own houses, other independent theaters, and finally television stations.[57] By the early 1950's Telenews was said to be furnishing more than 90 per cent of television news film across the nation.[58] With the subsequent founding and expansion of newsreel film units by networks and local television stations, however, such distribution dropped to a fraction of its former volume.

Over the years each of the major newsreel producers built and maintained a huge stock-shot library, containing old newsreel footage. This material was oftentimes used to fill gaps in otherwise incomplete newsreel sequences. It was also made available, at a price, to producers of fiction films who needed exotic or historically important scenes for continuity purposes.

Fox Movietone had one of the largest of these libraries. By the mid-1940's its vaults contained more than forty-two million feet of film, photographed throughout the world and elaborately and painstakingly indexed with respect to subject matter, dates, personalities, political issues, and other headings.[59] This vast collection of pictorial material was supplemented by a smaller but still extensive sound-film library which included every kind of sound effect needed for newsreel or feature-film production. Pathé also had a fine library; some of the footage in it dated back to 1898.

Bert Holst, librarian for Fox Movietone, wrote on one occasion of the curious and amusing requests which sometimes came from feature-film producers, reflecting their unique and peculiar needs:

"Have you a shot," we were once asked, "of an English railroad train running without lights during a blackout?" Another time a lady editor seriously wired for—and this is the exact description she sent us—two love doves cooing, one gets vexed and draws away, the other seems to pine.

A West Coast producer once asked us for an alligator waving an American flag!

A religious organization in the process of making a biblical picture wired us, "What have you got in your library on Abraham and Moses?"

A big powder manufacturing company making a commercial wired us to send them a 2-ft. shot showing a close-up of the impact of an explosive shell hitting an iceberg.

A famed explorer wishing to illustrate the fiction he dishes out in his lectures wrote us that we would greatly help his film presentation if we could supply him with a pelican diving for fish; camera to follow him under water; pelican to catch school of fish; fish swimming in pelican's bill.

Then, as innocently as a newborn babe, another West Coast producer wired us for "A Wednesday afternoon scene—Landscape." This is a complete description of his request![60]

Holst also received requests for sound effects. Certainly one of the oddest he ever got was, "Can you send us the sound of a moccasin on soft snow?"

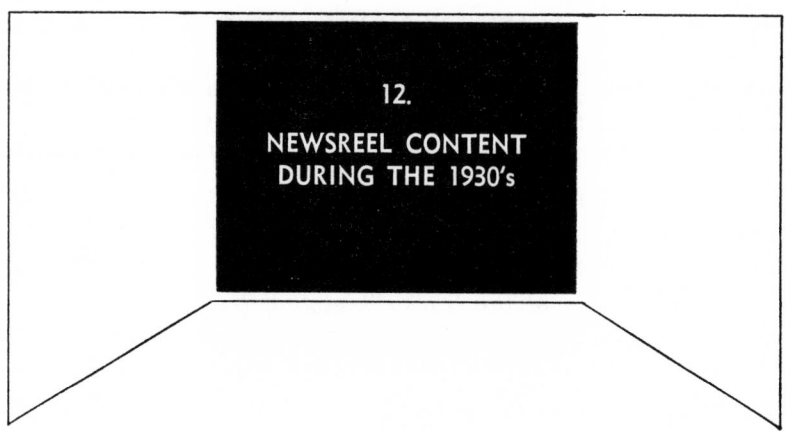

The newsreel of the 1930's benefited greatly from the sensational news events of the period. These were years of growing tensions, mounting fears, international unrest, and military aggression. They were years of economic distress and unusual economic and political innovations—years of polemic discourse, social hysteria, and crackpot panaceas. It was a troubled but always colorful decade, whose image was continuously, if not always meaningfully, mirrored by the newsreel cameras of America. Even the least newsworthy events of the 1930's would, in previous decades, have provided any single year's most sensational subject matter for the newsreels. A few examples will suffice.

The riots of 1934 in Salisbury, Maryland, followed the arrest of four Salisbury men for conducting a lynching. Irate citizens rioted and attempted to rescue the prisoners from the authorities. Paramount News sent Harry Tugander, outfitted with a complete camera and sound-truck ensemble, to Maryland to photograph the violence. Tugander described what followed:

As we were nearing Salisbury we saw eight busses of troops rushing out of the town towards Baltimore. Behind the troops we saw a photographer we knew. As he passed in his car he waved his hand, but we didn't know whether he was trying to stop us or was just saying hello. Behind him was a sedan filled with four tough looking men that seemed to be escorting him out of town.

We didn't quite know what to make of it, but continued on towards Salisbury. We had no sooner arrived in town than we saw a mob chasing someone down a street. We started to follow the mob when a Western Union messenger jumped on the running board on one side of the truck. "Get that truck out of sight— your lives aren't worth a nickle [sic]!" he yelled. The messenger was still shouting at us when a reporter for a local paper jumped on the other running board and said:

"The mob is after reporters and photographers. Get out while you can get out."

We turned the truck into a side street and about half way up the block we found a garage. We put the truck away in the back where it couldn't be seen easily.

Then I walked back to the corner. I could see the mob smashing up a car down the street. . . .

While I was standing on the corner a red-haired boy came tearing down the street leading a mob. They were headed for the garage in which the truck was parked. There was no stopping them. It would have meant fighting the whole town. In a minute they had the truck and were pushing it down the street. . . . I followed them. When they got to the west side of the Wicomico River, they pushed the truck over an embankment head on. It went into the river out of sight. $25,000 worth of equipment— gone![1]

The destruction of the truck merely delayed the Paramount organization, which assigned other cameramen, including Urban Santone, to reinforce Tugander. Despite the mob's interference Paramount's photographers finally managed to cover the riots with hand-held silent cameras.

Sometimes, of course, the cameramen were not so successful. On one occasion, in West Virginia, another Paramount sound truck was thrown into the river by irate striking miners, and the cameramen were hustled out of town at gunpoint.[2] On still another occasion Fox Movietone cameraman Dennis Welch, of Philadelphia, was sent out to photograph striking coal miners. Violence flared daily in the area, and outsiders—particularly cameramen—were no more welcomed by the police than by the strikers. After two days' delay without word from Welch, the Fox editors began to worry whether his footage would arrive in time for the semiweekly release. It never did. All they received from Welch was a telegram, which arrived just before deadline time:

Kindly request technical department check all valves [sound-recording tubes] and repair lens mount also broken side door my camera which expressing immediately stop send my pay check Mercy Hospital Pittsburgh care Welch.[3]

The Chinese-Japanese War provided some of the grimmest but most spectacular footage of the 1930's. The brutal bombing of Shanghai civilians was photographed by several American cameramen, including Harrison Forman of *The March of Time*, Hearst's Wong Hai-Sheng ("Newsreel" Wong), and T. Taguchi, and Universal's George Krainukov. According to an article in *Time*, Forman, Wong, and Krainukov were on hand to photograph the Japanese bombing of the Cathay and Palace hotels on August 14, 1937, in which 220 people were killed:

The March of Time's *Cameraman Harrison Forman, an aviator, explorer and author just down from Tibet, was sitting inside the Cathay when the terrifying explosion took place. The Hearst News of the Day's Shanghai man, a daredevil called "Newsreel" Wong, was behind the counter of his camera shop, two blocks away. Universal's George Krainukov, who had just had his camera shot out of his hand in the Chinese evacuation of Peiping, was also almost within hailing distance of the tragedy....*

Judged by the progressive destruction of a Lincoln Zephyr which, rammed head on into the curb, burns throughout Forman's, Wong's and Krainukov's films, Wong was the first man on the scene. (Presumably Forman lost time by having to rush up-stairs from the Cathay bar to get his machine.) But, according to the best guesses of U.S. newsreel people, Wong must have been turned back by the police after making his first shots, for it is Krainukov whose camera turns in the most gruesomely inclusive report of the bombing. . . .

Wong, Forman and Krainukov were once more on the spot to film the gore when a bomb from either the Japanese or Chinese shattered the roof of Sincere Co.'s department store nine days later. Somewhat surpassed by his competitors in both the explosions, March of Time's Forman scooped the pair of them with three other remarkable shots of the Shanghai shambles. He filmed a Japanese plane dropping a bomb on the native quarter, was the only one permitted aboard the Augusta *after she was struck by a one-pounder. Better than that, almost miraculously he happened to be taking a night view of the* Augusta *when she was hit.*[4]

Almost as unusual as the footage itself was the fact that Chinese censors allowed it out of the country. Continued *Time*:

The Chinese censors, who are among the world's most vigilant and who do not like even so moderately seamy a subject as the city's houseboat dwellers to be filmed for export, were as demoralized as the rest of the population when the shooting began. Photographer Forman was able to throw his cans of film to a departing friend as her tender pulled away. A Clipper* brought his pictures to the U.S. in time for the March of Time's current issue, released this week. Wong and Krainukov put their films on the Clipper a week later.[5]

A few months later, on December 12, 1937, the most news-worthy footage of all the Far Eastern coverage was shot when the

---

* The *Clipper* was a "flying boat"—a passenger airplane designed to land on water. Appearing before the long-distance land-based plane, it allowed for trans-Atlantic and trans-Pacific flights during the 1930's, and was frequently utilized by newsreel companies for the speedy transport of film from foreign countries to the United States.

United States gunboat *Panay*, steaming in the Yangtze River, was sunk by bombs from a Japanese plane. In a rare stroke of cameraman's luck, Universal's Norman Alley and Fox Movietone's Eric Mayell were on board the ship when it was bombed. Herbert Aller wrote:

Disregarding their personal safety, concentrating on doing their job in hand well, they ably took pictures of an incident that shocked the world, illustrating how the Panay *was bombed, fired upon, what occurred during the bombardment, the scramble to shore, how the victims fled for safety, tramping through the marshes and swamplands.*[6]

Their photographs were considered so valuable by both their employers and the United States government that the footage was rushed by a United States destroyer to Manila and from there, closely guarded, was flown to the West Coast on the *Clipper*. From there it was flown to New York by chartered airplane and transported from the airport to the laboratory in an armored car. It was estimated that more than twenty-five thousand dollars had been spent getting the pictures back to the laboratories.[7] The money was well spent, however, for the release was widely publicized and attracted large crowds at motion picture theaters across the country.[8] Albert Benham, of the National Council for Prevention of War, wrote, not very happily, of the resulting release:

Never before—or since—has the newsreel received the publicity that was accorded its coverage of the bombing of the Panay. *Front-page headlines in the daily press proclaimed that a film record of the incident had been obtained—that the visual evidence was being rushed to America—and finally, like a Hollywood premiere, the first screenings brought out column after column in the papers. While public interest in news value was logical justification for showing the films, the editorial comment which accompanied it was not. Despite the fact that in one company's release a title explained that the scenes were presented without editing or censorship, the commentator provided a running track of dialogue weighted with fiery tirades against the Japanese and undoubtedly calculated to arouse the American temper. . . .*

Among more pungent remarks about these newsreel pictures was that of Walter Winchell, hardly a pacifist, who said that while the newspaper writers had refused to become hysterical over the Panay *bombing, "the newsreel narrators put on the jingo act— noticeably those over the soldiering age."*[9]

A number of newsreel cameramen were killed in the line of duty during this period, and life-insurance rates rose accordingly. By 1938, George Krainukov's insurance company in Tokyo had begun issuing policies for lengths of ninety, sixty, and thirty days. At about this time he decided that "it would be longer and healthier for me if I made my home in America. . . . It was time to go some place and that place was not Shanghai."[10]

The kidnapping of Charles Lindbergh's baby in 1932, and the arrest and trial of Bruno Richard Hauptmann for the act in 1934–35 were covered by the newsreels with a vigor and thoroughness which many people found offensive. Even before Hauptmann had been taken into custody, the newsreel companies had been tipped off about his imminent arrest so that they could prepare background footage in advance. Following the arrest police officials even allowed newsreel men to photograph the original interrogation of Hauptmann at the Greenwich Street Police Station in New York. Later, newsreel men were allowed to shoot both silent and sound footage within the courtroom between sessions, by means of a rota pool system whereby the footage produced from two cameras was made available to all the newsreel companies.[11]

This was not the first appearance of newsreel cameras in courts of law. The court had previously allowed them to operate during the famed "monkey trial" of Tennessee schoolteacher John T. Scopes in 1925. Movies were also made of the courtroom proceedings of "Machine Gun" Kelly's murder trial in Oklahoma City. Abroad newsreel cameras photographed the military court in

Havana trying and convicting rebels during the 1930's. The Nazis photographed the courtroom testimony of Communists following the Reichstag fire of 1933, and the Soviets filmed appearance of witnesses in the trial of "counterrevolutionaries" in 1922.[12] At the Hauptmann trial, at Flemington, New Jersey, however, newsreel cameramen, together with newspaper and radio reporters, managed to convert what was an otherwise sobering tragedy into a grisly side show. Pathé cameramen, in a particularly repellent example of photojournalistic initiative, toured the streets of Flemington with a camera truck, asking passers-by to cast their vote about Hauptmann's guilt or innocence for the benefit of the sound newsreel camera.[13]

Following protests by David Wilentz, prosecutor of the case, and alleged pressure on the film industry from Wall Street banking houses, Fox and Paramount withdrew their coverage of the trial from release, but Hearst and Metrotone withdrew their film only in New York and New Jersey. Pathé and Universal held their ground and continued to release their footage throughout the country.[14]

In some areas of the country the newsreels beat the newspapers with the announcement of the death verdict against Hauptmann. As in newspaper practice, some of the newsreels had prepared alternate summary reels ahead of time—one for conviction, the other for acquittal—both of which were sent to exchanges and theaters. Within five minutes after the verdict had been handed down, theater owners had been notified by telegraph, and the appropriate reel was on the screens of hundreds of theaters.[15]

Rounding out this already ample coverage, Paramount somehow managed to get onto death row with its cameras for a sound-film interview with Hauptmann in his cell as he awaited execution. Paramount subsequently refused to disclose how it had secured this morbidly absorbing footage.[16]

Some of the other events of the thirties which provided exciting subject matter for the newsreels included the birth of the Dionne quintuplets in 1934;[17] the second Byrd expedition to Antarctica in

1934–35;[18] the earthquake of 1933 in southern California;[19] the 1932 and 1936 Olympics at Los Angeles and Berlin;[20] the 1932, 1936, and 1940 presidential-election campaigns;[21] the abdication of the Duke of Windsor, his marriage, and the coronation of George VI in 1937;[22] the visit of the king and queen of England to the United States in 1939;[23] the Republic Steel strike riots of 1937;[24] the burning and sinking of the *Morro Castle* in 1934; Haile Selassie's appeal to the League of Nations (which was re-created by Warner Brothers for the 1943 feature film *Mission to Moscow*);[25] Neville Chamberlain at a London airport after his return from Munich, waving a memorandum and talking of "peace in our time";[26] the Cuban rebellion of 1933;[27] Amelia Earhart landing at Newark, New Jersey, after her 2,175-mile nonstop flight from Mexico City;[28] the dynamiting of the Alcazar at Toledo, Spain;[29] and many other extraordinary scenes.

Of all the sensational newsreel material, however, two events in particular attracted the most attention and were in years to come remembered longest and most vividly by editors and cameramen, for whom they represented the greatest scoops in the history of the newsreel. The first was the assassination of King Alexander I of Yugoslavia. The second was the explosion of the German zeppelin *Hindenburg*.

Alexander I, the ruling monarch of Yugoslavia, had by the mid-1930's acquired an unenviable reputation in European political circles. He had carved an empire out of the Balkan States following World War I, waged vicious and unremitting internal warfare to maintain his position of leadership—and destroyed a number of his enemies in the process. By 1934 he was hated in many political quarters. His life had been threatened on several occasions, and assassination attempts were commonplace.

On October 9, 1934, Alexander traveled by ship to Marseilles, where preparations had been made for him to negotiate a new alliance with the French. The occasion was one which called for pomp and ceremony, and French officials went to some trouble to prepare a suitably gala welcome to the city. Precautions had been taken for his protection, but they were far less severe and thorough than they would have been in the monarch's own country. The possibility of foul play in France had apparently not been taken very seriously. Ordinarily such an event, although of some political importance, would not have attracted more than perfunctory newsreel coverage. Its immediate importance was apparent only in Paris and Belgrade, and worldwide release of the footage ordinarily would not have resulted. Also, the day before his arrival, revolutionary riots broke out in Spain, and many news cameramen were sent to cover them. Still, every newsreel company had at least one or two persons covering Alexander's arrival at Marseilles.[30]

On this occasion circumstances transpired to bring a full crew of Fox Movietone cameramen to the scene. Fox had just sent a new sound truck to Europe for its Paris office, and French cameramen Georges and Raymond Mejat, brothers, were told to break in the new truck by taking it to Marseilles to cover the ceremonies. In order to make up for the expense involved, Georges Mejat decided to make a spectacle of the event. Accordingly, he stationed his brother, Raymond, on top of the customs house to photograph from a high angle the meeting of King Alexander and French Foreign Minister Jean Louis Barthou at the dock and the automobile procession down the streets of Marseilles. The sound-camera crew, with its new truck, was stationed down the street ahead of the motorcade, to record natural sounds while photographing the smiling, waving officials as they approached in their open limousine. Georges Mejat himself took a small, hand-held, spring-wound camera and ran the police lines alongside the big automobile to obtain intimate shots of the major political figures. Both Georges and his brother were photographing the approach of the limousine when shots rang out. Georges ran toward the car and photographed the assassin on the running board and the guards who cut him down with their sabers. Georges followed with shots of the dying king, stricken women who had been accidentally shot by the assassin, the killer's straw hat, and the automatic pistol with which the murder had been accomplished.[31]

The footage which Mejat secured was of very good quality, considering the conditions under which it was shot. It was augmented by equally good coverage by the sound-truck crew. However, as newsreelmen oftentimes discover, it is one thing to photograph a great event but another thing to escape with the footage and get it back to the laboratories. Fearing that his film would be confiscated by the police, Mejat gave it to his brother, Raymond. Later, at the demand of the police, Georges turned over to them a worthless reel of film. In the complicated series of events which followed, Raymond lost the film Georges had given him, the police found it, and the Mejat brothers were back where they had started, trying to get out of the city with their precious film record. After negotiation and further maneuvers, the film was recovered from the police and transported to the Fox laboratories in America.[32] Movietone prepared a special issue which featured the event, complete with the original, on-the-spot sounds, the extra coverage photographed by Mejat's associates, and subsequent coverage of the transporting of Alexander's body to his homeland by the same ship on which he had arrived. The finished film, which was narrated by Lowell Thomas, was successfully released as a feature newsreel throughout the world.

The Fox Movietone coverage of the assassination was undoubtedly the most spectacular, especially since it was accompanied by first-hand synchronous sound. Other newsreelmen secured similarly good footage, however, and, like the Mejat brothers, had serious problems getting it out of the country. The French government was acutely embarrassed about its failure to protect the king and attempted at every turn to prevent shipment of the footage. In the end most of the film reached screens in Britain and the United States but was banned from exhibition in Switzerland, France, Germany, Italy, and Austria.[33]

For sensational subject matter and the quality of the motion picture coverage, the assassination film was not to be matched for another quarter of a century, until the assassinations of Japanese

Socialist leader Inejiro Asanuma in 1960, President John F. Kennedy in 1963, and Senator Robert F. Kennedy in 1968.

One could hardly imagine a more dramatic newsreel subject than the killing of a king. And then the *Hindenburg* exploded.

By 1937 arrivals and departures of the zeppelin *Hindenburg* and of other hydrogen-filled airships, had become fairly commonplace. By that time any early fears about the use of highly flammable hydrogen in the ships had been largely forgotten—at least by the public. Zeppelin designers would have preferred to use helium, but that rare gas was manufactured in quantity only in the United States and was not available to German industry. Most of the cameramen who were sent to Lakehurst, New Jersey, on May 6 of that year went to their assignments unwillingly. Al Gold, of Fox Movietone, was particularly unhappy. "This wasn't news any more," he wrote later. "Suppose we had to cover every boat that came over the Atlantic. Here was a big air liner that made the trip many times before with clock-like precision."[34] Still, this was the first arrival of the year, and there was always the chance to photograph celebrities among the trans-Atlantic passengers. For these reasons there was quite a crowd of cameramen on hand by sunset waiting for the arrival of the ship. Cameramen Al Gold, Larry Kennedy, and Deon DeTitta, contact man A. A. Brown, and sound man Addison Tice represented *Fox Movietone News*. James J. Seeley was on hand for Hearst's *News of the Day*. Bill Deekes represented *Pathé News*. Paramount sent Al Mingalone to cover the event. Universal had a man at the airfield, too; he was eager to get back to New York to attend a Broadway play for which he and a girlfriend had tickets. There was also a scattering of still photographers at the scene, representing, among other papers, the *Philadelphia Bulletin*, the *New York Sunday Mirror*, and the *New York Daily News*.

By rare circumstance the National Broadcasting Company, which until this date had never played an electrical transcription of program material over its radio network, had sent announcer

Herbert Morrison, engineer Charles Nelson, and a disk-recording sound truck to the airport that afternoon to secure background sounds for the company's sound-effects collection and to describe the arrival of the *Hindenburg* for its recording library. There was never any intention of broadcasting the recording as such over the air.

On this particular day the usually punctual *Hindenburg* was late. A thunderstorm had broken about an hour before its arrival, soaking the cameramen and their equipment. Said Al Gold, "We all sat, wringing wet, beside our cameras mounted on the roof of our trucks and exchanged vituperatives about the weather and the editors who assigned us to the story."[35] As darkness approached, it became apparent that satisfactory photographs could no longer be made, and the Universal cameraman left with his girlfriend for the Broadway play.[36] Finally, at 7:20 P.M., the pride of Germany's airship fleet arrived, settled toward the mooring mast, and prepared to anchor. "We [the Fox cameramen] didn't even bother to get up from our squatting positions to focus until she began to drop ballast. Then as they dropped the landing ropes we got busy."[37]

In the NBC recording truck engineer Charles Nelson turned on his disk-recording apparatus, and announcer Herbert Morrison spoke into his microphone describing the securing of the graceful airship:

It's practically standing still now. They've dropped ropes out of the nose of the ship, and they've been taken hold of down on the field by a number of men. It's starting to rain again. The rain had slacked up a little bit. The back motors of the ship are just holding it just enough to keep it from—It burst into flame! Get this, Charley! Get this, Charley!

[Crying hysterically] It's fire, and it's crashing! It's crashing terrible! Oh, my! Get out of the way, please! It's burning and bursting into flames, and it's falling on the mooring mast . . . and all the folks . . . this is terrible, this is one of the worst catastrophes

in the world! Oh, flames four or five hundred feet into the sky! It's a terrific crash, ladies and gentlemen, the smoke and the flames now . . . crashing to the ground, not quite to the mooring mast. Oh, the humanity and all the passengers . . . I can't talk, ladies and gentlemen. Honest, it's a mass of smoking wreckage . . . lady, I am sorry . . . Honestly, I can hardly breathe. I'm going to step inside where I cannot see it. Charley, that's terrible. Listen, folks, I'm going to have to stop for a minute because I've lost my voice—this is the worst thing I've ever witnessed.[38]

From beginning to end the explosion and crash of the zeppelin lasted only a few seconds. Such was the shock of the event and the concentration of the cameramen upon their work that later they could give only half-coherent testimony regarding the events which had transpired. James Seeley described his reactions:

I was panning my camera across the body of the ship when the terrific explosion took place near the stern. Suddenly flames leaped hundreds of feet into the air. I was stunned by what I was witnessing, but the training of [sic] every newsreel man gets to hold his ground stood me in good stead. By pure reflex action I kept grinding, even while passengers and crew were spewed out of the cabin windows of the monster and scrambled from beneath the mass of flaming fabric, their figures silhouetted against the background of seething fire. Not until my film ran out did I cease grinding.[39]

Movietone's Al Gold elaborated upon his experience:

When the explosion occurred I was shooting the ground crew grappling with the ropes. Instinctively, without a thought, I panned up to the silver bag looking in my finder to see what was happening. From then on what happened to me or my camera is a confused memory.

It only took about thirty seconds for the big bag to strike the ground after the explosion. But if the Board of Investigation calls me, I could never swear to that. It seemed an age or a moment. I couldn't believe that what I was seeing was true. "I'm dreaming,"

I said to myself over and over. The sense of time was like that in a dream.

I could hear only the grinding of my camera. Whatever other sounds were around the blazing pile never came to my ken. That there must have been hollering and screeching and the roar of flames I know, but I didn't hear them. My wet belt [the camera's take-up belt] was working. The film was unwinding before my lens. "I've got everything I can from this angle," I thought. . . .

Shutting the motor off and putting a lens shade on my two-inch, I hoisted the camera to [soundman Addison Tice] . . . asking Brownie . . . to take the batteries as Ad and I went forward to the pyre for close-ups. As we hurried forward dodging through men running hither and thither I still thought I was dreaming. All around the blazing mass we moved, the three of us. We must have made ten set-ups before Brownie called a halt and said we had better begin thinking of getting our film on the way to New York.

"When they come to," he said, "they may confiscate our film. It has happened before on stories of this kind."

We then recalled Larry Kennedy and his assistant Deon De Titta, from our company, who were with us on the assignment getting a different angle. The last we had seen of them they were directly under the tail of the ship. We started looking for them. From one cameraman to another we ran. Finally we found them. Like us they had been moving around the ship making every possible angle. They had been saved by a gust of wind that came up as the ship settled. It blew it over their heads and it landed about fifty feet from where they were standing. They had gotten many of the marvelous shots you saw on the screen in the Movietone News special. I was the only man given screen credit but many of the great shots in our release were photographed by Kennedy.[40]

In the confusion and shock of the moment none of the many cameramen present knew whether he had really succeeded in capturing the explosion on film (all of them did). "Among ourselves," wrote Al Gold, ". . . we almost fought in sheer relief. We kept telling each other, 'You've got it all. I haven't a thing.' We did this until there was hysterical bitterness among us."[41] Back at the newsreel laboratories suspense mounted as roll after roll arrived for processing. No editor was more apprehensive than Max Klein, of Paramount:

The stringer cameraman [Al Mingalone?] working for our "Reel" could only tell us that he apparently kept his camera running until that final second when personal survival transcends all—he himself ran, as fast as he could from the immediate scene of the holocaust. Then, he continued his coverage, of the victims fleeing the Hindenburg, their clothes aflame, of the dramatic scenes of rescue and aftermath. But did he get the Hindenburg actually bursting into flames? One Eyemo roll would answer that terribly pressing query—one hundred feet of film which would make or break the sensational story.

. . . the negatives were developed, and we waited in the screening room—running off first one roll, another—until at last only that important Eyemo roll remained. Paradoxically, in the rush of developing and joining the negative rolls for projection, camera run continuity had to be ignored; first in importance was last on the screen! What happened? The scenes flashed from the projection booth aperture, an audience of hardened newsreel men sat in hushed anticipation—then, brilliant in exposure, razor-sharp in focus, the camera record of the sudden death of the Hindenburg! In barely more than one minute of negative was the nucleus for a story that with each passing year has become more valuable as an unmatched example of newsreel spot coverage.[42]

Parenthetically, NBC Radio also shared in the scoop. That evening, for the first time in its history, its rigid rule against broadcasting recorded programs was broken so that the radio audience could hear Morrison's eyewitness account.[43]

13.

FILM-INDUSTRY
ATTITUDES
TOWARD
NEWSREEL PRODUCTION
AND RELEASE

As we have seen, the early news film not only served to introduce and popularize the early motion picture medium but survived for some years as a distinct "feature" attraction. As the competing fictional, dramatic film gained in popularity, however, the news film declined proportionately until by 1910 its exhibition was rare and was occasioned only by intermittent coverage of genuinely newsworthy events. Conceivably, if the newsreel had not been introduced in 1911, journalism might have disappeared from motion picture screens altogether, thus rendering the film a wholly dramatic medium.

The newsreel survived, but the role which industry leaders had picked for it to play destroyed its individuality as a program attraction and seriously compromised its journalistic integrity. After 1911, with the exceptions already noted, the film industry no longer regarded the newsreel as a feature attraction to be advertised on theater marquees and sold directly to the public at the box office. Instead of being presented intermittently, on those occasions when coverage and newsworthiness of content made it appropriate, the newsreel was now presented regularly, whether its content was newsworthy or not.

Theater owners generally viewed the newsreel as nothing more than a convenient house-clearing device to be inserted between feature attractions. Indeed, in the earliest days of the motion picture, exhibitors' resistance to the newsreel was so great that issues were provided at cut rates or even free of charge by the distributor to establish a market for the product.[1] In time, because of its apparent popularity with audiences, it became an established part of the program. As long as the newsreel represented a quasi-journalistic attraction which featured celebrities, humor, sensation, sports, technology, and catastrophe—suitably visualized, noncontroversial in nature, and capable of presentation without interpretation—exhibitors were willing to run it in their theaters, recognizing an apparent audience demand for its inclusion in the prepackaged motion picture program. The newsreel was intended to function as a relatively unimportant program component which supported the main feature. The exhibitors' attitude in this respect was illustrated in a revealing anecdote recounted by Edgar Hatrick, general manager of Hearst's *International Newsreel*:

> . . . *when Admiral Byrd flew from Spitzbergen to the North Pole and back, a Hearst cameraman made great shots of the epic flight. After he took his pictures, this cameraman plodded overland with them by dogsled, rode an icebreaker in the Arctic Ocean, flew to Norway, was forced down, flew to England, caught the Aquitania just as it was leaving the dock, went through six days of North Atlantic storms and finally arrived in New York. In New York, the newsreel company rushed the films to the office, kept men overtime, broke records in processing the pictures, slapped a big "exclusive" on them, and then rushed them over by special messenger to the late Major Edward Bowes, who was then managing the Capitol Theater in New York.*
>
> *Bowes glanced at the reel, yawned and put it up on a shelf.*
>
> *"Aren't you going to use it?" the messenger shrieked.*
>
> *"No," said Bowes. "I just added a dog act to my vaudeville show, and we don't have the running time."*[2]

Exhibitors, moreover, seldom failed to express their reluctance to run controversial news material as part of what they considered an exclusively entertainment enterprise and to edit out such material at will. In this respect the exhibitor's point of view was clearly stated by Martin Quigley, owner and editor-in-chief of the exhibitor's trade paper, *Motion Picture Herald*, in 1937:

. . . *newsreels have no social obligation beyond those of the amusement industry and theatres they are supposed to serve. Newsreels have an obligation, if they are to be purveyed as entertainment in theatres, to be entertaining. They have no obligation to be important, informative. They can successfully present neither one side, both sides, nor the middle of any social condition or issue.*[3]

A year later, at the time that *The March of Time* released one of its more controversial issues, Quigley wrote:

We hold that the motion picture theatre is and should remain devoted to the mission of providing entertainment. Entertainment in the sense used here must of course be accorded a latitudinous definition but certainly not one that may be stretched to include controversial political material. . . .

The exhibitors of the country ought to tell "The March of Time" that it is welcomed when it behaves itself but only then. . . . They should tell it . . . that they expect it to be mindful of the proprieties of theatrical presentation—that they do not want controversial political material which is calculated to destroy the theatre as the public's escape from the bitter realities, the anguishes and the turmoil of life.[4]

In 1945, as the world's most devastating war finally drew to a close, the *Motion Picture Herald* had not budged one inch in its view of the motion picture theater as an escapist refuge for anguished audiences. In opposing the public screening of scenes of the German death camps at Dachau and Buchenwald, as well as scenes of Mussolini's death, *Herald* editor Terry Ramsaye wrote: "It sets the picture back to the dime museum, or the Chamber of Horrors of the Eden Musee's frenzied wax works. No competent excuse exists for the presentation. . . . The news obligation of the newsreel is happily trivial. . . . No one goes to the theater to get the news."[5] This insight into industry sentiment becomes all the more revealing when it is noted that Ramsaye had worked earlier in his career as editor of the *Kinograms* newsreel, the *Mutual Screen Telegram* (Mutual Films' issue), and the Pathé newsreel.[6]

Another indication of exhibitors' reaction to controversial footage was revealed in an account provided by newsreel editor Ray Hall of Rothapfel's appraisal of news footage released following Lenin's funeral in 1924:

Lenin died in Russia. As dictator of the Soviet Government he had forced his way into prominence as a world figure. Pictures reviewing his life were collected by one of the news reels and sent along with their regular editions for such theatres as might care to use them. I happened to be in S. L. Rothapfel's office when the reel was run off. He is one of Broadway's great showmen and famous to millions of radio fans as "Roxy." Together we sat in his projection room.

"Great pictures," said Mr. Rothapfel; "wonderful and interesting, but I wouldn't show them in my theater for $10,000."

Asked why, he reached two conclusions evidently so inconsistent that he explained: "In a cosmopolitan city like New York there are all sorts of people. Undoubtedly, there are sympathizers with Lenin. If I showed the picture they might applaud. Then someone might hiss. Instantly, everyone in the house is uncomfortable. It might develop into a real unpleasantness; someone might have to be evicted. Anyway, it would be sure to engender controversy. And in any theatre that I manage we will do everything to avoid controversy."[7]

This intense desire to avoid controversy on motion picture screens led Pennsylvania's exhibitors to enter into an agreement in 1936 that no newsreel footage bearing upon political issues would be run in their theaters.[8]

Distributors held the newsreel in somewhat higher esteem,

though not because of any apparent respect for its journalistic or artistic potential. In order to compete effectively, each of the major production-distribution organizations sought to provide a complete program to exhibitors. This usually comprised a feature (later a double bill); a cartoon, novelty, or travelogue; trailers; and a newsreel. The producer-distributor unable to offer any one of these program components took the risk that its independent-exhibitor accounts would rent from other companies' exchanges. In the film business such nonexclusivity was considered bad business, and every effort was made to contract exclusively with independent theaters by offering complete program packages, block-booked in advance.

Although information bearing upon distribution policy and financial operations in the film business is always hard to find, at least one piece of evidence is available which throws light on the role the newsreel played in the economic structure of the motion picture industry during the 1920's and 1930's. In 1930 the Harvard Business School undertook a study of film-industry economics, which was subsequently published under the auspices of the George F. Baker Foundation. In the report Howard Thompson Lewis described an attempt made in 1929 to combine all newsreels then operating into one giant newsreel association roughly analogous to the newspaper press associations. Although the scheme appeared attractive as a means of reducing excessively high production costs, both the Paramount and Metro-Goldwyn-Mayer (Hearst) newsreel organizations declined to enter into the agreement, thus ensuring its failure. According to Lewis:

One of their chief reasons for entering the newsreel field had been their desire to be in a position to furnish their customers with a complete program. This would not be prohibited under the joint newsreel service, but these companies had invested a large sum of money in the establishment of their newsreels and believed that they were in a strong competitive position. Each of them ap-

*parently expected to become a leader in the newsreel field despite
the intense competition of the other companies.*[9]

Distributors thus may be said to have regarded the newsreel as
an economically necessary part of the block-booked program. Inasmuch as the economic structure of motion picture production
and distribution was built upon the practice of block booking—
at least before antitrust actions successfully prosecuted by the
federal government in the 1930's and 1940's[10]—newsreel production by each of the major studios was an economic necessity. The
point that seems worth emphasizing, however, is that distributors
assigned no greater intrinsic value to the newsreel than to the
cartoons, travelogues, and novelties which were also essential to
their block-booked bills.

The producers of newsreels often professed a kinship to the
traditional newsprint media. Nonetheless, most evidence indicates
that their values belonged to show business rather than to journalism and that they viewed their "readership" or "circulation" as
being an entertainment-hungry audience rather than a well-
informed public.

Attempts by particular producers to describe the manner in
which they managed to arrive at a knowledge of the needs, character, and preferences of their audiences were not very revealing.
The editor of the Fox newsreel tried to explain it this way:

*How does a news-reel editor know the reactions of his audiences
to the subtleties of a subject? The editor of a newspaper learns
what his readers think through occasional letters, usually from
persons he has displeased. A news-reel editor who receives a
hundred letters a year from theater patrons would be getting a
record number. But if he wants to know how they like the reel,—
how they respond to any given treatment of a subject,—he may
step into the nearest theatre and a thousand people will uncon-
sciously tell him. On this point he is never in doubt.*[11]

Suggested another newsreeler, probably a little closer to the truth, "Of course first of all one must have a fixed idea in mind as to what would be a thriller or have screen value for entertainment."[12]

I know of no attempt by a newsreel producer to conduct a systematic, objective analysis of audience preferences. Moreover, except in newsreel theaters, the newsreel producer lacked access to the one barometer which was considered infallible in the motion picture industry—financial returns at the box office. The newsreel, as we have seen, was presented as an unfeatured program component. Apart from the operation of theaters which featured newsreels exclusively, any connection between the success or failure of a motion picture program and the presence of a newsreel on the same bill was considered accidental. For these reasons, any knowledge or insights which producers may have had regarding the taste and interests of their audiences may be assumed, in the main, to have been gained intuitively rather than empirically.

This is not to say that producers' judgments in such matters— any more than the general run of judgments made in show business—were necessarily incorrect, but simply that they appeared to be based upon assumed rather than demonstrated facts. Whether valid or invalid, producers' notions regarding their audiences' preferences influenced the style and content of the newsreels. Some producers, such as Emanuel Cohen, felt so sure of their insights that they did not hesitate to offer broad generalizations about them:

What kinds of pictures are most popular with audiences?

Soldiers, airplanes, battleships—and babies! A picture of a laughing baby, or of a crying one, stirs a ripple of amusement. And a picture of a white baby and a colored one together gets a big laugh.[13]

Another newsreel editor categorized newsreel values, together with accompanying examples. They included major political, social, or economic events (the opening of Parliament and the Irish question); great physical events (fires, explosions, volcanoes, avalanches, floods); scientific progress (the development of a method for tempering copper and a machine for printing envelopes); human interest (a blind soldier knitting and a trained earthworm); and spectacles (navy airplanes sinking former German battleships, and the completion of a large dam).[14]

Still another unidentified newsreel editor (possibly Emanuel Cohen) outlined his "sure-fire" newsreel subjects. According to him, the parade of the Twenty-seventh Division down Fifth Avenue in New York was the most emotionally successful film he had ever released, followed by the Black Tom explosion at the munitions docks in Jersey City, New Jersey, in 1916, and the bomb explosion on Wall Street, in New York City, in 1920. His most successful human-interest picture was of a Robersonville, North Carolina, family with thirty-four children. Among other things the film showed the family using a tub for a butter plate.[15] According to the editor, audiences were still talking about it years later.

A third editor provided still another estimation of audience content interests. He told an interviewer that his biggest human-interest film was a duck leading a blind bull to water.

As Ramsaye concluded in 1934: "The newsreel is not a purveyor of news and never is likely to become one. . . . The newsreel ought to be an entertaining and amusing derivative. . . . Whether they know it or not, the newsreels, as they call them, are just in the show business."[16]

14.

**CRITICISM
OF THE
SOUND NEWSREEL
1929–60**

*From the beginning we have had newsreels, but dim records
they seem now of only the evanescent and the essentially unreal,
reflecting hardly anything worth preserving of the times they recorded. . . . The newsreel has gone dithering on, mistaking the
phenomenon for the thing in itself, and ignoring everything that
gave it the trouble of conscience and penetration and thought.*
JOHN GRIERSON, 1937[1]

The newsreel: A series of catastrophes, ended by a fashion show.
OSCAR LEVANT, 1965

The addition of sound brought the newsreel into public prominence. The exciting and highly pictorial news events of the 1930's
kept it there. The number of popular articles and the amount of
serious attention which newspaper and periodical writers devoted
to the newsreel increased markedly after the introduction of sound
and continued to increase throughout the 1930's. Articles appeared in popular periodicals, scholarly journals, trade magazines,
and daily newspapers. Such critical attention would probably have
revealed flaws in the most polished of dramatic productions if it
had been pursued for an equally long period of time. In the case
of the newsreel the criticism became devastating as writers grew
aware of its artistic and journalistic shortcomings.

If the addition of sound had led to a more cinematic form, a more fluid or even theatrical style, then a new kind of American newsreel might have evolved, with actuality footage, newsworthy interviews, authentic sound for the raw material, and interpretative narration where suitable, all edited in counterpoint with nonredundant music and sound effects. If nothing else, the addition of sound might have allowed for a moderately smooth and cinematic transition between sequences of radically different subject matter. The addition of sound had no such effect, however. The fragmented, sometimes incoherent structure of the newsreel continued to be patterned after that of the newspaper—an ill-ordered series of static visualizations of dubious news value— what Andrew Buchanan once called "jumpy little postcard collections."[2]

Such a structure was by no means inevitable. In the late 1930's the Nazi German government introduced a different sort of newsreel—*Die Deutsche Wochenschau* (*The German Newsreel*)— which, despite the purpose to which it was put, provided a much more intellectually exciting and cinematically appropriate model for newsreel production.[3]

The American newsreel, in newspaper fashion, began each issue with its most important story, following it with progressively less important material. The reel usually ended with sports and the newsreel equivalent of the comic section—Lew Lehr and the monkeys or their equivalent. Such a presentation might work well in conventional journalism, but it could be argued that it did not make for very good film making. Instead of building toward a climax, each successive scene was of less and less significance.

The Nazi film makers generally structured their newsreels in just the opposite manner, building toward the exciting, skillfully edited battle footage from current military campaigns with which they ended their reels. The Nazi films were at least twice as long as their American counterparts. They rarely ran less than fifteen minutes and sometimes ran as long as forty minutes, depending upon the subject matter. The American newsreels of the same period ran no more than ten minutes, and were shortened even further during World War II. The German newsreel took itself seriously and presented its political, economic, and technological subject matter in an editorially sober fashion. Because of the manner in which it approached its subjects, its audience—with whom it was apparently popular—also took it seriously. The American newsreel, on the other hand, included so much frivolous material that the audience found it difficult to take it very seriously. The American newsreel employed newspaper-style captions which briefly introduced the subject of each sequence. The German reels were much less fragmented. They used no captions. Instead, individual sequences were blended smoothly by means of fades, dissolves, accompanying narration, and music bridges.

Of course *Die Deutsche Wochenschau* was by no means the only potential kind of newsreel. As early as 1922 the Soviet film director Dziga Vertov had introduced a newsreel featuring dynamic cutting and montage effects. There were also a few film series here and there which tried with varying success to bridge the gap between newsreel and documentary, between reportage and commentary. One of these was *The March of Time*, a radically different kind of motion picture short subject which first appeared on American and foreign theater screens in the spring of 1935. It was produced by the former newsreel cameraman Louis de Rochemont for the publishers of *Time* and *Fortune* magazines. Released once a month, this unusual series of films survived for sixteen years, from the spring of 1935 to the fall of 1951—the only series, newsreel or not, to exploit political issues regularly during that period upon commercial motion picture screens. At a time when depression-ridden audiences sought relief from the harsh realities of the period, *The March of Time* rudely reminded them of bread lines, unemployment, and political demagoguery. While film producers in other newsreel studios eschewed controversial political and military items, *The March of Time* stubbornly paraded the faces and deeds of the world's most controversial figures. Hitler, Stalin, Mussolini, and Tojo—they and their exploits appeared in *Time*'s fast-moving reviews, a dazzling display of controversial material which ultimately provoked the most intense and unrelenting program of censorship ever inflicted upon a motion picture series anywhere in the world.

Its style was revolutionary, a curious mixture of cinematic exposition and journalistic punctuation that defied both convention and analysis. The static camera and nervous editing, the *vox e sepulchro* strained with alarm, the posture of omniscience, and the calculated air of fearlessness—all combined to delight a contemporary audience otherwise bored with the inanities of intermission travelogues and farces. *Time* editorialized openly, infuriating its enemies and oftentimes alienating its friends. And it did all of this with a vigor, artistry, and showmanship which shamed its less-daring competitors.

There is no need here to elaborate upon the structure, content, and evolution of *The March of Time*. Its history has been treated elsewhere.[4] Moreover, whatever it was, it was not a newsreel. It was a kind of documentary film whose structure represented a compromise between the traditional newsreel and the socially conscious discursive forms of the British and American documentary traditions. As critic Andrew Buchanan observed, "Strictly speaking, and judging by present newsreel standards, *The March of Time* isn't a newsreel at all or if it is *then all the others aren't!*"[5]

A number of differences distinguished *The March of Time* from the common newsreel:

1. It made no pretense of reporting up-to-the-minute news. It was released only once a month. The regular newsreel was released twice weekly.

2. It dealt with a limited number of subjects in each issue (after May, 1938, with only one subject in each issue). The newsreel dealt with as many as a dozen different topics in each release.

3. Each issue ran as long as twenty minutes, allowing for a fairly leisurely and detailed exposition of subject matter. The American newsreel never ran more than ten minutes, oftentimes less.

4. It was an interpretive, discursive reel which elaborated with

maps, narration, diagrams, titles, and supplementary footage upon the issues which it treated. The newsreel, with rare exceptions, treated only the superficialities of day-to-day events.

5. It spent fifty to seventy-five thousand dollars on each issue. The average newsreel company spent eight to twelve thousand dollars on each issue.

6. Both the newsreel and *The March of Time* staged and re-created events, but *The March of Time* did so to a far greater extent, sometimes to the almost complete exclusion of authentic footage. Moreover, it frequently used impersonators of celebrities when it was found that actual footage was not available.

7. The intention of *The March of Time* was to create and exploit controversy and to provoke discussion of politically, economically, and socially touchy subjects. Newsreel producers tried to avoid controversial subject matter at all costs.

8. *The March of Time* was sometimes openly partisan; the newsreel, rarely, and never avowedly so.

The most important distinction to be made is that *The March of Time* was a bona fide documentary production, dramatic in structure and pace and moderately fluid and cinematic in exposition (although never narratively lyrical, as was the case in many British and Continental documentaries). The American newsreel, on the other hand, was inflexibly bound to the fragmented news-item structure of the newspaper. As one critic noted, "For some reason or other, probably through lack of time, newsreels are never produced—they merely happen."[6] The question which concerns us here is whether *The March of Time*, with its unusual style and production innovations, exerted any noticeable influence upon the content, structure, or production of the major American newsreels. Certainly many people had hoped that it would do so. As early as 1936, Andrew Buchanan optimistically saw

signs that news films will ultimately be made which shall be so intelligent, absorbingly interesting and completely different . . . that, in time . . . we shall go to see a news-reel with the same thrill

*we experience when about to view a production by Grierson,
Pudovkin, or Rotha. The most significant of such signs is "The
March of Time."*[7]

Added the producers of *The March of Time*, smugly:

*It must also be noted that during the year there has been a
marked increase in the significance and coherence of the traditional newsreel....*

If The March of Time *has stimulated some of this activity, the
publishers are gratified."*[8]

On March 4, 1937, two years after *Time* introduced its controversial series, the Academy of Motion Picture Arts and Sciences
presented it with a special award for its "significance to motion
pictures and for having revolutionized one of the most important
branches in the industry—the newsreel."[9] In fact, however, the
awarding of an Oscar to *The March of Time* was solely in recogni-
tion of the film's own peculiar qualities, rather than for any real
influence upon the regular newsreel. Insofar as I can tell, *The
March of Time* had not the slightest effect upon the structure,
content, or style of the American newsreel. Indeed, the granting
of an Academy Award to *The March of Time* was bitterly pro-
tested within the newsreel business as a slur upon the quality of
the regular newsreel service. Gilbert Seldes concluded: "I may be
unduly pessimistic but it seems to me that ... *The March of Time*
has had little influence on the newsreels. They continue to be
almost appallingly unimportant."[10]

At best, the journalistic contribution of the conventional newsreel had always been second rate, both in intent and in performance. Producers, distributors, and exhibitors had never taken its
journalistic potential very seriously. As early as 1931, for example,
Twentieth-Century Fox, owner of America's largest newsreel
company, announced that its theaters would not be allowed to
show newsreels of a controversial nature.[11] (Interestingly, by the
end of the troubled 1960's, some independent television stations
in the United States had announced a similar policy regarding
news films of civil disorder.) As for distributors and exhibitors,

233

they too generally disregarded or denied the journalistic character and responsibility of their own newsreels. Economically speaking, the newsreel was considered merely an entertainment component in the block-booked program. In this respect the sound newsreel differed from the silent newsreel not at all. In 1931, shortly after sound was introduced, Terry Ramsaye wrote:

The zest has gone out of the newsreel camera men and their editors chiefly because the fate of the product is being decided not by performances in the field of adventure and on the screen, but around the tables in sales conferences and trade-offs of playing time. The truth is that a really important feature picture can in a fashion drive through its own way to the screen and the market, but the best newsreel on earth could not importantly affect its gross by sheer quality of performance.[12]

If the quality of the sound newsreel was falling in 1931, it was to sink far lower in the years to come, as disenchanted audiences were quick to note. Within a few years after the introduction of sound, film critics were indicating their complete disillusionment with the newsreel:

1932: *... criticism might be levelled at any of the news reels which are so prominent to-day, for it is debatable whether their editors have as yet truly discovered what does and does not constitute news in the screen sense of the word. . . . There should be nothing crude about the presentation of a newsreel, no abrupt, badly-finished sequences, leaving the audience suspended in mid-air. Too often we are confronted by statesmen and other notabilities making speeches which, without warning, finish abruptly half-way through, and before we have realized the fact, we are watching an abbreviated version of a football match.*[13]

1933: *As history, as bottled samples of what is happening now, to be handed down to our great grandchildren, the newsreels are more often than not trivial, lazy, and misleading.*

As witnesses of great contemporary events, as impartial eyes and ears which wander over the world to record red-hot actuality, they have degenerated rather than improved with time. Even as entertainment, as something served up to the public between Mickey Mouse and Greta Garbo, they are too often silly and dull. . . . I wish, indeed, to indict the newsreels on three counts, viz:

They have largely abandoned the service of history and set up shop as entertainers, with the result that the bulk of their offerings is no longer news, but a collection of stale, recurring athletic events, dare-deviltries and sideshows such as can be seen to better advantage at any circus or county fair.

They have ceased to run after history or to try to catch her unawares, preferring to consult the calendar and wait until, as in a St. Patrick's Day parade, she marches past the corner with a brass band.

Third, they have formed the lazy habit of prearranging and rehearsing events, and, instead, of going hunting in the jungles where history lurks or even waiting until she goes by, they have tamed the once camera-shy muse so that she will now turn up and show her profile at the studio by appointment. Which inevitably results in a portrait that does not do her justice.[14]

1937: *I criticize the news-reel, for I think their editors do not fulfil their responsibilities as journalists, as do editors of newspapers. . . . No news-reel has yet had the courage to set up as the equivalent of a Liberal or Labour twopenny daily. . . . None have the courage to be a little more complete or considered in what they chronicle than the rest. . . . The great proportion of important events are not recorded, or at most given cursory notice. So for all its apparent "service," the newsreel isn't giving us the real news.*[15]

One of the most annoying features of the sound newsreel was

the stereotyped "backing" of dramatic footage with accompanying solemn narration and overly powerful music, the effect of
which, at least for critic John Erskine, writing in 1935, was an
irritating redundancy of picture and narrative:

> For example, if the title on the screen announces the wreck of
> the Morro Castle, I must first listen to a snatch of music before I
> see the picture. There will probably be a few measures of Wagner's
> fire-music. This is to let me know there is a storm coming, and
> tragic disaster, but I knew that before. I recognize Wagner and I
> must waste a second disentangling myself from memories of the
> opera house and getting down to what actually happened on the
> Jersey coast. As soon as I am free of the music, and the picture
> starts, a firm voice, modulated to a properly tragic tone, begins a
> lecture on the causes of the accident, the number of lives lost, the
> progress of the official investigation. Now of course, when the
> wreck took place, . . . there was no accompanying lecture. The
> introduction of artificial elements has cheated me of what I came
> for—the opportunity of seeing exactly what happened. The
> pleasure should be primarily for the eye. But the firm voice pur-
> sues me, distracts my eye, and wrecks my pleasure. . . .
>
> The announcer has forgotten that an actor can't make his
> audience cry by shedding his own tears. His listeners may be sorry
> for him, but not in a complimentary sense, and they will be more
> inclined to laugh.[16]

In many articles of the period writers took malicious delight in
reviewing the banal contents of typical newsreels selected at ran-
dom from the season's releases. Robert Littell wrote in 1933:

> . . . the students of 2133 will take out their notebooks, and gaze
> with growing bewilderment (not to say disillusion) upon the fol-
> lowing items rescued from the newsreels of the flaming, fluid, fate-
> laden 1930's:
> A parade of babies, some of them dressed as butterflies.
> Several hundred adolescents in white uniforms throwing their
> visored caps in the air.

A man in tights, leaping feet foremost at another man, also in tights.

Three dozen girls in bathing suits, sliding down a snow slope on their tails.

A very ordinary looking young man, playing the piano with black mittens on his hands.

Several polar bears, breaking cakes of ice inside of which are frozen fish.

Automobiles going around and around and around an inclined track.

Horses running around and around and around a track which is not inclined.

A pair of midgets, one male, one female, dressed as bride and groom.

A middle-aged citizen in horn-rimmed glasses, talking haltingly about some unintelligible aspect of government.

A small and rather frightened boy, with a crown on his head.

Two dozen girls in rompers high-kicking on the deck of a battleship....

And this, say to themselves the student sons of our great grand-children, is what our ancestors found interesting to record of the age of Gandhi, Stalin and Einstein.[17]

Of all the newsreel's failures, however, none more irritated such critics as Littell than the announcers' gratuitous, heavy-handed attempts at humor:

When a water sport festival is held in Paris, and a very fat man is toppled into the water, the announcer calls out "Yes sir, halitosis wins" (he says "Yes sir" every two minutes). When the midgets get married in Chicago he remarks "Everything's midget size at the wedding except the kiss." When the American Davis Cup players are winning from the Australians, his confidential, breezy voice says "It looks like that old mug is coming back to poppa." When Italian trade unionists, carrying the emblems of their patron saints through the streets of Gubbio, pause for a drink, he tells us they are taking on "some of that special high test gas called Chianti." When we are shown pigs feeding at a Berlin nature fair, he hopes that "they won't make hogs of themselves." When the picture is one of a dog show, he remarks that the dogs "are making their bows and bow-wows." And the announcer who can get off the worst puns and allude to Mr. Pig and Mr. Dog in the oiliest bedtime story manner is probably the one who draws the highest salary (or perhaps somebody else writes the drool, and he only speaks it—for this is the age of specialization).[18]

Novelist Carlton Brown provided a devastating description of newsreel production methods which he observed over a period of several weeks in the spring of 1947 while working as a narration writer for one of the major newsreel companies (designated by him, for anonymity's sake, as "Cosmic News"):

It was my first experience in this sort of work, and I put in only two days a week at it, and so I am not qualified as an expert on the subject. But the job gave me a new curiosity about a far-reaching medium of communication which I had previously taken pretty much for granted, as I believe a great proportion of its vast audience take it. . . .

Jenks, [Brown's mentor] on my first day with Cosmic, showed me the stop-watch in my desk drawer and gave me a fast briefing —which I found meaningless—on its application. He evidently wanted to be helpful, but he had been writing lines to fit newsreel footage for eight or ten years and had such an automatic mastery of the technique that he could not explain it in terms a novice could understand. Gradually, in practice, I picked up the mechanical rules of the craft, managed to mimic the hackneyed prose style which is imposed by tradition, and divined some of the unwritten laws governing editorial approach; but when I came back to the office with the basket-hat assignment, I was still very much in the dark.

"I never had any idea this fashion stuff was written," I said to Jenks. "I always thought the dame just stood there while the pic-

ture was being taken and said whatever came into her pretty little head."

"That's the way it's supposed to sound, I guess," Jenks said.

I sat at the typewriter and tried to think of something cute to say about basket hats. Finally, I wrote, "A tisket, a tasket, she wears a yellow basket," and another ten or fifteen lines in the same vein. At Jenk's suggestion, I let the script cool for an hour or two before taking it to the editor, who removed "yellow" from the opening line, because, he explained, the film was not in technicolor. Otherwise, my script was acceptable, and, by a happy accident, about the right length.

A few hours later, I heard the chatty voice of a woman fashion commentator, greatly amplified, echoing through the halls from the sound-recording studio. Hearing one's own semi-literate writing thrown back in overwhelming volume is an unsettling experience not encountered in other sorts of hack work, and it may help to account for the high consumption of alcohol among newsreel people.[19]

As the years passed, the amount, vehemence, and passionate immediacy of newsreel criticism gradually declined, not because the newsreel got any better but probably because its critics lost hope for its improvement. By the end of the 1940's most writers appeared to have largely written off its journalistic potential as incapable of realization.

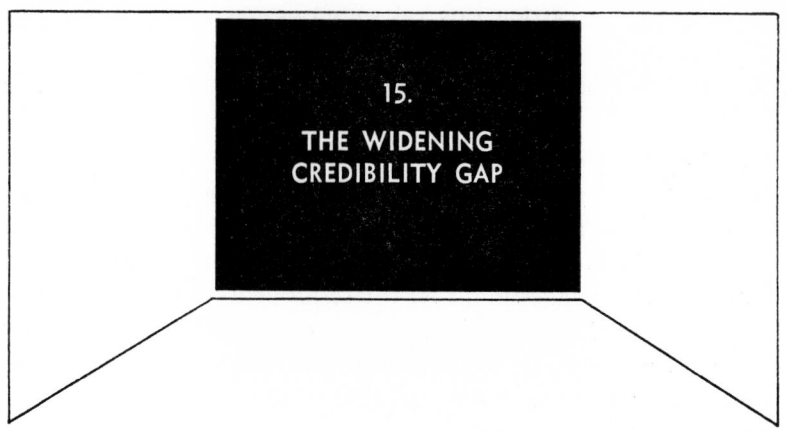

If the opportunities for journalistic fraud were great during the silent newsreel days, the addition of sound doubled them, inasmuch as manipulation of content could be executed in both dimensions. The same general practice of content manufacture and alteration continued, of course, but with a whole new set of techniques contributed by the sound technician. An article in the *New York Times* described them:

> *A sound librarian has no shame and very little of what is known as the historical conscience.*
>
> *Say that Honolulu sends over a "silent" shot of the surfboard antics at Waikiki; unembarrassed, the sound man will dig out a little roll of sound-tracked film marked "Ocean Waves," try it out on a loud-speaking gadget, nod his head approvingly and tack it onto the print, even if those particular waves actually broke back in 1931 on the coral strands of Long Beach, N.J. Pounding hoofs sound as realistic in one Derby as in another. Assorted riots (race, breadline, WPA, Communist) always are available in the sound library, and much more tidily than they would be at the scene of conflict.[1]*

Such technical virtuosity seems fairly innocent. Other forms of newsreel deception represented blatant fraud. Critic Anthony

North described how a silent newsreel sequence featuring George Bernard Shaw was "hoked up" into a bogus sound attraction:

Last year [1933] when Bernard Shaw arrived in the United States on a world cruise the newsreels sent their men down to the boat to get him to say something. Mr. Shaw was diffident, not to say temperamental. He wouldn't cooperate at all. He wouldn't talk. He just wouldn't do anything. Back in the studio with only some scanty shots of the great Shaw backing and cavorting about the deck, one of the reels dubbed on some very interesting sound. Several of the boys in the studio contributed a running chatter of informal comment. Such shouts as "Mr. Shaw, can't you stand still a minute!" "Will you stop moving around and let us get a picture!" etc. etc. were heard through a general babble of voices. The critic for one of the leading trade publications in the amusement field was completely fooled and congratulated the cameraman for that particular newsreel for letting his camera run and picking up the informal comments of the exasperated reporters and photographers. All the sound was actually faked in the studio.[2]

Once the technique of sound-film editing was perfected, it allowed for considerable alteration of the original meaning and emphasis in any particular sequence. A British technician put it this way:

We claim that with judicious cutting and an adroit use of camera angles, it is simple to make a fool of anybody. We can distort the emphasis and meaning of Ministers' speeches not only by cutting out statements but by the simple use of long shot, medium shot, and close-up. For any statement said in close-up is given greater significance on the screen than one said in long shot. There is no end to the tricks we can play with this simple device.[3]

The time-honored practice of staging news events expressly for the newsreel camera also continued. Columnist Stanton Delaplane described such a staging which occurred in 1940:

In a photographically correct scene and with a script rewritten to the tastes of the newsreel patrons, Captain Leland E. Hawkins received the highest decoration which the Japanese government gives an alien—the Fifth Class Order of the Rising Sun.

Last Year Captain Hawkins' tanker Associated picked up 209 people from the nitrate-fired Bokuyo Maru. Yesterday on the after sundeck of the Asama Maru, at Pier 11, he was given the red-and-white stripped [sic] ribbon and ruby medallion entitling him to attend special functions held for the Emperor....

As usual, the newsreels took charge.

Before the participants had arrived, the newsreel men were busy rearranging the scene and the speeches. A pair of tables and bundled American and Japanese flags were whisked away.

The fifth class was dropped from the title of the decoration.

"Gives it more class," explained the sound men.

Kluver of the newsreels slipped on his head phones, spun his lenses and squinted through the eyepiece. The Consul looked around for confirmation and then said that he was happy to present this medal from the Emperor.

He took the medal from a black lacquered box and hung it in Captain Hawkins' buttonhole.

Captain Hawkins said to tell the Emperor he was grateful and anyone in his position would have done the same. The longshoremen began to argue on the deck just below the microphone.

Kluver slipped off his headphones and yelled "Quiet!"

"Let's try it again," he said. "Turn toward me when you say, 'and I feel anyone in my position and so and so.'"

"I'm cold," said Captain Hawkins. The Japanese all smiled politely.

"Please give my thanks to the Emperor and I feel—"the medal fell off his coat. The Captain juggled it back into his buttonhole and continued—"I feel that anyone in my place would have done the same...."

The cameras were moved up to a close-up and the Captain re-

peated his speech, adding this time that anyone would have done the same "where humanity is concerned. . . ."

"We really ought to tell what it's for," said Kluver. They set up the cameras again and someone asked the Captain how it happened.

"We were on a return trip from Manila," said the Captain, while the newsreel men squinted in their eyepieces. "We got an SOS from the Bokuyo Maru, and we were the nearest ship. When we arrived we found the lifeboats and floating wreckage and we took the people aboard."

"We ought to get in something about it exploded and burned to the water's edge, or something like that," said Kluver. "Let's do it over."

"It all depends on whether you want the truth or a story," said Captain Hawkins. . . .

Under prodding, the Captain gritted his teeth and told the staring camera that he had come to the Bokuyo Maru, which had fire in the hold, and later exploded and burned to the water's edge, in response to an SOS. The part about his being the nearest ship was deleted.[4]

The practice of re-creating events also continued, particularly in the coverage of political or governmental affairs. Hines reported that

such practice actually is encouraged by some politicians who don't like to have their original blurted and sometimes garbled statements recorded by the unprejudiced automaton which is the sound camera. In these cases, the original action often will be photographed by a hand camera; and a later, more staid and controlled reading of the controversial speech, statement or manifesto will be filmed with sound under ideal conditions. In the final newsreel, the two will be combined; the silent track will run with a commentator's remarks and blend from time to time into flashes of the staged speech. Nobody is really cheated; the politician gets a chance to look his best and the newsreel audience gets the more idealized version of what really went on.[5]

Occasionally newsreel re-creation had less pleasing consequences. William Montague, assignment editor for Paramount News, wrote:

Some years ago when the newsreels were less experienced, a kidnapping took place in San Jose, California. The son of a wealthy department store owner was kidnapped, murdered, and thrown into the bay. A couple of suspects were held in the San Jose jail. Well, one newsreel re-enacted the crime, showed where the kidnapping took place, how the man was killed, and thrown off the bridge. This was staged with the assistance of the police. . . .

The prints were rushed out. They reached the San Jose theatres one morning. The same night a mob took the San Jose jail apart and lynched those two suspects. The newsreel got the picture of the lynching, too. . . .[6]

On another occasion Paramount newsreel cameraman Henry de Sienna was hustled out of a strike-torn town by the police who suspected him of fomenting a riot so that he could secure some exciting newsreel shots of the resulting violence.[7]

The issue of authenticity is just as complicated in newsreel coverage as it is in newspaper publishing and television reporting. The ethical problems involved are complicated by the fact that there do not appear to be clear-cut standards—among either professional communicators or the general public—which distinguish legitimate "arrangement" of the elements of a news story from outright fraud. Three philosophical questions are involved: What is reality? What is truth? and, What is ethically right?

On the one hand, in a week's time there is very little hard news —that is, actual events which happen whether or not reporters and cameramen are on hand to record it. The news is hard by virtue of its significance and immediate relevance to human beings. Not only is there little hard news from day to day, but the chances that a cameraman or reporter will be on hand to witness and record it are generally slight.

If newspapers, television newscasts, and the now-defunct motion picture newsreels had had to depend upon first-hand records of such events, they would have had to go out of business years ago. Instead, the press spends most of its time either re-creating hard news or manufacturing an artificial news event—as when a reporter asks a political figure what his reaction will be if an opponent pursues a hypothetical course of action. If the politician responds, then the reporter has a story. If, better still, the man's opponent responds to the first man's reaction, then the reporter has another story, all of which fills the columns of the newspaper from day to day and allows the newspaper and its reporters to survive economically.

So it was for the motion picture newsreel. What I have described is a form of soft news—the reportage of events which did not happen entirely spontaneously but which were partly caused to happen by newsmen or photographers. Historian Daniel Boorstin terms this kind of incident a "pseudo event" and in his writings has provided a frightening picture of contemporary Americans whose perceptions are overwhelmed and confused by the mass media's never-ending manufacture of such events.[8]

In 1961, Walter Wilcox, professor of journalism in the University of California at Los Angeles, conducted a study which sought to determine the attitudes of both laymen and professional newsmen regarding the ethics of the staged photograph or motion picture news scene. A set of ten ethical problems was presented to several hundred members of the public, still photographers, television newsmen, and managing editors of newspapers. The respondents were asked to rate each of the situations with respect to the ethics involved in their operation. Two examples of the ten situations will suffice to illustrate the nature of the study:

Situation 1: Murder Trial. A photographer attempts to get a shot of a woman murder trial defendant, but she consistently evades him by shielding her face or ducking behind her escorting wardens. The photographer spots another woman who looks like the defendant, and by diffusing the light and adjusting the focus he gets a striking picture which no one will challenge as being faked.

Situation 2: Ground breakers. A photographer covers a ground breaking ceremony for a new church. Local dignitaries have already turned the first spadeful of earth, before the photographer arrives. He asks that the ceremony be repeated. The dignitaries cooperate, and he gets his picture.[9]

After treating the results of the study statistically, Wilcox concluded that, "despite certain significant differences, the four groups of respondents were in remarkable agreement."[10] For example, the overwhelming majority of all respondents agreed that situation 1 was unethical but that situation 2 was not unethical. According to Wilcox: "Disagreement occurred to the highest degree in situations that involved hard news, and that also were somewhat complex. . . . photographers regard their interpretive prerogatives more liberally than do the other groups."[11] Of particular interest was Wilcox's conclusion that "the public has become conditioned to standard staging practices and, in general, interprets the practice in the same context as do the newsmen."[12]

In the history of newsreel production the faking of newsreel content to augment deficient or insufficient footage for the week's release was a frequent practice, commonly admitted and sometimes boasted of by newsreel editors and cameramen. However, the purposeful inclusion of political propaganda was another matter. It is the matter of communication *intent* that seems most pertinent here, for, although a study of the American newsreel reveals occasional evidence of content manipulation for political purposes, it is an entirely different matter to find conclusive evidence of any consistent and organized propaganda campaign. No one in the history of the American newsreel has ever admitted to such an intent or effort. Lacking any such damning admissions, the best that one can do in a history such as this is to examine the flood of critical literature which followed the introduction of sound in the newsreel, on the assumption that where commentators and critics professed to find fire there may at least have been a few wisps of smoke. The following quotations, each from a different critic (some of them with political axes of their own to grind), suggest the virulence with which newspapers and periodical writers questioned the impartiality of the motion picture sound newsreel. They contrast sharply with the trusting endorsements of newsreel objectivity which were written during the silent newsreel period:

1935:   *The newsreel is without doubt the most effective type of film for propagandizing....*

There exist at least two ways of combating fascism and militarism on the screen. The first is to protest such films as ... "The March of Time" and Hearst Metrotone News, with an organized campaign of letters and phone calls to impress the theatre managers....

A second method, which has been suggested by Richard S. Ames, is to demand a congressional investigation of the film industry, similar to the munitions investigation.[13]

1935:   *... "newsreels" arrange sequences of events in such a way as to point a definite moral while ostensibly confining themselves to the presentation of news.*[14]

1936:   *A camera records actuality; and there are some who say that it is the only approach to the absolute in description. Yet anyone who has written captions, or has edited film, knows that no spoken witness may be suborned so easily as can a mute photograph.*[15]

1937:   *... the adage that "the camera never lies" is, of course, nonsense.*[16]

1945:   *News has divorced Truth and eloped with Politics. Their offspring is Propaganda....*

As in journalism, screen news displays an ever-increasing

*tendency to become tied up with views. Long before 1939,
partaking of partiality, the news reel and the news bulletin
apparently had no alternative but to ally themselves to
politics, a move involving an ever-greater projection of
propaganda. . . .*

    Film lends itself to skilful shaping. It is dangerous.[17]

1947:   *The motion picture camera in particular is a natural liar;
and it lies more artfully with the aid of a willing cameraman
or editor. Among the five United States newsreels today, as
a consequence, there is no more attempt at pure objectivity
than there is in ordinary "straight" news reporting.*[18]

1948:   *As for authenticity, some newsreels are almost as phony as
the old staged photographs of the sinking of the* Maine *in
1898, which were shown in the nickelodeons. . . . The films
are saturated with anti-Communist and pro-military propaganda.*[19]

The newsreel release most frequently criticized for its alleged
propaganda intent was that of the Hearst organization, *News of
the Day*, released by MGM. Possibly Hearst's reputation for colorful newspaper journalism was transferred in many people's minds
to his motion picture operation. In matters of this sort the detection of bias remains very much a matter of opinion. Certainly,
liberal writers of the day were eager to find and expose propaganda
effort in all of Hearst's journalistic enterprises. Justified or not,
reaction against the Hearst newsreel became so strong that by the
mid-1930's it was fairly common for audiences to boo the reel and
to picket the theaters that ran it. Energetic boycott efforts were
conducted by liberal, pacifist, and Communist groups and publications, and formal protests were delivered to theater owners and
managers.[20] In a number of motion picture houses—for example,
those located at Amherst and Williams colleges—the Hearst newsreel was dropped entirely from the program. The harassment of
certain New York theaters, through picketing, boycott, and threat,
finally became so pronounced that the state of New York began

The largest and best financed of the sound newsreels was *Fox Movie-tone News,* which achieved distinction during the 1930's under the supervision of Truman Talley. Of all the American newsreel firms Fox Movietone was the best equipped for on-the-spot sound recording. By 1934 nearly all the one hundred Movietone cameramen on salary had complete sound equipment available to them, and they were expected to use it whenever circumstances allowed them to do so. (From Fox Movietonews, Inc.)

For many years the very popular Lowell Thomas served as Fox's chief commentator. (From Fox Movietonews, Inc.)

Some of the names who make **FOX MOVIETONE NEWS** the world's greatest newsreel

LOWELL THOMAS
Chief Commentator

TRUMAN TALLEY
Producer and General Manager

BENJAMIN MIGGINS
European Director

LAURENCE STALLINGS
Editor In-Chief

SIR MALCOLM CAMPBELL
British Editor

HARRY LAWRENSON
Foreign Editor and
Makeup Supervisor

GERALD SANGER
British Producer

RUSSELL MUTH
Central European Supervisor

ED THORGERSEN
Sports Commentator

LEW LEHR
Newsettes Commentator

LOUISE VANCE
Fashion Commentator

BONNEY POWELL
Far Eastern Supervisor

VYVYAN DONNER
Fashion Editor

EDMUND REEK
News Editor

You haven't a show without **FOX**

Facing page: The principal figures in the Fox Movietone international organization are shown at left in this 1935 advertisement. Within the next two years Sir Gordon Craig had joined the overseas Fox team as the British general manager; while, in the United States, Edmund Reek had moved up to become general manager under producer Truman Talley, Jack Haney succeeded Reek as news editor, Harry Lawrenson continued as foreign editor, and Arthur de Titta joined the firm as political editor. (From *Motion Picture Herald*, June 8, 1935.)

Fox Movietone's sound newsreels of Lindbergh were so successful that the company sent its crews all over the world to photograph famous celebrities as they spoke for the sound camera. One of the reluctant notables to be approached was George Bernard Shaw, who in 1928 finally consented to appear, but only on the condition that he could direct his own "show." Fox agreed, and an altogether delightful interview resulted. (From Fox Movietonews, Inc.)

Now playing every month in 11,000 theatres throughout the world

THE MARCH OF TIME

RKO RADIO

PRODUCED BY THE EDITORS OF LIFE AND TIME

"...the most significant motion picture development since the invention of sound."

DAVID SELZNIC[K]

"WHERE CAN I SEE THE MARCH OF TIME EACH MONTH...

IN NEW YORK'S GREAT RADIO CITY MUSIC HALL, each issue of THE MARCH OF TIME is shown for a full week, is seen by some one hundred and fifty thousand theatre goers.

Three years ago, the Editors of TIME introduced THE MARCH OF TIME in 432 theatres. This month it is being shown in over 11,000 theatres throughout the world, more theatres than play any other regular motion picture feature. On this and the next four pages are the names of every theatre in the United States and Canada now showing THE MARCH OF TIME every month.

..AND WHEN?"

To make sure of seeing each new issue of THE MARCH OF TIME write or phone the manager of your local theatre (as listed here) and ask him to let you know each month the exact days the new issue is to be shown in his theatre. He is prepared to give you this reminder service every month by telephone or postcard.

THEATRES NOW SHOWING THE MARCH OF TIME

ALABAMA	Goodwater	Rex
Alabama City	Rita	Greensboro	Strand
Alexander City		Greenville	Ritz
	Strand	Hanceville	Ritz
Aliceville	Palace	Huntsville	Lyric
Andalusia	Paramount		Merrimack Mills
Anniston	Ritz		Princess
Arab	Arab	Jacksonville	Princess
Ashland	Strand	Jasper	Jasper
Auburn	Tiger	La Fayette	La Fayette
Athens	Ritz	Leeds	Dixie
Atmore	Strand	Livingston	New
Bessemer	Grand	Lavern	Luverne
Birmingham		Marion	Bonita
Alabama, Famous,		Mobile	Century
Five Points,			Pike Roosevelt,
Woodlawn			Saenger
Brewton	Rita	Monroeville	Monroe
Brilliant	Boston	Montevallo	Strand
Brundidge	Brundidge	Montgomery	Maxwell
Camden	Camden		Field, Paramount
Clayton	Wadesnitze	Opelika	Opelika
Clayton	Clayton	Ozark	Ozark
Cordova	Dixie	Pell City	Lyric
Cullman	Lyric	Piedmont	Fox
Decatur	Princess	Prattville	Lyric
Dadeville	Ritz	Prichard	Rex
Demopolis	Marengo	Roanoke	Rita
Dothan	Houston	Samson	Broad
Elba	Elba	Scottsboro	Ritz
Ensley	Ensley	Selma	Academy
Eufaula	Lee	Sheffield	Ritz
Evergreen	Pix	Sylacauga	Ritz
Fairfax	Fairfax	Talladega	Ritz
Fairfield	Fairfield	Tallassee	Roxy
Fairhope	Fairhope	Troy	Enjoy
Fayette	Betsy	Tuscaloosa	Bama
Flomaton	Jackson		

Tuscumbia	Strand
Tuskegee	Macon
Union Spgs.	Lilfred
Uniontown	Strand
Warrior	Warrior
Wetumpka	Plaza
York	Sumter
ARIZONA	
Ajo	Oasis
Bisbee	Lyric
Buckeye	Buzie
Casa Grande	
	Paramount
Chandler	Rowena
Clarkdale	Grand
Clifton	Princess
Coolidge	Coolidge,
	Mesk
Cottonwood	Rialto
Douglas	Grand
Duncan	Duncan
Flagstaff	Liberty,
	Orpheum
Florence	Isis
Gilbert	Gilbert
Glendale	El Ray,
	Glendale
Globe · Fox, Alden
Grand Canyon	
	Community
Hayden	Rex
Holbrook	Roxy
Jerome	Rita
Kingman	Longs
McNary	Rivoli
Mesa	Nilu]
Miami	Grand

Facing page: In the spring of 1935, Time, Inc., introduced a radically different kind of newsreel called *The March of Time*. Its style was revolutionary—a unique mixture of cinematic exposition and journalistic punctuation that defied convention. It editorialized openly, infuriating its enemies and often alienating its friends. And it did all of this with a vigor, artistry, and showmanship which put to shame its less daring competitors. (From Time, Inc.)

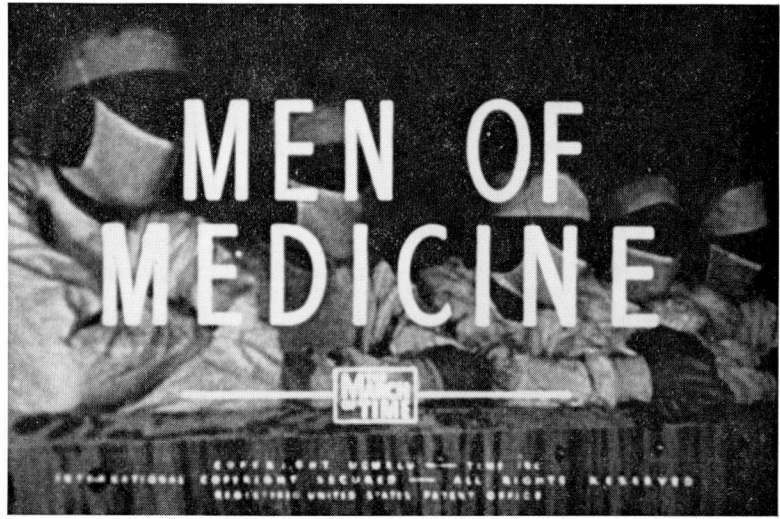

After a couple of years of experimentation, *The March of Time* arrived at a format which treated only one subject in each twenty-minute issue. In 1937 the series received an Academy Award "for having revolutionized one of the most important branches in the industry—the newsreel." In fact, however, *The March of Time* had not the slightest effect upon the structure, content, or style of the American newsreel. (From Time, Inc.)

By far the most dramatic coverage in newsreel history occurred on the evening of May 6, 1937, when cameramen gathered for routine filming of the landing of the German zeppelin *Hindenburg* at Lakehurst, New Jersey. On that day the usually punctual *Hindenburg* was late, and as darkness approached, at least one cameraman gave up and left.

Suddenly, as the airship approached the mooring mast and prepared to anchor, fire broke out, and the extremely flammable hydrogen gas ignited from one end of the ship to the other. The giant zeppelin slowly settled to the earth, carrying its passengers with it.

Stunned cameramen continued to grind out footage as the bulk of the ship, now totally engulfed in flame, struck the ground.

In less than a minute the *Hindenburg* lay in flaming ruins. More than a third of the passengers perished in the disaster, and most of the survivors were seriously injured. For newsreel cameramen this epic film represented the high point of hard-news film coverage. The scenes shown here are from the footage shot by *Fox Movietone News* cameraman Al Gold. (All four photographs from Fox Movietonews, Inc.)

If it moves, shoot it! Violence, action, and speed were qualities valued highly by newsreel editors. Automobile racing and daredevil riding were especially popular subjects. These *Fox Movietone News* shots were made in the 1930's. (From Fox Movietonews, Inc.)

Disasters—natural and man-made—were standard newsreel fare. Nothing has more journalistic or pictorial excitement. Above: The periodic floods on the Mississippi River and its tributaries in the 1930's provided both awe-inspiring and heart-rending material. Audiences identified with the homeless, and the newsreel played a role in encouraging federal legislation that led to the control of the river. One of the first American newsreels, issued in 1911, featured a staged train collision. In the 1930's newsreels were still showing train wrecks (below). (Both photographs from Fox Movietonews, Inc.)

Not all newsreel fare dealt with momentous subjects. The latest women's fashions, conventional and bizarre, were regularly featured. Some companies hired fashion specialists to research and stage these sequences. The see-through dresses below appear to be made of cellophane. These clips are from the 1930's. (Both photographs from Fox Movietonews, Inc.)

MGM's 1938 production *Too Hot to Handle* capitalized on the alleged glamour and romance of the newsreel business. Clark Gable starred as the cameraman and Myrna Loy as his girl. (Copyright by Metro-Goldwyn-Mayer Studios and reproduced with its permission.)

The most unforgettable scene of the Chinese-Japanese War was this shot of a helpless baby crying in the rubble of the Shanghai South Station (a civilian target) immediately after Japanese planes bombed the area in August, 1937. Fifteen babies and two hundred adults were killed in the raid. The scene was photographed by Hearst cameraman Wong Hai-Sheng ("Newsreel Wong"). *Fox Movietone News* also ran the footage, and this still photo was reproduced in newspapers and magazines throughout the world. It was estimated that more than 136 million people saw this shot on motion picture screens or in print. (From *The Hearst Metrotone News*.)

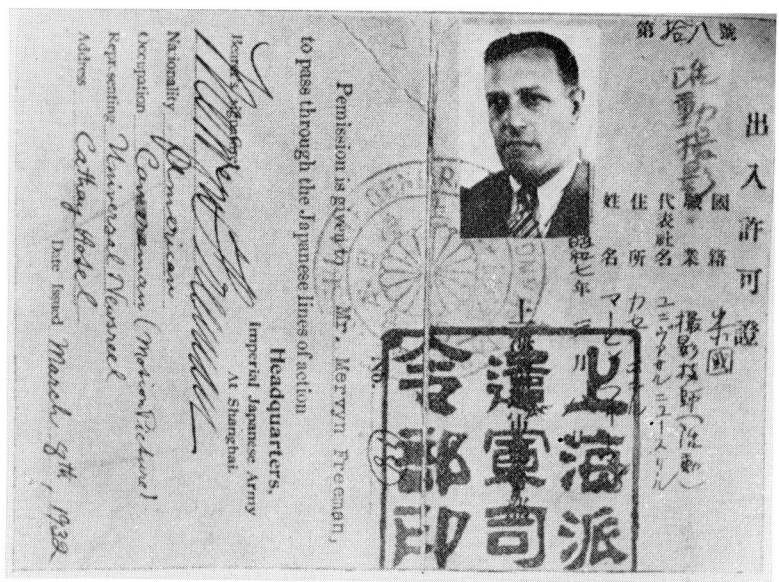

Before the entry of the United States into World War II, American newsreel cameramen were able to photograph the Chinese-Japanese War from both sides of the battlefield. This identification pass, issued by the Imperial Japanese Army at Shanghai, allowed Universal cameraman Mervyn Freeman to pass through Japanese lines. (From the author's collection.)

Perhaps the newsreel's most poignant scene is the one above, showing
British Prime Minister Neville Chamberlain at London Airport on
September 30, 1938. He has just returned from the Munich Conference,
where Czechoslovakia was sacrificed to Nazi Germany for "peace in
our time." Chamberlain is waving a document he and Adolf Hitler
signed renouncing war. World War II was less than a year away. (From
the author's collection.)

The Japanese attack on Pearl Harbor, Hawaii, December 7, 1941. Despite the surprise with which the enemy forces moved, American military photographers secured some excellent shots of the disaster— all of which were immediately suppressed by military censors. Here the ammunition magazine of the U.S.S. *Shaw* explodes. (U.S. Navy photograph.)

Above: A U.S. Navy photographer made this shot of American planes burning on the runway at the Naval Air Station at Pearl Harbor. The Japanese attack was so unexpected that few American planes made it into the air. Most still photographs and motion-picture footage of scenes such as this were not released to the public for more than a year after the attack, in contrast to the almost instantaneous coverage of the Vietnam War via electronic satellite.

Below: The U.S.S. West Virginia burns out of control following the attack on Pearl Harbor. Badly damaged, the ship was not returned to service until late 1942. (Both photographs from U.S. Navy.)

considering legal action against the protestors under provisions of the penal code and the United States Department of Justice began investigating the matter—apparently considering deportation of alien agitators on the ground that their activities were subversive. Most of those involved in protests and subsequent arrests were young persons, ranging in age from 17 to 23.[21] Finally, in 1936, Hearst removed his name from the newsreel altogether and re-named it *News of the Day*, the title under which it continued to operate until its demise in 1967.[22]

By contrast, the only newsreel which seemed to command some respect from politically independent writers and which generally escaped charges of either left-wing or right-wing propaganda was *Paramount News*. Paramount was the only newsreel organization to assign men to the Memorial Day demonstration—which turned into a riot—at the Republic Steel plant in South Chicago in 1937. It was also the only newsreel to cover the march of pro-Fascist Sir Oswald Mosley through London's East End in 1937.[23] Newton Meltzer points out that

Paramount News, in a "Strike Report," summarized the major strikes of early 1946 quite fairly, concluding with a remarkable treatment of the support which the town of Bloomfield, N.J., gave to its embattled electrical workers. . . . It was Paramount News which alone presented an unbiased report on the Chinese Communists. And while the Greek crisis was aflame, only Paramount dared touch it."[24]

Added another writer:

Not all the newsreels are equally guilty [of propaganda]. The Hearst Metrotone News seems to have been the worst offender with Pathé News coming second, while casual observation leads one to conclude that Paramount News is far less given to propaganda.[25]

Charges of propaganda intent made during this period usually came from liberal writers who professed to detect militaristic themes, antilabor sentiment, and an over-all right-wing tone in newsreel sequences. One writer, Selden Menefee, even conducted his own content analysis which, so he alleged, revealed that

militaristic scenes make up 10.4 percent of all items shown. In forty-five newsreels there were thirty-two shots of such fascinating subjects as military reviews, naval maneuvers and bombing planes. Twelve more shots of civil aviation contain military implications. By way of contrast, there were only ten shots, 3.3 percent of all, that could be construed as pacifistic in effect.[26]

Added Oswald Villard, editor of *Nation*:

I do not go to the movies very often, but not in a year have I seen a newsreel which did not play up the military or the navy. I have never seen a Hearst movie yet that did not contain deliberate propaganda of this kind. . . . I saw the worst piece of propaganda I have ever seen some two weeks ago when the pictures of three recent criminals, or alleged criminals, were shown. It was stated that all three of these men had been in jails and insane asylums, and the voice behind the films enunciated the theory that we were emptying our jails and insane asylums in order that their inmates might continue to commit horrible crimes. There was no explanation as to who stood behind this piece of propaganda. It was not news. It had no scientific background nor did it cite any authorities. It was actually a direct argument that if any man ever got into jail or into an insane asylum he should never be released.[27]

Kracauer and Lyford* added:

When Cardinal Spellman and President Truman spoke on St. Patrick's Day, it was the anti-Communist portions of their addresses that were singled out for screening. Extensive shots of army maneuvers, diving planes, smoking rockets and General Mac-

---

*This and subsequent quotations in this chapter from "A Duck Crosses Main Street," by Siegfried Kracauer and Joseph Lyford, are cited in the notes at the end of this book and are reprinted by permission of *The New Republic*, Copyright 1948 Harrison Blaine of New Jersey, Inc.

Arthur reviewing his troops in Japan are screened while sound tracks blare do-or-die college marching songs. . . .

Labor conflicts are usually treated with ill-concealed bias. During the soft-coal strike last year, elaborate shots of abandoned mines and joking, idle miners invited movie-goers to ponder the destructive effects of the shutdown. The cameras did not go into the miners' side of the story. The newsreels' way of treating the packing-house workers' strike was to give prominence to signs in butcher shops proclaiming the rising cost of meat.[28]

Newsreel editors and managers defended their selection of content on the basis of popular interest and entertainment value. It was argued, for example, that military subjects, although charged with political implications, furnished the same sort of exciting movement and pictorial display as that other popular category, sports.[29]

From time to time suits for libel and slander were filed against newsreel companies for allegedly perpetrating untruths.[30] However, I have been able to find only one instance when a major newsreel company retracted a story. The incident was described in a 1933 trade-paper news item:

This week for the first time in history of newsreels, so far as is known, a reel is flashing a retraction. Paramount several weeks ago made a clip of Prof. Tugwell, one of the Rooseveltian brain trustees, in which the Prof. used a certain name to identify certain brands of patent medicines. It so happened that the name is that of a New York chemist. Word got back to the U.S. Dept. of Agriculture and this week the Department announces the error, via the Par reel.[31]

Much newsreel criticism of the 1930's can possibly be traced to politically oversensitive writers who confused a general lack of imagination, taste, skill, and intelligence in the newsreels' make-up for political bias and militaristic fervor. Still there were occasional instances of unmistakable propaganda content, the most blatant of which involved the manufacture of a series of bogus sound newsreels called *The Inquiring Reporter*, issued during the 1936 political campaign in California, when Socialist Upton Sinclair ran for state governor under the slogan "End Poverty in California." Among the many projects which Sinclair planned to launch during his administration was one which called for the state of California to produce films and operate theaters in competition with those of the commercial industry.[32]

According to *New York Times* critic Bosley Crowther, these bogus newsreels were photographed and edited by a Metro-Goldwyn-Mayer crew on orders from production head Irving Thalberg.[33] Harry Pringle, of the *New Yorker*, described the newsreel coverage of the campaign:

The strategy was simple and effective. Cameras and sound trucks travelled up and down the state, and hundreds of shots were made of average Californians. These were . . . tacked onto the twice-a-week newsreel releases. The plot of these miniature dramas was stark in its brevity. One question was asked of the surprised Californians upon whom, as they worked at their daily chores, the sound apparatus and cameras swooped: "Are you going to vote for Sinclair or Merriam?"

Strangely, when the releases were shown in California's movie houses, they proved to be the best comedies since Charlie Chaplin's two-reelers. The pro-Merriam voters were unspectacular enough. They consisted of hard-working filling-station men, honest clerks, homely housewives, well-dressed business executives, and intelligently pretty girls. They said earnestly that Merriam was their man because they loved their homes and their state. The guffaws came when the pro-Sinclair enthusiasts were flashed on the screen. They scratched themselves as they spoke. They were dishevelled, bleary-eyed, shabby and scrofulous. They stammered or lisped or spoke in squeaky voices. They proclaimed that they were for Sinclair because he meant soft jobs and easy money. A few admitted openly that they were Communists.[34]

Added Thomas Sugrue: "The scenes were staged, if not actually faked, and I, seeing them in San Francisco and Los Angeles theaters that summer, thought the freedom of the reels had come to an end. Nothing like it has happened since."[35]

Most criticism of the newsreels during this period came from liberals. On at least one occasion, however, equally vocal conservatives reacted to left-wing propaganda in the newsreels when New Dealer Harry Hopkins contracted with Pathé, on behalf of the Works Progress Administration, for a series of New Deal newsreels designed to feature the successes and triumphs of the Roosevelt administration. The idea for a WPA-sponsored newsreel was said to have struck Hopkins in February, 1936, when he viewed a Pathé newsreel which highlighted WPA activities in Indiana.[36] Impressed with the propaganda potential of the newsreel—and with the presidential elections only nine months away—Hopkins invited bids from forty-one motion picture producers for the production of thirty WPA newsreel issues "to present to the citizens of a particular State, or area, information about the operations of WPA in that State, or area."[37] Only five companies responded, and Pathé won the contract with a bid of $4,280 a reel. Without additional charge Pathé also agreed to distribute one such WPA newsreel each month as part of its own regular newsreel release. Predictably, this WPA-Pathé production provoked a good deal of criticism. Managers of the competing newsreels charged that the contract violated reportorial integrity. The *Motion Picture Herald* headlined: "WPA Setting Out to Buy Way to Theater Public."[38] Republican House leader Bertrand Snell stated, "I, for one, vigorously protest this shocking distortion of the relief program to the direct services of the New Deal Presidential campaign."[39] The Republican National Committee called it "propaganda . . . paid for out of relief funds."[40] All in all, the incident provided a refreshing change from the usual charges of right-wing newsreel propaganda.

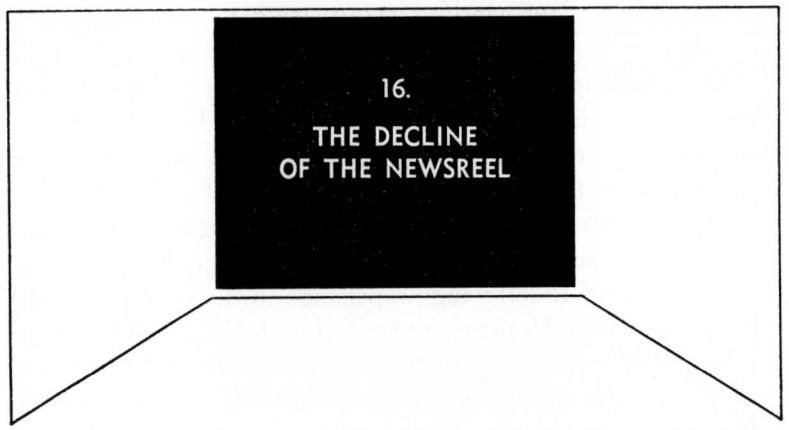

16.
THE DECLINE
OF THE NEWSREEL

Following the introduction of sound a number of factors began to contribute to the decline of newsreel quality and the eventual failure of America's newsreel organizations in the 1950's and 1960's. These factors included a decline in newsreel competition, an increase in the severity of newsreel censorship, the introduction of journalistically unhealthy production innovations during World War II, and the postwar competition of television news services.

Once the novelty of sound had faded, so too did the fierce rivalries which had become characteristic of newsreel production during the silent-film era. Whereas the cameramen of the 1920's had gone to any lengths to secure scoops, to rush their footage into release first, and even to sabotage their competitors, the cameramen of the 1930's cooperated with one another, participated in rota pools, and scorned the old-fashioned individualistic brand of journalistic rivalry. As early as 1934 a writer for the *New Yorker*, Morris Markey, observed that "little remains of the fierce competition between rival organizations which marked so boisterously the early days of the newsreel business."[1]

Such a decay in competitive spirit followed from a number of causes, all of which were apparent by the middle 1930's. First, the chances of securing exclusive footage decreased once the industry had reached the point where major news events in the world were covered by all the major newsreel organizations. The coverage of scheduled events was carefully preplanned by all five newsreel producers, sometimes in concert, weeks in advance. Political personalities, commercial manufacturers, governmental agencies, and other groups conscious of public relations took care to see that all the newsreel firms were treated with fair and equal consideration. Sports events were nearly always photographed jointly, and the chances of an unexpected major news break occurring anywhere on the globe in the presence of fewer than two or three competing cameramen became slim indeed.

Second, from 1930 on it was the practice of American firms to exchange footage not only with their foreign competitors but with each other as well. A monotonous similarity of newsreel content crept into the newsreel programs throughout the industry— to an increasing extent each of the five newsreel companies began screening identical footage. Noted one writer in 1936, "If one of Pathé's cameras had broken down at Governor Landon's notification ceremonies in Topeka, probably Fox or Universal would have helped out with an extra print."[2]

Third, cameramen unionized. By the late 1930's virtually every staff cameraman belonged to one of the four locals of the International Alliance of Theatrical Stage Employees: Local 644 in New York, Local 666 in Chicago, Local 659 in Los Angeles, and Local 665 in Toronto, Canada.[3] Union organization served to emphasize the commonality of the cameramen's interests and to discourage lively competition. As Kracauer and Lyford observed in 1948, "The cameramen travel in a tightly knit group, shoot the same stuff, and look with a fishy eye at colleagues who attempt to get exclusive stories."[4] A cameraman who had the bad taste to scoop his rivals was sometimes discriminated against.

George Krainukov, Universal's lone-wolf Far Eastern representative, was a cameraman who persisted in perpetuating traditional newsreel rivalries. Krainukov stated that on one occasion in the late 1930's safe passage had been arranged for Far Eastern newsreelmen to travel between the Japanese and Chinese lines to

271

allow for a few hours' coverage of Japanese military activity. An automobile was provided for the transportation of the cameramen, but after everyone else had piled into the car, Krainukov was informed that "there was no more room available," and the automobile took off without him. Infuriated, he shouldered his camera and tripod and began walking across no-man's land by himself. As he approached the Japanese lines, he was shot and wounded, rushed to a Japanese field hospital, and treated.

The Japanese military authorities were so impressed by his devotion to duty that they gave him the run of the area for several days, during which time he managed to scoop his competitors on every subject of news value. When Krainukov finally left the Far East, traveled to America, and took out United States citizenship, he was not allowed to join the cameramen's union. He spent the last years of his life working as a technician at the campus camera shop of the University of Southern California.[5]

Perhaps the most vivid example of the decline in competitive spirit occurred when Norman Alley and Eric Mayell, veteran newsreelmen representing Universal and Fox Movietone, filmed the bombing of the American gunboat *Panay* in 1937, the release of which has already been described. Having filmed one of the greatest scoops of the decade, the two competing cameramen not only cooperated in the follow-up coverage of the story but also agreed to guard each other's footage in the event of an unforeseen catastrophe. Union official Herbert Aller described the arrangement:

... *the Panay incident was marked by a great scoop being tossed aside because of professional loyalty and the mutual promise of two brother IA members.*

Norman Alley's fine gesture in guarding the film of another newsreel company [Fox] while in shipment from Shanghai to the U.S.A. was a splendid example of how a pact between two brother newsreel cameramen is carried out despite the fact that the men are competing against each other. When the bombard-

*ment commenced, neither Eric Mayell nor Norman Alley knew
who would come out alive [they both did], but being fellow
workers and loyal to each other, an understanding was made and
when circumstances developed as they did, Alley carried out
his promise in fine sportsmanship style.*[6]

Finally, the introduction of the rota pool-coverage system destroyed whatever vestiges of intercompany competition may have
survived by the end of the 1930's. The rota system provided for the
assignment of a single cameraman, or a limited number of cameramen, to a particular news event. The footage was shared by all
interested newsreel producers. Such pools were in operation as
early as 1935, when cameramen Roy Kluver, of Hearst; Seebach
and MacGrath, of Fox; and John Herrmann, of Paramount,
filmed the cruise of the American "Black Fleet" on maneuvers in
Alaskan waters.* The combined footage was shared by the parent
companies.[7] Much of the Far Eastern coverage of the late 1930's
was also pooled.

With the outbreak of World War II it became necessary for
the United States government to establish rota pools to provide
satisfactory civilian coverage of the war. Clearly, there were too
many military operations underway to make it possible for any
one newsreel firm to cover all of them. Colonel William Mason
Wright, head of the Pictorial Branch of the Bureau of Public
Relations of the Department of War, described the mechanics of
the system:

*I propose the idea of pooling our resources for the duration of
the war. If each newsreel company will provide us with two cameramen for each theater of operations, I think we can adequately
cover all theaters. The work of all cameramen will be censored
and processed by the War Department and the Navy Depart-*

---

* The "Black Fleet" was a fleet of American warships assembled for six weeks of
war games during April and May, 1935, in Alaskan waters near Unalaska and Dutch
Harbor. The ships included the *Minneapolis*, the *Saratoga*, and the *Utah*.

ment, and then distributed to the five newsreel organizations, along with all the work of the Army and Navy cameramen. You will all use the same films, of course, and there will be no more competition among you, but we feel that this is the only way of bringing the war in film to the American people.[8]

With the introduction of the rota system the plan for a newsreel association which Educational Pictures had futilely proposed back in 1929, had finally come to fruition. Such wartime pools were necessary, of course, but the effect was to destroy competition for the duration of the war. The system very nearly ruined the newsreel theater chains, too, most of which subscribed to all five newsreel services. As a result of the rota system theater owners received virtually identical footage from all of them. The rota pool system was officially concluded in 1945,[9] but the practice continued by agreement in the coverage of many major news stories. As an editorial in *Sequence* magazine pointed out, there were clear financial savings for producers:

The five companies have exclusive rights to . . . [certain news events], . . . and "it does no harm to profits if you can buy pictures at one-fifth the cost of making your own." While individual cameramen may be expert and enterprising, half their assignments are trivial or stereotyped from the start, the material they obtain will be sliced up and handed round, and the results cannot be anything but fragmentary and uniform.[10]

In 1955, long after the rota system had been introduced and the many other factors already mentioned had begun to sap the competitive spirit of the newsreel industry, veteran cameraman Charles Peden, who had turned to television newsreel production for a living, looked back over his years of experience and reflected upon the effect which the decline in competition had had upon the destiny of the motion picture newsreel. Wrote Peden:

Those of us who make and love the newsreel know its value.

The public once held it in high esteem and would embrace it quickly. Honest exhibitors know in their hearts that it was a great asset, an attraction people sought. . . .

Even now, one by one the top men behind the cameras, disillusioned and broken-hearted, are leaving decades-old connections to join the ranks of TV newsreel producers because they know that the magic spark, so necessary to good reporting, exists there—the competitive spirit and drive. . . .

[Earlier assignment editors] were the men of vision and daring who sent their boys with Byrd to the Antarctic, over the North Pole, into volcanoes, through swamps and impenetrable jungles; the boys who okayed chartered aircraft, boats, trains and even dogsleds to get the story. And almost without exception their men came back with epics. Stories that caught the public fancy and made exhibitors paste one-sheets outside their theatres.

When an atmosphere of daring pervades a news shop it rubs on the men and gets into the story. That devil-may-care, to-hell-with-the-expense-account coverage that makes the auditors cringe, but the public applaud, and the cash registers sing.

Newsreels need a face-lifting and injection of new drive. They need fresh window dressing in the form of new techniques and a renewal of every trick in the bag—competition, not cooperation with each other.[11]

By 1955, however, it was far too late to salvage the motion picture newsreel. As early as 1939 the only kind of competition which was to flourish in the years to come had already begun to appear. At the opening of the New York World's Fair in May, 1939, the National Broadcasting Company had operated live television cameras alongside motion picture newsreel cameras for the first time in the United States as President Roosevelt opened the fair to the public.[12] In 1939, however, the TV cameras were something of a novelty, and no one seemed to take them very seriously.

Even during the era of the silent film the American motion picture newsreel had never been free of editorial control and censorship. With the addition of sound and the growth of political, economic, and military tensions in the 1930's, censorship became even more frequent, severe, and inevitable.

The term censorship is used latitudinously here to embrace not merely "prior restraint" by official bodies of review but also other forms of content control operating both from within (internal) and without (external) the motion picture industry. The varieties of newsreel content control appear to have fallen into three categories:

1. Control of cameramen, their access to news events, and their exposed negative (external control).

2. Editorial control of the newsreel subject matter and presentation (internal control, sometimes influenced by external coercion).

3. Control of distribution and exhibition of the finished newsreel (internal and external control).

Control of the mobility and activities of newsreel cameramen was exercised by a number of governments in Europe and Asia. Many countries, such as the Soviet Union and (toward the end of the 1930's) Nazi Germany did not allow any American cameramen to operate within their borders.* Others, such as China, Ethiopia, and Japan, placed severe restrictions upon the movements of foreign cameramen, supervised their work, and imposed unequivocal limitations upon the kinds of subject matter which they were allowed to photograph.

In China, for example, the Nanking government promulgated a set of regulations governing the pictorial reportage of newsreel cameramen. These regulations prohibited the photography of "(1) Things prejudicial to [the] racial dignity of the Chinese

---

* This statement is perhaps an oversimplification. For example, the documentary film maker Julian Bryan was allowed to take photographs in both countries, as were a few other cameramen from time to time, but only under unusual circumstances, for short periods of time, and under close supervision and restrictions. Continuous, comprehensive newsreel coverage in these countries was not permitted to Americans, however.

nation. (2) Actions contrary to the Three Peoples Principles. (3) Things not of good morals and customs of the country. (4) Things superstitious or grotesque."[13] Such restrictions oftentimes worked to the detriment of the Nanking government, however, since they precluded the release of pictures which would have helped to marshal world opinion against Japanese aggression in the Far East.

Sometimes government authorities discriminated against particular cameramen or newsreel companies. In 1937 the Hearst cameraman "Newsreel" Wong photographed the Japanese bombing of South Station in Canton. One of the scenes captured by his camera (sometimes alleged, but never proved, to have been staged) showed an injured baby sitting in the middle of the rubble, crying. The scene became one of the most celebrated symbols of the Far East conflict; over 136 million people were said to have seen it. As a consequence of its release the Japanese government was reported to have placed a price of fifty thousand dollars on Wong's head.[14]

During the execution of Cuban rebels in 1935, Universal cameraman Abelardo Domingo walked into the prison courtyard one morning, set up his camera, and photographed some exceptionally grisly scenes of a firing squad in action. No one objected at the time. When the Universal newsreel issue containing the footage reached Havana, however, infuriated officials arrested Domingo and sentenced him to be shot. Only frantic intercession by Universal representatives kept Domingo from the firing squad. Before the affair ended, the officials from Universal were also arrested, and then, a few days later, all of them, including Domingo, released without explanation.[15]

In some cases the subjects of newsreel coverage exercised control over the cameraman's work. Strikers and rioters often singled out newsreelmen for their wrath, since the footage photographed under such circumstances often ended up in the hands of a district attorney, who used it for prosecution and the securing of injunctions. Other individuals, such as distressed sharecroppers and migratory workers, resented intrusions upon their privacy and prevented cameramen from operating in their vicinity. The interference of police and the confiscation of film by company guards also occurred during this period in the coverage of aircraft disasters.[16]

As for the newsreel companies themselves there seemed to be no evidence of any internal prohibitions against the *photography* of subject matter. Managing editors appeared to encourage the *filming* of all newsworthy events, the footage of which, once processed, could then be edited and shaped to conform to the company's editorial point of view.

Distinct editorial policies existed within the newsreel business. Some of those policies were common to all the firms; others were observed only in particular studios. As mentioned earlier, all the studios eschewed controversial subject matter. For example, the Fox Corporation ruled in 1931 that its theaters and newsreels could not show scenes of a "controversial nature . . . on which reaction might be divided."[17] One of the major newsreel firms (possibly Fox) was also reported to have ruled that

no news from Germany whatever was to be used in the newsreel unless it was revolution against the Hitler regime. This applied not only to news of a political nature but of any nature at all. . . . "We won't publicize Hitler or Hitler's Germany," was the last word of those who controlled that particular newsreel.[18]

As late as 1938, at the time *The March of Time* released "Inside Nazi Germany—1938," the publishers of *Time* and *Life* stated that an industry-wide policy forbade the exhibition of scenes of Adolf Hitler.[19] The unfortunate and unintended effect of such prohibitions, of course, was to cloak in anonymity the machinations of the Nazi government during its early years at just the time public opinion should have been well informed.

To some extent foreign governments were able to control the editing of newsreels through coercion. In 1934 cameramen secured photographs of the French riots in the Place de la Concorde. The French authorities failed to confiscate all the negatives but ended by arresting a cameraman for an American firm whose film had been spirited out of the country. Anthony North reported:

Before the pictures could be released in England or re-shipped to the United States the London company head received a frantic wire from his Paris colleague pleading that the film be destroyed immediately lest he languish indefinitely in an unattractive French jail. . . . Ultimately pictures of the French riots were released by the newsreels but they were carefully censored. No shots of the actual attack on police and troops were permitted to be shown.[20]

As North observed: "It seemed incredible that the French government, from Paris, France, could dictate the newsreel fare of the people of Paris, Ill., or Phoenix, Ariz. But it can be done!"[21]

At the time of the marriage of the Duke of Windsor to the American divorcee Wallis Simpson in 1937, one cameraman—André Conquet, of Paramount—was allowed to photograph the ceremony, held on the grounds of the Chateau de Candé, near Tours, France. The footage was made available, rota-pool fashion, to the other newsreel companies. These films were widely exhibited throughout the United States. Within England and throughout the British Empire, however, the pictures were never shown. A news item in *Motion Picture Herald* explained why:

"Suggestions" from high authority convinced motion picture officials in England that there would be no interest in the pictures of the ceremony....

It was intimated that any company ignoring the hints might encounter difficulty in obtaining passes for the filming of official functions.[22]

Almost without exception, scenes of death and dead bodies, maiming, gross injury, and others of questionable taste were eliminated by the editors. Paradoxically, although cameramen went to great trouble, at their supervisors' urgings, to catch moments of violence and accident—particularly in the filming of auto races, airplane stunt flying, and other dangerous events—such scenes were usually cut either just before the moment of impact or before the reality of death or injury became apparent to the audience. Explained Emile Schnurmacher:

In making a dramatic newsreel sequence, it is not necessary to have a fatal ending, for the actual death scene is generally deleted by the newsreel editor. . . .

. . . suspense and not tragedy is the dominant theme sought by the newsreel man, and actual death scenes are left behind in the cutting room.[23]

The same prohibitions applied to war footage. Newsreel union official Herbert Aller wrote in 1938 that

only a small part of the actual horrors of war, recorded by the camera, has been shown to theatre patrons, because of the restrictions imposed by good taste and fear of shock to more sensitive natures from the astounding scenes.[24]

Editorial censorship of a relatively unimportant nature, tending to favor the public image of important celebrities and political figures, was carried on regularly. For example, one company shelved a unique sound-on-film shot of Lindbergh speaking in an aside to his wife. The scene, although innocuous in nature, was not released out of respect for Lindbergh's refusal to speak for the sound newsreel.[25] An article by Edward Harrison in *Ken*, the irreverent picture magazine of the 1930's, described a number of other examples of censorship of celebrity footage.[26] A ludicrously funny scene of the Duke of Windsor tripping over a sound cable at his wedding was eliminated. President Roosevelt was never photographed walking with his crippled gait or being pushed about in his wheelchair. Scenes of King Victor Emanuel of Italy (who was only slightly taller than a midget) were always edited to avoid showing him being lifted onto his horse or seating himself on his special elevated chair at the Opera House in Rome. Understandably scissored was a remark said to have been made in a sound newsreel showing a ceremony at which Vice-President John Nance Garner and House Speaker William Bankhead congratulated Associate Justice Hugo Black, who had been newly appointed to the Supreme Court. The Vice-President turned to Black and said, jokingly, "If anything ever happens, I'll know where to go when I want the right decision."[27]

Sometimes internal censorship assumed more serious proportions. On Memorial Day, 1937, CIO strikers and sympathizers congregated at the violence-torn Republic Steel plant in South Chicago for what was meant to be a peaceful demonstration. Many women and children were also present. Some of the demonstrators walked about carrying signs. Apparently only one company—Paramount—had considered the occasion important enough to send a cameraman and sound crew. They set up their equipment and began operating it at just about the time 1,000 to 2,000 strikers began to march toward the plant. The strikers were met by somewhere between 120 and 300 armed Chicago policemen.

What happened next is not clear.[28] In the motion pictures the Paramount cameramen took, strikers were seen arguing with the police. These pictures were taken with a long-focus lens. The cameraman stopped his camera and rotated the lens turret to show a wide-angle view of the crowd, an operation which took about seven seconds.[29] During that brief period, whether justifiably or not, the police opened fire upon the strikers. In all, ten people died from gunshot wounds received that day—seven of them shot in the back—and ninety others were injured.

The motion picture record of that riot was sensational, but Paramount's editor, A. J. Richard, decided to suppress it. In a telegram answer to an inquiry from University of Chicago Professor (later United States Senator) Paul Douglas, who presided over a hastily formed citizen's-rights committee, Richards stated:

Find your wire awaiting me upon my return to city. You asked fair questions which entitle you to fair and frank answer. Our pictures of the Chicago steel riots are not being released any place in the country for reasons reached after serious consideration of the several factors involved. First, please remember that whereas newspapers reach individuals in the home, we show to a public gathered in groups averaging 1,000 or more, and therefore subject to crowd hysteria while assembled in the theatre. Our pictures depict a tense and nerve-wracking episode which in certain sections of the country might very well incite local riot and perhaps riotous demonstrations in theatres, leading to further casualties. For these reasons of public policy, which we consider more important than any profit to ourselves, these pictures are shelved, and so far as we are concerned will stay shelved. We act under editorial rights of withholding from the screen pictures not fit to be seen. This parallels the editorial rights exercised by newspapers of withholding from publication news not fit to be read. Thanks for your inquiry.[30]

Shortly after Paramount's decision to suppress the footage Senator Robert La Follette, Jr., chairman of the Senate Civil Liberties Committee, subpoenaed the film, along with 16mm amateur motion pictures of the riots which had been photographed by a bystander, the Reverend Chester Fisk, pastor of the South Shore Community Congregational Church. Fisk's film had been confiscated by the Chicago police.[31] After Senator La Follette subpoenaed the footage Paramount released the sequence in a regular issue of its newsreel. It was banned by the police in Chicago as "unfit for women and children to see."[32] However, it was run widely elsewhere throughout the United States. In an article published the following year Paramount's managing editor, William Montague, claimed that Paramount had *not* suppressed the footage but had merely withheld it temporarily until the La Follette committee had examined it.[33] The testimony and available evidence, however, shows that this was not the case. The pictures were taken on May 30. Richards' telegram to Douglas, in which he expressly stated that he was shelving the film, was made public on June 8.[34] Steps were taken to secure the film for screening by the Senate committee on June 9, and the La Follette committee had viewed it by June 17.[35]

The control of newsreel exhibition by governmental authorities—censorship by so-called prior restraint—probably attracted more attention than any other kind, since it occurred in public and drew attention to itself. It existed on both national and international levels. On the international level, as early as 1933, British Home Secretary Sir John Gilmour threatened to censor American newsreels "if further objectionable news pictures were shown on British screens."[36] The film which had triggered this official reaction was one which included a re-enactment of the Brooke Hart murder case in California. In the case of this particular newsreel official pressure from the British government brought the desired results, and Sir John stated that "the offending newsreel had already been withdrawn by the distributing company here."[37] When, as in other cases, the newsreel firms did not yield so readily to official pressure abroad, direct suppression of the footage might follow. In April, 1937, Premier Mitchell Hepburn of Canada ruled that no newsreel footage of the Ford Motor Company strike at Oshawa, Canada, could be screened anywhere in Ontario. "He explained that he did not intend to allow any propaganda from either side to be shown on the screen."[38]

Foreign censorship of American newsreels was occasionally abetted by United States officials. In November, 1938, the British government acknowledged the assistance of American Ambassador Joseph P. Kennedy in suppressing a sequence from an American newsreel (Paramount's) which had been critical of the policies of Prime Minister Neville Chamberlain during the Munich Crisis in September. Sir John Simon, chancellor of the exchequer, explained Kennedy's role in the suppression:

The Ambassador of the United States . . . thought it right to

*indicate . . . [the British government's disapproval of the reel] to
a member of the Hays organization, which customarily deals with
matters of this kind. It was brought to the attention of Paramount News, who, from a sense of public duty and in the general
interest, decided to make certain excisions from the newsreel.*[39]

Added Sir John, "I am glad to think the Ambassador of the United
States and ourselves are in complete accord."[40]

Censorship of American reels in some foreign countries was
absolute—they simply were not allowed inside the borders. In
other countries they were severely and consistently censored. It
took many months of negotiation before the American quasi-
newsreel, *The March of Time*, was even allowed in France.[41] Indeed, censorship abroad became so commonplace by the late
1930's that it no longer attracted much attention.

Official censorship within the United States was much rarer,
however, and always provoked considerable controversy when it
occurred. During the 1930's several states—New York, Pennsylvania, Ohio, Kansas, Maryland, and Florida—as well as a number of municipalities, maintained censor boards to which all feature films were sent for preview. Many of these boards also exercised the right to review newsreels as well and occasionally directed producers to remove offending sequences. In 1937 the Ohio
Censor Board banned an entire Pathé newsreel sequence dealing
with the Spanish Civil War. The Ohio board ruled that

*the picture itself did not contain any harmful propaganda. How-
ever, the dialog of the narrator made the picture, we considered,
very harmful. We suggest that the narrators, in reporting on this
subject . . . keep their remarks neutral, or we will find it necessary
to make eliminations.*[42]

The narrator's remarks had included the following phrases:

*Prisoners marching to the rear often face firing-squads.
General Possasm observes the effects of shrapnel.*

The ring of steel around Madrid contracts and expands as its defenders counter-attack.

The tide of war surges in Spain as radical Madrid rushes troops to the front, including these Communist brigades, flying the red flag.

Meanwhile, France and Britain on the north, Italy and Germany in the Mediterranean, have begun their blockade. . . .

Rebel bombers, flying over the lines, rain death upon Madrid.

In this war without mercy, the innocent suffer with the guilty. This little girl is dug out of the debris still alive. She faced a fate terrified mothers in war-torn Spain fear for their little ones. A mere baby snatched from the jaws of death by the grace of God.[43]

Courtland Smith, managing editor of Pathé, replied to the Ohio board, protesting the ban:

You have no right to give us any such advice, or any advice, and we certainly do not intend to consider your ideas of what may, or may not, be neutral. The Constitution of the United States guarantees freedom of speech. You have therefore gone far beyond any authority you may have when you try to tell us what we may or may not say on any subject. . . . never again try to tell us what we may or may not say in a newsreel.[44]

In another case the politically appointed censor board of the state of Kansas excised a rebuttal argument *against* President Roosevelt's plan to pack the Supreme Court from a 1937 issue of *The March of Time.*[45]

Interference by state boards continued for many years, despite protests by newsreel firms and other journalistic media. In Louisiana a censorship act was pushed through the legislature in 1935 at the insistence of Senator Huey Long. Many people considered the act retaliation for the release of an issue of *The March of Time* in the same year which had ridiculed Long in describing his rise to power.[46]

The newsreel producers were incensed not only by the discrimination which was practiced against newsreels as compared with other news media but also by the costly charges levied by the boards for their "services." At the rate of three dollars a print, it was estimated in 1953 that the newsreel industry could save fifty-seven thousand dollars a year if censor-board review were abolished in the state of Ohio alone.[47] In retaliation against the Ohio board's expensive review regulations, Universal's newsreel conducted a camera boycott on news events in the state of Ohio for a while.[48]

During the 1950's a number of legal actions were undertaken to challenge the authority of such boards. In September, 1952, a "friendly" court action was brought by the State Division of Film Censorship of Ohio against theater owner Martin G. Smith, who had run a newsreel which had not been reviewed by the state board. Municipal Judge Frank Wiley ruled that the Ohio censorship laws were in violation of both the state and the federal constitutions.[49] At the same time public and legislative opinion began to form during the 1950's against all forms of motion picture censorship.

In 1952 the United States Supreme Court, in the case of *Joseph Burstyn v. Wilson*,[50] formally overruled legal precedents set in the 1915 Mutual Film case[51] and appeared to question the constitutionality of all motion picture censorship. Subsequently newsreels were excluded from censorship laws in both Virginia and Maryland,[52] censorship statutes in Florida were declared unconstitutional,[53] and the state censorship laws in Massachusetts, Pennsylvania, and Ohio were declared invalid by their respective state supreme courts.[54]

Still later the unofficial practice of "sitting" on a film—delaying a decision on its suitability for release—was forbidden by the United States Supreme Court in *Freedman v. Maryland* (1965).[55] The court now requires that if a censor board finds a film objectionable it must bring charges against the exhibitor and/or distributor within a reasonable period of time in a court of law, into whose hands the prosecution of the case is then handed.

Interestingly, although the Supreme Court's decisions have

rendered censor boards impotent, their existence is still sanc-
tioned by the court, which ruled in *Times Film Corp.* v. *Chicago*
(1960) that the requirement by a state or local government that
films be *submitted* to the censor board before release was not in
itself unconstitutional.[56] This decision, which embraces all kinds
of films, follows by many years a decision handed down by the
Appellate Division of the Supreme Court of New York in July,
1922, which ruled that the State Motion Picture Commission of
New York had the right to censor newsreels of current events.[57]

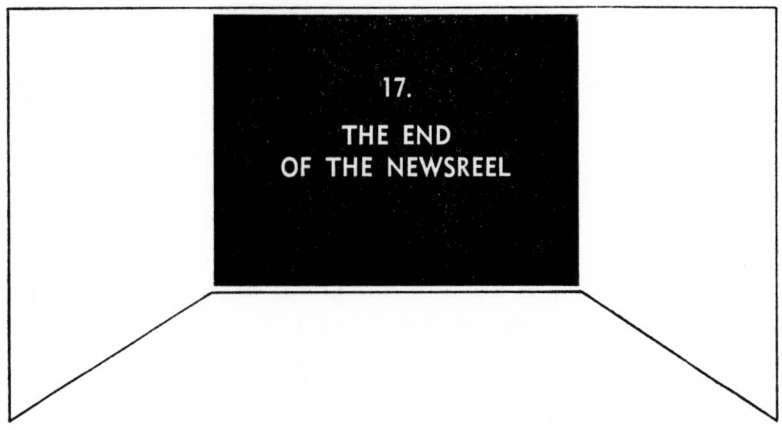

With the outbreak of World War II the output of civilian news-reels declined greatly. The laboratories continued to function, of course, but the overwhelming majority of scenes were photographed either by the military services or by civilian cameramen who operated under the control of the military. Each of the major newsreel companies assigned two cameramen to all the important fronts or battle areas around the world:

Civilian war photographers and cameramen are given the same rating as war correspondents, once they are assigned to a combat unit. That is to say, they enjoy the privileges of officers. They must be accredited in Washington before they are eligible for duty abroad, and they lose their civilian status to the extent at least that they are subject to the orders of the military or naval command to which they are attached and must accompany it into battle or wherever it goes, unless ordered to do otherwise.[1]

The greatest amount of combat footage which reached theater screens, however, was filmed by United States Signal Corps and Navy photographers,[2] many of whom had been trained in schools established by *The March of Time*, *Fox Movietone*, and Hearst's *News of the Day*.[3]

Despite the early resistance of theater owners to the exhibition of war footage and the occasional "No War News Shown Here" signs during the early days of conflict, the commitment of the United States in late 1941 to total war generated great interest among audiences in political and military subject matter in newsreels, and the amount of such footage increased steadily. *Look* estimated that four-fifths of all newsreel footage released from 1942 to 1946 was devoted to some aspect of war, a figure only a little higher than that provided in a content analysis of newsreel material conducted by Leo Handel and published in 1950. By 1943, according to Handel, 73.9 per cent of all newsreel footage released was devoted to a combination of (1) government news, (2) national-defense news, (3) political news, (4) news of war in Europe, and (5) news of war in the Pacific. Sports footage, which had provided the largest single category of newsreel material, dropped from 26.2 per cent in 1941 to 8.6 per cent in 1943 (see the table on page 290).[4]

By 1944, according to a *Paramount News* breakdown, 77 per cent of its total content was devoted to war news: 35 per cent to the European theater; 13 per cent to the Pacific theater; 16 per cent to home-front activities; 4 per cent to the armed forces in camps, in training, and in other activities; 7 per cent to foreign material on the war (Russian, British, Polish, Yugoslavian, and French); and 2 per cent to captured German and Japanese film.[5]

In addition, the newsreels regularly incorporated film segments supporting the Red Cross, War Bond drives, the National War Fund, and the March of Dimes and appeals for workers in critical manpower areas and for volunteers for the Wacs, the Waves, the nurse corps, and so on.[6]

In addition to the domestic commercial newsreels which operated during the war, the United States government financed its own newsreel for overseas viewers, entitled *United Newsreel*. The producer was a private, nonprofit corporation established in 1942 by the five major American newsreel firms—Paramount, Pathé, Fox Movietone, Universal, and News of the Day (MGM)—in association with the Office of War Information, and financed by the United States government. The reel was designed as a counter-

TABLE 1

TEN YEARS OF NEWSREEL ANALYSIS
1939–48

National news:	Topical content, per cent									
	1939	1940	1941	1942	1943	1944	1945	1946	1947	1948
Aviation	3.1	0.8	0.9	0.1	0.2	0.4	1.4	3.2	1.8	1.7
Disaster, fires, etc.	3.4	3.1	2.6	2.3	1.4	1.7	1.9	3.0	4.0	2.1
Farm	0.2	0.4	0.2	0.6	0.7	0.2	0.2	0.5	0.4	0.4
Fashions, styles	1.8	1.6	1.5	0.9	0.5	1.0	0.9	1.5	1.2	2.3
Governmental news	5.1	4.5	5.8	8.6	7.8	2.7	11.7	8.4	8.2	6.2
Health	0.4	0.4	0.2	0.1	0.6	0.9	0.1	0.6	0.4	*
Industrial progress	0.7	0.9	0.6	0.1	1.0	0.3	0.3	0.5	0.1	0.3
Labor news	0.8	0.1	1.5	0.3	0.7	0.3	0.8	2.4	1.3	1.0
National defense	4.1	13.7	24.7†	23.3†	22.2†	13.3†	3.4†	7.1	4.3	4.5
Political news	0.8	7.3	0.1	0.1	0.3	5.0	0.1	0.6	0.3	6.1
Religious news	1.0	0.6	0.7	0.4	1.0	1.5	0.8	2.3	0.8	1.0
Science	1.1	0.2	0.3	0.1	0.2	0.2	0.9	0.7	0.5	0.7
Sports	26.1	25.0	26.2	15.3	8.6	9.1	9.4	18.3	26.2	23.1
Weather	0.8	1.1	0.4	0.4	0.2	0.6	0.3	0.5	0.9	0.5
Miscellaneous	21.8	15.9	12.9	15.1	8.9	9.2	20.3	17.2	18.1	18.2
Foreign news	18.3‡	5.8‡	4.2‡	2.9‡	2.1‡	1.4†	23.7‡	29.7	29.3	30.3
War in Europe	10.5	18.6	15.8	15.0	28.9	37.7	9.7	…	…	…
War in Pacific	…	…	1.4	14.4	14.7	14.5	14.1	…	…	…
United Nations	…	…	…	…	…	…	…	3.5	2.2	1.6
	100.0	100.0	100.0	100.0	100.0	100.0	100.0	100.0	100.0	100.0
Total clips	4,940	4,947	4,948	4,454	3,810	3,491	3,133	3,559	3,484	3,541

Source: Compiled from Movietone News, News of the Day,
Paramount News, Pathé News (Warner Pathé News after August
15, 1947), and Universal Newsreel. Adapted from Leo Handel,
Hollywood Looks at Its Audience (Urbana, University of Illinois
Press, 1950).

* Less than 0.1%.
† Including domestic war activities after United States' entry
into World War II.
‡ Excluding World War II coverage.

propaganda medium and was reportedly released in sixteen languages. It not only was distributed in friendly, neutral, and doubtful countries but was also dropped behind enemy lines in a German-language version. The government's contract with United Newsreel Corporation came to a close on December 15, 1945.[7]

Certainly, the military production of newsreel footage and the wartime context in which newsreels were shown had their advantages. The extent of the coverage and the quality of combat photography were superb. Even more important, both the motion picture industry and the public took its newsreels seriously for the first time. Carlton Brown wrote:

During the war, the newsreels came close to realizing their tremendous potentialities. . . .

The newsreels very likely reached their peak of effectiveness during the war because they were made and supervised largely by individuals and government agencies genuinely concerned with the tremendous drama of global war. They probably registered their increase in public interest because the majority of Americans, even when they were not looking for individual faces, were far more concerned with world events than they usually are and found the most compelling account of them, for the first time, in the newsreels.[8]

For the first time in a long while serious critics of the cinema again began to write about the newsreel, half expecting its rebirth and rededication, half hoping that it might, in war, realize its always recognized potential for intelligent journalistic contribution. The usually reserved critic for *New Statesman and Nation* wrote enthusiastically of the invasion films of 1944:

Queues twenty-five yards long outside the news theatres testified to the main drama of this week and of many weeks to come. . . . Here, for once, was something worth standing in the rain for. . . . The invasion films (Gaumont British and British Paramount) gave us those close-ups and bird's-eye views that one missed from reading the newspapers. Marching men and "ducks" poured along a road from the Downs; the camouflaged boats touched sides in harbour; paratroops blackened their faces and turned over the first issue of French notes (the sight of these men brought the first spontaneous cheer I have heard in a cinema for months). . . . We have always been inclined, rather stupidly, to prune out war documentaries so that they shan't offend the queasy. This first installment of the invasion newsreels made by British and American cameramen promises well for the future.[9]

A few months later another critic, Edgar Anstey, reviewed the newsreels of the liberation of Paris:

Appropriately enough, in view of the majesty of the event, the liberation of Paris has given rise to the best newsreel pictures of the war. . . .

It is not often that the camera is able to be a completely un-heeded spectator. Yet emotion and the need for speed completely possess these men, women and children of Paris in the construction of their street barricades of cobblestones, railings and tree-trunks [photographed by French Forces of the Interior camera-men]. They must think, not of history, but of the enemy at the bottom of the street. Sniping from windows, hurling grenades from attics to the Nazi-patrolled streets below, the choice is between liberty and death, and the camera is a privileged but ignored spectator. Both sets of newsreels are full of revealing incidents, tiny cameos which one would like to examine time after time.[10]

Much admired for their honesty were the newsreel issues which featured the grisly scenes of Nazi death camps at Buchenwald and Dachau. Here and there some exhibitors refused to run the reels, but most presented them as scheduled, and were astonished by the mature concern with which audiences received them.[11] In comparison with early newsreel war footage, in which the dead and maimed were rarely shown, footage released toward the end of the war—particularly that of the Iwo Jima, Tarawa, Peleliu, and

Angaur battles in the Pacific—was grim indeed. Commented critic Bosley Crowther:

The newsreels, thank heaven, are getting tougher. They are letting us have it right between the eyes. . . . They are showing the theatre-going public, after three years, that war is truly hell. . . . One can realize the large advance toward frankness in the news films we are seeing now. In the interest of human comprehension, we must solemnly approve this advance.[12]

James Agee, *Nation*'s articulate critic, wrote glowingly of the newsreel's contribution in 1944:

If as a civilian, you feel the importance of experiencing what little you can about the war, you had better avoid practically every foot of fiction film which we have made about it, and you had of course better see all the newsreels and war-record films you can. At their weakest, they have things to show which non-record war films, not even the greatest that might be made, could ever hope to show. . . . The great things in such films are nearly always single shots. The good things, which sometimes approach and could attain greatness, are the cutting, the sound, the quality of the text and voice of the commentary. But even the weakest shots, and even some of the prepared or posed ones, seem to me to have great power and wonder.[13]

Writing a year later on the same subject, Agee remained enthusiastic about the wartime newsreels but had reached some new conclusions about their meaning for and effect on audiences:

Very uneasily, I am beginning to believe that, for all that may be said in favor of our seeing these terrible records of war, we have no business seeing this sort of experience except through our presence and participation. I have neither space nor mind, yet, to try to explain why I believe this is so; but since I am reviewing and in ways recommending that others see one of the best and most terrible of war films [the record of the Iwo Jima invasion], I can-

not avoid mentioning my perplexity. Perhaps I can briefly suggest what I mean by this rough parallel: whatever other effects it may or may not have, pornography is invariably degrading to anyone who looks at or reads it. If at an incurable distance from participation, hopelessly incapable of reactions adequate to the event, we watch men killing each other, we may be quite as profoundly degrading ourselves and, in the process, betraying and separating ourselves the farther from those we are trying to identify ourselves with; none the less because we tell ourselves sincerely that we sit in comfort and watch carnage in order to nurture our patriotism, our conscience, our understanding, and our sympathies.[14]

We wonder what this perceptive critic might have said—had he lived long enough to see it—of the extraordinary coverage of Viet Nam fighting which by the late 1960's American audiences were receiving daily by means of satellite.

The American newsreel benefited from its wartime experiences to the extent that it achieved a new maturity. However, it experienced other changes which were to work to its detriment, then and in the years to come.

First, competition between cameramen and studios, which before the war had dropped to a new low, now disappeared altogether. As long as the war continued, there was no need or excuse for competition. Under the rota system the government furnished every foot of film on combat that was released and made it available equally to all interested producers.

Second, a deadly sameness in coverage followed as each of the newsreel companies provided almost identical issues to their customers. As a consequence, the newsreel theaters which subscribed to all the services now found it difficult to fill out a complete bill. These theaters survived only because of the intense general interest in war news, as well as promotion schemes such as that which provided free photographic enlargements from combat footage to customers who recognized relatives and loved ones in the films.[15]

Third, footage which reached the theaters was heavily censored, particularly during the early days of the war. Whereas still photographs were cleared in the field, all newsreel footage was sent directly to Washington for review.[16] The newsreel footage of the attack on Pearl Harbor was not released for one year after the event, while that of the Battle of Tarawa was not released until months after its conclusion.[17] Such censorship extended not merely to military information but also to the presentation of certain other kinds of materials, such as scenes of American casualties and dead. Further, access to celebrities and news events in allied and neutral countries was greatly curtailed; governmental authorities carefully supervised cameramen's movements and activities. The footage which military officers did release was frequently dull and lifeless, and what they released was often weeks late.[18]

Sometimes, too, individual theater managers would edit footage from the war newsreels which they thought too gruesome. Radio City Music Hall, for example, refused to show newsreels of the death camps at Dachau and Buchenwald. G. S. Eyssell, the managing director, said that he did not want to chance "sickening any squeamish persons in the audience which usually is family trade, mostly women and children."[19] The effect of all these kinds of censorship was to further compromise the work and initiative of newsreelmen.

Fourth, the standard one-reel length of the American newsreel, which had never been long enough to allow for really satisfactory exposition in normal times, was abbreviated even further by government order because of raw-stock shortages—from 900 to 750 feet during the period 1942–45 and from 750 to 700 feet in 1945.[20]

Fifth, controversial issues, particularly those of a political nature, virtually disappeared from theater screens. Understandably, the war effort required that partisan politics, economic problems, social protest, interally dissension, and other such issues be ignored in the interests of national unity. However, the absence of controversial subject matter had effects which lasted long after the war and tended to render the newsreel even more innocuous. *The March of Time*, for example, previously one of the world's most polemic motion picture features, never again managed to recapture its prewar impudent, iconoclastic style and declined rapidly in the postwar years.

For people in the newsreel business, the postwar era began optimistically. The prospects for business as usual appeared so good that another newsreel, *Telenews*, entered the field as a supplier of footage to newsreel theaters and television,[21] while in August, 1947, Warner Brothers Studios acquired *Pathé News* and began releasing it through its own exchanges.[22] Now, for the first time—and for a brief span of time—every major motion picture studio was releasing its own independently produced newsreel: Fox's *Movietone News*, *Paramount News*, MGM-Hearst's *News of the Day*, *Universal Newsreel*, and *Warner Pathé News*. There was even some brave talk of "restructuring" the newsreel so as to meet the communications needs of the postwar era. In 1948, C. Clement Cave, managing editor of *Warner Pathé News*, wrote of the new role which the newsreel might play in the years to come:

> *A great newsreel public was built up during the war, when the reels had great and vivid pictures to show and stories of great daring to tell. . . . The time for new ideas and a complete change of mentality is now. . . .*
>
> *A new form of technique in presentation is required. The formal method of title and then story is as old and out of date as some of the news carried. It needs streamlining, and tricks used which give the reel a punch.*[23]

To a slight extent the newsreels did try to introduce some changes in their formats. By 1948, *Warner Pathé News* was occasionally featuring a style which was somewhat akin to that of *The March of Time*,[24] while by 1949 *Paramount News* occasionally featured what was termed a "full-length documentary treatment."[25] Greater numbers of local stories were photographed

With the American declaration of war on the Axis in December, 1941, initiative in combat photography passed from civilian hands to the armed forces, and for the next four years it was from the latter that most such footage came. Civilian cameramen were assigned to the various theaters of war, and their footage was pooled with that of service cameramen. All of the film was censored before it was released to the newsreel companies. Above: An army cameraman photographs the landing of American troops on Kiska Island in the Aleutians, August 15, 1943. (U.S. Army photograph.)

Of all the wartime celebrities none made better subject matter for newsreels than (left to right) Joseph Stalin, Franklin D. Roosevelt, and Winston Churchill, photographed by a U.S. Army Signal Corps cameraman at the Teheran Conference late in 1943. (U.S. Army photograph.)

One of the most dramatic military figures of World War II, General Douglas MacArthur, walks along the beach at Humboldt Bay, Dutch New Guinea, after the successful landing by American forces in April, 1944. (U.S. Navy photograph.)

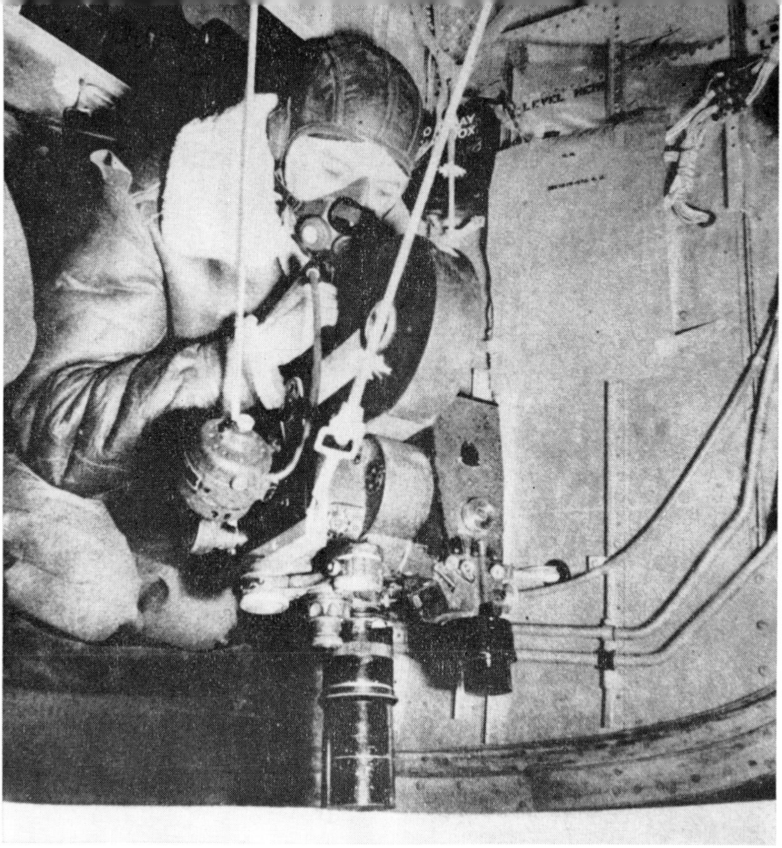

Above: An American Air Corps cameraman sights through the open bomb bay of a B-24 Liberator on a run over enemy territory, 1943.

Right: A combat cameraman photographs the scene as 500-pound bombs are dropped from a Flying Fortress on an oil refinery at Leghorn, Italy, 1943. (Both photographs from the U.S. Army Air Corps.)

Allied Supreme Commander General Dwight D. Eisenhower talks with paratroopers shortly before the D-day invasion of France, June 6, 1944. (U.S. Army photograph.)

Facing page: D-day, June 6, 1944. Above: Allied warships, protected by barrage balloons, mass in the English Channel as the invasion of Europe begins. (U.S. Navy photograph.) Below: Allied troops pour from a landing craft onto Normandy beaches. (U.S. Coast Guard photograph.) Unfortunately, most motion-picture footage of the invasion, which was collected and stored in one ship offshore, was destroyed when the ship was sunk.

In the Pacific the battles of Tarawa and (above) of Iwo Jima were brilliantly photographed by both civilian and service cameramen. However, the footage of these and other bloody battles, especially those of the early days of the war, was suppressed by military censors and was not released to theaters until months after the events. (U.S. Coast Guard photograph.)

The war in Europe ended with the capitulation of Germany and the signing of the surrender document in Reims, France, on May 7, 1945. Note the newsreel cameraman at the right. The war had about come to an end and, with television around the corner, so had the newsreel. (U.S. Army photograph.)

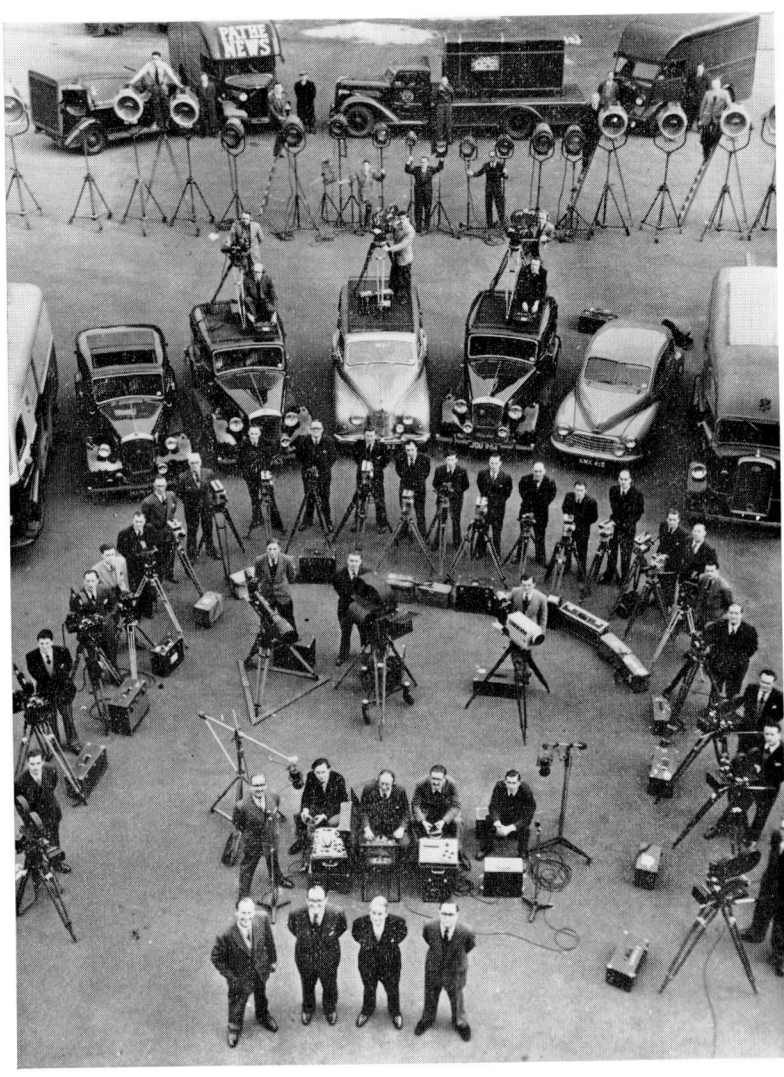

The newsreel had one last moment of glory—the coronation of Elizabeth II of England in 1953. In the photograph above is shown all of the equipment used by just one company, Pathé, to film the event. (From British Film Institute.)

expressly for particular American markets, and attempts were made to speed up delivery of all kinds of newsreel footage to the subscribing theaters. Later some newsreels began to offer color-film news coverage.[26] But the changes were superficial and minor. They could be expected merely to alleviate the symptoms of news-reel decline rather than to cure its causes.

By 1949 the commercial-television industry was well estab-lished, and its news services had already begun to offer real compe-tition to motion picture newsreel producers. It was some time, however, before the nature and magnitude of television compe-tition became apparent in the motion picture industry. At first, in the late 1940's, newsreel producers ignored the new medium. Then, as television antennas sprouted across the nation and the new entertainment attraction caught on, the same producers ridiculed it for its temporarily clumsy coverage and inferior image quality. The newsreel industry even refused to service television networks and stations with footage in the late 1940's.[27]

Charles Lazarus, writing in *Motion Picture Herald* in 1952, ap-peared to speak for the industry:

Theatrical newsreels are expertly and smoothly edited and pre-sented with no interruptions, whereas TV footage all too often is catch-as-catch-can with the presentation interrupted by com-mercials.

The television newscasters' contracts call for them to be tele-vised while talking, thus a major part of the news period is occu-pied with the TV camera on the commentator's face instead of the action he's talking about.

The personal preferences of sponsors often dictate the contents of a television news period, often with emphasis on what is dull and tedious.

Theatrical newsreels are presented once during a program, whereas at home the TV news period is presented only at specific times.[28]

Actually, television coverage of news events—both live and on film—had been undertaken throughout the world on an experimental basis during the 1930's. The Germans transmitted live television images of the 1936 Olympic games in Berlin to an audience estimated at 150,000.[29] In 1937 the British Broadcasting Corporation televised scenes of the coronation of George VI in London to an estimated audience of fifty thousand in an area of seventy-five hundred square miles. Reception was reported to be excellent within this area, and was reported to be clear as far away as Brighton and Ipswich, fifty miles from London.[30]

As for television-film coverage, as early as 1935 the Germans were broadcasting a regular motion picture newsreel called *The Mirror of the Day* over their Berlin television station on Monday, Wednesday, and Saturday evenings. They even outfitted a remote-location truck with a film laboratory and electronic equipment which allowed for processing of the camera footage within one minute, scanning of the film images, and transmission of them by cable to the Berlin television station for instantaneous retransmission to the public. The quality of the image was poor by today's standards, but it all worked just the same. As an American trade paper prophetically observed in 1935: "Against this time delay of only about one minute (or even five) the ordinary newsreels cannot compete. The only hope, then, of the newsreel industry is to improve the technique of newsreel production."[31]

Newsreel technicians had experimented with electronic systems for rapid transmission of footage as early as 1934. Had the experiments proved practical, they might have allowed the theater newsreel to compete more realistically with the television services of the future. In November, 1934, Gaumont-British transmitted eight to ten feet of newsreel footage, frame by frame, from Australia to London by wireless-telephoto service. The individual photographs—about 160 frames in all—were then rephotographed on motion picture film and rushed to theaters. The footage showed aviators Scott and Black after they touched down in Melbourne, winning the international air race from England to Australia. Owing to poor weather the transmission took sixty-eight hours to complete. Nonetheless, Gaumont scooped everyone by many days with the footage. As one would expect, the cost was high. At $189 a frame, the total bill came to $30,264. In the months that followed, *Paramount News* experimented with wireless transmission of newsreel footage and toyed with the idea of setting up its own transmission stations throughout the United States and around the world. In the end the scheme was abandoned, presumably because of the very high costs involved.[32]

With the passing of time, postwar television news coverage improved rapidly, as did the quality of its picture. By the time of President Harry S Truman's inauguration in 1949, the television industry was able to scoop its motion picture competition by a number of hours from New York to Chicago, and with considerably more coverage.[33] (Television cameras had not been allowed to broadcast the inauguration of President Roosevelt in 1945.)[34] More important, the depth and quality of coverage had also improved. The broadcasting industry had a long tradition of mature radio news reporting to fall back upon. One by one, distinguished radio commentators augmented the growing television news and public-affairs staffs.

By 1950 many newsreel theaters had closed across the nation. On November 6, 1949, exactly twenty years to the week after it opened its doors, New York's Embassy Newsreel Theater closed them for good. It was estimated that more than eleven million paid admissions had been transacted at its box office.[35] According to W. French Githens, president of Newsreel Theaters, Inc.:

Television has been a major factor in the decline of the newsreel theatre. Sports always made up an important section of our shows. Saturday nights used to find our theatre packed with sports fans watching local football games we had filmed that afternoon. Now these patrons can see sporting events as they occur.[36]

By the summer of 1950 only one of Trans-Lux's fourteen houses still played newsreels exclusively—the others ran regular motion picture programs.[37] Many conventional motion picture theaters across the country stopped playing newsreels altogether.

With increasing clarity newsreel producers perceived the magnitude of their competition and began allying themselves with television interests. Paramount began supplying newsreel footage to its own and other independent television stations. Fox entered into an association with United Press International to supply footage to television stations. *Telenews* was already firmly entrenched in the television market. MGM-Hearst's *News of the Day* provided film for Edward R. Murrow's brilliant television documentary series *See It Now*.[38] Concomitantly, economic panic struck the motion picture industry as box-office receipts shrank, theaters closed, backlogs of features were sold to television syndicates, and Hollywood's production payrolls were slashed. By 1953 the status of the newsreel had sunk so low that parent studios required their own newsreels to feature pseudo–news coverage of gala premieres and publicity events which advertised their own features. In 1953, according to *Daily Variety*, such publicity accounted for 3.5 per cent of all newsreel footage; in 1954 it accounted for 4.4 per cent.[39]

One by one the great newsreel companies began to close shop. In the autumn of 1951 *The March of Time* ceased production of its theatrical release and began work on a television series entitled *Crusade in the Pacific*. It sold its extensive, two-million-foot stock-shot library to NBC. On August 23, 1956, *Warner Pathé News* ceased operations. By this time the company's vaults held over twenty-four million feet of film, some of which went back as far as 1898. A news item reporting its demise stated that less than half of the nation's 19,200 theaters then operating still booked a news-reel.[40] On February 15, 1957, Paramount's "The Eyes and Ears of the World" stopped production, although its laboratory facilities in New York continued to operate for the convenience of the parent studio. A spokesman for Paramount stated that discontinuance of the newsreel was "in line with the changes in communications methods these days and Paramount's policy to diversify interests. While Paramount News is still showing a profit, the returns, unfortunately are not commensurate with the time, energy, and investment in the newsreel."[41] In 1963 its vast film library was sold to Wolper Productions.[42]

Fox Movietone News, once the largest of the newsreels, closed shop in September, 1963;[43] and *Hearst Metrotone* (*News of the Day*), on November 30, 1967,[44] although both continued their overseas issues for a while. Hearst finally discontinued its overseas reel on January 1, 1968, allegedly, so *Variety* charged, when the United States Information Agency withdrew its secret financial support. According to the *Variety* account, the money was channeled through the USIA under the code name "Kingfish." The story said that USIA "made no attempt to influence domestic editions of the newsreel, but sometimes 'inserted material not used in domestic editions of the newsreel.' "[45]

The last to go was *Universal Newsreel*, the oldest and longest lasting of them all.* Although produced by different people over the years, it had been released through the same company for over half a century. On December 26, 1967, its final six-minute issue was prepared in New York City, narrated by Ed Herlihy, who had succeeded Graham McNamee as the voice of Universal. According to retiring general manager Thomas Mead, the *Universal Newsreel* had serviced thirty-three hundred theaters at its peak. When it finally ceased operations, however, only sixteen hundred theaters were showing it, and the series was losing five thousand dollars a week for the parent company.[46]

---

* By 1968 a radical film series called *Newsreel* was being distributed by Newsreel Features, of New York City. According to the distributors, "Newsreel hopes to serve as a medium of agitation, diffusion and exchange of revolutionary experiences." *Newsreel Catalogue No. 4*, March, 1969, p. 1. It was in no way a conventional newsreel, however, but was similar to the irregularly released quasi-newsreel of labor conflicts, hunger marches, and other manifestations of social and political unrest produced by the Film and Photo League as early as 1928. A. William Bluem, *Documentary in American Television*, 49. Insofar as the conventional newsreel is concerned, its history ends with the demise of *Universal Newsreel*.

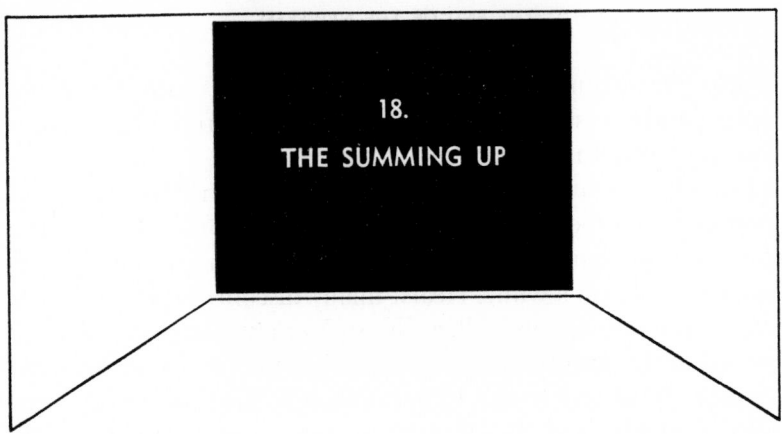

18.

THE SUMMING UP

Evolving out of the news film of the 1890's, the American news-reel finally appeared in a more or less permanent, recognizable form around 1911, a child of journalism and motion picture commerce. By the early 1920's the newsreel industry had managed, at great expense, to perfect a distribution system by means of which —twice weekly—news-hungry Americans were able to view the laying of cornerstones, the judging of beauty contests, and the training of monkeys.

Judged by commonly held journalistic standards, the traditions and aims of the American newsreel were only superficially similar to those of the printed news-reporting media. The known instances of content manufacture, re-creation, personality impersonation, and blatant fraud were so great in number, so common in nature, and so continuous in occurrence throughout the history of the American newsreel that its over-all veracity and fidelity as a medium of public information is rendered suspect. The implications of this awareness for responsible producers of archive-documentary features seem obvious: the substance, meaning, and historical accuracy of all newsreel footage should be scrutinized and appraised with great care, lest the documentarian's integrity is unintentionally compromised by the dishonesty of his materials. The performance of the newsreel in presenting newsworthy information to the public was inferior to that of the printed media with

310

respect to the speed with which it reported the news, the extent of coverage, the depth and quality of interpretation, and the degree to which censorship and editorial timidity precluded discussion of controversial issues.

The inability of the motion picture newsreel to compete successfully with the printed media cannot be satisfactorily explained, however, simply by acknowledging the several factors described earlier in this history which limited its speed of publication, length of "dispatches," and extent of coverage. It can be argued, for example, that other motion picture productions, such as the American *March of Time* and the British *Modern Age* series, treated contemporary issues with a maturity and insight equal to that of the better quality newspapers and periodicals. The journalistic failure of the American newsreel can only be explained by contrasting the aims of newsreel producers and the intended functions of their films with the aims and functions typical of traditional journalists. The producers of newsreels, when it was convenient, often professed a kinship to the older news-reporting media. Nonetheless, available evidence leads to the conclusion that their values belonged to show business rather than to journalism and that they viewed their "readership" or "circulation" as an entertainment-hungry audience rather than a well-informed public.

In the newspaper business an hour's reminiscences from a veteran reporter would probably provide examples of a number of outstanding stories of Pulitzer Prize caliber in the history of American journalism: a revealing exposé of municipal corruption, an insightful treatment of a labor-management dispute, a penetrating political analysis of a presidential campaign, and so forth. By contrast, when cameramen, supervisors, editors, and industry trade-paper writers wrote of triumphs in the newsreel business, the coverage usually most valued by them featured scenes of raw violence, sensation, and catastrophe. Many such sequences which appeared over the last fifty years have been described in this book. One of them in particular, the explosion of the *Hindenburg*, was generally regarded by newsreel people as the greatest single sequence ever filmed. The professionals' recollections of that extraordinary event, even of those who did not actually participate in filming it, were characterized by an almost mystical rapture. If there is a Valhalla to which brave newsreel cameramen retire at death, it is probably one in which large German zeppelins explode on a regular schedule for the benefit of those who could not be on hand during life to photograph the *Hindenburg*.

Generalizing both from evidence of the newsreel's performance and from the testimony of its producers, I would venture to say, then, that the mission of the newsreel was, first, to satisfy the appetites of an entertainment-seeking audience, and second, to encapsulate newsworthy events by "freezing" their superficialities. In this respect, the briefer the sequence and the sharper its condensation, the more successful it seemed to be considered in newsreel circles. A third mission was to present a "pictorial fact" which was as devoid of ramification as possible, which was complete in itself, and which required little or no explanation or interpretation. Fourth, the newsreel was to avoid controversial subjects and editorialization whenever possible. Fifth, it was to interpret intellectual issues, when they could not be avoided, along lines of strong pictorial action—to reduce to a minimum the intellectual participation of the audience.

The most compelling problem in the preparation of this book has been to provide a perspective which would explain the eventual decline of the American motion picture newsreel. The word "decline" is used here to refer not merely to the immediate causes of its failure and disappearance in the 1950's and 1960's but also to the contributory causes which operated over a prolonged period of time.

As for the more apparent causes, two postwar factors figured most directly in the failure of the newsreel. The first of these was the introduction of commercial television, which severely disrupted the economy of the film industry. The second was the aggressive exploitation of television's news-reporting potential. If the economy of the motion picture industry had continued on an even keel during the years that followed the war, and if competing television news services had not appeared, it seems likely that the newsreel would have survived unchanged, still performing its modest function as an unimportant program component, together with the travelogues and the Mickey Mouse cartoons. However, the introduction of commercial television, with its inherently greater facility and speed for reporting on-the-spot news and current events, changed all that. It did so by offering a faster and, in time, a better newsreel service, and by precipitating an economic crisis which destroyed the old big-five major-studio system of production. The financial failure of more than a dozen independently produced newsreels during the seventy-five-year history of the American cinema has demonstrated that only the majors were in a position to sustain the financial burden of newsreel production. When they curtailed production in the 1950's and cut back costs to meet television competition, their least important properties— the newsreels—were the first to be jettisoned.

Still, it would be an oversimplification to blame the decline and failure of the newsreel on television competition alone. Subsequent events in the entertainment business have shown that television competition in itself is not sufficient to rival seriously those products of the motion picture industry which have genuine merit and which satisfy the needs and tastes of the public. The feature film is still with us; it remains one of the most prominent features of American show business, representing in recent estimate a gross annual revenue from American theaters alone of $1,097,000,000 a year—a figure which the United States Department of Commerce estimates as representing 48.05 per cent of the total annual spectator amusement expenditures in the United States.[1]

Intelligent showmen, sensitive to changes in audience taste and expectations, have always varied the content and style of their feature films to conform to the fashions and values of the time. The form and character of the newsreel, however, became petrified shortly after the introduction of sound. Unnoticed, unheralded, the decay of newsreel quality had already begun by the mid-1930's and would surely have been apparent at that time had not the tension-filled subject matter of the period obscured the fact that there was really nothing new in the newsreel.

If the newsreel had served a genuinely important function in the American entertainment business, it would have survived, just as the feature film survived. On virtually no occasion after 1911 was the regular newsreel advertised or promoted as an individual item on a multi-feature program. Without an identity as a program attraction, the newsreel could never be taken seriously by motion picture audiences. At the same time, lacking a separate and measurable box-office response to its release, the newsreel could never be taken seriously by film producers either. Deprived of any substantial appeal to either audiences or film executives, the newsreel was hardly missed when it disappeared from motion picture screens in the late 1960's.

In every way the newsreel had seemed foredoomed to failure. It was doomed artistically because of its domination by former newspapermen who perpetuated an outmoded, inappropriate style. It was doomed journalistically because of its inability to compete realistically with either newspapers or television and because of its producers' reluctance to provide mature treatments of contemporary issues. It was doomed as political commentary because of the entertainment context in which it was screened and the severity of censorship with which it was afflicted. It was doomed as a reliable record of the contemporary scene because of the ease with which it lent itself to artifice and deceit. And finally, it was doomed economically by its own system of exhibition, which guarantee that it would never be placed in a position where it could compete with feature productions as a separate and distinct motion picture attraction.

Even judged by its own peculiar quasi-journalistic standards, the newsreel may be said to have flourished for only two brief periods in its history. The first of these extended from about 1920 to 1927 when editorial innovators such as Emanuel Cohen provoked interstudio competition, spent lavish sums of money to support large staffs of internationally based cameramen, and encouraged zealous, almost fanatic attempts on the part of newsreel workers to capture exotic and exciting footage which, though it may have been intellectually thin, was at least never dull. A second and even briefer period of newsreel accomplishment lasted from about 1927 to 1932 when a new kind of newsreel coverage presented unmanipulated sound-on-film interviews with internationally famous political personalities. Given a more congenial exhibition environment in which to flourish, a little more vision on the part of motion picture producers, and an insulation from the deleterious effects of sound-track manipulation and technical sophistication, the motion picture newsreel might have ultimately begun to offer the same sort of mature news and public affairs commentary that *The March of Time* attempted and network television finally achieved.

In view of the increasingly poorer quality of newsreel production from the mid-1930's onward, the really central question is not why the newsreel declined, but rather why it survived as long as it did. No one answer will suffice, and any combination of answers is speculative. First, although it is difficult to demonstrate, we may certainly assume that, at least during the late silent and early sound periods, the newsreel enjoyed a measure of real popularity with audiences. The early success of newsreel theaters provides evidence of this, as does the extravagantly successful release of the very early sound-newsreel interview films, which were released and promoted as individual feature attractions. Indirect evidence is also provided in the testimony of exhibitors during this early period. As Howard Thompson Lewis concluded after conducting a survey of motion picture conditions in 1933:

Practically every exhibitor agrees that no program is complete without a newsreel. There seems to be a general unanimity of opinion that, while other short subjects such as comedies may be used to supplement the feature picture, the newsreel must be used.[2]

315

Second, although the form of the newsreel medium did not change or improve after the early 1930's, it may be assumed that the exciting news events it presented continued to appeal to motion picture patrons until the conclusion of World War II. In view of the obvious decline in newsreel quality following the war, and the obvious fall-off in popularity of the newsreel theaters, the only explanation which seems persuasive for the continued survival of the newsreel after 1945 is one which emphasizes the traditional economic role the newsreel played in distribution circles— a program component offered partly for prestige purposes and partly to discourage subscribing exhibitors from purchasing part of their program from distribution sources other than those offering the feature attractions.

And so, farewell to the newsreel. Unlike other fast-blooming cultural innovations which startled societies with their brilliance, influenced artists and intellectuals, and then faded from the scene, the newsreel cannot be said ever to have contained the seeds of its own destruction in its bloom, for the newsreel never really bloomed at all. Like some species of the hardy cactus plant, it had simply survived, barely sustaining itself from year to year—a symbiotic marvel, unnourished and unchanged by the dynamic environment in which it had always been rooted.

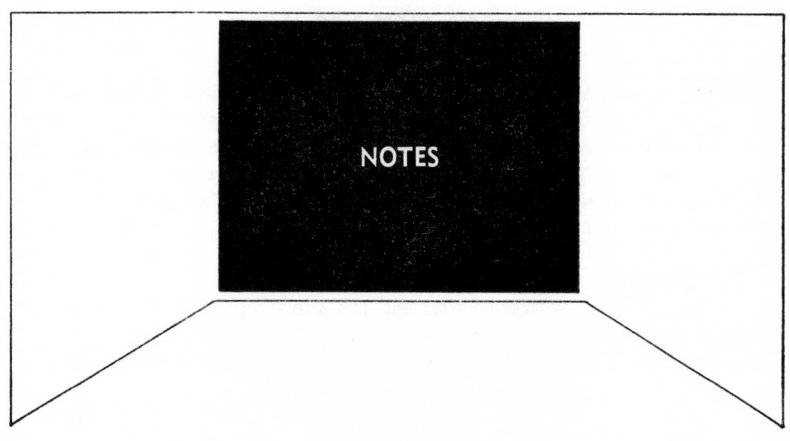

CHAPTER 1

1. W. K. L. Dickson and Antonia Dickson, *The Life and Inventions of Thomas Alva Edison*, 319.

2. Accounts from Scottish newspapers, quoted in Rachael Low and Roger Manvell, *The History of the British Film*, I, 23.

3. Thomas Armat, "My Part in the Development of the Motion Picture Projector," *Journal of the Society of Motion Picture Engineers*, Vol. XXIV (March, 1935), 247.

4. For an account of one of the first known instances of money being spent for news-film coverage (at the McKinley inaugural of 1896), see Earl Theisen, "Story of the Newsreel," *International Photographer*, September, 1933, p. 3.

5. Gordon Hendricks, *The Kinetoscope*, passim; Harold G. Bowen, "Thomas Alva Edison's Early Motion Picture Experiments," *Journal of the Society of Motion Picture and Television Engineers*, Vol. LXIV (September, 1955), 508.

6. Georges Sadoul, *Histoire Générale du Cinéma*, I, 276–77, 281; and Anonymous, *Hommage à Louis Lumière*, 7.

7. Francis Doublier, "Reminiscences of an Early Motion Picture Operator," *Image*, June, 1956, pp. 134ff.; Georges Sadoul, *French Film*, 3; Jean Benoit-Levy, *The Art of the Motion Picture*, 104; and Jay Leyda, *Kino*, 18–19.

8. Doublier, *loc. cit.* See also Anonymous, "Pioneer Newsreels," *Image*, September, 1953, p. 39, according to which the number of dead in this disaster was estimated at between 1,138 and 1,282.

9. Doublier, *loc. cit.*, 135.

10. *Ibid.*

11. Felix Mesguich, *Tours de Manivelle*.

12. Sidney Birt Acres [son of Birt Acres], "Kinematography and the Kiel Canal," *Cinema Studies*, Vol. I, No. 6 (December, 1962), 130–31; and H. Tummel, "Birt Acres," *Cinema Studies*, Vol. I, No. 7 (June, 1963), 157–60.

13. Anonymous, "The Prince's Derby Shown by Lightning Photography,"

Strand Magazine, Vol. XII (1896), 134–40; Kenneth Gordon, "The Early Days of News-Reels," *British Kinematography*, Vol. XVII (August, 1950), 47; Anonymous, "The Story of the News Reel," *Moving Picture World*, March 26, 1927, p. 322; Frederick A. Talbot, *Moving Pictures: How They Are Made and Worked*, 116–17, and illustration facing p. 118; and Robert Paul, "Kinematographic Experiences," *Journal of the Society of Motion Picture Engineers*, Vol. XXVII (November, 1936), 495.

14. Ray Allister, *Friese-Greene: Close-Up of an Inventor*, 96.

15. Albert Norath, "Oskar Messter and His Work," *Journal of the Society of Motion Picture and Television Engineers*, Vol. LXIX (October, 1960), 733.

16. Peter Baechlin and Maurice Muller-Strauss, *Newsreels Across the World*, 10.

17. For details about this and the other early British newsfilms, see Anonymous, *National Film Library Catalogue, Part I: Silent News Films, 1895–1933*, 3ff.

18. Irving Browning, "Through an Eyemo Finder I Saw Champions Fall," *American Cinematographer*, September, 1944, p. 297; Terry Ramsaye, *A Million and One Nights*, I, 108; and Theisen, *loc. cit.* For a general discussion of early fight films, see John Patrick, "The Drama That Staged Itself," *I.A.T.S.E. Official Bulletin*, Winter, 1965, pp. 16ff.

19. See Gordon Hendricks, *The Edison Motion Picture Myth*, 195, n. 50.

20. See Ramsaye, *A Million and One Nights*, I, 109.

21. *Ibid.*, 110. See also Leslie Lieber, "Solved!" The Mystery of Thomas Edison's First Fight Film," *This Week Magazine*, (December 3, 1961), 9. There are records of other Edison fight films of the same period, including a match between the Glenroy brothers, filmed on October 6, 1894, and scenes of boxer Billy Edwards, made in 1895. Gordon Hendricks, "A Collection of Edison Films," *Image* (September, 1959), 157.

22. Patrick, *loc. cit.* (Winter, 1965), 16ff.

23. Ramsaye, *A Million and One Nights*, I, 134.

24. Talbot, *Moving Pictures*, 47; and Ramsaye, *A Million and One Nights*, I, 134.

25. See, for example, Ramsaye, "A Chronology of Film Beginnings," *A Million and One Nights*, I, facing p. 214.

26. At the Grand Café, Paris, December 28, 1895.

27. At the Cotton States Exhibition, Atlanta, Georgia, September, 1895.

28. At the Finsbury Technical Institute, February 28, 1896.

29. For photographic enlargements from the original film, see *Image* (December, 1959), 199; and Ramsaye, *A Million and One Nights*, illustration facing p. 286.

30. Ramsaye, *A Million and One Nights*, I, 286.

31. Patrick, *loc. cit.*, 17.

32. Ramsaye, *A Million and One Nights*, I, 288.

33. *Ibid.*, 289.

34. Editorial, *Brooklyn Eagle*, July 4, 1897, quoted by Ramsaye, *A Million and One Nights*, I, 287.

35. See Albert E. Smith, *Two Reels and a Crank*, 12–25. The testimony in this

book should be appraised carefully; there are many errors of fact and many exaggerations. See also *New York Evening Telegram*, November 6, 1899, for what Smith stated was a garbled version of the circumstances under which the film was shot. See also Ramsaye, *A Million and One Nights*, II, 408–13.

36. Although the authentic films of this fight were ruined, Sigmund Lubin produced and released a fake recreation, using impersonators. See United States copyright entry, "Reproduction of the Fitzsimmons-Jeffries Fight in Eleven Rounds Showing the Knock-Out," Nos. 1–2, copyright by S. Lubin, June 12, 1899, No. 38632–38633. See also George Pratt, "No Magic, No Mystery, No Sleight of Hand," *Image* (December, 1959), 207; and photographic enlargements from the Lubin film reproduced in *American Cinematographer* (December, 1939), 546.

37. Smith, *Two Reels and a Crank*, 17.

38. *Ibid.*, 19.

39. *Ibid.*, 23.

40. For descriptions of the exhibition of both the Vitagraph and Biograph versions, see Pratt, *loc. cit.*, 207. The Edison film was copyrighted by White as "The Battle of Jeffries and Sharkey for Championship of the World," November 4, 1899, No. 72364; and "The Jeffries-Sharkey Contest," November 4, 1899, No. 72363. The American Mutoscope and Biograph Company copyrighted the film as the "Jeffries-Sharkey Contest," Nos. 1–8, November 10, 1899, Nos. 73505–12; Nos. 9–22, November 11, 1899; Nos. 73784–97; Nos. 23–30, November 13, 1899, Nos. 74281–88; and Nos. 31–36, November 15, 1899, Nos. 74690–95.

41. See Smith, *Two Reels and a Crank*, 25.

42. Copyrighted as "Reproduction of the Jeffries and Sharkey Fight," September 9, 1899, No. 57771.

43. Unless otherwise noted, information regarding these early United States news films has been secured from the copyright records and from the salvaged films themselves in the Library of Congress. See Howard Lamarr Walls, *Motion Pictures, 1894–1912*; and Kemp Niver, *Motion Pictures from the Library of Congress Paper Print Collection, 1894–1912*.

44. See Theisen, "Story of the Newsreel," *International Photographer*, September, 1933, p. 3; see also the many United States film copyright entries of the Edison Company in 1897.

45. See Pratt, *loc. cit.*, 202.

46. See Gordon Hendricks, *Beginnings of the Biograph*, 34, 40.

47. *Ibid.*, 38; see also copyright entries No. 69092, December 19, 1896; No. 68815, December 18, 1896; and No. 3543, January 7, 1897.

48. Copyrighted by American Mutoscope Company, December 18, 1896, No. 69091; and November 11, 1896, No. 61793; and January 7, 1897, No. 3558.

49. Quoted by Ramsaye, *A Million and One Nights*, I, 323ff.; see also Hendricks, *Beginnings of the Biograph*, 41–43.

50. See Ramsaye, *A Million and One Nights*, I, 326.

51. An interesting artist's sketch of the Vatican filming has survived which shows the motor-driven, battery-powered pre-1900 Biograph camera in operation. See Pratt, "No Magic," *Image* (December, 1959), 197. Another sketch of the

giant Biograph camera in operation shows it being used by Casler and Dickson to photograph the Penn R. R. Limited Express. See *Scientific American* (April 17, 1897).

52. See Kenneth Gordon, "Early Days of News-Reels," *British Kinematography,* Vol. XVII (August, 1950), 48.

53. At least this many Edison news films are listed and described in the Kemp Niver catalogue under the categories "Newsreel," "Newsreel (Catastrophe)," and "Newsreel (Human Interest)." Actually, the number of films listed here is greater; however, Niver's classification of films is rather arbitrary, and many of the titles which he has cast into these categories are not what we would consider "news films." Niver, *Motion Pictures from Library of Congress Collection.*

CHAPTER 2

1. For example, Low and Manvell presented, in Vol. I of the highly regarded three-volume *History of the British Film,* a photograph of a motion picture camera-man, back-to, filming a scene from the Boer War (illustration 19, following p. 80). They identify the cameraman as Joseph Rosenthal, an Englishman. The identical photograph is presented by the American motion picture pioneer Albert E. Smith in his memoirs. (*Two Reels and a Crank,* second illustration following p. 128). Smith claimed that it was he who was pictured in the photograph. South African film historian Pieter Germishuys agrees with Low and Manvell's identification of Rosenthal. However, Germishuys disputes their statement that Rosenthal was the first "professional war cameraman" and states that by the time Rosenthal arrived in Cape Town, Edgar Hyman, John Bennett Stanford, and W. K. L. Dickson had already filmed in the country. Pieter Germishuys, "Flickering Past," *South African Panorama,* May, 1963, pp. 3, 5; and Low and Manvell, *History of the British Film,* I, 66.

2. Edison copyrighted two similar films which had been made even earlier. In these films, by means of stop motion, a Cuban flag was replaced with an American flag. See these films in the Library of Congress collection, each entitled "Old Glory and the Cuban Flag," copyright No. 17706, March 15, 1898; and No. 18131, March 17, 1898.

3. Smith, *Two Reels and a Crank,* 54–55. Sentences rearranged for greater clarity.

4. Copyright No. 25325, April 21, 1898. See illustrations from Library of Congress collection reproduced in *Life,* September 20, 1943, p. 18.

5. Copyright No. 25323, April 21, 1898.

6. Smith, *Two Reels and a Crank,* 54.

7. Edison's film is copyright No. 38239, June 22, 1898.

8. Smith, *Two Reels and a Crank,* 56.

9. See copyrighted films of 1898 on these subjects, described in Niver, *Motion Pictures from Library of Congress Collection;* and Howard Lamarr Walls, *Motion Pictures, 1894–1912.*

10. Niver, *Motion Pictures from Library of Congress Collection.*

11. Smith, *Two Reels and a Crank*, 62–63. See also Homer Croy, *How Motion Pictures Are Made*, 257, which suggests that Smith's film of the San Juan charge may have been a fake.

12. Illustrations from the film in "Pioneer Newsreels," *Image*, September, 1953, p. 39.

13. Smith, *Two Reels and a Crank*, 66ff.

14. From a recording of Smith speaking at the Academy Award ceremonies in Hollywood in March, 1947. The recording is from the collection of Charles Clarke.

15. Arthur Krows, "Motion Pictures—Not for Theaters," *Educational Screen*, October, 1938, p. 249.

16. Blackton, speaking in a broadcast in 1940, claimed that this was the world's first motion picture newsreel (from a recording of the broadcast in the collection of Charles Clarke). Clearly, however, it was neither the "first" nor a newsreel—at least not as the term is generally defined. There are also contradictions in the recollections of Blackton and Smith about the manner in which the footage was secured. All the principals in this event have long since died, and there seems little chance of ever resolving such contradictions.

17. See copyrighted films of the years 1898 and 1899 on these subjects, described by Niver, *Motion Pictures from Library of Congress Collection*, and Walls, *Motion Pictures, 1894–1912*.

18. Pieter Germishuys, *loc. cit.*, 2–7.

19. Low and Manvell, *History of the British Film*, 25–26, 65ff.; and Cecil Hepworth, *Came the Dawn*, 39.

20. Low and Manvell, *History of the British Film*, 66ff.; see also Anonymous, *National Film Library Catalogue, Part I, Silent News Films, 1895–1933*, pp. 4–7; and Hepworth, *Came the Dawn*, 48.

21. Published in book form under the title *The Biograph in Battle*.

22. *Ibid.*, 75.

23. *Ibid.*, 63ff.

24. *Ibid.*, 62.

25. Smith, *Two Reels and a Crank*, 97–125.

CHAPTER 3

1. Maurice Bessy and Giuseppe Lo Duca, *George Méliès, Mage*, passim.

2. Lewis Jacobs, *The Rise of the American Film*, 22ff.

3. Copyrighted by Lubin as "Reproduction of the Jeffries and Sharkey Fight," September 9, 1899, No. 57771.

4. Smith, *Two Reels and a Crank*, 102.

5. *Ibid.*, 120.

6. See numerous fight films copyrighted by Sigmund Lubin between 1899 and 1908 and described in Niver, *Motion Pictures from Library of Congress Collection*; and Walls, *Motion Pictures, 1894–1912*. With the exception of the 1905 Britt vs. Nelson reproduction, these films apparently no longer exist and are known only by their record in the copyright files.

7. Ramsaye, *A Million and One Nights*, I, 390. See also Theisen, *loc. cit.*, 3.

8. Ramsaye, *A Million and One Nights*, 391; Baechlin and Muller-Strauss, *Newsreels Across the World*, 10; Maurice Bardèche and Robert Brasillach, *The History of the Motion Pictures*, 30.

9. Copyrighted films No. D16704, August 16, 1900; No. H18369, May 31, 1902; No. H18371, May 31, 1902; and No. H18370, May 31, 1902. See also illustrations of some of these scenes reproduced from the Library of Congress collection published in *Life*, September 20, 1943, p. 19.

10. Frank Lewis Dyer and Thomas Commerford Martin, *Edison—His Life and Inventions*, 547.

11. See copyrighted films No. H75677, May 2, 1906; No. H34100, August 3, 1903; No. H43618–H43620, H44025, March 23, 1904; No. H60289, May 3, 1905; No. H24896, December 9, 1902; No. H69962, December 12, 1905; No. H25968, December 31, 1902, described in Niver, *Motion Pictures from the Library of Congress Collection*; and Walls, *Motion Pictures, 1894–1912*.

12. Review in the *Rochester Democrat and Chronicle*, May, 1900, quoted by Pratt, *loc. cit.*, 206.

13. Presumably this is copyrighted film No. H77924, May 19, 1906.

14. Theisen, *loc. cit.*, 4.

15. Leslie Wood, *The Miracle of the Movies*, 191.

16. Theisen, *loc. cit.*

17. *Ibid.* Biograph also released three films on the San Francisco disaster which were apparently authentic: No. H77925, May 19, 1906; H77926, May 19, 1906; and No. H77927, May 19, 1906. Were these perhaps the films which Harry Miles shot and which ended up being released by Biograph? Sigmund Lubin also released a film on the disaster. Knowing his reputation, I would assume that it was a fake. See film copyright No. H77058, May 9, 1906.

18. Rachel Low and Roger Manvell, *The History of the British Film*, 68.

19. Leslie Wood, *Miracle of the Movies*, 192.

20. Lecture by Colonel A. C. Bromhead to the British Kinematographic Society, February 3, 1936, quoted in Low and Manvell, *The History of the British Film*, 69.

21. Henry, "The Historian of the Future," *Moving Picture World*, July 8, 1911, p. 1565.

22. T. S. Matthews, "What Makes News," *Atlantic*, December, 1957, p. 80. The paragraphs of this quotation have been reversed for greater clarity.

23. Ramsaye, *A Million and One Nights*, I, 392–93.

24. Smith, *Two Reels and a Crank*, 68.

CHAPTER 4

1. Helmut Gernsheim, *The History of Photography*, 357–72.

2. *Ibid.*, 371; see also Vincent S. Jones, "The Challenge of Photo-Journalism," *Image*, September, 1957, pp. 153ff.

3. See, for example, James Peck, "Sun and Shade, 1888–1896," *Image*, November, 1955, pp. 60ff., for a description of an early, short-lived picture magazine

entitled *Sun and Shade: A Record of Events by the Photographic Process of Reproduction*, which first appeared in 1888. Because of financial difficulties, the magazine's photographic coverage ceased shortly after its introduction.

4. Beaumont Newhall, *The History of Photography*, 177.

5. Gernsheim, *History of Photography*, 372.

6. Unless otherwise indicated, information regarding these early news films was secured from the United States copyright records. See Walls, *Motion Pictures: 1894–1912*; and Niver, *Motion Pictures from Library of Congress Collection*.

7. From an Edison catalogue of 1901, reprinted in Jacobs, *The Rise of the American Film*, 15.

8. Smith, *Two Reels and a Crank*, 125–29.

9. See films copyrighted September 24, 1900, Nos. D18560–D18567, H14295. See also photographic enlargements from some of these films published in *Life*, September 20, 1943, p. 19.

10. See films copyrighted September 11, 1901, Nos. H8588–H8590. For footage of McKinley's funeral, see films copyrighted January 22, 1903; No. H27388; November 11, 1902, No. H23805; September 26, 1901, No. H9084; September 21, 1901, No. H8914; September 21, 1901, No. H8915; September 26, 1901, No. H9083; and September 26, 1901, No. H9085. For the execution of Czolgosz, see film copyrighted November 9, 1901, No. H10605 (this is a reproduction).

11. Smith, *Two Reels and a Crank*, 132ff.

12. From an early Edison catalogue, quoted in the subtitle of a Museum of Modern Art archive compilation film entitled *Early Films of Interest*.

13. See film copyrighted May 14, 1906, No. H77297.

14. See *Moving Picture World*, January 30, 1909, p. 118.

15. See Oscar A. Depue, "My First Fifty Years in Motion Pictures," *Journal of the Society of Motion Picture Engineers*, Vol. XLIX (December, 1947), 488. See also film copyrighted by Biograph, May 2, 1906, No. H76577, which is a reproduction. Niver gives the copyright number as H75677 and Walls as H76577.

16. See films copyrighted February 15, 1904, No. H42176; February 12, 1904, No. H42054; February 12, 1904, No. H42055; February 19, 1904, No. H42310. See also photographic enlargements from some of these films published in *Life*, September 20, 1943, p. 19.

17. *Moving Picture World*, July 1, 1911, p. 1516.

18. *Ibid.*

19. See numerous films copyrighted between 1902 and 1905 and listed in the Walls and Niver catalogues.

20. See "Scientific Nature-Faking," *Collier's*, July 3, 1909, p. 13.

21. See Ramsaye, *A Million and One Nights*, II, 519–22.

22. *Ibid.*

23. Smith, *Two Reels and a Crank*, 151–53.

24. See numerous films copyrighted between 1901 and 1909 and listed in the Walls and Niver catalogues.

25. Copyright entries No. H1311–H1313, February 16, 1901; see also items listed in *National Film Library Catalogue of the British Film Institute*, Part I (1951), 7–8.

26. *Moving Picture World*, March 11, 1911, p. 526.

27. For authentic footage, see items listed in *National Film Library Catalogue of the British Film Institute*, Part I (1951), 9–10. A reproduction of the event which, according to Niver, was produced by Méliès, was copyrighted by American Mutoscope and Biograph on August 8, 1902, No. H20562.

28. *Ibid.*, 20–21.

29. *Ibid.*, 31–33. See also *Moving Picture World*, July 22, 1911, p. 115. The coronation footage is criticized in this account, which states that since "the titles are misplaced, making the descriptions untrue and misleading, only those possessed of the knowledge of English customs know whereby they can rightly interpret the picture for themselves." The report adds, "As a spectacle it is not what was expected, and unless we get some pictures giving more details, these films are not destined to become more than musty historical records."

30. *Moving Picture World*, March 11, 1911, p. 526.

31. *National Film Library Catalogue of the British Film Institute*, Part I (1951), 20–22.

32. *Moving Picture World*, June 4, 1910, p. 935.

33. *Ibid.* See also Thomas Sugrue, "The Newsreels," *Scribner's Magazine*, April, 1937, p. 16, for a photographic enlargement made from the original footage.

34. *Moving Picture World*, June 4, 1910, p. 930.

35. *Ibid.*

36. Kenneth Gordon, "The Early Days of News-Reels," *British Kinematography*, Vol. XVII (August, 1950), 49. For an even more detailed account, see Talbot, *Moving Pictures*, 120–22. See *National Film Library Catalogue of the British Film Institute*, Part I (1951), 35, for descriptions of particular surviving films in that collection.

37. *National Film Library Catalogue*, Part I (1951), 37ff.; and Low and Manvell, *The History of the British Film*, I, 65.

38. Entry copyrighted March 23, 1912, Nos. J167590–J167593. Apparently the footage of this entry no longer exists; only its mention in the copyright records remains.

39. Kenneth Gordon, "A Newsreel Man's Story," *Cine-Technician*, March, 1955, p. 36.

40. *Ibid.* See also Gordon, "The Early Days of News-Reels," *loc. cit.*, 49.

41. The Charles Urban Trading Company was founded in 1903 by an American entrepreneur whose name it bore. Before that time Urban had headed the American-owned Warwick Trading Company. See D. B. Thomas, *The First Colour Motion Pictures*.

42. See Theisen, "Story of the Newsreel," *loc. cit.*, 5, for a photographic enlargement.

43. Depue, *loc. cit.*, 489.

44. Abel Green and Joe Laurie, Jr., *Show Biz from Vaude to Video*, 54.

45. Ramsaye, *A Million and One Nights*, II, 570.

46. Depue, *loc. cit.*, 489.

47. Gordon, "The Early Days of News-Reels," *loc. cit.*

48. See Leo A. Handel, *Hollywood Looks at its Audience*, 170.

49. Copyrighted May 26, 1902, No. H18125; November 19, 1903, No. H38332; November 16, 1903, No. H38239. Green and Laurie have erroneously stated that "the first football game to be recorded for the cameras was the 1915 Yale-Harvard match." See Green and Laurie, *Show Biz from Vaude to Video*, 153.

50. See Niver, *Motion Pictures from Library of Congress Collection*, 384, for a list of the various America's Cup races which were filmed by early newsreel cameramen, and their copyright dates and numbers.

51. See films copyrighted in 1904.

52. *Moving Picture World*, October 22, 1910, p. 925.

53. *Ibid.*

54. *Ibid.*

55. See films copyrighted between 1901 and 1910 and listed in the Walls and Niver catalogues. Some of these films apparently no longer exist; only their mention in the copyright records survives.

56. For a retrospective account of the fight and the circumstances surrounding its presentation, see Al Bine, "The 'Battle of the Century,'" *Los Angeles Examiner*, July 4, 1960, Section 4, p. 3.

57. See Smith, *Two Reels and a Crank*, 220.

58. See Ramsaye, *A Million and One Nights*, II, 694.

59. *Ibid.* Cf. Smith, *Two Reels and a Crank*, 22, which gives a loss figure of $200,000. I consider the Ramsaye account more reliable.

60. Act of Congress, 37 Stat. 240 (July 31, 1912), Chap. 263, Sec. 1, Misdated by Smith as 1910 in *Two Reels and a Crank*, 222.

61. Ramsaye, *A Million and One Nights*, II, 698.

62. Films copyrighted August 4, 1904, No. 48851; April 12, 1904, No. H44434; April 8, 1904, No. H44263; March 12, 1904, No. H43183.

63. See scenes copyrighted August 14, 1905, No. H64509; and August 15, 1905, No. H64599. See also photographic enlargements from these scenes published in *Life*, September 20, 1943, 18ff.

64. See films copyrighted between 1901 and 1907 and listed in the Walls and Niver catalogues.

65. Copyrighted October 29, 1904, No. H52333.

66. See films copyrighted September 1, 1905, No. H65080; November 1, 1905, No. H68148; January 11, 1902, No. H13040; May 3, 1906, No. H76605; August 22, 1903, No. H34980.

67. Copyrighted April 18, 1902, No. H16735. See also Pratt, *loc. cit.*, 200ff. for photographic enlargements from the original footage.

68. Depue, *loc. cit.*, 487.

69. Theisen, "Story of the Newsreel," *loc. cit.*, 4ff.

70. Copyright January 12, 1903, No. H26890.

CHAPTER 5

1. David S. Hulfish, *The Motion Picture—Its Making and Its Theater*, 70.

2. Green and Laurie, *Show Biz from Vaude to Video*, 50.

3. Robert Grau, *The Theatre of Science*, 116; Jacobs, *The Rise of the American Film*, 56.

4. Walls, *Motion Pictures*, 1894–1912, viii.

5. This argument is developed by Nicholas Vardac, *Stage to Screen*. See also Allardyce Nicoll, *Film and Theatre*, for historical and theoretical discussions on the relations and distinctions between theater and cinema.

6. Anonymous, "The Topical Picture," *Moving Picture World*, July 16, 1910, p. 132.

7. The firm was founded by four Pathé brothers, with a total capital investment of about two thousand dollars. In panic two of the brothers withdrew from the organization shortly after its founding. Anonymous, "The Romance of a Great Business," *Education*, February, 1916, p. 395. In the English-language literature cited in this study, the French acute accent sometimes appeared in the name Pathé, and sometimes did not. For the sake of consistency, it is always shown here.

8. Anonymous, "Charles Pathé Honored," *Image*, October, 1954, p. 47.

9. Sadoul, *French Film*, 9.

10. See joint Museum of Modern Art and RKO-Pathé news release dated September 28, 1940, on the occasion of Pathé's gift of fifteen million feet of historical Pathé newsreel negative to the museum. From the collection of the museum.

11. There is some disagreement about the date of the opening of the *Pathé Journal*, estimates ranging from 1906 to 1910. The most likely date seems to be 1910 (*ibid.*); Grau, *The Theatre of Science*, 323; Anonymous, "The Romance of a Great Business," *loc. cit.*, 396; Anonymous, "The Weekly News Reel," *Moving Picture World*, July 21, 1917, p. 419; Theisen, "Story of the Newsreel," *loc. cit.*, 24; Sugrue, *loc. cit.*, 13; Krows, *loc. cit.*, 250; Bardèche and Brasillach, *The History of Motion Pictures*, 40; T. F. Woods, "Headlines in Celluloid," *Saturday Evening Post*, August 11, 1945, p. 22; Anonymous, *The Factual Film*, 136; and Baechlin and Muller-Strauss, *Newsreels Across the World*, 11. See also Léon Franconi, quoted in *New York Times*, October 29, 1939, Sec. 9, p. 4; and a letter from George P. Mills of *Pathé News*, New York, to historian Jay Leyda, dated March 9, 1939, in the files of the New York Museum of Modern Art, which dates the introduction of the French *Pathé Journal* as 1910.

12. Theisen, "Story of the Newsreel," *loc. cit.*, 24; and Jean Vivie, *Histoire et Dévelopement de la Technique Cinématographique*, Vol. I of Traite Général de Technique du Cinéma.

13. Baechlin and Muller-Strauss, *Newsreels Across the World*, 11.

14. *Ibid.*; see also Anonymous, "Animated Journalism," *World's Work*, October, 1910, p. 13476; and Anonymous, "The Romance of a Great Business," *loc. cit.*, 396.

15. Anonymous, "Animated Journalism," *loc. cit.*

16. Gordon, "The Early Days of Newsreels," *loc. cit.*, 48.

17. See interview with Léon Franconi, *New York Times*, October 29, 1939, Sec. 9, p. 4. See also Grau, *The Theatre of Science*, 323; Theisen, "Story of the Newsreel," *loc. cit.*, 24; Anonymous, "The Story of the News Reel," *loc. cit.*, 322; Sugrue,

loc. cit., 10, 13; Krows, *loc. cit.*, 250; and T. F. Woods, *loc. cit.* See also joint Museum of Modern Art and RKO-Pathé news release dated September 28, 1940. In a letter dated March 9, 1939, from George P. Mills of the Pathé News company to Jay Leyda of the Museum of Modern Art, Mills states that the first issue of *Pathé News* was released in America on November 11, 1910. From the collection of the museum.

18. Interview with Léon Franconi, *New York Times*, October 29, 1939, Sec. 9, p. 4.

19. Advertisement in *Moving Picture World*, August 19, 1911, p. 431.

20. Anonymous, "The Pathé Weekly," *Moving Picture World*, September 23, 1911, p. 871.

21. Ramsaye, *A Million and One Nights*, II, 518. Cf. tape-recorded interview of pioneer cameraman Arthur Miller, April 3, 1965. One of Miller's first jobs in the film industry was as a newsreel cameraman for Pathé.

22. At that time the ten participating organizations were Edison, Pathé, Méliès, Selig, Essanay, Lubin, Biograph, Vitagraph, Kleine, and Kalem. For a comprehensive history of the Motion Picture Patents Company and its distributing arm, the General Film Company, see Ralph Cassady, Jr., "Monopoly in Motion Picture Production and Distribution: 1908–1912," *Southern California Law Review*, Vol. XXXII, No. 4 (1959), 325–90.

23. Anonymous, "The Weekly News Reel," *loc. cit.*, 419.

24. Advertisement, *Moving Picture World*, July 29, 1911, p. 179. See also *Moving Picture World*, September 2, 1911, p. 653, and August 5, 1911, p. 315.

25. Editorial, *Moving Picture World*, July 29, 1911, p. 187.

26. Review, *Moving Picture World*, August 12, 1911, pp. 359–60.

27. Anonymous, "The Pathé Weekly," *loc. cit.*, 871. See also news item, *Motography*, August, 1911, which discusses the introduction of both the Pathé and the Vitagraph newsreels.

28. Anonymous, "The Weekly News Reel," *loc. cit.*, 420.

29. Theisen, "Story of the Newsreel," *loc. cit.*, 24.

30. Anonymous, "The Weekly News Reel," *loc. cit.*, 420.

31. Tape-recorded interview with Arthur Miller.

32. *Ibid.*

33. *Ibid.*

34. *Ibid.*

35. Theisen, "Story of the Newsreel," *loc. cit.*

36. Tape-recorded interview with Arthur Miller. According to Miller, who went to work for Pathé News in 1912, Hoagland was one of the general supervisors of the entire Pathé operation, but by that time had little to do with the newsreel unit. It was Franconi, who in 1912 was in charge of Pathé's newsreel operations, hired and fired personnel, and handed out assignments. See also Sugrue, *loc. cit.*, additional biographical information about Franconi.

37. Grau, *Theatre of Science*, 323.

38. Anonymous, "The Weekly News Reel," *loc. cit.*, 420.

39. Anonymous, "A Combination of Interesting Subjects," *Moving Picture World*, April 13, 1912, p. 118.

40. Tape-recorded interview with Arthur Miller.

41. Anonymous, "Pathé Putting Out News Daily," *Moving Picture World,* June 13, 1914, p. 1524.

42. *Ibid.*

43. *Ibid.*

44. *Moving Picture World,* May 16, 1914, p. 975.

45. Anonymous, "Pathé Putting Out News Daily," *loc. cit.;* and Anonymous, "The Romance of a Great Business," *loc. cit.,* 397.

46. In addition, before World War I, Pathé's *weekly* issue was printed on safety stock as a matter of course. See *Moving Picture World,* June 13, 1914, p. 1524, and June 27, 1914, p. 1841. Agfa Film Company also manufactured a non-flammable film stock in 1914.

47. *Moving Picture World,* July 21, 1917, p. 420.

CHAPTER 6

1. Anonymous, "How We Vitagraphed the Hudson-Fulton Marine Celebration," *Moving Picture World,* October 9, 1909, p. 482.

2. Advertisement, *Moving Picture World,* July 29, 1911, p. 180, and August 19, 1911, p. 432.

3. See news item regarding the introduction of the Pathé and Vitagraph newsreels in *Motography,* August, 1911, p. 56. See also *Moving Picture World,* August 5, 1911, p. 283 for another such news item.

4. Advertisement, *Moving Picture World,* July 29, 1911, p. 180. For an illustration from the film, see *Moving Picture World,* August 12, 1911, p. 379.

5. Review, *Moving Picture World,* August 5, 1911, p. 283.

6. Smith, *Two Reels and a Crank,* 223ff.

7. *Ibid.*

8. Anonymous, "Gaumont Weekly for Film Supply Company," *Moving Picture World,* August 3, 1912, p. 431.

9. Francis Collins, *The Camera Man,* 93ff., for a brief description of Mutual's operations. See also *Moving Picture World,* February 14, 1914, p. 824; January 4, 1913, p. 87, January 24, 1914, p. 427; and many references regarding Mutual's war coverage cited in Chapter 7.

10. See, for example, advertisements in *Exhibitors Herald,* November 15, 1919, p. 18, and December 13, 1919, at front of issue. See also Arthur Krows, "Motion Pictures—Not for Theatres," *Educational Screen,* October, 1938, p. 251.

11. Ramsaye, *A Million and One Nights,* II, 812ff. See also Howard Thompson Lewis (ed.), "Associated Newsreels, Incorporated: Producer and Distributor—Motion Pictures," in *Harvard Business Reports,* VIII, 126–31.

12. *Exhibitors Herald,* January 22, 1921, p. 43; March 5, 1921, p. 11; March 26, 1921, p. 59; April 16, 1921, p. 19; May 14, 1921, p. 7; February 11, 1922, p. 61; February 12, 1921; January 15, 1921; and February 5, 1921, p. 70.

13. *Motion Picture Herald,* December 13, 1947.

14. *Moving Picture World,* April 23, 1927, p. 737.

15. Unidentified news clipping in the Theater Collection of the New York Public Library, dated December 15, 1931, supplied to the author on microfilm.

16. See issues of *Exhibitors Herald* for February 21, 1920, p. 48; March 3, 1920, p. 6; March 27, 1920, pp. 6 and 38; April 17, 1920, p. 50; May 22, 1920, p. 20; May 29, 1920, p. 46; June 26, 1920, p. 13; February 12, 1921; February 19, 1921; March 19, 1921; August 27, 1921, p. 13; February 4, 1922, p. 36; April 8, 1922, p. 68; September 2, 1922, p. 96; September 16, 1922, p. 64; and October 7, 1922, front ad. It is not known when *Selznick News* went out of business; however, as late as December 23, 1922, a review of the reel appeared on page 53 of the *Exhibitors Herald*.

17. Advertisements, *Moving Picture World*, January 24, 1914, p. 463, and February 7, 1914.

18. *Exhibitors Herald*, July 2, 1921, and July 16, 1921.

19. Boyle's obituary, *Journal of the Society of Motion Picture and Television Engineers*, Vol. LXIX (January, 1960), 60.

20. Herbert Aller, "News Reels: Enterprise Personified," *International Photographer*, April, 1938, p. 37; and Anonymous, "The First News Reel," *International Photographer*, September, 1929, p. 26.

21. *Moving Picture World*, January 17, 1914, p. 334, and April 25, 1914, p. 537.

22. Aller, "News Reels," *loc. cit.*, 38. See also Sugrue, *loc. cit.*, 13.

23. Theisen, "Story of the Newsreel," *loc. cit.*, 24; and Ramsaye, *A Million and One Nights*, II, 655ff.

24. Theisen, "Story of the Newsreel," *loc. cit.*, states that Selig produced news films from 1905 onward. Actually, Selig copyrighted two news films as early as 1903, while in 1904 he copyrighted three fake news films. In any case, Selig was certainly involved in news-film production as early as 1903.

25. *Ibid.*

26. Advertisement, *Moving Picture World*, March 7, 1914, p. 1263. Norman Alley, however, states that the first issue was released on February 14, 1914 (*I Witness*, 57). For early advertisements and articles regarding this reel, see the issue of *Selig Polyscope Company Release* containing synopses of releases, August 17–31, 1914, p. 14, and *ibid.*, Vol. I, No. 4, pp. 5ff. See also advertisement, *Moving Picture World*, March 14, 1914, p. 1331.

27. Krows, *loc. cit.*, 250; and Anonymous, "The Weekly News Reel," *loc. cit.*, 420; Alfred A. Cohn, "A Film Newspaper in the Making," *Photoplay Magazine*, April, 1916, p. 46.

28. Anonymous, "The Weekly News Reel," *loc. cit.*

29. *Time*, November 23, 1936, p. 25.

30. Advertisement, *Moving Picture World*, March 7, 1914, p. 1263. The word "newsreel" appears there as two words. See also brochure, "Facts About Newsreels —1940 Edition," published by the Newsreel Theaters of New York City, an association which included the Embassy Theater, in the collection of the Museum of Modern Art. The brochure claims that the Hearst newsreel was the first to use the term "newsreel." See also Cohn, *loc. cit.*, 46–47; and *Moving Picture World*,

July 21, 1917, p. 419, for early uses of the word "newsreel." See *Variety*, January 8, 1930, for mention of Hearst's use of the term as early as 1914.

31. Cohn, *loc. cit.*

32. Krows, *loc. cit.*

33. Cohn, *loc. cit.*

34. *Ibid.*, 46ff.

35. Theisen, "Story of the Newsreel," *loc. cit.*, 24. The copyright date of the first issue was April 20, 1913, according to the copyright records.

36. Anonymous, "Local 'War' Scenes," *Moving Picture World*, October 17, 1914, p. 352.

37. *Moving Picture World*, November 28, 1914, p. 1218.

38. *Exhibitors Herald*, October 11, 1919, p. 64. For typical advertisements of the period, see the following issues of *Exhibitors Herald*: October 18, 1919, p. E4; November 1, 1919, front ad; August 14, 1920, following p. 66; March 4, 1922, front ad; July 15, 1922, following p. 10; September 2, 1922, p. 16; September 23, 1922, front ad; November 11, 1922, front ad.

39. *Ibid.*, September 13, 1919, p. 48.

40. *Ibid.*, October 4, 1919, p. 55.

41. *Ibid.* See also *ibid.*, October 11, 1919, p. 64.

42. *Ibid.*, October 4, 1919, p. 55.

43. *Ibid.*

44. *Ibid.*

45. *Ibid.*, October 11, 1919, p. 64; and November 15, 1919, p. 105.

46. *Ibid.*, October 4, 1919, p. 55.

47. *Ibid.*, December 23, 1922, p. 53.

48. *Ibid.*

49. *Ibid.*, November 13, 1920.

50. *Ibid.*, February 11, 1922, p. 70; April 1, 1922, p. 8; January 29, 1921, p. 81; and June 10, 1922, p. 37.

51. *Ibid.*, March 4, 1922, p. 63; and February 4, 1922, pp. 12–13.

CHAPTER 7

1. Sugrue, *loc. cit.*, 17.

2. Ariel Varges, "Ace Newsreeler Gives Light on How He Films News of the World," *American Cinematographer*, July, 1938, p. 275; and Aller, "News Reels: Enterprise Personified," *loc. cit.*, 37.

3. Anonymous, "Capturing Mexico with a Camera," *Literary Digest*, June 6, 1914, p. 1390; and Aller, "News Reels: Enterprise Personified," *loc. cit.*

4. Anonymous, "Wagner in Mexico," *Moving Picture World*, July 18, 1914, p. 440; and *Moving Picture World*, January 24, 1914, p. 403.

5. Anonymous, "Wagner in Mexico," *loc. cit.*

6. Anonymous, "Capturing Mexico with a Camera," *loc. cit.*

7. *New York Times*, January 8, 1914, p. 2; and Ramsaye, *A Million and One Nights*, II, 671.

8. *New York Times*, January 7, 1914, p. 1. See also advertisements in issues of *Moving Picture World*, February 7, 1914, p. 703, and February 28, 1914, p. 1133.

9. Homer Croy, *How Motion Pictures Are Made*, 258; and Ramsaye, *A Million and One Nights*, II, 671.

10. *Moving Picture World*, September 12, 1914, p. 1487, and January 24, 1914, p. 421.

11. *New York Times*, January 7, 1914, p. 1.

12. Ramsaye, *A Million and One Nights*, II, 672. See also *New York Times*, January 8, 1914, p. 2.

13. See Theodore Irwin, "Camera! Feeding the News Reels," *Popular Mechanics*, May, 1930, p. 797; and Ramsaye, *A Million and One Nights*, II, 673.

14. For an account of the New York exhibition of the newsreel footage of the battle at Torreón, shown at the Lyric Theater for the first time on May 9, 1914, see *New York Times*, May 10, 1914, Sec. 4, p. 7. See also W. Stephen Bush, "Mexican War Pictures," *Moving Picture World*, February 7, 1914, p. 657; and advertisements in *Moving Picture World*, June 20, 1914, p. 1648, and February 7, 1914, p. 703.

15. Editorial, *New York Times*, January 8, 1914, p. 10.

16. Editorial, *London Evening News*, quoted in *New York Times*, January 9, 1914, p. 2.

17. Editorial, London *Daily Citizen*, quoted in *New York Times*, January 9, 1914, p. 2.

18. See Homer Croy, "It Looks Easy," *Saturday Evening Post*, November 5, 1921, p. 14.

19. Charles Rosher, quoted in "No Cameras Going to the Front," *Moving Picture World*, September 12, 1914, p. 1487.

20. Croy, *How Motion Pictures Are Made*, 259; Collins, *The Camera Man*, 14; and Anonymous, "All War Pictures Fakes," *Moving Picture World*, October 3, 1914, p. 50.

21. Joseph Ward Swain, *The Harper History of Civilization*, II, 566ff.

22. Stephen Bush, "War Films," *Moving Picture World*, September 19, 1914, p. 1617.

23. *Ibid.*

24. Letter from John D. Tippett, September 5, 1914, *Moving Picture World*, October 3, 1914, p. 50.

25. Anonymous, "Fake War Movies," *Literary Digest*, November 13, 1915, p. 1079. The article is composed mostly of quotations from an article appearing in *Popular Science and the World's Advance*, November, 1915.

26. A. K. Dawson, quoted in Collins, *The Camera Man*, 7ff.

27. *Ibid.*, 9.

28. Charles I. Reid, "The Adventures of the 'Movie' Camera Man," *Photographic Times*, June, 1915, p. 236.

29. Anonymous, "Faking War Pictures," *Picture World*, November 28, 1914, p. 1249.

30. The *St. Stephen* was sunk by two Italian gunboats in the Adriatic on June

10, 1918. The newsreel sequence is included in a reel entitled *Early Films of Interest* in the collection of the New York Museum of Modern Art.

31. For information about this unusual camera design, see Charles I. Reid, *loc. cit.*, 236; Ernest Dench, "Methods by Which the European War Has Been Filmed," *Scientific American*, March 20, 1915, p. 277; Anonymous, *Proceedings, British Kinematographic Society*, No. 21 (1933), No. 28 (1935), No. 38 (1936); Gordon, "The Early Days of Newsreels," *loc. cit.*, 48; Austin Lescarboura, *Behind the Motion Picture Screen*, 232; L. C. Goldsmith, "Grinding Out History," *Sunset Magazine*, July, 1925, p. 33; Croy, *How Motion Pictures Are Made*, 260ff.; and Geoffrey Malins, *How I Filmed the War*, passim. Several photographs of the Aeroscope camera appear in Malins' book, shown being operated by the author. This flamboyantly titled book is an interesting account of the work of a British War Office newsreel cameraman. See also *Nickelodeon*, July, 1909, p. 25.

32. Croy, *How Motion Pictures Are Made*, 259.

33. Dench, "Methods by Which the European War Has Been Filmed," *loc. cit.*

34. *Ibid.*

35. *Ibid.*

36. James Mock and Cedric Larson, *Words That Won the War*.

37. *How the War Came to America*.

38. Elmer E. Cornwell, Jr., "Wilson, Creel and the Presidency," *Public Opinion Quarterly*, Vol. XXIII (Summer, 1959), 196.

39. *Ibid.*, 192.

40. Earl Theisen, "The Photographer in the World War," *International Photographer*, November, 1933, p. 4.

41. Croy, *How Motion Pictures Are Made*, 265ff.

42. George Creel, *How We Advertised America*.

43. Theisen, "The Photographer in the World War," *loc. cit.*

44. Quoted from Alexander Khanzhonkov, *The First Years of Russian Cinematography* (Moscow, 1937), in Leyda, *Kino*, 92.

45. Anonymous, "Tragedy and Comedy in Making Pictures of the Russian Chaos," *Current Opinion*, February, 1918, p. 106ff.

46. *New York Times*, December 10, 1917, p. 15.

47. For example, see the description of the coverage of Lenin's 1924 funeral by John Dored, "Soviets Imprison A.S.C. Member for News 'Scoop' in Filming Lenin's Funeral in Moscow," *American Cinematographer*, May, 1924, p. 4; John Dored, "Newsreeler's Dilemma," *American Cinematographer*, June, 1949, p. 213; and John Dored and Robert Low, *I Shoot the World*, 47.

CHAPTER 8

1. Sadoul, *French Film*, 20ff.

2. *Ibid.*, 16.

3. Stuart Mackenzie, "How the Movie News Man Gets Pictures of World Events," *American Magazine*, January, 1924, p. 40; see also *Exhibitors Herald*, October 25, 1922, p. 63.

4. George J. Lancaster [*Paramount News* cameraman], "Tragedy Follows News Cameramen," *International Photographer*, May, 1932, p. 12.

5. Emanuel Cohen, "The Business of International News by Motion Pictures," *Annals of the American Academy of Political and Social Science*, Vol. XXVIII (November, 1926), 76.

6. Mackenzie, *loc. cit.*

7. *Ibid.*

8. A. Hubl, "Cultural Films and Sound News Reels," *International Review of Educational Cinematography*, April, 1932, p. 268. The company involved here, however, was not Pathé.

9. S. L. Rothapfel, "Dramatizing Music for the Pictures," *Reel Life*, September 5, 1914, p. 23.

10. *Exhibitor's Trade Review*, January 12, 1918, p. 515.

11. The statistics provided in this section are taken from the following sources: Howard Thompson Lewis, "Associated Newsreels, Incorporated," in *Harvard Business Reports*, VIII, 126ff.; Cohen, *loc. cit.*; Mackenzie, *loc. cit.*; Arthur Pound, "When Movies Tell the News," *Independent*, November 28, 1925, p. 615; John Amid, *With the Movie Makers*, 52ff.; Charles P. Morrison, "Topical Cinematography," *American Photography*, March, 1927, pp. 152ff.; Howard Lewis, *The Motion Picture Industry*, 54ff.; Sugrue, *loc. cit.*, 9ff.; Collins, *The Camera Man*, 93ff.; and tape-recorded interview with Arthur Miller. See also Sanford E. Greenwald, "The Good Old Days," *International Photographer*, April, 1965, p. 16.

12. Greenwald, "The Good Old Days," *loc. cit.*

13. Herbert McKay, "Hints for News Cameramen," *Motion Picture Photography for the Amateur*," 174ff.; Morrison, "Topical Cinematography," *American Photography*, loc. cit., 640ff.; and Colin Noel Bennett, *The Handbook of Kinematography*, 35ff.

14. Bill Davidson, "The Newsreel Business," *Cosmopolitan*, September, 1946, p. 149.

15. The section was entitled "Newspictures." For a typical issue see *Exhibitors Herald*, April 15, 1922, p. 61.

16. Pound; *loc. cit.*; Lescarboura, *Behind the Motion Picture Screen*, 226; Davidson, *loc. cit.*; and Robert Humfrey, *Careers in Film*, 72.

17. *Exhibitors Herald*, October 7, 1922, p. 55.

CHAPTER 9

1. Theisen, "Story of the Newsreel," *loc. cit.*, 3.

2. Lescarboura, *Behind the Motion Picture Screen*, 234ff.

3. *Ibid.*, 236ff.

4. Letter from Joe Gibson to Ray Fernstrom in *International Photographer*, February, 1933, p. 18.

5. *Exhibitors Herald*, January 1, 1921.

6. Croy, "It Looks Easy," *loc. cit.*, 59. See also Mackenzie, "How the Movie

News Man Gets Pictures of World Events," *loc. cit.*, 40; and Anonymous, "Braving Death for News Films," *Literary Digest*, May 28, 1927, p. 48.

7. Morris Markey, "A Reporter at Large: Newsreel," *New Yorker*, September 22, 1934, pp. 68ff.; Anthony North, "Let's Wait for the Newsreel," *New Outlook*, October, 1934, p. 25; and Davidson, "The Newsreel Business," *loc. cit.*, 149. For information about "bought pictures" in Great Britain, see Gordon, "A Newsreel Man's Story," *loc. cit.*, 37.

8. Gordon, "A Newsreel Man's Story," *loc. cit.*, 37.

9. Robert Humfrey, *Careers in Film*, 74.

10. *Motion Picture Herald*, April 6, 1935, p. 17.

11. *Ibid.*

12. Anonymous, "Olympics—Ltd.," *Time*, July 26, 1948, p. 65.

13. Markey, "Reporter at Large: Newsreel," *loc. cit.*, 70.

14. *Exhibitors Herald*, November 11, 1922, p. 53.

15. Ray Hall, "Seeing is Believing," *Independent*, September 18, 1926, p. 327.

16. Editorial, *Leslie's Weekly*, January 6, 1900, quoted in Jacobs, *The Rise of the American Film*, 13ff.

17. Henry, "The Historian of the Future," *loc. cit.*, 1565.

18. *Moving Picture World*, July 29, 1911, p. 187.

19. Talbot, *Moving Pictures*, 279.

20. Bush, "War Films," *loc. cit.*, 187.

21. "Newspictures," *Exhibitors Herald*, June 24, 1922, p. 93.

22. Charles P. Morrison, "The News Film," *American Photography*, December, 1926, p. 640.

23. Emanuel Cohen, "The Business of International News by Motion Pictures," *loc. cit.*, 76.

24. *Ibid.*

25. Lescarboura, *Behind the Motion Picture Screen*, 230. Italics added.

26. Reid, "The Adventures of the 'Movie' Camera Man," *loc cit.*, 235.

27. Eugene Lyons, "Louis de Rochemont, Maverick of the Movies," *Reader's Digest*, July, 1949, p. 23. See also Maurice Zolotow, "Want to be a Movie Star?" *Saturday Evening Post*, March 29, 1952, p. 25.

28. Lancaster, "Tragedy Follows News Cameramen," *loc. cit.*, 11.

29. Tracy Mathewson, quoted in Betty Shannon, "The Prince and the Pictures," *Photoplay*, March, 1920, p. 56.

30. *Ibid.*, 56 and 118.

31. Green and Laurie, *Show Biz from Vaude to Video*, 153; and news items based upon a Hearst press release published in *Exhibitors Herald-World*, June 29, 1929, p. 137, and *New York American*, June 23, 1929, p. 16L.

32. *Moving Picture World*, January 22, 1927, p. 247; April 2, 1927, p. 464.

33. Anonymous, "Obituary: Terry Ramsaye," *Films in Review*, October, 1954, p. 386.

34. For an analysis of the financial position of Educational Pictures, Inc., see Lewis, "Educational Pictures, Incorporated," in *Harvard Business Reports*, VIII, 115–25.

35. Theisen, "Story of the Newsreel," *loc. cit.*, 25.

36. *Moving Picture World*, February 12, 1927, p. 475; March 5, 1927, p. 12; March 19, 1927, p. 155; and April 2, 1927, cover ad.

37. E. C. Schnurmacher, "Get the Story: They Risk Their Lives to Live," *Popular Mechanics*, March, 1932, p. 410.

38. Lewis, "Associated Newsreels, Incorporated," *loc. cit.*, 126.

39. *Ibid.*, 130. See also *Exhibitors Daily Review*, December 2, 1928.

40. *Ibid.*, 131.

CHAPTER 10

1. Edison Caveat No. 110, handwritten draft in the archives of the Thomas Alva Edison Foundation, West Orange, N.J., published in Bowen, *loc. cit.*, 510.

2. Hendricks, *The Kinetoscope*, 118–25, and illustrations 48 and 49.

3. For an exhaustive, authoritative historical survey of sound–motion picture technology, see Edward W. Kellogg, "History of Sound Motion Pictures," *Journal of the Society of Motion Picture and Television Engineers*, Vol. LXIV (June, 1955), 291–302; (July, 1955), 356–74; and (August, 1955), 422–37. See also Earl Sponable, "Historical Development of Sound Films," *Journal of the Society of Motion Picture Engineers*, April, 1947, pp. 275–303; May, 1947, pp. 407–22; and Will H. Hays, *See and Hear*. For contemporaneous description of sound-film equipment and technique, see Anonymous, "Be Your Own Producer and Newsreel Cameraman," *International Photographer*, November, 1934, p. 15; Walter McInnis, "The Newsreel Cameraman," *Journal of the Society of Motion Picture Engineers*, Vol. XLVII (November, 1946), 368–71; Warren McGrath, "News Mikes Hear but Not Seen," *International Photographer*, June, 1938, pp. 19–21; Harold Smith, "Sound in News Ten Years Old," *International Photographer*, April, 1937, pp. 13ff.; Harry Jones, "The Modern Newsreel," *Journal of the Society of Motion Picture Engineers*, Vol. XIV (February, 1930), 204–208; Fitzhugh Green, *The Film Finds Its Tongue*; and Warren McGrath, "Newsreel Sound," *Journal of the Society of Motion Picture Engineers*, Vol. XLVII (November, 1946), 371–75.

4. Not to be confused with the Photophone sound-on-film system introduced by RCA in the late 1920's. See Kellogg, *loc. cit.*, 301, who states that "the first commercial uses of RCA Photophone recording equipment were for newsreel service."

5. *Ibid.*, 295.

6. E. I. Sponable, *loc. cit.*, 292–93, includes a production photograph of the La Follett interview. See also rare examples of De Forest test sound films in the collection of the American Film Institute.

7. Kellogg, *loc. cit.*, 296; Sponable, *loc. cit.*, 408; and Hays, *See and Hear*, 53. See also *New York Times*, April 30, 1927, p. 25. Finally, see Ben Hall, *The Best Remaining Seats*, 248. According to Hall, *What Price Glory?* and its accompanying Movietone shorts opened at the Sam Harris Theater on November 28, 1926. However, all three of the other writers above agree on the date January 21, 1927. Without detracting from Hall's otherwise very informative book, I accept the date

given by Sponable, Hays, and Kellogg, all of whom were involved either in the introduction of the sound film in America, or in the later sophistication of it.

8. See Sponable, *loc. cit.*, 409; Hays, *See and Hear*, 53; and Hall, *The Best Remaining Seats*, 248. (Hall misdates this event as 1926.) According to Hall, the Movietone scene of Lindbergh's takeoff had been slipped into a silent-film program at the Roxy Theater four days earlier, on May 21, at the moment when the news of Lindbergh's safe arrival in Paris reached New York City.

9. Frederick Lewis Allen, *Only Yesterday*, 245ff. Originally published by Harper & Row, Publishers, Inc., and reprinted with their permission.

10. The Lindbergh newsreel sequences—both of the takeoff and of the Washington welcome ceremonies—are available for study in their original form from the Film library of the Museum of Modern Art, New York.

11. Charles Gilson operated the camera and E. H. Hansen the sound equipment. See Sponable, *loc. cit.*, May, 1947, p. 409.

12. There is a cut at midpoint from a long shot to a medium long shot, but both shots were taken from exactly the same position, head-on, presumably by two cameras operating side by side.

13. See Jerome Beatty, "Shooting the Big Shots," *American Magazine*, February, 1931, p. 69.

14. See Sponable, *loc. cit.*, May, 1947, pp. 409–10.

15. See continuity copy describing these two issues in the collection of the Museum of Modern Art, New York.

16. Information about these early sound-film interviews has been secured from the following sources: Beatty, *loc. cit.*, 68–69, 138–41; Harry Lawrenson, "Foreign Editions," *Journal of the Society of Motion Picture Engineers*, Vol. XLVII (November, 1946), 361–64; Stuart Chesmore, *Behind the Cinema Screen*, 58–61, and Sponable, *loc. cit.*, May, 1947, p. 409.

17. Sponable, *loc. cit.*, May, 1947, p. 409.

18. See Beatty, *loc. cit.*, 70.

19. *Ibid.*, 143.

20. *Ibid.*, passim. See also Hays, *See and Hear*, 54–55; and *Films in Review*, August–September, 1961, p. 413.

21. A print of the Shaw film is available for study from the film library of the Museum of Modern Art, New York.

22. Burns Mantle, quoted in Anonymous, "American Debut of G.B.S.," *Literary Digest*, July 28, 1928, p. 21.

23. Warren McGrath, "Newsreel Sound," *loc. cit.*, 372ff.

24. J. A. Battle, "Newsreel Sound Quality Is Greatly Improved," *International Projectionist*, August, 1935, pp. 23–25.

25. Sugrue, *loc. cit.*, 13; Hays, *See and Hear*, 54; and Sponable, *loc. cit.*, May, 1947, p. 413.

26. Anonymous, "Seeing the World in Ten Minutes," *Popular Mechanics*, May, 1939, p. 698.

27. *Variety*, April 13, 1929; and *Exhibitor's Daily Review*, February 28, 1930; January 7, 1930; and February 14, 1930.

28. George Baynes, quoted in *Exhibitor's Herald-World*, November 16, 1929.

29. *Moving Picture World*, March 5, 1927, p. 11; and May 2, 1927, p. 781. See also Lewis, "Associated Newsreels, Inc.," in *Harvard Business Reports*, VIII, 126.

30. News items in *Exhibitor's Herald-World*, June 29, 1929, and *New York American*, June 23, 1929, p. 16L. Before these dates rumors circulated that Hearst was about to enter into a similar arrangement with Warner Brothers Studios. *Variety*, April 3, 1929, and *Exhibitor's Daily Review*, April 1, 1929; *New York Journal*, July 31, 1929; *New York American*, August 14, 1929.

31. *Exhibitor's Daily Review*, February 14, 1929.

32. Unidentified newspaper clipping dated August 25, 1931, part of the MGM clipping file in the Theater Collection of the New York Public Library.

33. Unidentified newspaper clipping dated November 17, 1931, in the Theater Collection of the New York Public Library.

34. Abram Myers, "Allied Makes Progress in 1931," *The 1932 Film Daily Year Book of Motion Pictures*, 532.

35. Ramsaye, *A Million and One Nights*, II, 813; and citations given in Chap. 3, note 63.

36. *Film World*, January, 1964, pp. 8–10. Most of the footage of this newsreel became part of the Historical Film Collection of the Ford Motor Company, which was formally presented to the National Archives, Washington, D.C., by Ford Motor Company on November 13, 1963.

37. Apparently introduced on March 1, 1932, as an independent newsreel for the states'-righter market. See Lewis, *The Motion Picture Industry*, 135.

38. Fernstrom, "Something New in Newsreels," *International Photographer*, December, 1934, p. 9; and Ray Fernstrom, "The Junior Newsreel Is Here," *International Photographer*, September, 1934, p. 4.

39. Paul Wyand, *Useless If Delayed—Adventures in Putting History on Film*, 253.

40. Magdalon Grahl, "Home State Newsreel Got Start on Gridiron," *Motion Picture Herald*, August 14, 1937, p. 92.

41. Produced by Charles Ford, who later became managing editor of the Universal sound newsreel. See Sugrue, *loc. cit.*, 14.

42. Anonymous, "Negro Newsreel Seen by 4,000,000," *American Cinematographer*, November, 1943, p. 408. See also Baechlin and Muller-Strauss, *Newsreels Across the World*, 61; Woods, *loc. cit.*, 22; and a typical continuity sheet for Vol. 2, No. 95, of the *All-American News* in the collection of the Museum of Modern Art, New York.

43. Anonymous, "News Parade," *Time*, June 21, 1937, p. 42. See also the *New York Times*, July 4, 1937, Sec. 10, p. 4.

CHAPTER 11

1. Sugrue, *loc. cit.*, 14.

2. *Motion Picture Herald*, July 7, 1934, p. 22; June 8, 1935, p. 58; and June 17, 1937, pp. 32–33. See also Charles S. Aaronson, "Forty Years of Screen Journalism,"

Motion Picture Herald, August 29, 1959, p. 15; *Motion Picture Herald*, June 8, 1935, p. 58; *Film Daily*, January 20, 1930.

3. *Motion Picture Herald*, March 24, 1945, p. 33.

4. Morris Markey, "A Reporter at Large: Newsreel," *New Yorker*, September 22, 1934, p. 67.

5. *Ibid.*, 68.

6. *Motion Picture Herald*, August 10, 1935.

7. Janet Mabie, "Reeling Up the Newsreels," *Christian Science Monitor Magazine*, June 19, 1935, p. 3; and Naomie Jones, "The Invisible Vyvyan and the Voice of Fashion," *Woman*, May, 1947, p. 5. See also Anonymous, "Screen: Newsreels Seek Gains with 'Super-Commentators,' " *News-Week*, October 6, 1934, p. 22.

8. "She Makes Movies," *Independent Woman*, October, 1934, p. 315.

9. *Motion Picture Herald*, April 20, 1935, p. 26.

10. Newton Meltzer, "Are Newsreels News?" *Hollywood Quarterly*, Vol. II (April, 1947), 271. Meltzer was associated with *Telenews*, a competing release in the 1940's.

11. Roy Tash, "Shooting the 'Quints,' " *International Photographer*, December, 1935, pp. 19 and 32. See also Alley, *I Witness*, 161 ff.; and *Motion Picture Herald*, September 1, 1934, pp. 23 and 55.

12. *New York Times*, July 2, 1940, p. 17.

13. Browning, *loc. cit.*, 320.

14. Theisen, "Story of the Newsreel," *loc. cit.*, 25. An obituary describing the work of Pathé cameraman Will E. Hudson appears in Patsie Sinkey, "Farewell, Traveller," *International Photographer*, December, 1945, p. 14.

15. Lewis, *The Motion Picture Industry*, 54.

16. Meltzer, *loc. cit.*, 271. See also Lewis, *Motion Picture Industry*, 50.

17. Handel, *Hollywood Looks at Its Audience*, 170; and Carlton Brown, "What's Wrong with the Newsreels?" *Tomorrow*, October, 1947, pp. 15ff.

18. *Motion Picture Herald*, May 29, 1937, p. 55; and June 12, 1937, p. 40.

19. *Ibid.*, September 22, 1934, p. [23]; and June 15, 1935, p. [41].

20. Anonymous, "Hearst's News of the Day," *Time*, November 23, 1936, p. 25.

21. *Moving Picture World*, March 5, 1927, p. 11; May 2, 1927, p. 781.

22. Anonymous, "Screen: Newsreels Seek Gains with 'Super-Commentators,' " *loc. cit.*, 22; and Kellogg, *loc. cit.*, 296.

23. *Motion Picture Herald*, September 29, 1934, p. 10; *Greater Amusements*, September 28, 1929; *Exhibitors Herald-World*, September 28, 1929; and *Variety*, August 28, 1927.

24. *Ibid.* See also *Motion Picture Herald*, September 1, 1934, p. 55.

25. Anonymous, "Better News Reels," *Outlook and Independent*, October 2, 1929, p. 179.

26. Sugrue, *loc. cit.*, 14.

27. Theisen, "Story of the Newsreel," *loc. cit.*, 25.

28. Wallace West, *Paramount Newsreel Men with Admiral Byrd in Little America*; and Lancaster, *loc. cit.*, 12.

29. *Motion Picture Herald,* April 13, 1935, p. 3.

30. Anonymous, " 'Educational' Newsreels for WPA," *Literary Digest,* August 8, 1936, p. 32.

31. Norman Alley, "Shoot, I've Got You Covered," *loc. cit.,* 18. For a typical advertisement of this period, see *Motion Picture Herald,* May 2, 1936, p. 31.

32. Mabie, *loc. cit.,* 3; and E. C. Schnurmacher, "Get the Story," *loc. cit.,* 405.

33. Theisen, "Story of the Newsreel," *loc. cit.,* 25.

34. Tape recording of an address delivered by George Crane at the University of Southern California, Department of Cinema, February 20, 1959, in the collection of the author. See also George Krainukov, "Universal's Thrill Hunter in China," *International Photographer,* July, 1941, pp. 3–7; and *Time,* September 13, 1937, p. 33.

35. *Humiston v. Universal Film Mfg. Co.* (1917), *New York Law Journal,* August 10, Ordway. The original verdict was for the plaintiff, later reversed by the appellate court. *Humiston v. Universal Mfg. Co.* (1919) 178 N.Y.S. 752, 755 (or 189) and App. Div. 467. For a discussion of the original case, see Charles Schwartz and Louis Frolich, *The Law of Motion Pictures and the Theater.* For a discussion of the Appellate Court decision, see Roger Marchetti, *Law of the Stage, Screen and Radio,* 147. See also *Motion Picture Herald,* March 30, 1935, p. 18.

36. Judge Joseph Sprouls, quoted in "Newsreels Not Liable for Picture Shocks," *Motion Picture Herald,* March 30, 1935, p. 18.

37. Anonymous, "Twenty-Two Soho Square," *Great Britain and the East,* July 29, 1937, p. 162.

38. *Ibid.,* 163.

39. Davidson, *loc. cit.,* 150.

40. Lawrenson, *loc. cit.,* 361.

41. Anonymous, *The Factual Film,* 137.

42. *Ibid.,* 136.

43. *Ibid.,* 137.

44. Laurence Stallings, [Editor of *Fox Movietone News*], "Words and Pictures," *Saturday Evening Post,* November 21, 1936, pp. 9ff.

45. H. Piron, quoted in Anonymous, "Newsreels in Europe to Appeal to League of Nations for Fairness," *Motion Picture Herald,* July 31, 1937, p. 25.

46. *Ibid.*

47. 1940 edition of information booklet published by Newsreel Theaters, Inc., of which the Embassy Theater was a part, from the collection of the author. See also *New York Times,* November 6, 1949, Sec. II, p. 5; *Motion Picture News,* November 9, 1929; *Exhibitors Daily Review,* November 2, 1929; and *Variety,* October 10, 1929.

48. Wood, *The Miracle of the Movies,* 190. Wood offers no documentation for this claim. He also states that a kind of "newsreel" theater was opened in Paris by Alexander Rapoutat in 1897—an eighty-seat house in which Rapoutat presented footage which he shot each day in the streets of Paris. If this information is reliable, perhaps it might better be called an "actuality theater."

49. Caroline Lejeune, "The News Theater," in *Cinema*, 208–15.

50. 1940 edition of *Facts About Newsreels*, a brochure published by Newsreel Theaters, Inc., and distributed free to its patrons, from the author's collection.

51. W. French Githens, "Hail and Farewell," *New York Times*, November 20, 1949. See also *Exhibitors Herald-World*, November 9, 1929.

52. *Ibid.* See also *Motion Picture Herald*, August 31, 1935, p. 41.

53. Githens, *loc. cit.*

54. Creighton Peet, "The New Movies: Trans-Lux," *Outlook and Independent*, March 25, 1931, p. 442.

55. Sugrue, *loc. cit.*, 9; and *Motion Picture Herald*, January 5, 1935, p. 45; August 31, 1935, p. 24; August 7, 1937, p. 40; May 22, 1937, p. 15; June 5, 1937, p. 40; August 14, 1937, p. 44; December 9, 1944, p. 38; March 24, 1945, p. 40; March 31, 1945, p. 49; and October 27, 1945, p. 32.

56. Woods, *loc. cit.*, 66.

57. "Telenews Hails 20th Year," *San Francisco News-Call Bulletin*, September 4, 1959, p. 24; Anonymous, "War Booms Newsreel Chains," *Daily Variety*, July 19, 1950, p. 4; Carlton Brown, "What's Wrong with the Newsreels?" *Tomorrow*, October, 1947, p. 16; and Baechlin and Muller-Strauss, *Newsreels Across the World*, 61 ff.

58. Anonymous, "The Newsreel Boxoffice: A San Francisco Newsreel Movie House Looks Back on History," *Fortnight*, September 1, 1952, p. 14.

59. See Bert Holst, "The Film Library," *Journal of the Society of Motion Picture Engineers*, November, 1946, p. 365.

60. *Ibid.*, 366.

CHAPTER 12

1. Harry Tugander, quoted in John Beecroft, "The Salisbury Riots," *International Photographer*, January, 1934, 20 ff.

2. Marshall McCarroll, "Shot Under Protest," *International Photographer*, April, 1940, p. 3.

3. Stallings, "Words and Pictures," *loc. cit.*, 85.

4. Anonymous, "Shanghai Shambles," *Time*, September 13, 1937, p. 33, reprinted by permission of *Time, The Weekly Newsmagazine*, © Time, Inc. 1937. See also *Motion Picture Herald*, September 11, 1937, p. 30, and September 25, 1937, p. 10.

5. Anonymous, "Shanghai Shambles," *loc. cit.* See also Anonymous, "This Is Arthur's," *Time*, October 25, 1937, p. 25.

6. Herbert Aller, "Gable Becomes Newsreeler," *International Photographer*, March, 1938, p. 10. See also A. J. Ezickson, *Get That Picture!* 197ff.

7. Anonymous, "Seeing the World in Ten Minutes," *loc. cit.*, 126A; and Robert Desmond, "News About the Newsreel," *Christian Science Monitor Magazine*, September 28, 1938, p. 5.

8. *New York Times*, January 2, 1938, Sec. 10, p. 5; December 18, 1937, p. 10; December 19, 1937, p. 37; December 25, 1937, p. 4; December 27, 1937, p. 1;

December 28, 1937, p. 14; December 29, 1937, p. 3; December 30, 1937, p. 3; and December 31, 1937, p. 3. See also Anonymous, "A Universal Cameraman Documents American History: The Panay Incident," *Life*, January 10, 1938, pp. 11–17.

9. Albert Benham, "The 'Movie' as an Agency for Peace or War," *Journal of Educational Sociology*, Vol. XII (March, 1939), 411.

10. George Krainukov, "Universal's Thrill Hunter in China," *loc. cit.* 7.

11. *Motion Picture Herald*, September 29, 1934, p. 10.

12. *Ibid.*, January 19, 1935, p. 29. See also sequences from footage of the Soviet trials which originally appeared in issues of Dziga Vertov's *Kino Pravda*, available for study in the collection of the Museum of Modern Art, New York.

13. *Motion Picture Herald*, January 19, 1935, p. 29.

14. *Ibid.*, February 9, 1935, p. 11. See also Terry Ramsaye, "Newsreel Rights and the Flemington Hysteria," *Motion Picture Herald*, February 9, 1935, pp. 9ff.

15. *Motion Picture Herald*, February 23, 1935, p. 28.

16. *Ibid.* For additional commentary on newsreel coverage of the Lindbergh case, see Charles Peden, *Newsreel Man*, 113–26; Ray Fernstrom, "The Newsreel World," *International Photographer*, December, 1933, p. 28; and Kyle Crichton, "Photo Mugs," *Collier's*, November 28, 1936, p. 19.

17. Tash, *loc. cit.*, 19 and 32.

18. Anonymous, "A Hollywood Cameraman in the Land of a Billion Faces," *International Photographer*, May, 1935, pp. 4–5 and 22.

19. Anonymous, "When the Newsreels Shoot an Earthquake," *International Photographer*, April, 1933, p. 34.

20. Ray Fernstrom, "Olympic Newsmen Real Champions," *International Photographer*, September, 1932, p. 24; and Laurence Stallings, "Pomp and Circumstance," *Stage*, October, 1936, p. 70.

21. Frank Blackwell, "With President Roosevelt at Boulder Dam," *International Photographer*, January, 1936, pp. 14ff.; Anonymous, "Newsreels Set Pace for Lively Campaign; Refute Charges," *Motion Picture Herald*, February 29, 1936, p. 18; and Paul Koons, " 'Vacationing' With Wilkie," *International Photographer*, October, 1940, p. 10.

22. Anonymous, "Duke of Windsor's Wedding Films Banned in Britain by 'Agreement,' " *Motion Picture Herald*, June 12, 1937, p. 54; James Cunningham, "The Coronation in Color," *Commonweal*, June 25, 1937, p. 246; Stuart Legg, "The Cinema: The Coronation Films," *Spectator*, May 28, 1937, p. 991; and Anonymous, "Twenty-Two Soho Square," *Great Britain and the East*, July 29, 1937, p. 163.

23. Anonymous, "Newsreel Takes Prize," *International Photographer*, December, 1939, p. 19.

24. Anonymous, "Newsreel Shows Chicago Memorial Day Riot in Which Ten Were Killed," *Life*, July 12, 1937, p. 72.

25. T. F. Woods, "Headlines in Celluloid," *Saturday Evening Post*, August 11, 1945, p. 23.

26. *Ibid.*

27. Fernstrom, "The Newsreel World," *loc. cit.*, 23.

28. Mabie, *loc. cit.*, 3.

29. See still photograph enlarged from the original Paramount newsreel footage in Sugrue, *loc. cit.*, 15.

30. *Motion Picture Herald*, October 27, 1934, p. 23.

31. Georges Mejat, quoted in Laurence Stallings, "Words and Pictures," *loc. cit.*, 80 ff.

32. *Ibid.*, 82.

33. *Motion Picture Herald*, October 27, 1934, p. 23.

34. Al Gold, "Zep Crash Through Newsman's Eyes," *International Photographer*, June, 1937, p. 16.

35. *Ibid.*

36. Davidson, *loc. cit.*, 149.

37. Gold, *loc. cit.*

38. Herbert Morrison, quoted in A. A. Schechter and Edward Anthony, *I Live on Air*, 257ff. Schechter was director of news and special events for NBC at the time of the *Hindenburg* disaster.

39. James J. Seeley, quoted in Hal Hall, "James J. Seeley, A.S.C.," *American Cinematographer*, March, 1945, p. 79.

40. Gold, *loc. cit.*, 16ff.

41. *Ibid.*, 17.

42. Max Klein, "How the Newsreels Do It," in Anonymous, *Mike and Screen Press Directory*, 1954–55, p. 12. See also *New York Times*, May 8, 1937, p. 3, and May 23, 1937, p. 3.

43. Schechter and Anthony, *I Live on Air*, 258.

CHAPTER 13

1. Talbot, *Moving Pictures*, 278; Davidson, *loc. cit.*, 149; Sugrue, *loc. cit.*, 13.

2. Edgar Hatrick, quoted in Davidson, *loc. cit.*, 152.

3. Editorial, *Motion Picture Herald*, June 26, 1937.

4. Martin Quigley, "The Exhibitor's Screen—How Shall It Be Used?" *Motion Picture Herald*, February 5, 1938, p. 7.

5. Terry Ramsaye, "Blood and Guts," *Motion Picture Herald*, May 26, 1945.

6. *Motion Picture Herald*, April 21, 1945; *Films in Review*, October, 1954, p. 386.

7. Ray L. Hall, "Seeing is Believing," *Independent*, September 18, 1926, pp. 327 and 336.

8. *Motion Picture Herald*, February 1, 1936, p. 7.

9. Lewis, "Associated Newsreels, Incorporated," in *Harvard Business Reports*, VIII, 128.

10. In its legal brief, prepared in reply to the Federal Trade Commission in the late 1920's, the Famous Players–Lasky Corporation provided a concise, albeit partisan, history of the practice of block booking as it existed from about 1920 on. It is quoted in *ibid.*, 230–32. For a more recent study on the same subject, see Michael Conant, *Antitrust in the Motion Picture Industry*.

11. Hall, *loc. cit.*, 326. Hall was editor of Fox's newsreel during the 1920's and had been production manager of the Division of Films of the Creel Committee on Public Information during World War I.

12. Lancaster, *loc. cit.*, 12.

13. Emanuel Cohen quoted in Mackenzie, *loc. cit.*, 120.

14. Unidentified newsreel editor, quoted in Croy, "It Looks Easy," *loc. cit.*, 59.

15. Unidentified newsreel editor [possibly Emanuel Cohen], quoted in *ibid.*, 60. The news events mentioned here were those which had been particularly well covered by Pathé, and the answers are somewhat similar to those secured by Mackenzie in his interview with Cohen.

16. Terry Ramsaye, "News and Corpses," *Motion Picture Herald*, September 3, 1934, editorial page.

CHAPTER 14

1. John Grierson, *Grierson on Documentary*, 162.

2. Andrew Buchanan, *The Art of Film Production*, 72.

3. Raymond Fielding, "The Nazi-German Newsreel," *Journal of the University Film Producers Association*, Vol. XII (Spring, 1960), 3.

4. Raymond Fielding, "Mirror of Discontent: *The March of Time* and Its Politically Controversial Film Issues," *Western Political Quarterly*, Vol. XII (March, 1959), 145ff.; Raymond Fielding, "Time Flickers Out," *Quarterly of Film, Radio and Television*, Vol. XI (Summer, 1957), 354–61; and Raymond Fielding, "The March of Time, 1935–1942," unpublished Master's Thesis, University of California at Los Angeles, 1956.

5. Andrew Buchanan, *Going to the Cinema*, 109.

6. Buchanan, *The Art of Film Production*, 72.

7. *Ibid.*

8. Anonymous, *Four Hours a Year*, 20.

9. Academy Award Citation, quoted in *Life*, January 10, 1938, p. 42.

10. Gilbert Seldes, "Screen and Radio," *Scribner's Magazine*, July, 1937, p. 58.

11. Anonymous, "Trans-Lux," *Outlook and Independent*, March 25, 1931, p. 442.

12. Terry Ramsaye, writing in the *Motion Picture Herald*, November 14, 1931, quoted in Lewis, *The Motion Picture Industry*, 135.

13. Andrew Buchanan, *Films: The Way of the Cinema*, 195 and 198.

14. Robert Littell, "A Glance at the Newsreels," *American Mercury*, November, 1933, pp. 264ff.

15. Charles Grinley, "Notes on the News-Reels," *Life and Letters-Today*, Winter, 1937, pp. 123, 125, and 127.

16. John Erskine, "Newsreels Should Be Seen and Not Heard," *American Mercury*, June, 1935, pp. 219 and 221.

17. Littell, "A Glance at the Newsreels," *loc. cit.*, 263ff.

18. *Ibid.*, 266.

19. Brown, *loc. cit.*, 12ff.

CHAPTER 15

1. Anonymous feature article, apparently in *New York Times*, published sometime in 1935, furnished to the author on microfilm by the New York Public Library from the Theater Collection newspaper clipping file.

2. Anthony North, *loc. cit.*, 22.

3. Anonymous British technician, quoted in Baèchlin and Muller-Strauss, *Newsreels Across the World*, 31. The original quotation appeared in a front-page article in *London Tribune*, August 5, 1949.

4. Stanton Delaplane, "Very Too Happy Please," *San Francisco Chronicle*, December 14, 1940, reprinted in *International Photographer*, February, 1941, 18ff.

5. Al Hine, "Movies: Covering a Convention," *Holiday*, July, 1948, p. 24, reprinted with permission from *Holiday*, © 1948, The Curtis Publishing Co.

6. William Montague, "The Newsreel and Public Opinion," *High Points*, June, 1938, p. 11.

7. Fernstrom, "The Newsreel World," *loc. cit.*, 28.

8. Daniel J. Boorstin, *The Image, or What Happened to the American Dream*.

9. Walter Wilcox, "The Staged News Photograph and Professional Ethics," *Journalism Quarterly*, Vol. XXXVIII, No. 4 (Autumn, 1961), 498.

10. *Ibid.*, 500.

11. *Ibid.*, 502–503.

12. *Ibid.*, 504.

13. Selden Menefee, "The Movies Join Hearst," *New Republic*, October 9, 1935, 241 ff.

14. Anonymous, "Are Newsreels News?" *Nation*, October 2, 1935, p. 369.

15. Laurence Stallings, "Cannon Fodder on the Road to Jijiga," *Stage*, July, 1936, p. 30.

16. Legg, *loc. cit.*, 991.

17. Andrew Buchanan, *Film and the Future*, 38 and 42.

18. Meltzer, *loc. cit.*, 270.

19. Siegfried Kracauer and Joseph Lyford, "A Duck Crosses Main Street," *New Republic*, December 13, 1948, pp. 13 and 15.

20. *New York Times*, August 11, 1935, p. 3; Montague, *loc. cit.*, 10; Anonymous, " 'Newsreel' Policy," *Motion Picture Herald*, June 26, 1937; Anonymous, "Are Newsreels News?" *loc. cit.*, 369; Menefee, *loc. cit.*, 242; *Motion Picture Herald*, August 31, 1935, p. 16; *Time*, November 23, 1936, p. 25; and *Motion Picture Herald*, August 31, 1935, p. 6.

21. *Motion Picture Herald*, September 7, 1935, p. 28; and October 5, 1935, p. 16.

22. Anonymous, "Hearst's News of the Day," *loc. cit.*, 25.

23. Grinley, *loc. cit.*, 125.

24. Meltzer, *loc. cit.*, 270–71.

25. Anonymous, "Are Newsreels News?" *loc. cit.*, 370.

26. Menefee, *loc. cit.*, 241.

27. Oswald Villard, "Issues and Men, Propaganda in the Movies," *Nation*, December 12, 1934, p. 665.

28. Kracauer and Lyford, *loc. cit.*, 15.

29. For a defense of the newsreels, see Montague, *loc. cit.*, 5–12. Montague was assignment editor for *Paramount News* during the 1930's.

30. *Ibid.*, 6ff.

31. See unidentified motion picture trade-paper news item dated November 21, 1933, provided to the author on microfilm by the New York Public Library from the Theater Collection newspaper clipping file.

32. *Motion Picture Herald*, September 8, 1934, p. 10.

33. Bosley Crowther, *Hollywood Rajah*, 225–28.

34. Henry Pringle, "The Movies Swing an Election," *New Yorker*, April 4, 1936, p. 28.

35. Sugrue, *loc. cit.*, 17. See also Menefee, *loc. cit.*, 241.

36. Anonymous, "WPA: Pathé Wins Film Contract as New Deal 'Goes Hollywood,' " *News-Week*, August 15, 1936, p. 18.

37. *Ibid.*

38. *Motion Picture Herald* headline, quoted in " 'Educational' Newsreels for WPA," *Literary Digest*, August 8, 1936, p. 32.

39. Bertrand Snell, quoted in Anonymous, "WPA: Pathé Wins Film Contract as New Deal 'Goes Hollywood,' " *loc. cit.*, 18.

40. *Ibid.*

CHAPTER 16

1. Markey, *loc. cit.*, 67.

2. Anonymous, " 'Educational' Newsreels for WPA," *loc. cit.*, 32.

3. Herbert Aller, "News Reels: Enterprise Personified," *International Photographer*, April, 1938, 36.

4. Kracauer and Lyford, "A Duck Crosses Main Street," *New Republic*, December 13, 1948, 14.

5. See tape recording of address by George Krainukov, delivered at the Department of Cinema, University of Southern California, February 20, 1959, from the collection of the author.

6. Herbert Aller, "Gable Becomes Newsreeler," *International Photographer*, March, 1938, 10.

7. Anonymous, "A Cruise with the Black Fleet," *International Photographer*, July, 1935, 6.

8. Colonel Wright, quoted in Davidson, *loc. cit.*, 150ff.

9. Anonymous, "Newsreel Race," *Business Week*, January 5, 1946, 41.

10. Editorial, *Sequence*, Summer, 1949, 48.

11. Charles Peden, "Guts, Vision—Crying Needs to Rejuvenate Newsreels," originally printed in *Motion Picture Herald*, July 9, 1955; reprinted in *American Cinematographer*, August, 1955, 471–72 and 486.

12. See photographs and caption in Anonymous, *Mike and Screen Press Directory*, 1954–55, p. 19.

13. *China Weekly Review*, April 11, 1936, p. 216.

14. Davidson, *loc. cit.*, 150.

15. *Motion Picture Herald*, May 25, 1935, p. 26, and May 18, 1935, p. 15.

16. McCarroll, *loc. cit.*, 3.

17. Anonymous, "Trans-Lux," *loc. cit.*, 442.

18. North, *loc. cit.*, 23.

19. Anonymous, "Movie of the Week," *Life*, January 31, 1938, p. 24. See also Anonymous, *Four Hours a Year*, 19.

20. North, *loc. cit.*, 24.

21. *Ibid.*

22. Anonymous, "Duke of Windsor's Wedding Films Banned in Britain by 'Agreement,' " *Motion Picture Herald*, June 12, 1937, p. 54.

23. Emile Schnurmacher, "The Cameraman Foretells Disaster," *loc. cit.*, 840.

24. Aller, "Gable Becomes Newsreeler," *loc. cit.*, 10.

25. Beatty, *loc. cit.*, 69.

26. Edward Harrison, "What the Newsreels Never Show," *Ken*, June 16, 1938, p. 80.

27. Vice-President Garner, quoted in *ibid.*

28. Anonymous, "Newsreel Shows Chicago Memorial Day Riot in Which Ten Were Killed," *Life*, July 12, 1937, p. 72.

29. *New York Times*, July 10, 1937, p. 32.

30. William Montague, quoted in *New York Times*, June 8, 1937, p. 8. See also news item, *Motion Picture Herald*, June 12, 1937, p. 54.

31. *New York Times*, June 4, 1937, p. 15.

32. *Ibid.*, p. 5.

33. Montague, "The Newsreel and Public Opinion," *loc. cit.*, 8.

34. *New York Times*, June 8, 1937, p. 8.

35. *Ibid.*, June 9, 1937, p. 2; June 17, 1937, p. 3; June 13, 1937, Sec. 11, p. 3; June 18, 1937, p. 1; June 20, 1937, p. 4; June 23, 1937, p. 2; July 11, 1937, p. 2; July 20, 1937, p. 22; and July 23, 1937, p. 1.

36. Sir John Gilmour, quoted in *New York Times*, December 5, 1933, p. 11.

37. *Ibid.*

38. *Ibid.*, April 17, 1937, p. 3.

39. Sir John Simon, quoted in a dispatch by Ferdinand Kuhn, Jr., *New York Times*, November 24, 1938, p. 1.

40. *Ibid.* See also *ibid.*, November 30, 1938, p. 14; December 2, 1938, p. 5; and December 8, 1938, p. 23.

41. Anonymous, *Four Hours a Year*, 15.

42. Anonymous, "Sound and Fury over Free Speech," *Literary Digest*, May 1, 1937, p. 3.

43. *Ibid.*

44. *Ibid.*

45. Fielding, "The March of Time, 1935–42," unpublished master's thesis, University of California at Los Angeles, 1956, pp. 52–57.

46. "Louisiana Adopts Censorship Law," *Motion Picture Herald*, July 13, 1935, p. 14; and news item, *ibid.*, April 27, 1935, p. 18. See also Fielding, "The March

of Time, 1935–42," unpublished master's thesis, University of California at Los Angeles, 1956, 21–22.

47. *Daily Variety*, May 27, 1953, p. 10.

48. "Not the Answer," *Motion Picture Herald*, July 6, 1935, p. 7.

49. *New York Times*, September 11, 1952, p. 36.

50. 343 U.S. 495 (1952).

51. *Mutual Film Corp.* v. *Industrial Commission*, 236 U.S. 230, 244 (1915).

52. *Daily Variety*, April 6, 1955, p. 8.

53. Comment, 49, *Yale Law Journal*, 87, 93n.41 (1939).

54. *Brattle Films, Inc.* v. *Commission of Public Safety*, 333 Mass. 58, 127 N.E. 2d 891 (1955); *Hallmark Productions, Inc.* v. *Carroll*, 383 Pa. 348, 121 A.2d 584 (1956); *R.K.O. Radio Pictures, Inc.* v. *Department of Education*, 162 Ohio St. 263, 122 N.E. 2d 769 (1954).

55. 380 U.S. 51 (1965).

56. In this five-to-four decision Associate Justice Thomas Clark delivering the opinion of the Court, stated that "the broad justiciable issue is therefore present as to whether the ambit of constitutional protection includes complete and absolute freedom to exhibit, at least once, any and every kind of motion picture. It is that question alone which we decide. We have concluded that Section 155-4 of Chicago's ordinance requiring the submission of films prior to their public exhibition is not, on the grounds set forth, void on its face." See United States Supreme Court pre-print, No. 34, October term, 1960 (January 23, 1961), Justice Clark's decision, p. 3. Chief Justice Earl Warren, in delivering the dissenting opinion, stated that "the decision presents a real danger of eventual censorship for every form of communication be it newspapers, journals, books, magazines, television, radio or public speeches. . . . I am aware of no constitutional principle which permits us to hold that the communication of ideas through one medium may be censored while other media are immune. . . . I submit that in arriving at its decision the Court has interpreted our cases contrary to the intention at the time of their rendition and, in exalting the censor of motion pictures, has endangered the First and Fourteenth Amendment rights of all others engaged in the dissemination of ideas." United States Supreme Court preprint, No. 34, October term, 1960 (January 23, 1961), Chief Justice Warren's dissenting opinion, p. 1. The practical consequences of this decision are not yet apparent. However, it is obvious that the way is clear for the establishment of new censor boards on both state and municipal levels—whatever their powers may be.

57. "Newspictures Subject to Censor Court Rules," *Exhibitor's Herald*, July 22, 1922, p. 17.

CHAPTER 17

1. Jack O'Brine, "Studios on the Battlefield," *Popular Science*, March, 1943, p. 113.

2. One writer estimated that civilian cameramen photographed only 20 per cent of the total World War II newsreel footage (Davidson, *loc. cit.*, 113). Even that figure seems high.

3. Thomas Pryor, *New York Times*, February 8, 1942, Sec. 9, p. 5; Davidson, *loc. cit.*, 151; O'Brine, *loc. cit.*, 216.

4. Handel, *Hollywood Looks at its Audience*, 170.

5. Reported in *Motion Picture Herald*, February 3, 1945, p. 14.

6. *Ibid.*

7. The newsreel organization was directed by Lacy W. Kastner, who was in charge of the overseas motion picture division of the U.S. Office of Coordinator of Information, and its successor, the U.S. Office of War Information (which was, in turn, succeeded in time by the U.S. Information Agency). Kastner was assisted by Martin Quigley, Jr., and Harry W. Sturges. Its first editor was E. C. Buddy, later succeeded by Fred Abbott. Joseph Seidelman was its first president, later succeeded by Murray Silverstone. On behalf of the government Robert Riskin assumed charge of the newsreel when he was named director of OWI's overseas motion picture division in August, 1942. He in turn was succeeded by Louis Lober in 1945. See *Motion Picture Herald*, October 6, 1945, p. 43; December 1, 1945, p. 8; December 15, 1945, p. 21; December 22, 1945, p. 35; and Thomas Pryor, "Our Newsreel Across the Seas," *New York Times*, May 14, 1944.

8. Brown, *loc. cit.*, 14.

9. William Whitebait, "The Movies," *New Statesman and Nation*, June 17, 1944, p. 404.

10. Edgar Anstey, "The Cinema," *Spectator*, September 8, 1944, p. 219.

11. Bosley Crowther, "Between the Eyes," *New York Times*, May 6, 1945; and *Motion Picture Herald*, May 5, 1945, p. 8, and May 12, 1945, p. 14.

12. Bosley Crowther, "Matters of Actual Fact," *New York Times*, March 18, 1945.

13. James Agee, "Films," *Nation*, June 24, 1944, p. 743.

14. *Ibid.*, 342.

15. Woods, *loc. cit.*, 22.

16. O'Brine, *loc. cit.*, 216.

17. "War and Newsreel," *Motion Picture Herald*, June 24, 1944, editorial page.

18. Bosley Crowther, "Too Little Too Late," *New York Times*, March 21, 1943.

19. Reported in *Motion Picture Herald*, May 5, 1945, p. 8.

20. Brown, *loc. cit.*, p. 14; and *Motion Picture Herald*, February 3, 1945, p. 14, and February 10, 1945, p. 25.

21. For a description of *Telenews'* operations, see Baechlin and Muller-Strauss, *Newsreels Across the World*, 61 ff.

22. Handel, *Hollywood Looks at Its Audience*, 170, note 1, Table 64.

23. G. Clement Cave, "Newsreels Must Find a New Policy," *Penguin Film Review*, No. 7, September, 1948, pp. 53ff.

24. *Ibid.*, 52. Pathé's new format began as early as October 4, 1944, with a newsreel on the entry of the Allies into Germany. The entire reel was devoted to the one subject, in what was described as a "one-story magazine style." *Motion Picture Herald*, October 7, 1944, p. 8.

25. Anonymous, "Newsreel Not to Shift Now, Editors Say," *Motion Picture Herald*, May 28, 1949, p. 39.

26. *Kinematograph Weekly*, December 12, 1963, p. 7; April 4, 1963, p. 9; November 26, 1964, p. 7; and May 2, 1963, p. 7; and *Variety*, June 3, 1964, p. 15.

27. "Press Services Plan Newsreels for Television," *Motion Picture Herald*, November 1, 1947, p. 36.

28. Charles Lazarus, "The Newsreel Fights Back," *ibid.*, March 8, 1952, p. 14.

29. See photographs and captions, Anonymous, *From Semaphore to Satellite*, 187–88.

30. *Motion Picture Herald*, June 5, 1937, p. 72.

31. *Ibid.*, July 13, 1935, p. 49; and June 29, 1935, p. 62.

32. *Ibid.*, November 17, 1934, p. 32; and December 29, 1934, p. 10.

33. *Ibid.*, January 29, 1949, p. 21.

34. *Ibid.*, January 27, 1945, p. 32.

35. *New York Times*, November 6, 1949, Sec. 2, p. 5.

36. *New York Times*, November 20, 1949.

37. *Daily Variety*, July 19, 1950, p. 11.

38. Lazarus, "The Newsreel Fights Back," *loc. cit.*; and *Motion Picture Herald*, January 29, 1949, p. 21. See also *Broadcasting-Telecasting*, July 29, 1957, pp. 96ff.

39. *Daily Variety*, January 19, 1955, p. 6.

40. *New York Times*, July 24, 1956, p. 20.

41. *Ibid.*, January 24, 1957, p. 34. See also *Daily Variety*, January 23, 1957, p. 1.

42. UCLA *Librarian*, April, 1969, p. 21.

43. Letter to author from Jonas Rosenfield, Jr., vice-president of Twentieth-Century Fox, May 19, 1969. See also *Los Angeles Times*, September 7, 1963, Sec. 3, p. 6.

44. *Des Moines Register*, November 25, 1967; *New York Times*, November 24, 1967, p. 56; and letter to author from Dan S. Terrell, vice-president of Metro-Goldwyn-Mayer, May 12, 1969.

45. *Daily Variety*, May 7, 1969; May 14, 1969; and *Des Moines Register*, May 8, 1969.

46. *New York Times*, November 24, 1967, p. 56; December 22, 1967, p. 37; *Des Moines Register*, November 25, 1967, and December 23, 1967; and *Time*, December 29, 1967, p. 35.

CHAPTER 18

1. These figures are provided by the U.S. Department of Commerce, Office of Business Economics, National Income Division, and the Survey of Current Business (July, 1970), quoted in Anonymous, 1971 *International Motion Picture Almanac*, p. 52A.

2. Lewis, *The Motion Picture Industry*, 133.

Books

Allen, Frederick Lewis. *Only Yesterday*. New York, Bantam Books, 1946.

Alley, Norman. *I Witness*. New York, Wilfred Funk, 1941.

Allister, Ray. *Friese-Greene: Close-Up of an Inventor*. London, Marsland Publications, 1948.

Amid, John. *With the Movie Makers*. Boston, Lothrop, Lee and Shepard, 1923.

Anonymous. *The Factual Film*. London, Oxford University Press, 1947.

———. *Four Hours a Year*. New York, Time, Inc., 1936.

———. *From Semaphore to Satellite*. Geneva, International Telecommunications Union, 1965.

———. *Homage à Louis Lumière*. Paris, Ville de Paris, Musée Galliera, 1935.

———. *International Motion Picture Almanac—1971*. New York, Quigley Publications, 1970.

———. *Mike and Screen Press Directory, 1954–55*. New York, Radio-Newsreel-Television Working Press Association of New York, 1955.

———. *National Film Library Catalogue, Part I: Silent News Films, 1895–1933*. London, British Film Institute, 1951.

Baechlin, Peter, and Maurice Muller-Strauss. *Newsreels Across the World*. Paris, UNESCO, 1952.

Bardèche, Maurice, and Robert Brasillach. *The History of Motion Pictures.* New York, Norton, 1938.

Bennett, Colin Noel. *The Handbook of Kinematography.* London, Kinematography Weekly, 1911.

Benoit-Lévy, Jean. *The Art of the Motion Picture.* New York, Coward-MacCann, 1946.

Bessy, Maurice, and Giuseppe Lo Duca. *Georges Méliès, Mage.* Paris, Les Editions Prisma, 1945.

Bluem, A. William. *Documentary in American Television.* New York, Hastings House, 1965.

Boorstin, Daniel. *The Image, or What Happened to the American Dream.* New York, Atheneum Publishers, 1962.

Buchanan, Andrew. *The Art of Film Production.* London, Pitman and Sons, 1936.

———. *Film and the Future.* London, Allen and Unwin, 1945.

———. *Films: The Way of the Cinema.* London, Pitman and Sons, 1932.

———. *Going to the Cinema.* London, Phoenix House, 1947.

Chesmore, Stuart. *Behind the Cinema Screen.* London, Nelson and Sons, 1934.

Collins, Francis. *The Camera Man.* New York, Century, 1916.

Conant, Michael. *Antitrust in the Motion Picture Industry.* Berkeley, University of California Press, 1960.

Creel, George. *How We Advertised America.* New York, Harper and Brothers, 1920.

Crowther, Bosley. *Hollywood Rajah.* New York, Dell, 1961.

Croy, Homer. *How Motion Pictures are Made.* New York, Harper and Brothers, 1918.

Crump, Irving. *The Boy's Book of Newsreel Hunters.* New York, Dodd, Mead, 1936.

Dale, Edgar. *The Content of Motion Pictures.* New York, Macmillan, 1935.

Dench, Ernest A. *Making the Movies.* New York, Macmillan, 1915.

Dickson, William Kennedy Laurie. *The Biograph in Battle.* London, Unwin, 1901.

———, and Antonia Dickson. *The Life and Inventions of Thomas Alva Edison.* London, Chatto and Windus, 1894.

Dored, John, and Robert M. Low. *I Shoot the World*. New York, Lippincott, 1938.

Dyer, Frank Lewis, and Thomas Commerford Martin. *Edison—His Life and Inventions*. New York, Harper and Brothers, 1910. (Republished in 1929.)

Ezickson, A. J. *Get That Picture!* New York, National Library Press, 1938.

Fang, Irving. *Television News*. New York, Hastings House, 1968.

Gernsheim, Helmut. *The History of Photography*. London, Oxford University Press, 1955.

Gore, George. *The People I Shot*. New York, Vantage Press, 1968.

Grau, Robert. *The Theatre of Science*. New York, Broadway Publishing Co., 1914.

Green, Abel, and Joe Laurie, Jr. *Show Biz from Vaude to Video*. Garden City, N.Y., Garden City Books, reprint edition, 1952.

Green, Fitzhugh. *The Film Finds Its Tongue*. New York, Putnam's Sons, 1929.

Grierson, John. *Grierson on Documentary*. New York, Harcourt, Brace, 1947.

Hall, Ben. *The Best Remaining Seats*. New York, Bramhall House, 1961.

Handel, Leo A. *Hollywood Looks at Its Audience*. Urbana, University of Illinois Press, 1950.

Hays, Will H. *See and Hear*. Los Angeles, Motion Picture Producers and Distributors of America, 1929.

Hendricks, Gordon. *Beginnings of the Biograph*. New York, Beginnings of the American Film, 1964.

———. *The Edison Motion Picture Myth*. Berkeley, University of California Press, 1961.

———. *The Kinetoscope*. New York, Beginnings of the American Film, 1966.

Hepworth, Cecil. *Came the Dawn*. London, Phoenix House, 1951.

Hoadley, Ray and Roman Freulich. *How They Make a Motion Picture*. New York, Crowell, 1939.

Hulfish, David. *The Motion Picture—Its Making and Its Theater*. Chicago, Electricity Magazine Corporation, 1909.

Humfrey, Robert. *Careers in Film*. London, Isaac Pitman and Sons, 1938.

Jacobs, Lewis. *The Rise of the American Film*. New York, Harcourt, Brace, 1939.

Lejeune, Caroline. *Cinema*. London, MacLehose, 1931.

Lescarboura, Austin. *Behind the Motion Picture Screen*. New York, Scientific American Publishing Co., 1919.

Lewis, Howard Thompson. *The Motion Picture Industry*. New York, D. Van Nostrand, 1933.

Leyda, Jay. *Films Beget Films*. New York, Hill and Wang, 1964.

———. *Kino*. New York, Macmillan, 1960.

Low, Rachael, and Roger Manvell. *The History of the British Film*. I. London, Allen and Unwin, 1948.

Low, Warren. *The Film Game*. London, Warner Laurie, 1937.

McKay, Herbert C. *Motion Picture Photography for the Amateur*. New York, Falk, 1924.

Malins, Lieut. Geoffrey. *How I Filmed the War*. New York, Stokes, [1919].

Marchetti, Roger. *Law of the Stage, Screen and Radio*. Los Angeles, Sutton House, 1936.

Mesguich, Felix. *Tours de Manivelle*. Paris, Éditions Bernard Grasset, 1933.

Mock, James, and Cedric Larson. *Words That Won the War*. Princeton, Princeton University Press, 1939.

Newhall, Beaumont. *The History of Photography*. New York, Museum of Modern Art, 1964.

Nicoll, Allardyce. *Film and Theatre*. New York, Crowell, 1936.

Niver, Kemp. *Motion Pictures from the Library of Congress Paper Print Collection, 1894–1912*. Berkeley, University of California Press, 1967.

Noble, Ronald. *Shoot First! Assignments of a Newsreel Cameraman*. London, Harrap [1955].

Peden, Charles. *Newsreel Man*. New York, Doubleday, 1932.

Ramsaye, Terry. *A Million and One Nights*. 2 vols. New York, Simon and Schuster, 1926.

Sadoul, Georges. *French Film*. London, Falcon Press, 1953.

———. *Histoire Générale du Cinéma*, I. Paris, Éditions Denoël, 1948.

Schechter, A. A., and Edward Anthony. *I Live on Air*. New York, Stokes, 1941.

Schwartz, Charles, and Louis D. Frohlich. *The Law of Motion Pictures and the Theater.* New York, Baker, Voorhis, 1918.

Seldes, Gilbert. *Movies for the Millions.* London, Batsford, 1937.

Sinclair, Upton. *I, Candidate for Governor; and How I Got Licked.* Pasadena, Calif., privately printed by the author, [1935].

Smith, Albert. *Two Reels and a Crank.* Garden City, N.Y., Doubleday, 1952.

Swain, Joseph Ward. *The Harper History of Civilization.* New York, Harper and Brothers, 1958.

Talbot, Frederick A. *Moving Pictures: How They are Made and Worked.* London, Heinemann, 1912.

Thomas, D. B. *The First Colour Motion Pictures.* London, Her Majesty's Stationery Office, 1969.

Vardac, Nicholas. *Stage to Screen.* Cambridge, Harvard University Press, 1949.

Vivié, Jean. *Histoire et Dévelopement de la Technique Cinématographique.* Vol. I of Traité Général de Technique du Cinéma. Paris, B.P.I., 1946.

Walls, Howard Lamarr. *Motion Pictures, 1894–1912.* Washington, D.C., Copyright Office, Library of Congress, 1953.

Waples, Douglas. *Print, Radio and Film in a Democracy.* Chicago, University of Chicago Press, 1942.

West, Wallace. *Paramount Newsreel Men with Admiral Byrd in Little America.* Racine, Whitman, 1934.

Wood, Leslie. *The Miracle of the Movies.* London, Burke, 1947.

Wyand, Paul. *Useless If Delayed—Adventures in Putting History on Film.* London, Harrap, 1959.

Articles in Books

Baechlin, Peter, and Maurice Muller-Strauss. "How the Newsreels Grew." In Anonymous. *Mike and Screen Press Directory, 1954–55.* New York, Radio-Newsreel-Television Working Press Association of New York, 1955, 9.

Donahue, Robert. "The News Cameraman." In Charles Jones (ed.). *Breaking into the Movies.* New York, Unicorn Press, 1927, 186.

Klein, Max. "How the Newsreels Do It." In Anonymous, *Mike and Screen Press Directory, 1954–55.* New York, Radio-Newsreel-Television Working Press Association of New York, 1955, 9.

Kling, Bill. "Film Editor vs. Cameraman." In Anonymous, *Mike and Screen Press Directory*, 1954–55. New York, Radio-Newsreel-Television Working Press Association of New York, 1955, 40.

Lewis, Howard Thompson, ed. "Associated Newsreels, Incorporated," in *Harvard Business Reports*. VIII. New York, McGraw-Hill Book Co., 1930.

Malkames, D. Karl. "Camera History." In Anonymous. *Mike and Screen Press Directory*, 1954–55. New York, Radio-Newsreel-Television Working Press Association of New York, 1955, 22.

Myers, Abram. "Allied Makes Progress in 1931." In Anonymous, *The 1932 Film Daily Year Book of Motion Pictures*. New York, Film Daily, 1932, 532.

Smith-Ross, J. "News on the Screen." In Anonymous, *The World Film Encyclopedia: A Universal Screen Guide*. London, Amalgamated, 1933, 467.

Theses and Dissertations

Drowne, Peter P. "An Investigation into the Evolution of Motion Picture Photography and Film Usage in the United States Marine Corps 1940–45." Unpublished master's thesis, University of California at Los Angeles, 1965.

Fielding, Raymond. "A History of the American Motion Picture Newsreel." Unpublished Ph.D. dissertation, University of Southern California, Los Angeles, 1961.

———. "The March of Time, 1935–42." Unpublished master's thesis, University of California at Los Angeles, 1956.

Randle, Robert B. "A Study of the War Time Control Imposed on the Civilian Motion Picture Industry and with Some Reference to Those Affecting the Army Motion Pictures During World War II." Unpublished master's thesis, University of Southern California, Los Angeles, 1950.

Vincent, Ross H., Jr. "A Historical Study of the Army Air Forces First Motion Picture Unit (18th AAFBU) in World War II. Unpublished master's thesis, University of Southern California, Los Angeles, 1959.

Signed Articles

Aaronson, Charles S. "Forty Years of Screen Journalism," *Motion Picture Herald*, August 29, 1959, p. 15.

Acres, Sidney Birt. "Kinematography and the Kiel Canal," *Cinema Studies* (British), December, 1962, p. 130.

Agee, James. "Films." *Nation*, June 24, 1944, p. 743.

———. "Films." *Nation*, March 17, 1945, p. 314.

———. "Films." *Nation*, March 24, 1945, p. 342.

Allen, Leigh. "News Sense, Perseverance Necessary for Newsreeling," *American Cinematographer*, March, 1956, p. 161.

Allen, Spencer M. "Film Problems in Television News Reporting." *Journal of the Society of Motion Picture and Television Engineers*, August, 1955, p. 413.

Aller, Herbert. "The Colorful Career of the Newsreel Man—His Life a Constant Sacrifice," *International Photographer*, February, 1937, p. 14.

———. "Gable Becomes Newsreeler," *International Photographer*, March, 1938, p. 9.

———. "News Reels: Enterprise Personified," *International Photographer*, April, 1938, p. 34.

Alley, Norman. "Shoot, I've Got You Covered," *International Photographer*, May, 1940, p. 12.

———. "Vive Les Vincennes," *International Photographer*, September, 1939, p. 5.

Anstey, Edgar. "The Cinema," *Spectator*, September 8, 1944, p. 219.

Armat, Thomas. "My Part in the Development of the Motion Picture Projector," *Journal of the Society of Motion Picture and Television Engineers*, March, 1935, p. 247.

Battle, J. A. "Newsreel Sound Quality Is Greatly Improved," *International Projectionist*, August, 1935, p. 13.

Beatty, Jerome. "Shooting the Big Shots," *American Magazine*, February, 1931, p. 68.

Beecroft, John. "The Salisbury Riots," *International Photographer*, January, 1934, p. 20.

Benham, Albert. "The 'Movie' as an Agency for Peace or War," *Journal of Educational Sociology*, Vol. XII (March, 1939), 410.

Bine, Al. "The 'Battle of the Century,'" *Los Angeles Examiner*, July 4, 1960, Sec. 4, p. 3.

Blackwell, Frank. "With President Roosevelt at Boulder Dam," *International Photographer*, January, 1936, p. 14.

Bland, W. S., "Development of the Sound Newsreel," *British Kinematography*, August, 1950, p. 50.

Bowen, Harold G. "Thomas Alva Edison's Early Motion-Picture Experiments," *Journal of the Society of Motion Picture and Television Engineers*, September, 1955, p. 508.

Bracker, Milton. "U.S. Newsreel Held Vital in 'Cold War,' " *New York Times*, June 5, 1950, p. 7.

Brown, Carlton. "What's Wrong with the Newsreels?" *Tomorrow*, October, 1947, p. 12.

Browning, Irving. "Through an Eyemo Finder I Saw Champions Fall," *American Cinematographer*, September, 1944, p. 296.

Bush, W. Stephen. "Camera on the Firing Line," *Moving Picture World*, January 31, 1913, p. 522.

———. "Mexican War Pictures," *Moving Picture World*, February 7, 1914, p. 657.

———. "War Films," *Moving Picture World*, September 19, 1914, p. 1617.

Cassady, Ralph, Jr. "Monopoly in Motion Picture Production and Distribution, 1908–1912," *Southern California Law Review*, Vol. XXXII, No. 4 (1959), 325.

Cave, G. Clement. "Newsreels Must Find a New Policy," *Penguin Film Review*, No. 7 (September, 1948), 50.

Churchill, Winston. "You Get It in Black and White," *Collier's*, December 28, 1935, p. 32.

Cohen, Emanuel. "The Business of International News by Motion Pictures," *Annals of the American Academy of Political and Social Science*, November, 1926, p. 74; republished, with slight changes, in *Journal of the Society of Motion Picture Engineers*, February, 1927, p. 296.

Cohn, Alfred A. "A Film Newspaper in the Making," *Photoplay Magazine*, April, 1916, p. 44.

Cooke, Alistair. "History in the Making," *Listener*, November 20, 1935, p. 931.

Cornwell, Elmer E., Jr. "Wilson, Creel, and the Presidency," *Public Opinion Quarterly*, Summer, 1959, p. 189.

Cowling, Herford Tynes. "Bringing the Ends of the Earth to Your Movie House," *American Magazine*, April, 1926, p. 62.

Crichton, Kyle. "Photo Mugs," *Collier's*, November 28, 1936, p. 19.

Crosby, John. "Newsreeland," *Atlantic*, December, 1948, p. 126.

Crowther, Bosley. "Between the Eyes," *New York Times*, May 6, 1945, Sec. 2, p. 1.

——. "Matters of Actual Fact," *New York Times*, March 18, 1945, Sec. 2, p. 1.

——. "The Solemn Facts," *New York Times*, April 29, 1945, Sec. 2, p. 1.

——. "Time Marches Off," *New York Times*, July 15, 1951, Sec. 2, p. 1.

——. "Time Marches On and On," *New York Times*, October 31, 1937, p. 6.

——. "Too Little Too Late," *New York Times*, March 21, 1943, Sec. 2, p. 3.

Croy, Homer. "Handing It Down to Posterity," *Photoplay*, September, 1919, p. 70.

——. "It Looks Easy," *Saturday Evening Post*, November 5, 1921, p. 14.

Cunningham, James. "The Coronation in Color," *Commonweal*, June 25, 1937, p. 246.

Dale, Edgar. "Need for Study of the Newsreels," *Public Opinion Quarterly*, July, 1937, p. 122.

Dangerfield, George. "Time Muddles On," *New Republic*, August 19, 1936, p. 43.

Davidson, Bill. "The Newsreel Business," *Cosmopolitan*, September, 1946, p. 54.

Delaplane, Stanton. "Very Too Happy Please," *San Francisco Chronicle*, December 14, 1940; reprinted in *International Photographer*, February, 1941, p. 18.

Dench, Ernest A. "Methods by Which the European War Has Been Filmed," *Scientific American*, March 20, 1915, p. 277.

Depue, Oscar A. "My First Fifty Years in Motion Pictures," *Journal of the Society of Motion Picture Engineers*, Vol. XLIX (December, 1947), 481; republished in *American Cinematographer*, April, 1948, p. 124.

Desmond, Robert. "News About the Newsreel," *Christian Science Monitor Magazine*, September 28, 1938, p. 5.

Dodge, Natt N. "Adventures of a News Hound," *Sunset*, July, 1930, p. 34.

Doherty, Dan. "Editing the Newsreel," *Journal of the Society of Motion Picture Engineers*, November 1, 1946, p. 357.

Donner, Vyvyan. "Women's Fashions," *Journal of the Society of Motion Picture Engineers*, November, 1946, p. 364.

Dored, John. "Newsreeler's Dilemma," *American Cinematographer*, June, 1949, p. 201.

———. "Soviets Imprison A.S.C. Member for News 'Scoop' in Filming Lenin's Funeral in Moscow," *American Cinematographer*, May, 1924, p. 4.

Doublier, Francis. "Reminiscences of an Early Motion Picture Operator," *Image*, June, 1956, p. 134.

Duff, David. "The First Victorian Newsreel," *Home and Garden*, October, 1964, p. 128.

Ellis, Peter. "Fascism Marches On," *New Masses*, September 3, 1935, pp. 29ff.

———. "The March of Time," *New Masses*, July 9, 1935, p. 30.

Erskine, John. "Newsreels Should Be Seen and Not Heard," *American Mercury*, June, 1935, p. 219.

Felbinger, Red. "Peace—Except to the Newsreelers," *International Photographer*, June, 1945, p. 7.

Ferguson, Otis. "Time Steals a March," *New Republic*, February 9, 1938, p. 19.

Fernstrom, Ray. "Improvising for the Newsreels," *American Cinematographer*, March, 1934, p. 442.

———. "The Junior Newsreel Is Here," *International Photographer*, September, 1934, p. 4.

———. "The Newsreel World," *International Photographer*, December, 1933, p. 28.

———. "Olympic Newsmen Real Champions," *International Photographer*, September, 1932, p. 24.

———. "Royal Families News Material," *International Photographer*, February, 1931, p. 15.

———. "Something New in Newsreels," *International Photographer*, December, 1934, p. 9.

Fielding, Raymond. "Mirror of Discontent: *The March of Time* and Its Politically Controversial Film Issues," *Western Political Quarterly*, March, 1959, p. 145.

———. "The Nazi-German Newsreel," *Journal of the University Film Producers Association*, Spring, 1960, p. 3.

———. "Time Flickers Out," *Quarterly of Film, Radio and Television*, Summer, 1957, p. 354.

Genock, Edouard P., and John Flory. "Techniques for Newsreel Cameramen," *Journal of the University Film Producers Association*, Spring, 1957, p. 5.

Genock, Ted. "A Newsreel Man Shoots the War," *American Mercury*, August, 1942, p. 158.

Germishuys, Pieter. "Flickering Past," *South African Panorama*, May, 1963, p. 2.

Gib. "Close-Ups—Norman Alley: Best Known Cameraman in the World," *International Photographer*, February, 1939, p. 17.

Githens, W. French. "Hail and Farewell," *New York Times*, November 20, 1949, Sec. 2, p. 4.

Gleason, David. "The People Gore Shot," *Pittsburgh Press*, November 17, 1968, p. 4.

Gold, Al. "Zep Crash Through Newsman's Eyes," *International Photographer*, June, 1937, p. 16.

Goldsmith, L. C. "Grinding Out History," *Sunset Magazine*, July, 1925, p. 32.

Gordon, Jack. "The Field Unit," *Journal of the Society of Motion Picture Engineers*, November, 1946, p. 367.

Gordon, Kenneth. "The Early Days of News-Reels," *British Kinematography*, August, 1950, p. 47.

———. "A Newsreel Man's Story," *Cine-Technician*, March, 1955, p. 36.

Grahl, Magdalon. "Home State Newsreel Got Start on Gridiron," *Motion Picture Herald*, August 14, 1937, p. 92.

Greenwald, Sanford E. "Extra—Extra—MacArthur Surrenders," *International Photographer*, May, 1951, p. 6.

———. "The Good Old Days," *International Photographer*, April, 1965, p. 16.

———. "You Can't Outguess the Quarterback," *International Photographer*, November, 1949, p. 5.

Grinley, Charles. "Notes on the News-Reel," *Life and Letters—Today*, Winter, 1937, p. 122.

Hall, Hal. "James J. Seeley, A.S.C.," *American Cinematographer,* March, 1945, p. 79.

Hall, Ray. "Seeing is Believing," *Independent,* September 18, 1926, p. 325.

Harrison, Edward. "What the Newsreels Never Show," *Ken,* June 16, 1938, p. 80.

Hastings, Charles Edward. "A Cameraman Runs into a War," *Moving Picture World,* January 29, 1927, p. 327.

Heitzner, Irving. "I 'Shot' the President," *International Photographer,* October, 1955, p. 16.

Hendricks, Gordon. "A Collection of Edison Films," *Image,* September, 1959, p. 157.

Henry. "The Historian of the Future," *Moving Picture World,* July 8, 1911, p. 1565.

Hine, Al. "Movies: Covering a Convention," *Holiday,* July, 1948, p. 22.

Hochberg, Joel. "The Vanishing Newsreel," *Films in Review,* June–July, 1959, p. 344.

Holst, Bert. "The Film Library," *Journal of the Society of Motion Picture Engineers,* November, 1946, p. 365.

Hopper, Hedda. "Demise of Newsreel Ends Film Tradition," *Los Angeles Times,* September 7, 1963, sec. 3, p. 6.

Hubl, A. "Cultural Films and Sound News Reels," *International Review of Educational Cinematography,* April, 1932, p. 268.

Irwin, Theodore. "Camera! Feeding the News Reels," *Popular Mechanics,* May, 1930, p. 794.

Johnson, Paul W. H. G. "Newsreel or Viewsreel?" *International Photographer,* November, 1958, p. 8.

Jones, Harry. "The Modern Newsreel," *Journal of the Society of Motion Picture Engineers,* February, 1930, p. 204.

Jones, Naomie. "The Invisible Vyvyan and the Voice of Fashion," *Woman,* May, 1947, p. 5.

Jones, Vincent S. "The Challenge of Photo-Journalism," *Image,* September, 1957, p. 153.

Kanter, Doris. "Memories of an Old-Time Newsreel Photographer," *Washington Star Pictorial Magazine,* March 14, 1954, p. 18.

Kellogg, Edward W. "History of Sound Motion Pictures," *Journal of the Society of Motion Picture and Television Engineers,* June, 1955, p. 291.

King, Frank. "And . . . That Was Flying," *International Photographer*, December, 1942, p. 4.

Koons, Paul. " 'Vacationing' with Wilkie," *International Photographer*, October, 1940, p. 10.

Kracauer, Siegfried, and Joseph Lyford. "A Duck Crosses Main Street," *New Republic*, December 13, 1948, p. 13.

Krainukov, George. "Universal's Thrill Hunter in China," *International Photographer*, July, 1941, p. 3.

Krows, Arthur. "Motion Pictures—Not for Theaters," *Educational Screen*, October, 1938, p. 249.

Kuhn, Ferdinand, Jr. "Kennedy Helped Censor Newsreel Commons Learns." *New York Times*, November 24, 1938, p. 1.

Lancaster, George J. "Tragedy Follows News Cameramen," *International Photographer*, May, 1932, p. 11.

Lawrenson, Harry. "Foreign Editions," *Journal of the Society of Motion Picture Engineers*, November, 1946, p. 361.

Lazarus, Charles. "The Newsreel Fights Back," *Motion Picture Herald*, March 8, 1952, p. 14.

———. "Newsreels Face Big Test, Come Through in Korea," *Motion Picture Herald*, August 12, 1950.

Legg, Stuart. "The Cinema: The Coronation Films," *Spectator*, May 28, 1937, p. 991.

Lieber, Leslie. "Solved! The Mystery of Thomas Edison's First Fight Film," *This Week Magazine*, December 3, 1961, p. 9.

Littell, Robert. "A Glance at the Newsreels," *American Mercury*, November, 1933, p. 263.

———. "Hard on Heroes," *Reader's Digest*, July, 1936, p. 89.

Lyons, Eugene. "Louis de Rochemont, Maverick of the Movies," *Reader's Digest*, July, 1949, p. 23.

Lyons, Leonard. "Lyons Den—In Which Photographers Offer Other Pictures of People in the News," *New York Post*, April 23, 1936.

Mabie, Janet. "Reeling Up the Newsreels," *Christian Science Monitor Magazine*, June 19, 1935, p. 3.

McCarroll, Marshall. "Shot Under Protest," *International Photographer*, April, 1940, p. 3.

McGrath, Warren. "News Mikes Hear but Not Seen," *International Photographer*, June, 1938, p. 19.

———. "Newsreel Football Specials," *International Photographer*, December, 1938, p. 13.

————. "Newsreeling on the Golden Gate Bridge," *International Photographer*, May, 1934, p. 18.

————. "Newsreel Sound," *Journal of the Society of Motion Picture Engineers*, November, 1946, p. 371.

————. "Spot News Half a Mile Down," *International Photographer*, May, 1938, p. 19.

McInnis, Walter. "The Newsreel Cameraman," *Journal of the Society of Motion Picture Engineers*, November, 1946, p. 368.

Mackenzie, Stuart. "How the Movie News Man Gets Pictures of World Events," *American Magazine*, January, 1924, p. 38.

Markey, Morris. "A Reporter at Large: Newsreel," *New Yorker*, September 22, 1934, p. 64.

Matthews, T. S. "What Makes News," *Atlantic*, December, 1957, p. 80.

Meltzer, Newton L. "Are Newsreels News?" *Hollywood Quarterly*, Vol. II (April, 1947), 270.

Menefee, Selden. "The Movies Join Hearst," *New Republic*, October 9, 1935, p. 241.

Miller, Don. "The Visual Chronicle," *Films in Review*, December, 1957, p. 513.

Montague, William. "The Newsreel and Public Opinion," *High Points*, June, 1938, p. 5.

Morrison, Charles P. "The News Film," *American Photography*, December, 1926, p. 640.

————. "Topical Cinematography," *American Photography*, March, 1927, p. 152.

Norath, Albert. "Oskar Messter and His Work," *Journal of the Society of Motion Picture and Television Engineers*, October, 1960, p. 733.

Norman, Philip. "The Newsreel Boys," *Sunday Times Magazine* (London), January 10, 1971, p. 8.

North, Anthony. "Let's Wait for the Newsreel," *New Outlook*, October, 1934, p. 21.

O'Brine, Jack. "Studios on the Battlefields," *Popular Science*, March, 1943, p. 108.

Palmer, Lewis E. "The World in Motion," *Survey*, June 5, 1909, p. 355.

Patrick, John. "The Drama That Staged Itself." *I.A.T.S.E., Official Bulletin*, Winter, 1965, p. 16.

Paul, Robert. "Kinematographic Experiences," *Journal of the Society of Motion Picture Engineers*, November, 1936, p. 495.

Peck, James. "Sun and Shade, 1888–1896," *Image*, November, 1955, p. 60.

Peden, Charles. "Guts, Vision—Crying Needs to Rejuvenate Newsreels," *Motion Picture Herald*, July 9, 1955; reprinted in *American Cinematographer*, August, 1955, p. 471.

Peet, Creighton. "The New Movies: Trans-Lux," *Outlook and Independent*, March 25, 1931, p. 442.

Pound, Arthur. "When Movies Tell the News," *Independent*, November 28, 1925, p. 615.

Pratt, George. "No Magic, No Mystery, No Sleight of Hand," *Image*, December, 1959, p. 207.

Pringle, Henry. "The Movies Swing an Election," originally published in *New Yorker*; republished in *Reader's Digest*, August, 1936, p. 4.

Pryor, Thomas M. "An Adventurous Life for the Newsreel Man," *New York Times Magazine*, January 1, 1939.

———. "New Slant on the Newsreels," *New York Times*, February 25, 1945, Sec. 2, p. 3.

———. "Our Newsreel Across the Seas," *New York Times*, May 14, 1944, Sec. 2, p. 3.

Quigley, Martin. "The Exhibitor's Screen—How Shall It Be Used?" *Motion Picture Herald*, February 5, 1938, [p. 7].

Ramsaye, Terry. "Blood and Guts," *Motion Picture Herald*, May 26, 1945, editorial page.

———. "News and Corpses," *Motion Picture Herald*, September 1, 1934, editorial page.

———. "Newsreel Problem," *Motion Picture Herald*, January 13, 1945, editorial page.

———. "Newsreel Rights and the Flemington Hysteria," *Motion Picture Herald*, February 9, 1935, p. 9.

———. "White House Pictures," *Motion Picture Herald*, November 11, 1944, p. 7.

Reid, Charles I. "The Adventures of the 'Movie' Camera Man," *Photographic Times*, June, 1915, p. 235.

Reynolds, Capt. Bob. "Filming a News Event for the Screen," *Moving Picture World*, July 21, 1917, p. 421.

Ritchie, David. "That News-Reel Villainy," *Sight and Sound*, Autumn, 1934, p. 113.

Rogerson, J. C. "Tribune Hits at Newsreels," *Cine-Technician*, September–October, 1949, p. 136.

Rothapfel, S. L. "Dramatizing Music for the Pictures," *Reel Life*, September 5, 1914, p. 23.

Sarthe, Jean. "She Makes Movies," *Independent Woman*, October, 1934, p. 315.

Schnurmacher, Emile C. "The Cameraman Foretells Disaster," *Popular Mechanics*, December, 1933, p. 836.

———. "Get the Story: They Risk Their Lives to Live," *Popular Mechanics*, March, 1932, p. 404.

Seldes, Gilbert. "Screen and Radio," *Scribner's Magazine*, July, 1937, p. 56.

Shannon, Betty. "The Prince and the Pictures," *Photoplay*, March, 1920, p. 56.

Shepard, Richard F. "The Movie Newsreel Flickers Its Last and Dies," *New York Times*, December 22, 1967, p. 37.

Shorey, Jerome. "The Romance of the News Reel," *Photoplay*, February, 1919, p. 74.

Sibley, Hi. "That Dam Film," *Motion Picture Magazine*, October, 1916, p. 121.

Sinkey, Patsie V. "Farewell, Traveller," *International Photographer*, December, 1945, p. 14.

Smith, Harold. "Sound in News Ten Years Old," *International Photographer*, April, 1937, p. 13.

Sponable, Earl I. "Historical Development of Sound Films," *Journal of the Society of Motion Picture Engineers*, April, 1947, p. 275; May, 1947, p. 407; reprinted in *International Projectionist*, August, 1947, p. 12.

Stallings, Laurence. "Cannon Fodder on the Road to Jijiga," *Stage*, July, 1936, p. 30.

———. "Pomp and Circumstance," *Stage*, October, 1936, p. 70.

———. "Sermons in Silver," *Stage*, April, 1936, p. 36.

———. "Words and Pictures," *Saturday Evening Post*, November 21, 1936, p. 8.

Steene, E. Burton. " 'Shooting' the Generals with the Movie Camera," *Literary Digest*, December 8, 1917, p. 78.

Sugrue, Thomas. "The Newsreels," *Scribner's Magazine*, April, 1937, p. 9.

Sullivan, Neil. "News Cinematography Speeds Up," *Agfa Motion Picture Topics*, March–April, 1938, p. 11.

Tash, Roy. "Shooting the 'Quints,' " *International Photographer*, December, 1935, p. 19.

Theisen, Earl. "The Photographer in the World War," *International Photographer*, November, 1933, p. 4.

———. "Story of the Newsreel," *International Photographer*, September, 1933, p. 3.

Thomas, Howard. "Evolution of the News-Reel," *British Kinematography*, August, 1950, p. 47.

———. "The Future of the News-Reel," *British Kinematography*, August, 1950, p. 53.

Tummel, H. "Birt Acres," *Cinema Studies* (British), June, 1963, p. 157.

Varges, Ariel. "Ace Newsreeler Gives Light on How He Films News of the World," *American Cinematographer*, July, 1938, p. 275.

———. "Newsreel Cameraman in the War," *International Photographer*, March, 1942, p. 8.

Villard, Oswald. "Issues and Men, Propaganda in the Movies," *Nation*, December 12, 1934, p. 665.

Waller, Tom. "Checking the Newsreels," *Variety*, January 2, 1934.

Warner, Bob. "Question of Ethics on Staged Pictures," *Editor and Publisher*, January 13, 1962, p. 48.

———. "Staged Pix Draw Comments and Survey," *Editor and Publisher*, January 27, 1962, p. 44.

Welter, Rush E. "The 'Factual' Film in a Visual Age," *Etc.: A Review of General Semantics*, Winter, 1950, p. 137.

Whitebait, William. "The Movies," *New Statesman and Nation*, June 17, 1944, p. 404.

Wilcox, Walter. "The Staged News Photograph and Professional Ethics," *Journalism Quarterly*, Vol. XXXVIII, No. 4 (Autumn, 1961), 497.

Woods, T. F. "Headlines in Celluloid," *Saturday Evening Post*, August 11, 1945, p. 22.

Zolotow, Maurice. "Want to be a Movie Star?" *Saturday Evening Post*, March 29, 1952, p. 25.

Anonymous Articles

"Advent of the Topical Picture—Vitagraph to Release News Film," *Moving Picture World*, August 5, 1911, p. 283.

"All War Pictures Fakes," *Moving Picture World*, October 3, 1914, p. 50.

"American Debut of G.B.S.," *Literary Digest*, July 28, 1928, p. 21.

"American Interests Acquire Control of Pathé Exchange," *Exhibitors Herald*, July 2, 1921, p. 36.

"Animated Journalism," *World's Work*, October, 1910, p. 13476.

"Apportionment of Raw Stock for the Newsreels," *Motion Picture Herald*, February 10, 1945, p. 25.

"Are Newsreels News?" *Nation*, October 2, 1935, p. 369.

"Berlin Television News Broadcast Challenges Reels and Exhibitors," *Motion Picture Herald*, July 13, 1935, p. 49.

"Better News Reels," *Outlook and Independent*, October 2, 1929, p. 179.

"Be Your Own Producer and Newsreel Cameraman," *International Photographer*, November, 1934, p. 15.

"Braving Death for News Films," *Literary Digest*, May 28, 1927, p. 48.

"The Camera Press Man," *Moving Picture World*, September 23, 1911, p. 868.

"Cameras on Deck for Storming of Europe," *Motion Picture Herald*, May 13, 1944, p. 14.

"Capturing Mexico with a Camera," *Literary Digest*, June 6, 1914, p. 1390.

"Charles Pathé Honored," *Image*, October, 1954, p. 47.

"Cinema Moves with Invasion Fronts," *Motion Picture Herald*, June 10, 1944, p. 13.

"A Combination of Interesting Subjects," *Moving Picture World*, April 13, 1912, p. 118.

"The Coronation in Kinemacolor," *Moving Picture World*, August 5, 1911, p. 274.

"A Cruise with the Black Fleet," *International Photographer*, July, 1935, p. 6.

"Daring Death with Nervy News Photographers," *Literary Digest*, May 11, 1929, p. 36.

"Depinet Is Named Pathé News Head as Smith Resigns," *Motion Picture Herald*, May 29, 1937, p. 55.

"Disgraceful Fake Pictures," *Moving Picture News*, December 16, 1911, p. [5]; and December 23, 1911, p. 6.

"Duke of Windsor's Wedding Films Banned in Britain by 'Agreement,' " *Motion Picture Herald*, June 12, 1937, p. 54.

"E. B. Hatrick Explains M-G-M's New Newsreel," *Moving Picture World*, March 5, 1927, p. 11.

" 'Educational' Newsreels for WPA," *Literary Digest*, August 8, 1936, p. 32.

"Fake War Movies," *Literary Digest*, November 13, 1915, p. 1079.

"Faking War Pictures," *Moving Picture World*, November 28, 1914, p. 1249.

"Film Interests Answer Riots with Legal Moves Against Reds," *Motion Picture Herald*, October 5, 1935, p. 16.

"Films to Show WPA's Work," *Motion Picture Herald*, April 18, 1936, p. 48.

"First Issue of Time's Two-Reel News Opens in Theatres Dec. 20," *Motion Picture Herald*, November 17, 1934, p. 9.

"The First News Reel," *International Photographer*, September, 1929, p. 26.

"First Newsreels of the Invasion Take Audiences to the Beachheads," *Motion Picture Herald*, June 17, 1944, p. 9.

"Ford Film Collection Documents Americana," *Film World and A-V News Magazine*, January, 1964, p. 8.

"4,000 Theatres Will Show First of News Kinograms," *Exhibitors Herald*, January 22, 1921, p. 43.

"Forty Years of Screen Journalism," *Motion Picture Herald*, August 29, 1959, p. 15.

"Free Comment," *Sequence*, No. 8 (Summer, 1949), 47.

"Future of Newsreels," *Motion Picture Herald*, November 17, 1951, p. [1].

"Gaumont Weekly for Film Supply Company," *Moving Picture World*, August 3, 1912, p. 431.

"Hearst Product Will Continue Through MGM," *Exhibitors Herald-World*, June 29, 1929, p. 137.

"Hearst's *News of the Day*," *Time*, November 23, 1936, p. 25.

"Hearst Sound Newsreels Will Appear in September," *New York American*, June 23, 1929, p. 16-L.

"A Hollywood Cameraman in the Land of a Billion Faces," *International Photographer*, May, 1935, p. 4.

"Hollywood Starts War Cycle, as Newsreels Get Battle Scenes," *Motion Picture Herald*, October 9, 1935, p. 18.

"Horror Pictures," *Motion Picture Herald*, May 5, 1945, p. 8.

"Horror Pictures Shock Patrons but None Protests," *Motion Picture Herald*, May 12, 1945, p. 14.

"How Moving Pictures of the American Trip of Admiral Togo, Japan's Great Sea Fighter, Were Obtained," *Moving Picture News*, October 7, 1911, p. 28.

"How We Vitagraphed the Hudson-Fulton Marine Celebration," *Moving Picture World*, October 9, 1909, p. 482.

"King Alexander's Reel," *Time*, October 29, 1934, p. 18.

"Last Two Newsreels to Be Discontinued," *New York Times*, November 24, 1967, p. 56.

"Lindbergh Case Pawn in Newsreel Private Fight," *Motion Picture Herald*, February 9, 1935, p. 11.

"Local 'War' Scenes," *Moving Picture World*, October 17, 1914, p. 352.

"Look Out for Newsreel, It Does for You," *Berkeley Barb*, Vol. XVII, No. 18, issue 167 [October 25–31], 1968.

"Louisiana Adopts Censorship Law," *Motion Picture Herald*, July 13, 1935, p. 14.

"Matinee Idols of the News Reels," *Literary Digest*, September 5, 1931, p. 32.

"Million Gross High Point for Fight Pictures," *Motion Picture Herald*, December 20, 1947, p. 12.

"Move to Protect Newsreel Rights After Invasion," *Motion Picture Herald*, June 3, 1944, p. 30.

"Movie of the Week," *Life*, January 31, 1938, p. 24.

"Movietone Portrays King George Speaking," *New York Times*, November 28, 1928, p. 2.

"Movietone Reel to Carry Ads," *Daily Variety*, September 10, 1963, p. [1].

"Moving Pictures of the Powers Fire," *Moving Picture World*, July 1, 1911.

"Nanking Government Stresses Regulations Foreign Photographers in Interior of China," *China Weekly Review*, April 11, 1936, p. 216.

"NBC Telecasts Iwo Invasion," *Motion Picture Herald*, March 17, 1945, p. 27.

"Negro Newsreel Seen by 4,000,000," *American Cinematographer*, November, 1943, p. 408.

"A New Home for Pathé," *Motion Picture Herald*, October 6, 1945, p. 39.

"Newscasting: A Change of Screens," *Time*, December 29, 1967, p. 35.

"News Parade," *Time*, June 21, 1937, p. 42.

"Newspictures Ignore Profit and Loss," *Fortune*, September, 1930, p. 60.

"Newspictures Subject to Censor Court Rules," *Exhibitors Herald*, July 22, 1922, p. 17.

"The Newsreel," *Motion Picture Herald*, June 24, 1944, p. 42.

"Newsreel Analysis," *Christian Science Monitor Magazine*, August 26, 1950, p. 19.

"The Newsreel Boxoffice: A San Francisco Newsreel Movie House Looks Back on History," *Fortnight*, September 1, 1952, p. 14.

"Newsreel Camera in Shadow of Palace of the Lion of Judah," *Motion Picture Herald*, September 14, 1935, p. 17.

"News Reel Cameraman Tells How He Learned His Trade," *New York Herald Tribune*, July 15, 1928.

"Newsreel Camera News," *International Photographer*, December, 1939, p. 19.

"Newsreel Censorship in Japan Launches Government Control," *Motion Picture Herald*, September 28, 1935, p. 262.

"Newsreelers at Republican Convention," *International Photographer*, August, 1944, p. 23.

"Newsreel Not to Shift Now, Editors Say," *Motion Picture Herald*, May 28, 1949, p. 39.

" 'Newsreel' Policy," *Motion Picture Herald*, June 26, 1937, p. [1].

"Newsreel Race," *Business Week*, January 5, 1946, p. 41.

"Newsreel Rivalries Flame Again in Race with Assassination Films," *Motion Picture Herald*, October 27, 1934, p. 23.

"Newsreels Act to Strengthen Units," *Motion Picture Herald*, April 20, 1935, p. 42.

"Newsreels Adopt New Standard Reproduction to Improve Sound," *Motion Picture Herald*, February 23, 1935, p. 13.

"Newsreels and Pictures," *New Republic*, March 11, 1931, p. 96.

"Newsreels Are Now TV's Cup of Tea," *Broadcasting-Telecasting*, July 29, 1957, p. 96.

"Newsreels Bring Bloody Iwo Home," *Motion Picture Herald*, March 10, 1945, p. 36.

"Newsreels Changing Coverage," *Daily Variety*, January 19, 1955, p. 6.

"Newsreels Cover Steeplechase; and the Trouble Starts," *Motion Picture Herald*, April 6, 1935, p. 17.

"Newsreels Find Inauguration an Easy Assignment," *Motion Picture Herald*, January 27, 1945, p. 32.

"Newsreels First with Hauptmann Verdict," February 23, 1935, p. 28.

"Newsreels Foresee 57G Annual Saving If They Can End Ohio Censorship," *Daily Variety*, May 27, 1953, p. 10.

"Newsreels Give 80% of Footage to War News," *Motion Picture Herald*, February 3, 1945, p. 14.

"Newsreels Give Speedy Coverage of Lindbergh Kidnapping Arrest," *Motion Picture Herald*, September 29, 1934, p. 10.

"Newsreel Shows South Chicago Memorial Day Riot in Which Ten Were Killed," *Life*, July 12, 1937, p. 72.

"Newsreels in Europe Appeal to League of Nations for Fairness," *Motion Picture Herald*, July 31, 1937, p. 25.

"Newsreels Not Liable for Picture Shocks," *Motion Picture Herald*, March 30, 1935, p. 18.

"Newsreels Off to Ethiopian War; Stallings Heads Fox Expedition," *Motion Picture Herald*, August 10, 1935.

"Newsreels Race Video for Inaugural Honor," *Motion Picture Herald*, January 29, 1949, p. 21.

"Newsreels Set Pace for Lively Campaign; Refute Charges," *Motion Picture Herald*, February 29, 1936, p. 18.

"Newsreels Shift Cameramen in War Theatres," *Motion Picture Herald*, January 27, 1945, p. 32.

"Newsreels Show Canned Footage on Candidates," *Motion Picture Herald*, October 16, 1948.

"Newsreel Takes Prize," *International Photographer*, December, 1939, p. 19.

"Newsreel Television Reported in Germany," *Motion Picture Herald*, June 29, 1935, p. 62.

"Newsreel Turn from Baby Parade to Recording History Is Reflected," *Motion Picture Herald*, December 21, 1935, p. 30.

"No Cameras Going to the Front," *Moving Picture World*, September 12, 1914, p. 1487.

"Not the Answer," *Motion Picture Herald*, July 6, 1935, p. 7.

"Obituary: Terry Ramsaye," *Films in Review*, October, 1954, p. 386.

"Olympics—Ltd.," *Time*, July 26, 1948, p. 65.

"100 Newsreel Cameramen Cover Inaugural for Nation's Screens," *Motion Picture Herald*, January 23, 1937, p. 15.

"Only in Boston (and on Sunday) Are Newsreels Still Censored in U.S.," *Daily Variety*, April 6, 1955, p. 8.

"Paramount News Ready for War with Crews Lined Up in Europe," *Motion Picture Herald*, April 13, 1935, p. 3.

"Paramount to Cease Release February 15, 1957," *New York Times*, January 24, 1957, p. 34.

"The Passing of a King," *Moving Picture World*, June 4, 1910, p. 930.

"The Pathé Journal," *Moving Picture World*, August 12, 1911, p. 359.

"Pathé News Makes Housing Propaganda," *Motion Picture Herald*, February 2, 1935, p. 18.

"Pathé News Tieup Involves French and British Units," *Motion Picture Herald*, December 22, 1945, p. 35.

"Pathé Opens Exchanges," *Moving Picture World*, May 16, 1914, p. 975.

"Pathé Putting Out News Daily," *Moving Picture World*, June 13, 1914, p. 1524.

"Pathé's Rooster Crows to Mark Its 30th Year," *New York Herald Tribune*, November 10, 1940.

"The Pathé Weekly," *Moving Picture World*, September 23, 1911, p. 871.

"Pioneer Newsreels," *Image*, September, 1953, p. 39.

"Politics-on-Screen Issue Getting Warm with Anti–New Deal Short," *Motion Picture Herald*, February 15, 1936, p. 24.

"Press Services Plan Newsreels for Television," *Motion Picture Herald*, November 1, 1947, p. 36.

"The Prince's Derby Shown by Lightning Photography," *Strand Magazine*, Vol. XII (1896), p. 134.

"Radio Bows to Newsreel's Power, Apologizes for Gossip Broadcast," *Motion Picture Herald*, March 9, 1935, p. 13.

"Raw Stock Is Cut 20,000,000 Feet," *Motion Picture Herald*, January 6, 1945, p. 32.

"Reels of Royal Slaying Banned; Flier Drowned," *Motion Picture Herald*, October 20, 1934, p. 21.

"Reels Stress U.S., Not Global, Events," *Daily Variety*, June 27, 1957, p. 6.

"The Romance of a Great Business," *Education*, February, 1916, p. 395.

"Scene to Screen in 12 Hours," *Science Illustrated*, April, 1947, p. 34.

"Scientific Nature-Faking," *Collier's*, July 3, 1909, 13.

"The Screen: The March of Time," *New Masses*, October 8, 1935.

"Screen: Newsreels Seek Gains with 'Super-Commentators,'" *News-Week*, October 6, 1934, p. 22.

"Seeing the World in Ten Minutes," *Popular Mechanics*, May, 1939, p. 696.

"Shanghai Shambles," *Time*, September 13, 1937, p. 33.

"Siege of Antwerp Shown in Pictures," *Moving Picture World*, November 28, 1914, p. 1218.

"Sound and Fury over Free Speech," *Literary Digest*, May 1, 1937, p. 3.

"Speaking of Pictures . . . Library of Congress Unearths First Newsreels," *Life*, September 20, 1943, p. 18.

"State-Operated Studios Promised by Sinclair," *Motion Picture Herald*, September 8, 1934, p. 10.

"The Story of the News Reel," *Moving Picture World*, March 26, 1927, p. 322.

"Telenews Hails 20th Year," *San Francisco News-Call Bulletin*, September 4, 1959, p. 24.

"Telephoto Newsreels Will Go to Theatres Two Hours After Event," *Motion Picture Herald*, December 29, 1934, p. 10.

"Theatres Fight Red Dictation in Effort to Halt Picket Nuisance," *Motion Picture Herald*, August 31, 1935, p. 16.

"There's Drama Too in Newsreel Coverage of Hauptmann Trial," *Motion Picture Herald*, January 19, 1935, p. 29.

"This is Arthur's," *Time*, October 25, 1937, p. 25.

"The Topical Picture," *Moving Picture World*, July 16, 1910, p. 132.

"Tragedy and Comedy in Making Pictures of the Russian Chaos," *Current Opinion*, February, 1918, p. 106.

"Trans-Lux," *Outlook and Independent*, March 25, 1931, p. 442.

"20th-Fox Newsreel Setup is 26 Years Old," *Motion Picture Herald*, March 24, 1945, p. 33.

"Twenty-Two Soho Square," *Great Britain and the East*, July 29, 1937, p. 162.

"Two Newsreels Show Scenes of War in Shanghai," *Motion Picture Herald*, September 11, 1937, p. 30.

"Ultra-Speed Pan in the Newsreel Cinematography," *Agfa Motion Picture Topics*, January–February, 1938, p. 10.

"United Newsreel Releases First Under New Regime," *Motion Picture Herald*, December 22, 1945, p. 35.

"United Newsreel to Be Dissolved Effective December 15," *Motion Picture Herald*, October 6, 1945, p. 43.

"U.S. Justice Department Studies Reds' Boycott and Picket Drive," *Motion Picture Herald*, September 7, 1935, p. 26.

"A Universal Cameraman Documents American History: The *Panay* Incident," *Life*, January 10, 1938, p. 11.

"Universal War Service," *Moving Picture World*, May 2, 1914, p. 681.

"Wagner in Mexico," *Moving Picture World*, July 18, 1914, p. 440.

"War and Newsreel," *Motion Picture Herald*, June 24, 1944, editorial page.

"War Booms Newsreel Chains," *Daily Variety*, July 19, 1950, p. 4.

"Warner Brothers Newsreel to End August 23, 1956," *New York Times*, July 24, 1956, p. 20.

"Weekly Dramatic Newsreel Will Be Launched by 'Time' October 1," *Motion Picture Herald*, August 25, 1934, p. 13.

"A Weekly Film of the World's Events," *Moving Picture World*, July 29, 1911, p. 187.

"The Weekly News Reel," *Moving Picture World*, July 21, 1917, p. 419.

"When the Newsreels Shoot an Earthquake," *International Photographer*, April, 1933, p. 34.

"When the Newsreels Were Young," *New York Times*, October 29, 1939, Sec. 9, p. 4.

"Wide Study of Newsreels Is Planned," *Motion Picture Herald*, November 26, 1949, p. 47.

"WPA: Pathé Wins Film Contract as New Deal 'Goes Hollywood,' " *News-Week*, August 15, 1936, p. 18.

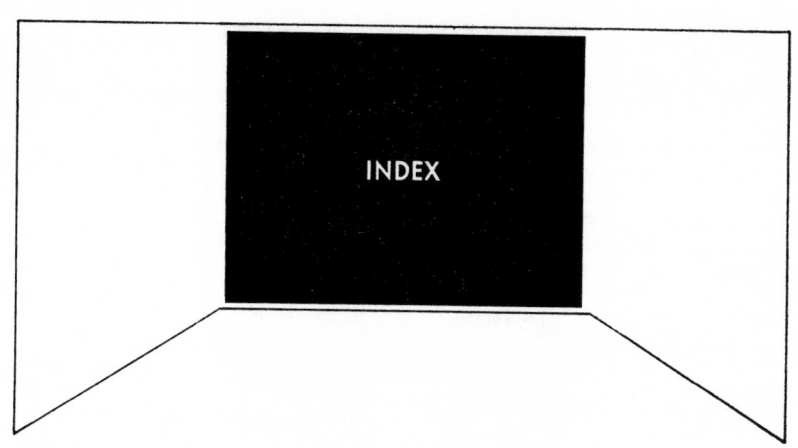

INDEX

The paper on which *The American Newsreel, 1911–1967* was printed bears the watermark of the University of Oklahoma Press and has an effective life of at least three hundred years.

UNIVERSITY OF OKLAHOMA PRESS

NORMAN

DATE DUE